CANADIAN
LAW

CANADIAN LAW

fourth edition

LAW

an introduction

Neil Boyd

Simon Fraser University

NELSON / EDUCATION

NELSON / EDUCATION

Canadian Law, An Introduction, Fourth Edition
by Neil Boyd

Associate Vice President, Editorial Director:
Evelyn Veitch

Publisher:
Joanna Cotton

Marketing Manager:
Lenore Taylor

Senior Developmental Editor:
Rebecca Rea

Permissions Coordinator:
Indu Ghuman

Production Editor:
Karri Yano

Copy Editor:
Elizabeth Phinney

Proofreader:
Liba Berry

Indexer:
Andrew Little

Senior Production Coordinator:
Hedy Sellers

Design Director:
Ken Phipps

Interior Design:
Tammy Gay

Cover Design:
Eugene Lo

Cover Image:
Brand X Pictures/Fotosearch (Top)
© 2001 Library of Parliament (Bottom)

Compositor:
Integra

Printer:
Webcom

Library and Archives Canada Cataloguing in Publication

Boyd, Neil, 1951–
Canadian law: an introduction / Neil Boyd.—4th ed.

Includes index.
ISBN 0-17-640716-2

1. Law—Canada—Textbooks. I. Title.

KE444.B69 2006   349.71
C2005-906409-9

KF385.ZA2B69 2006

To all my students, past, present, and future

Brief Contents

Contents

Part 2 Building Blocks of the Canadian Legal System

Preface

This text has had a lengthy development. Originally, after teaching a university-level introductory law course for 20 years, I found that I was uncomfortable with the existing learning materials. No text seemed to combine the basic building blocks of Canada's system of public law with a relatively broad social analysis of that system, giving the reader competing perspectives on the role of law, sources of law, the significance of the Canadian Charter of Rights and Freedoms, the value of statutory interpretation, criminal law, the law of divorce, and so on.

The purpose of this book, now in its fourth edition, remains consistent with the goals of the first edition: to introduce Canadian public law to college and university students, using specific case law to prompt debate and discussion. Law is a changing human construction, and it is my hope to interest students in the principles, powers, and privileges that law conveys. In its idealized form, law can be conceptualized either as the instrument of democracy or as a force to be employed, in axiomatic fashion, against the powerless. In practical terms, law is both a democratic institution and an instrument of control or oppression, depending on the specific historical context, and the lens that one adopts in the study of law. And that mix of critical values, changing culture, and conflict is what makes this enterprise both interesting and worth the effort.

Acknowledgements

I would like to thank Nelson Thomson Learning for its support and enthusiasm for this project. My legal colleagues at Simon Fraser University have also been generous in their insights and contributions: thanks go particularly to Paul Brantingham, David MacAlister, and Simon Verdun-Jones. Finally, I would like to thank my wife, Isabel Otter, for her continuing support.

Introduction

This text is designed to introduce students to Canadian law: first, to its role and origins; second, to the building blocks of the system: statutory interpretation, the Constitution, the courts, and the legal profession; and third, to areas of substantive law and their fundamental principles: tort law, family law, administrative law, and criminal law.

Each chapter concludes with discussion questions, Web links, and a listing of references and further readings. Case law is used to highlight competing perspectives, as well as to provide teachers and students with a focus for further analysis and debate. This fourth edition contains an appendix, with the full text of the Canadian Charter of Rights and Freedoms, and a glossary. Terms defined in the glossary are in bold at their first relevant occurrence in the text. In teaching introductory law, I have found that ancillary material comprising current judicial decisions and critical analyses, updated each semester, is a useful addition to any course text.

Part 1: Role and Origin, comprises three chapters. Chapter 1 sketches the different perspectives on the role of law in society, and explores the strengths and weaknesses of each perspective. Chapter 2 considers legal history and the question of how to understand sources of law in both specific and general contexts. Chapter 3 introduces what may be the primary task of the lawyer: statutory interpretation. The rules of interpretation and construction are canvassed and questioned, then applied to specific sets of facts.

Part 2: Building Blocks of the Canadian Legal System, also contains three chapters. Chapter 4 presents the most critical building blocks of Canadian law: the Constitution Act, 1982 and its fusion of the British North America Act, 1867 and the Canadian Charter of Rights and Freedoms. Chapter 5 is concerned with the Canadian court structure, its reform over time, and the functions and purposes of the different levels of courts. Chapter 6 focuses on the legal profession and the task of legal education: What is the essence of education about law? What are the priorities of the law school curriculum, and how does law school relate to the legal profession?

What standards of conduct do we expect from lawyers, prosecutors, and judges?

Part 3: Substantive Law, consists of four chapters. Chapter 7 sets out the key principles of tort law, the legal mechanism for the remedy of private wrongs. Intentional torts and torts of negligence are described, with excerpts from case law highlighting relevant principles and issues in dispute. Chapter 8 examines family law, focusing on the significant changes to the Divorce Act over the past 25 years. The social meaning of these changes is explored, and the major provisions of the Divorce Act are set out; legal provisions relating to same-sex marriage, matrimonial property, spousal support, and child custody are also discussed. Chapter 9 sets out the key principles of administrative law, charting the onus that the state has placed upon itself in relation to the conduct of its affairs. Finally, Chapter 10 surveys the often-discussed terrain of criminal law: the principles of mens rea and actus reus, the possible defences to criminal charges, and the principles to be employed in sentencing a guilty person.

Law is, in most important respects, a site of political, economic, and social conflict and debate. At the end of the day, this book will have accomplished its purpose if students see law as entirely human, changeable, and deserving of both institutional respect and continual criticism—as something in which we all have a stake and which we can influence.

PART 1

Role and Origin

CHAPTER 1

The Role of Law: Competing Perspectives on Legal Order

I myself have never been able to find out precisely what feminism is: I only know that people call me a feminist whenever I express sentiments that differentiate me from a doormat.

(Rebecca West, 1913)

Public morals are natural complements of all laws; they are by themselves an entire code.

(Napoleon Bonaparte)

The positivist thesis does not say that law's merits are unintelligible, unimportant, or peripheral to the philosophy of law. It says that they do not determine whether laws or legal systems exist. Whether a society has a legal system depends on the presence of certain structures of governance, not on the extent to which it satisfies ideals of justice, democracy, or the rule of law.

(Stanford Encyclopedia of Philosophy)

I find it hard to fathom that anyone disputes the truth of legal realism (lawyers don't, it's strictly some academics). It should hardly be surprising that legal realism is the correct descriptive account of appellate decision-making, if only for the simple reason that the cases selected for appellate review are disproportionately the ones where the legal reasons are indeterminate, and so the necessity for political and moral judgment is inescapable.

(Professor Brian Leiter, Faculty of Law, University of Texas)

Tracy Latimer was a 12-year-old child who suffered from a severe form of cerebral palsy; she was quadriplegic and had the mental capacity of an infant. Tracy had undergone many surgeries to correct various difficulties; she had a serious disability, but she was not terminally ill. She was often in pain, but could also express joy and pleasure. In late October of 1993, upon learning that his daughter needed yet another painful surgery,

Saskatchewan farmer Robert Latimer determined that her life was not worth living. On October 24, while his wife and other children were at church, Latimer carried Tracy to his pickup truck, seated her in the cab, and inserted a hose from the truck's exhaust into the cab. Tracy died from carbon monoxide poisoning. Latimer at first told police that Tracy had passed away in her sleep, but later confessed that he had taken her life. He also told police that he had considered giving Tracy an overdose of Valium or "shooting her in the head."

In January 2001 the Supreme Court of Canada determined, in a unanimous judgment, that Robert Latimer was properly found guilty of second degree murder for the killing of his daughter Tracy. The appeals against his conviction and sentence were dismissed. Like all individuals convicted of second degree murder, Mr. Latimer must spend 10 years in jail before he is eligible to apply for parole. Some Canadians have applauded Mr. Latimer's conviction and sentence as a demonstration of the value of human life; the punishment is said to be appropriate for the intentional killing of another human being. Others have sharply criticized the Supreme Court's decision, suggesting that Mr. Latimer was motivated by his love for Tracy, and arguing that he is worlds apart from those who are typically convicted of this offence.

How are we to evaluate the Supreme Court's decision in Latimer? We will all have immediate responses—opinions about the nature and scope of Mr. Latimer's criminal conduct and the punishment he should receive. Our views of the operation of criminal law reflect often passionately held moral, economic, and political points of view. In this chapter we will examine various perspectives or theories—grand designs for the role of law in Canadian society.

Individual Perspectives on the Law

Law is a vitally important force; it is the skeleton that structures our economic, social, and political lives. It is also a barometer of the nation's view of human relations, whether in the realm of criminal law, taxation, or constitutional law. It is as difficult to conceive of complex societies without law as it is to conceive of human beings without communication. Our attitudes toward law define us as citizens of our society, politically, economically, and morally.

If, for example, we turn to Canada's *Income Tax Act*, *Criminal Code*, and the *Canadian Charter of Rights and Freedoms*, we find legal structures that have, over time, defined and re-defined, among other things, the fair distribution of economic resources, the moral legitimacy of abortion, and the political legitimacy of preferential treatment for disadvantaged people.

Now let us consider three questions with roots in these economic, moral, and political realms: (1) Should high-income earners be more highly taxed than low-income earners? (2) Should women be able to obtain abortions without criminal sanction? (3) Should persons with disabilities be given preferential treatment in employment?

All of us will have opinions on these questions as well as justifications for our responses. For the law is a malleable human creation, which both reflects the movements of political actors and changing social mores, and influences those actors and mores. Our individual perceptions of **justice** and **injustice** define our relationship as citizens to the state.

Theoretical Perspectives on the Law

Theoreticians of law have staked out territories according to their perceptions of the law; there are positivists, natural lawyers, legal realists, Marxists, critical legalists, anarchists, libertarians, and feminists, among others. We will examine the most dominant, or perhaps the more traditional, of these perspectives first, using the three questions about economic resources, abortion, and persons with disabilities to highlight the central ideas of each perspective.

But first, consider the following five definitions of the meaning of law within our culture. The perspectives that are outlined following these definitions—the positivist, natural law, legal realist, Marxist, critical legalist, anarchist, libertarian, and feminist points of view—go beyond this first task of description to make normative arguments about the moral, economic, and political objectives of the legal process.

"Law is a set of rules which are generally obeyed and enforced within a politically organized society" (Professor Philip James, *Introduction to English Law*).

"Law is a rule established in a community by authority or custom; a body of such rules; the controlling influence of or obedience to this; the subject or study of such rules" (*The Oxford Reference Dictionary*).

"Law . . . is that part of the overall process of political decision making which has achieved somewhat more technical, more obvious, and more clearly defined ground rules than other aspects of politics. It is still, however, an integral subdivision of the overall political process" (Cheffins and Tucker, *The Constitutional Process in Canada*).

"Law in any society is the society's attempt to resolve the most basic of human tensions, that between the needs of the person as an individual, and her needs as a member of a community. The law is the knife edge on which the delicate balance is maintained between the individual on the one hand, and the society on the other" (Professor S.M. Waddams, *Introduction to the Study of Law*).

"Law is one of the devices by means of which men can reconcile their actual activities and behaviour with the ideal principles that they have come to accept, and can do it in a way that is not too painful or revolting to their sensibilities and in a way which allows ordered (which is to say predictable) social life to continue" (Paul Bohannan, "Law and Legal Institutions," in *The Sociology of Law* edited by William Evan).

Traditional Theories of the Role of Law

POSITIVISM AND THE POSITIVIST RESPONSE

Positivism is defined by *The Oxford Reference Dictionary* as "the theory that laws are to be understood as social rules, valid because they are enacted by 'the **sovereign**' or derive logically from existing decisions, and that ideal or moral considerations (e.g., that a rule is unjust) should not limit the scope or operation of the law."

Accordingly, positivism is a systematization of the law, seeking precision by an almost mechanical analysis of law as a matter of logic and interpretation; the values that lie behind the law can only muddy a clear vision of the legal process. In studying the scope or operation of the law, positivists seek quantitative and qualitative facts—to explain how the "machine" works.

Hence, for legal positivists, the answers to the three questions on page 5 are straightforward: yes, if this is the law; no, if it is not the law. The first question is, for example, defined by analyzing the *Income Tax Act*. As students and practitioners of the law, positivists are not concerned with its moral content. As citizens, they may have strong feelings about the direction that further amendments to law should take, but these concerns do not—and, they would argue, should not—enter legal analysis or legal practice.

Positivism essentially states that adherence to a just legal process is more important than the specifics of law, for these specifics will necessarily vary across time and space. The student of law should not be misled into thinking that those who espouse support for a positivist framework are inherently amoral or motivated by a desire to defer to the status quo. To the contrary, positivists argue passionately for a legal process that protects liberty and democratic institutions, and prevents the abuse of political power. Consider, for example, the danger posed by those ideologues who would disband courts, legislatures, and burdens of proof without recourse to legal process, all in the name of their own version of social justice. Simply put, the process of law is seen as more important than the specific content of law.

Positivists draw a firm line between the practice of law and the practice of politics. They regard the House of Commons and the legislative assemblies of the provinces as the proper places for debate—in this case, about appropriate levels of taxation. The task of lawyers, judges, or students of the law is technical and, accordingly, much more circumscribed. The advantage of creating this dichotomy between the content of law and the content of politics is said to be increased certainty, stability, and predictability. Law is the outcome of the political process, not a part of it. If individual views of the morality of economic relations were to dominate, there would be no consistent application of the law, only an anarchic distribution of economic resources.

Positivism is rooted in the British doctrine of parliamentary supremacy. This doctrine, described by constitutional scholars Dicey and Wade, dictates that Parliament is supreme: Parliament can make or unmake any law, and no person or body shall override or set aside its legislation. Parliamentary supremacy originated as a response to the arbitrary edicts of Britain's monarchical system of government; it reserves the practice of lawmaking—and the resolution of disputes about the content of those laws—to the political process. The task of the legalist is, at its most expansive, to interpret the intentions of lawmakers, not to make moral choices. Law is a valid set of rules, enforced through a system of economic and social sanctions. It is vital that the rules be applied correctly, but the morality of the law need not be subjected to scrutiny.

Positivism is also rooted in the notion of a **social contract**—that is, law ties individuals to the collective through a binding, democratically constructed agreement. Democratic elections are expressions of the will of the people and those who are successful in these elections are given the power to create laws. These laws then become binding and enforceable, for they flow from the will of the people. According to this view, the state, or the government of the day, is an expression of the sovereignty of the people who live within it.

There have been many variations of positivism. In its earliest variant, philosopher John Austin viewed law as a species of command, an instrument of government or bureaucracy. In 1832, Austin wrote in *The Province of Jurisprudence Determined*:

> The existence of law is one thing: its merit or demerit is another. Whether it be or not is one inquiry; whether it be or not conformable to an assumed standard, is another inquiry. A law, which actually exists, is a law, though we happen to dislike it, or though it vary from the text by which we regulate our approbation and disapprobation.[1]

For Austin, all human laws had to conform to God-given laws, an assertion that twentieth-century legal philosopher H.L.A. Hart has rejected as a "confusion." Hart suggests that this claim confuses law as it is and "law as morality would require it to be." "For him," Hart writes of Austin, "it must be remembered, the fundamental principles of morality were God's commands."[2]

H.L.A. Hart viewed law as a secular construction, although, like Austin, he believed that law and morality must be severed for purposes of legal practice and legal analysis. He was not, however, blind to its injustices:

> The step from the simple form of society, where primary rules of obligation are the only means of social control, into the legal world with its centrally organized legislature, courts, officials, and sanctions brings its solid gains at a certain cost. The gains are those of adaptability to change, certainty, and efficiency, and these are immense; the cost is the risk that the centrally organized power may well be used for the oppression of numbers with whose support it can dispense.[3]

In his best-known book, *The Concept of Law*, Hart argued that equating the validity of law with its morality will blind us to critical moral principles. What of the law that should now apply to German informers during the Nazi occupation? he asked. Hart conceded that the laws applying at the time were monstrous and immoral, but argued that "morality may also demand that the state should punish only those who, in doing evil, did what the state at the time forbade. This is the principle of ***nulla poena sine lege***."[4]

The Latin maxim quoted by Hart dictates that "there shall be no penalty without a valid law," a principled limitation on the power of the state to punish. In Hart's view, should the law's validity be analytically synonymous with the law's morality, retroactive punishment will be disguised as ordinary punishment. For Hart, while in the simple positivist doctrine, "morally iniquitous rules may still be law," positivism also "offers no disguise for the choice between evils which, in extreme circumstances, may have to be made."[5] The principle of "no penalty without a valid law" does not allow for repressive, retroactive law. However, this principle can comprehend retroactive law that benefits those touched by its imposition. For example, the Supreme Court of Germany ruled that Nazi law is not valid for those who suffered under its racist oppression. At the same time, however, those enforcing Nazi law in good faith (with a few exceptions) cannot be punished, because of the principle "no penalty without a valid law."

Sociologist Donald Black, in his controversial book *The Behavior of Law*, offered a further viewpoint on positivism. Black saw law as a quantitative variable; it increases in some contexts and decreases in others. When informal mechanisms of dispute resolution are strong, there is little need for law. But with modernization, centralization, and decreases in family and commmunity control, the need for law increases in quantitative terms.

Consider, for example, behaviour in a schoolyard during recess. During the 1950s and 1960s young children in Canada would often pick on other children, teasing and occasionally intimidating them to the point of provoking a physical response, either from the victim, friends, family, or teachers. This kind of informal dispute resolution can work well when there is a cohesive community. But in the year 2005, with less family and community control in the schoolyard setting, and with more urban and transient social contexts, the need emerges for a different definition or description of the behaviour—bullying—and for a more formal, legally based set of procedures to respond to a given behaviour.

Black also argued that the use of law varies directly with respectability; among "more respectable" people, one will find greater recourse to the law than among "less respectable" people. That is, the socially marginal citizens of a given society are less likely to call police and less likely to use law to resolve social disputes. Accordingly, Black has concluded, "a complaint by a respectable party against an unrespectable party is more likely than the reverse, and . . . more likely to succeed in every way."[6]

Although conceptions of "respectability" and "community" seem subjective and therefore difficult to define and measure, Black insisted that an objective, scientific explanation of law and legal order is possible. In a 1972 article in the *Yale Law Journal*, "The Boundaries of Legal Sociology," Black concluded that values have no place in any social analysis of law:

> We should be clear about the relation between sociological and legal scholarship. There is, properly speaking, no conflict of professional jurisdiction between the two. A legal problem is a problem of value

and is forever beyond the reach of sociology. Jurisdictional conflict arises only when the sociologist makes policy recommendations in the name of science: In matters of legal policy, the lawyer must rely on his own wits.[7]

Black's argument is solidly in the positivist tradition. Law is a valid set of social rules; considerations of morality or value are essentially unhelpful in any analysis of its operation. Like Austin's and Hart's, Black's strategy for understanding law is one that accepts that law has moral premises, but rejects the idea that the study of this morality is a part of the enterprise of legal analysis.

Positivists are conservative in the sense that they view law as a valid set of rules. However, this does not mean that positivists adhere to conservative positions on economic, moral, or political issues, for the content of the law may be premised on "radical," "liberal," or "conservative" moral values. For example, the positivist response to the question of the legitimacy of abortion posed at the start of this discussion mirrors that of the question of legitimacy in taxation. The existing law is a valid set of rules. Since there is an absence of criminal control of abortion, the practice is legally valid, i.e., legitimate. Likewise, positivists will answer the question about persons with disabilities on the basis of existing law. If a university decides to give preference to such candidates in a hiring competition, this decision will be valid, as long as the university has, in terms of its process, the legal power to insist upon such a preference.

NATURAL LAW AND THE NATURAL LAW RESPONSE

The natural law perspective is diametrically opposed to positivism. While positivists insist upon a strict separation of law and morality, the adherents of natural law insist on a clear link between law and morality. The essence of the natural law perspective is ***lex iniusta non est lex***: an unjust law is no law at all.

Natural law has a longer history than positivism; it can be traced through more than 2 500 years of Western development, from Plato, Socrates, and Aristotle to Hobbes, Spinoza, and Rousseau. Until the twentieth century, natural law theory was generally conceived to be based upon Christian theology or Judeo-Christian values. Those who believed in this necessary coincidence of morality and law argued that there are God-given moral values that must inform the operation and study of law and legality. Unlike Austin and the positivists, however, the natural lawyers could not be sure that God-given moral values would always find expression in law. There are also many variations of natural law: Christian law, Islamic law, Sikh law, and so on.

In this century, the secular basis of natural law has become more dominant, but the emphasis on determining moral values and principles remains. Philosopher David Lloyd explains, "We have a feeling of discontent with justice based on positive law alone, and strenuously desire to demonstrate that there are objective moral values which can be given a positive content."[8] However, the lack of clarity in such a perspective on law is nicely captured by law professor Gerald Gall: "The problem, of course, with natural law is defining the particular nature of the natural law to which [to] conform. The danger is that anyone can invoke his version of the natural law in order to suit his purposes."[9]

If law and morality are always to be coincident, which law and which morality are to prevail? In a largely secular society such as contemporary Canada, it is no answer to assert that "God's will must prevail." Even organized religions do not agree on important social issues. Moslems, Seventh-day Adventists, Jehovah's Witnesses, Hindus, Anglicans, Catholics, Jews, and Unitarians will provide different responses to the question of the morality of a given law. And for those whose beliefs are based on other foundations than religion, or for non-religious citizens, the proper coincidence of law and morality is a purely secular matter.

Legal theorist Roger Cotterrell has suggested that, as a perspective on law, natural law is virtually dead, eclipsed first by positivism and later by realist and Marxist conceptions. His argument is that the utility of a natural law approach has been limited because legal doctrine has become increasingly a compromise among diverse interests within the population of a given nation-state. It is difficult to discern a moral soul within such a product of conflict and compromise. Moreover, law is used, within specific geographic and temporal contexts, to create a certain kind of social order. What guides the operation of the law are not timeless moral principles, but time-specific pragmatism. The issue for lawmakers is less "what is moral" than "what works" in a specific time and place. According to Cotterrell,

> The problem is that even if there *are* universal principles of natural law, they may not offer a convincing guide or grounding for complex, highly technical and ever-changing modern law. After all, legal positivism does not deny that the substance of law can be subject to moral criticism. The issue is not whether law can be morally evaluated, but whether its essential character must be explained in moral terms.[10]

Nonetheless, there are many senses in which natural law remains very much alive. Both the U.S. Constitution and the *Canadian Charter of Rights and Freedoms* are statements of natural law ideals. In the latter, for instance, there is a guarantee of freedom from cruel and unusual punishment, and freedoms of conscience, religion, expression, and association. These are essentially moral precepts, having their roots in "some higher system to which mere positive law should conform."[11]

The problem for natural lawyers is to identify how natural law will be determined. For example, is the 25-year minimum sentence for first degree murder cruel and unusual punishment? If we subscribe to the tenets of natural law, do we look to the deterrent impact of the penalty, to its inherent "justness" (i.e., the extent to which it adequately reflects community denunciation of such a crime)? Or do we seek answers in the often contradictory writings of religious or moral thinkers? Since there is no single, clear morality to guide the operation of legality, an attempt to determine natural law can be compared to trying to nail Jell-O to the wall.

So, then, how would the adherent of the natural law perspective answer the questions on taxation, abortion, and persons with disabilities, which are, after all, clearly moral questions? If resources are seen to be morally distributed, if abortion is felt to be morally repugnant, if equality is considered a moral value to which all others should be subservient, then high-income earners should not be more highly taxed, women should not be able to obtain abortions, and persons with disabilities should not be given preferential treatment in matters of employment. On the other hand, if resources are seen to be unfairly distributed, if women are believed to have a moral right to reproductive freedom, if persons with disabilities are considered deserving of differential assistance, then high-income earners should be more highly taxed, abortion should not be criminally sanctioned, and persons with disabilities should be given preferential treatment in employment.

In these opposing answers, we find the Achilles' heel of the natural law perspective. There is no doubt that morality is at the heart of the legal process. However, a perspective that demands a linkage between law and morality *must* specify the moral premises that will be operative at any specific time and place.

LEGAL REALISM AND THE REALIST RESPONSE

The legal realist movement began in the United States in the early twentieth century, primarily as a reaction to the ongoing failure of legal doctrine to predict legal outcomes in specific instances. Legal realists are often referred to as skeptics; they argue that, in order to understand the legal process, one must be aware of the political, economic, and social contexts in which law arises, changes, and persists.

Legal realists see the personality and political orientation of individual judges, community sentiments, specific economic realities, and political imperatives as all contributing to the growth of statutory law and judicial decisions. Karl Llewellyn, perhaps the most prominent of American legal realists, has noted that realism is less a philosophy of law than a method or technology for achieving a more grounded understanding of law and legal process. "There is no school of realists," Llewellyn declared in 1931. "There is no group with an official or accepted, or even with an emerging creed. . . . There is, however, a movement in thought and work about law."[12]

The essence of this "movement in thought and work about law" is its rejection of the idea that a specific "correct" solution will inevitably emerge from the application of formal legal doctrine and formal logic to a particular legal problem. Indeed, the realist argues that legal doctrine cannot be understood without a serious empirical study of the social, economic, and political context in which that doctrine takes shape. Legal realists may be conservative, liberal, or radical in political, economic, or moral orientation, but all advocate the view that legal doctrine alone cannot explain legal decision making. There are many senses in which **legal realism** can be seen as the natural consequence of positivism. Legal realism provides the tools for a more nuanced interpretation of the content of law, one that positivism alone appears not to speak to or easily comprehend.

In answering the question whether higher-income earners should be more highly taxed, realists would respond that they would need to know more about the social environment before making any decision. What social circumstances led to different forms of taxation (e.g., income, sales, corporate, capital gains) and, more specifically, to the most recent amendments to taxation law and regulation? What are the moral, political, and economic issues surrounding these amendments? In empirical terms, how are resources taxed, and why? Likewise, in responding to the questions on abortion and the treatment of persons with disabilities, there will be empirical inquiry into the social, economic, and political conditions that gave rise to the current state of the law. That is, legal realists share an epistemology—a method or grounds for obtaining knowledge—but it does not follow that there is or need be a realist consensus on moral, economic, and political issues. Realists might ultimately be divided on all three questions, but they are likely to be better informed about the issues underlying the law than those who take either a positivist or a natural law perspective.

At the heart of the realist enterprise is a skeptical empiricism that creates an understanding of the law that is arguably distinct from both positivism and natural law. Llewellyn described the realist style of legal decision making as "grand style judging." He contrasted it with "the orthodox ideology," in which judicial precedents are seen as binding. In grand style judging, precedents are persuasive, but much more is involved: the reputation and approach of the judge writing the opinion, the general conceptual sense of the argument, and, most important, the possible consequences of the law under consideration. By contrast, the orthodox ideology is essentially a more limited, positivist position. It holds that difficult cases are to be decided by the rules of law alone. Policy is something to be debated by legislatures, not courts. The job of the court, as Llewellyn notes, is "to prune away those 'anomalous' cases or rules which do not fit."[13] In this process of pruning anomalies, judges are not creating new law, but discovering the meaning of existing law and clarifying the intent of the legislature.

At the time of its inception in the United States, legal realism presented a major challenge to established thinking and writing about law. Legal realists could point to the limits of the explanatory power of positivism and to the natural law perspective's poorly contoured definitions of morality. But critics of the realist school could, in turn, point to the lack of a coherent vision or morality within its regimen of skeptical empiricism. The Marxist view offered a new holy grail: a fusion of morality and science.

A MARXIST THEORY OF LAW AND THE MARXIST RESPONSE

The Oxford Reference Dictionary defines **Marxism** as "the political and economic theories of Karl Marx, especially that, as labour is basic to wealth, historical development, following scientific laws determined by **dialectical materialism**, must lead to the violent overthrow of the capitalist class. . . . Events would then progress toward the ideal of a classless society."

In most important senses, it is almost absurd to speak of a Marxist analysis of law and legal order; Marxists have traditionally urged "the withering away of the state" (and hence of law and legal order). They have also typically urged what must now be seen as the hopelessly naïve notion of the "dictatorship of the proletariat."

It is difficult to define a single Marxist approach to law. Are we referring to the writings and teachings of Karl Marx? Law as practised within self-described communist states? Indeed, is a Marxist approach ultimately reducible to a basic core? There appears to be no simple or universally agreed-upon answer to these questions. Moreover, there are those who work within a Marxist tradition, yet reject some of Marx's claims and analyses: his call for violence, the possibility or desirability of an end to contradiction, his omission of gender from his analysis, and his insistence that economic power determines law, and his failure to recognize the environmental need to limit production.

Marx argued that the relationship between material circumstances and human beings is dialectical in form. The economic organization of capitalism carries the seeds of its destruction. Being inherently oppressive, the distributive character of capitalism will be resisted by those who labour; it will therefore change, producing new contradictions that will require further remedy. The final result of these struggles, Marx believed, would be the "withering away" of the law; human beings would live in equality and harmony in a utopian communist state.

Capitalism has changed since Marx wrote of the contradictions of economic life in Europe and Czarist Russia. Although inequality in the distributive structure of economic relations is still very much with us in Western industrialized democracies, child labour laws, trade union legitimacy, universal social assistance, and universal health care have changed the social order in Europe, and, to a more limited extent, in North America.

How, then, are we to assess the Marxist analysis of law? Obviously, a literal adherence to the writings of Karl Marx has limited appeal. The problems that an avowedly communist Soviet Union faced during its last years were problems that Marx could not foresee: environmental limits to production, inefficiencies of state ownership, and the apparently ceaseless continuation of inequality and privilege, despite 1917 and the violent overthrow of the capitalist class.

Still, this does not mean that all elements of the Marxist view of law should be cast aside, and the perspective rejected as irrelevant. Robert Heilbroner has eloquently argued its continued usefulness:

> A dialectical view of reality, enlarging our view of things with a tension and contradictoriness that is lacking in other philosophic perspectives, should help clarify our knowledge of the world. A materialist view of history will enrich our understanding of the past and of the present, as long as the processes of production play a powerful role in human affairs and exert such enormous influences over the stratification of society. . . . And socialism—the grail of Marxism—must continue to exert its influence as long as humanity suffers the unnecessary bondages imposed by its own social organization, a condition that is certain to persist for generations.[14]

How, then, would a Marxist perspective view our three questions? First, should high-income earners be more highly taxed than low-income earners? Absolutely; the labour of certain citizens is disproportionately rewarded; increased taxation of the wealthy is a mechanism to ensure that those who expend similar amounts of labour are similarly rewarded. In the United States in 1990, the bottom 20 percent of families had an average gross income of approximately Can$9 000; the top 20 percent approximately Can$140 000; and the top 1 percent (about three million Americans) approximately Can$660 000.[15] From the Marxist perspective, the sheer magnitude of these discrepancies cannot be justified, even given a somewhat different time and effort typically expended in labour by the richer and poorer in American society.

Critics of the Marxist insistence upon economic equality argue that there are substantive differences in individual contributions to society. In the lowest-income quintile of the population, one typically finds large numbers of people unable or unwilling to labour productively. Moreover, economic rewards have historically created incentives for inventive contributions to the common good, such as new medicines and vaccines, computers, mass transit, and global systems of communication and transportation.

Perhaps the future of resource distribution is neither nineteenth-century **laissez-faire capitalism** nor Marxist economic equality. The New England ice cream corporation, Ben and Jerry's, initially set out a provocative 5 to 1 ratio for the salaries of its employees. No employee of this self-avowed socially and environmentally conscious company could make more than five times the salary of any other employee. Among American families, however, there is a ratio of more than 73 to 1 between the top 1 percent of earners and the lowest 20 percent.

The second question, that of a woman's right to abortion, falls outside the Marxist perspective, since the theory is economically rather than morally based. (Marx wrote virtually nothing about gender issues.) Given the emphasis of dialectical materialism, however, the right to abortion seems as likely to be criminalized as not. If a restriction of the birth rate is seen as economically desirable, abortion will not be criminalized. If an increase in the birth rate is seen as synonymous with greater economic well-being, the practice of abortion is likely to be criminally punished.

Finally, the question about preferential treatment in employment for those with disabilities might well be answered positively, given the Marxist emphasis on economic equality. Although the issue arose after the time of Marx, it might be argued that while dialectical materialism must ultimately produce legal remedies that give preference to disempowered minorities, it is not clear that such programs are particularly Marxist in their world-view.

Contemporary Theories of the Role of Law

THE CRITICAL LEGAL PERSPECTIVE

The critical legal studies movement arose in U.S. law schools during the late 1970s. Like the legal realist movement of the 1920s, it attracted law teachers and social scientists who had become increasingly disenchanted with current forms of legal analysis. Those first attracted to the so-called CLS movement

> were simply seeking to locate those people working either at law schools or in closely related academic settings with a certain vaguely perceived, general political or cultural predisposition . . . people on the left at least relatively sceptical of the State Socialist regimes . . . egalitarian, in a more far-reaching sense than those committed to tax-and-transfer-based income redistribution . . . those appalled by the routine Socratic discussions of appellate court decisions, repelled by their sterility, and thorough disconnection from actual social life . . . repelled by the supposition that neutral and apolitical legal reasoning could resolve charged controversies . . . put off by the hierarchical classroom style in which phony priests first crush and then bless each new group of initiates.[16]

The critical legal studies movement has not always been well received by the academic mainstream. Law professor Gerald Gall has suggested that critical legal studies is "an amalgam of traditional legal realism and modern cynicism." He argues that, while realists are often content to examine extra-legal factors influencing the operation of the law, critical theorists look to the purposes, values, and assumptions of the legal system, challenging their contemporary relevance, rationales, and validity. Gall has asserted that the critical legalists argue not from a sound philosophical basis but from personal and political values.[17]

Critical legal studies is clearly an assault on a positivist understanding of law and legal process, but its precise nature is not easy to discover. Law professor Mark Kelman has argued that it is more than simply a continuation of the realist critique; it also seeks to strip away the illusory certainty upon which the language of the law is based:

> We think in prepackaged categories, clusters, reified systems. We forget the degree to which we invent the social world. We come to think that rules make us act impersonally; we often forget that we must continually choose to act impersonally. . . . [S]oon we think that the rules make us do good rather than that we sometimes

> collectively choose to do the good things we do when applying rules. . . . [L]egalist practice . . . makes us passive by making us confused.[18]

There are elements not only of legal realism within this critique of law, but also of dialectical materialism and Marxist analysis. Kelman suggested that the aim of critical legal studies is to uncover illusion or delusion in the legal form, not to remedy simple ignorance. And while Kelman and other proponents of critical legal studies have recognized the limitations and weaknesses of the Marxist view of law, it is not clear that what they offer is either more than a derivative combination of legal realism and Marxist analysis, or a variation in kind rather than substance. The critical legal studies movement has, unlike legal realism, typically conceptualized matters in normative terms, and like Marxism, has pointed consistently to issues of social disadvantage.

Nonetheless, it is not clear how practitioners of critical legal studies would respond to our three questions. Most likely, they would view high-income earners as deserving of greater taxation, abortion as a matter of reproductive rights for women, and preferential employment for those with disabilities as advantageous. Yet none of these conclusions flow unequivocally from the critical legal studies perspective. Like legal realists, the adherents of this perspective speak to method, but like Marxists and natural lawyers, they often champion an understanding of law premised upon a specific vision of the role of law or the nature of morality in a specific society.

FEMINIST THEORIES OF LAW

A feminist theory of jurisprudence did not really begin to emerge until the 1960s, though its origins are appropriately traced to the **suffragette** movement of the early twentieth century. Feminists argue that history—and hence, law—has been written from a male point of view and, as such, cannot adequately reflect the contributions that women have made to the structure of social life. A **feminist theory of law** holds that both the language and the logic of law reinforce male values—that prevailing conceptions of law serve to perpetuate male power and female subordination. Feminist analysts of the legal system have worked to identify the "gendered" nature of law, pointing to laws affecting divorce, reproductive rights, domestic violence, and employment as areas of concern.

Feminist theories of jurisprudence have had a particularly significant effect on legal scholarship and legal practice within the past few decades. Contemporary law journals almost universally reflect this focus and interest. Many involved in feminist theory point to a number of waves of feminist thought: first-wave feminism, and second- and third-wave feminism. First-wave feminism was preoccupied with the social and legal inequalities inflicted on women in the late nineteenth and early twentieth centuries: the lack of access to educational opportunities, the subordination of women embodied in the laws of marriage, and the denial of the right to vote. First-wave feminists were, generally speaking, middle-class women whose challenge to legal order sprang from their own experiences of injustice.

Second-wave feminists emerged in the late 1960s and early 1970s in North America, Britain, and Europe. There were multiple concerns expressed with respect to the regulation and control of women: lack of access to birth control and the double standards of male and female sexual expression, the plight of working women, and discrimination against lesbians and women of colour. Unlike first-wave feminists, who voiced their displeasure with laws that reflected inequality, second-wave feminists went further, challenging the culture that was driving the subordination of women, and urging changes, not only in law, but in the lived experiences of women in their private and domestic lives. In second-wave feminism, the institution of law itself was seen as problematic and contributing to the subordination of women; this was a more profound critique than that offered by first-wave feminists, who strove largely to address their own concerns with respect to equality.

Third-wave feminism is explicit in its endorsement of social activism, and it is this third wave that has spawned much recent feminist legal theory. The third wave of feminism has emerged from the political consciousness of second-wave feminism, but with a more explicitly radical analysis of the role of law, and a critique of long-established legal notions such as reasonableness, objectivity, and neutrality. The feminist legal theorist Catharine MacKinnon has argued, for example, that positivism or what might be called mainstream legal theory actually hides a very explicit partiality or point of view behind what she terms its "point-of-viewlessness."[19] In denouncing such notions as reasonableness, objectivity, and neutrality, this kind of radical feminism necessarily opens the door to alternative methods for constructing knowledge—to what theorists term an alternate epistemology. Feminist narratives—the storytelling of experiences of subordination by gender and their intersecting realms of class and race—are viewed as sound epistemology, more deserving of the mantle of legal scholarship than any dispassionate analysis of legal doctrine.

In many ways a feminist theory of law represents a more substantial challenge to contemporary theories of the role of law than does any other theoretical framework. There is, however, no uniform or singular feminist analysis of law. While all feminists share a commitment to the moral, political, and social equality of men and women, beyond this vision substantial disagreement exists, especially in the everyday practice of feminism. Pornography is seen by some radical feminists as worthy of censorship and criminalization—as the embodiment of the male abuse of women. Yet other self-described radical feminists reject this criminalization or censorship of pornography as critical to the feminist agenda, urging that protection of sex trade workers constitutes a more worthy struggle. Similarly, some feminists celebrate differences between men and women, asserting that women tend to emphasize different values and skill sets in their everyday life; other feminists reject this kind of analysis, its empirical merits notwithstanding. A rejection of biological relevance leads these self-described radical feminists to suggest that the only sex differences of any consequence are those that reside within the realm of power.

A useful summary of the origins of a feminist theory of law and the range of definitions within it is offered by Obiora and Perry in the *International Encyclopedia of the Social Sciences*. Their analysis differs slightly from that set out above, but is offered as another lens through which to observe the continuing emergence of a feminist theory of law:

> Although it was only as recently as the 1970s that feminist legal theory or feminist jurisprudence were first heard as names for the diversity of gender-focused currents in legal scholarship and argumentation, these strands of contemporary thought have their roots in the "rights revolution" that took place in the political thought of seventeenth and eighteenth century Europe and the Americas. The foundations of early feminist thought can be traced to explicit efforts to appropriate the emancipatory liberal ideals for women.
>
> The extension of the right to vote was central to the nineteenth century feminist legal agenda. Informed by the social contract theory, early feminists believed that women's political enfranchisement would facilitate their emancipation from historical oppression. The women's rights movement was closely linked to the struggle for the abolition of slavery. In the United States, the campaign for women's vote is associated with the 1848 Seneca Falls convention and the Declaration of Sentiments that emerged from the meeting. It was at Seneca Falls that the former slave, Sojourner Truth, gave her celebrated "Ain't I a woman?" speech, which questioned the parallel that is often drawn between the legal status of white women and that of slaves in the rhetoric of early nineteenth century feminism.

Despite the significance of voting as the emblematic act of citizenship and of full participation in the *polis*, gender-based discrimination was no less pervasive in other spheres of life. Under the common law doctrine of coverture, a woman lived under the tutelage of her father or other male guardian, until through the sacramental covenant of marriage, her civil legal identity was subsumed by that of her husband under whose cover she derived protection. A woman was typically incapable of making contracts or testamentary dispositions, owning and alienating real property, testifying as a witness in court against her husband, suing or being sued in her own name, or controlling her earnings. She could not even protect her own physical integrity—her husband had the right to chastise her, although only with a switch no thicker than his thumb.

The legal fiction of the unity of spouses as well as the rise of separate spheres ideology exempted the private sphere of the family from state intervention, and rendered women vulnerable to an array of abuses, including rape by their husbands. Beginning in the middle of the nineteenth century, a series of statutes—generically called the Married Women's Property Acts—removed some of the most severe civil disabilities pertaining to women, and acknowledged their personhood for the purposes of the law. Ultimately, struggles for the right to vote, for property rights, for protective labor legislation, for access to education and professional careers, and for related entitlements helped transform the legal landscape. Over the past few decades, feminist strategies have continued to effect change in consciousness and in laws. Legal efforts have focused, *inter alia*, on expanding reproductive freedom, deterring sexual violence, and eliminating sex-based discrimination in employment, education, family, welfare, and related contexts.

Feminist legal theory is a legacy both of the nineteenth century campaigns for women's emancipation and of the renaissance of feminist activism in the United States and elsewhere since the 1960s. Although there is much debate about its definition, feminist legal theory can be understood as the manifestation in the legal academy of a range of efforts to understand the nature of women's subordination—especially the ways in which it is rationalized and naturalized—and to propose remedies for this subordinate condition. Drawing upon cross-cutting academic and activist traditions, feminist inquiry approaches law both as an ensemble of potential tactics for reform and, more generally, as a site of struggle for a more general political transformation. Most strands of contemporary feminist legal theory have conceptualized law as a historically and socially constructed artifact embedded in particular social relations. Feminist legal theory eluci-dates the ways in which law facilitates patriarchal dominance and control. Explicating how the doctrines, discourses, institutions, and cul-ture of law perpetuate gender hierarchy, feminist legal theory has pro-vided the impetus for reconceptualizing tightly bonded concepts and premises of legal thought.[20]

THE ANARCHIST AND LIBERTARIAN PERSPECTIVES: CRITICAL DIFFERENCES

There have been many other grand designs for understanding law besides those examined so far. The **anarchist perspective on law** and society is suspicious of all forms of state control, but anarchists also endorse a com-munitarian ethic that is quite distinct from contemporary libertarian per-spectives. In nineteenth-century Europe, however, libertarianism was generally thought of as synonymous with anarchism. Anarchism of this kind holds, even today, that all forms of government are unnecessary and oppressive—the state is seen as the mechanism responsible for the murder of more than 100 million human beings, for concentration camps, and for widespread famine. In this view, the economic system would ideally be organized on the basis of cooperatives and communal owner-ship. Unlike twentieth-century libertarians, anarchists are committed to a principle of egalitarianism; they argue that inequalities of wealth and power are obstacles to overcome—that these inequalities will neces-sarily give rise to the abuse of power by the state.

Libertarians, in contrast, celebrate the rights of the individual and reject the notions of social security that are often at the heart of the anarchist tradition. David Friedman, in his book *The Machinery of Freedom*, summarizes libertarian beliefs about the role of the state—and hence, the role of law.

> The central idea of libertarianism is that people should be permitted to run their own lives as they wish. We totally reject the idea that people must be forcibly protected from themselves. A libertarian society would have no laws against drugs, gambling, pornography—and no compulsory seat belts in cars. We also reject the idea that people have an enforceable claim on others, for anything more than being left alone. A libertarian society would have no welfare, no social security system. People who wished to aid others would do so voluntarily through private charity, instead of using money collected by force from the taxpayers. People who wished to provide for their old age would do so through private insurance.[21]

The Case of Robert Latimer: Testing Perspectives on Law

Let us now return to the case raised at the beginning of this chapter—namely the criminal conviction of Robert Latimer on a charge of second degree murder. We will examine the Supreme Court of Canada's assessment of this case, and then ask how adherents of the various perspectives on law might respond to the Court's decision.

At his first trial, Latimer was found guilty of second degree murder and sentenced to a term of life imprisonment without parole eligibility for 10 years. He appealed to the Saskatchewan Court of Appeal, which upheld both his conviction and his sentence. However, a further appeal to the Supreme Court of Canada was successful, resulting in the ordering of a new trial.

At the second trial, counsel for Latimer argued the defence of necessity, suggesting that Tracy's condition essentially forced Latimer to commit the offence for which he was convicted. The trial judge did not permit the defence of necessity to go to the jury, and the jury convicted Latimer of second degree murder. After the trial judge explained to the jury that there was a mandatory minimum sentence of between 10 and 25 years' imprisonment, some members of the jury appeared to be upset and sent a note to the judge asking him if they could recommend less than the 10-year minimum. The judge permitted the jury to make this unusual recommendation, and he then granted a constitutional exemption from the mandatory minimum, sentencing the accused to one year in prison and one year on probation. The Saskatchewan Court of Appeal affirmed Latimer's conviction, but reversed the sentence of the trial judge, imposing the mandatory minimum of 10 years' imprisonment.

On appeal to the Supreme Court of Canada, counsel for Latimer argued that the mandatory minimum sentence of 10 years' imprisonment constitutes cruel and unusual punishment, and was accordingly a violation of section 12 of the *Canadian Charter of Rights and Freedoms* (the *Charter*). Counsel also argued that the defence of necessity ought to have been placed before the jury during the second trial. Both these arguments were unsuccessful, and in January 2001, Robert Latimer was taken into custody to begin serving his life sentence for the commission of second degree murder.

Let's look a little more closely at the facts of the case before considering the validity of claims of necessity and cruel and unusual punishment. Tracy Latimer's physical condition did not allow her to communicate verbally; she could express herself only through facial expressions, laughter, and crying. She enjoyed music and bonfires and being with her family—typically expressing joy at seeing family members. She also apparently loved being rocked gently by her parents. Tracy was completely dependent on others to sustain her life. The severe cerebral palsy from which she suffered led to five or more seizures per day; she could only be spoon-fed and suffered weight loss from a resultant lack of adequate nutrition.

There was also evidence, however, that Tracy could have been fed through a feeding tube inserted into her stomach; this tube would have both improved her nutrition and health and permitted the administration of more effective pain medication. The Latimer family rejected surgery to insert a feeding tube, believing it was too intrusive and would preserve her life in an artificial manner.

In the 12 years that she was alive, Tracy Latimer had undergone many surgeries: in 1990 she had surgery to balance muscles around her pelvis, and in 1992 metal rods were implanted in her back to improve support to her spine. At the time of her death she was scheduled to undergo surgery to her dislocated hip; the procedure would have led to the removal of her upper thigh bone. The anticipated period of recovery was one year. At this point Robert Latimer decided to end his daughter's life—to stop what he perceived as "mutilation."

The Supreme Court of Canada rejected the application of the defence of necessity. The Court noted that this defence has three key elements: first, there is requirement of imminent peril or danger if one fails to commit the crime in question; second, the accused must have no reasonable legal alternative to the course of action undertaken; third, there must be a sense of proportion between the harm that the accused inflicted and the harm that the accused avoided in committing the crime. The Supreme Court indicated that the trial judge was quite correct in removing this defence from the jury's consideration: Latimer faced no danger; there was a reasonable legal alternative to his action (further surgery to minimize Tracy's pain); finally, the harm inflicted in killing his daughter was considerably more serious than the harm he avoided—further surgery.

The Supreme Court also rejected the claim that the 10-year minimum sentence for this crime constituted cruel and unusual punishment. The Court noted that the mandatory minimum sentence for second degree murder was not under attack by Latimer's counsel. Rather, Latimer and his counsel were arguing for a single constitutional exemption, based solely on the facts of this case. In such circumstances, the court is obliged to consider the gravity of the offence and the specifics of the offender and the offence. As the Supreme Court noted, the offence—the intentional killing of another human being—is a very serious crime. And the offender, though he was a caring and involved parent, did plan his daughter's death, made attempts to conceal his crime, and showed little remorse. The Court concluded that the mandatory minimum sentence plays an important role in denouncing murder, even if Mr. Latimer now poses no danger to society, is unlikely to re-offend, and does not appear to require rehabilitation.

The legal positivist would almost certainly support this interpretation by the Supreme Court. The Court is affirming a validly enacted law, a section of the *Criminal Code* prohibiting murder. Section 229 of the *Code* prohibits the crime. More specifically, section 229(a)(i) states: "Culpable homicide is murder (a) where the person who causes the death of a human being (i) means to cause his death."[22] There is no doubt that Robert Latimer fulfilled the terms of this section. Some positivists also might be skeptical of the role of the *Canadian Charter of Rights and Freedoms*, arguing that judicial decisions that can override legislation are undemocratic, substituting the judgment of non-elected individuals for the democratic will of representative government. At the same time, however, there is a positivist logic of support for the *Charter*. The *Charter* is, after all, a part of the Constitution, validly enacted law, and, as such, deserving of support; the law mandates judicial overview to protect what are thought to be timeless human rights. The manner in which section 12 of the *Charter* was interpreted in *R. v. Latimer*,[23] however, would probably be applauded by most all positivists. Stability, certainty, and predictability of law are enhanced by refusing to carve out a single judicially crafted exception to statutory law.

The natural lawyer is likely to applaud the decision in *Latimer*, at least insofar as the judgment stresses the value and sanctity of all life. Some of the interveners in this case were, in fact, groups that endorse a natural law perspective, one that flows from the specific realm of Christianity. The Catholic Group for Health, Justice and Life, the Evangelical Fellowship of Canada, the Christian Medical and Dental Society, and Physicians for Life all brought counsel to the Supreme Court hearing in *Latimer*. Some natural law adherents might, however, decry the sentence imposed as unjustly punitive—as failing to recognize the suffering that led Latimer to take his daughter's life. It is difficult, however, to construct a morality that justifies Mr. Latimer's taking of life in itself.

The legal realist and the critical legalist would want more information about the social and political context in which this decision was made— the public perception of Latimer, his conviction, and his sentence. As analysts of law, legal realists will, like positivists, be less concerned about the "justness" of the verdicts than about the internal logic of the decisions. Legal realists will cast their analytic nets more widely than positivists, employing more than doctrinal analysis. But their task will ultimately be quite similar: to understand how and why this case fits within existing precedents. Critical legalists, on the other hand, will be more inclined to fuse their analysis with moral judgment.

Those who work within a Marxist framework might well see Mr. Latimer as a victim of a social system that did not provide his family with adequate economic support. With the Marxist emphasis upon class oppression, Latimer's taking of life might be explained away or diminished as being the consequence of such victimization. On the other hand, self-described Marxist regimes have, to date, often endorsed especially punitive state responses to political opposition and to both criminal and quasi-criminal conduct.

The feminist theory of law does not appear to speak directly to the issues raised by the *Latimer* decision, but there is a good deal of subtext and potential for further exploration. Like 98 percent of convicted murderers, Robert Latimer is male. Further, he killed his daughter. Although only 2 percent of murderers are female, about 40 percent of victims are women and female children. Some feminists might, accordingly, applaud the *Latimer* decision, suggesting that it makes an important stand against patriarchy and male violence. Other feminists might suggest that an overly punitive treatment of Latimer is folly since such treatment could make the man a martyr and provoke an anti-female backlash.

Finally, anarchists and libertarians, with their skeptical view of state power, might well view at least the sentence imposed upon Robert Latimer as state abuse of power. This is especially true of laissez-faire libertarians, who are particularly suspicious of a potential tyranny of the collective. Latimer would be cast as a man trying to fend for himself and his family, simply attempting to survive—the victim of a big brother mentality on the part of the Canadian state. However, anarchists, who adopt a more communitarian ethic might well accept that Latimer's conduct violated a common code and, as such, deserves a common punishment.

Conclusion: The Importance of Competing Perspectives

Our views of law can be somewhat simplistically condensed into two opposing camps: those who view law and its transactions as morally neutral exercises of logic and interpretation, and those who view law and legal practice as a terrain for moral, political, and economic debate. The proponents of the first analysis embrace positivism, the dominant view among legal practitioners and, to a lesser extent, among legal academics. Those who embrace the natural law, realist, Marxist, anarchist, libertarian, feminist, or critical legal studies perspective argue that such a view is insufficient: to study and practise law is, they say, to engage the moral, political, and economic issues that infuse the legal process.

Yet we should be mindful of the limitations of these somewhat artificial categories. When Canadians speak of their views of law, these are not typically abstract, but concrete. Canadians do not identify themselves as positivists, realists, or Marxists, but speak either in favour of or against specific statutes and judicial decisions. Canadians are for and against capital punishment, for and against the legal recognition of homosexual marriage, for and against income surtax of the wealthy. The categories of positivism, natural law, realism, Marxism, and critical legal studies are more properly conceptualized as heuristic aids to understanding a range of perspectives or theories about law.

There are other perspectives on law besides these. One can claim, for example, that law is best understood as an instrument of social engineering, the will of God as revealed to human beings, or an implicit or explicit instrument of economic, gender, and racial oppression.

All these definitions of law will have merit for some Canadians in some circumstances. There is a sense in which law is an instrument of social engineering. But is this definition all-encompassing and ultimately definitive of an understanding of law? Or is it another conception of positivism, restated in different form? Then, for those who believe in an invisible deity ordering human affairs, law may well be formulated as the will of God. But can this perspective fully define the continuing amendment of law? Is it a conception of natural law, perhaps stated in its original form?

Finally, those who believe that law is an instrument of oppression distance themselves from both the natural law and the positivist perspectives, and show interest in some amalgam of the Marxist, legal realist, anarchist, libertarian, feminist, and critical legal studies perspectives. But, once again, can this definition fully inform an understanding of the law? The British historian E.P. Thompson has noted that although law can be an instrument of oppression, it can also be a tool for liberation.[24] Laws that serve to assist the disadvantaged—the granting of universal health care, compensation for disability, and the provision of a basic level of economic support—are not easily viewed as inherently oppressive.

For the typical Canadian citizen, however, the legal form may not be, as Thompson suggested, "an unqualified human good." Remarks and sentiments about law and legal process may be more likely to run in the direction of Shakespeare's exhortation (in *Henry VI*, Part 2), "The first thing we do, let's kill all the lawyers." Lawyers are often perceived as advocates for affluence and amorality, corrupted by privilege and motivated by material gain. Nevertheless, lawyers are also indispensable to the processes of dispute settlement in representative democracies, developing arguments, and creating effective advocacy. For how should disputes within societies be ordered, if not by law, and therefore by those expert in it? In its ideal form, law is the outcome of an informed verbal argument in which the interests of all relevant parties are adequately represented.

The various perspectives or theories about law suggest that the task of understanding cannot be too limited in focus. There is a need, as the positivists assert, to understand the form and structure of specific statutes and attendant judicial decisions. But the student of law and legal process must also seek to understand the political, economic, and moral values represented in statute law and judicial decisions—the issues that necessitate verbal argument and law.

Web Links

The Internet Encyclopedia of Philosophy
http://www.utm.edu/research/iep/l/law-phil.htm
The website at this URL is devoted exclusively to the philosophy of law. It is part of a larger site encompassing the Encyclopedia. The site is prepared by two philosophy professors and maintained at the University of Tennessee at Martin. It is an excellent resource for background material and definitions on philosophy.

JURIST: The Legal Education Network
http://jurist.law.pitt.edu/
This ambitious Internet project is designed to provide links to most legal resource materials available on the Internet. The main website is located at the University of Pittsburgh School of Law and has an international advisory board of legal academics. It is linked to the Canadian section at http://jurist.law.utoronto.ca/, which is hosted by the University of Toronto, Faculty of Law. The website is jointly maintained in other common law jurisdictions, including Canada, Australia, and the U.K. Links are especially good for law journals and online legal publications.

Robert Latimer
http://robertlatimer.com/english.htm
This website is maintained by the "friends of Robert Latimer" and contains information that supports the position that Robert Latimer was wrongly convicted and should not be imprisoned.

Decisions of the Supreme Court of Canada
http://www.lexum.umontreal.ca/csc-scc/en/index.html
Maintained by the University of Montreal, this site posts Supreme Court of Canada decisions and news. Cases on the site date back only to 1985, but there are plans to eventually make all the Court's decisions available online, without a subscription. A Boolean search engine is located at the bottom of the page, which makes searching for cases very simple.

Criminal Code of Canada
http://laws.justice.gc.ca/en/C-46/index.html
This site is accessed through the Department of Justice's laws page and provides the entire *Criminal Code* with all amendments. Searches can be conducted for specific information in the *Code* from the first page of the site.

Council of Canadians with Disabilities
http://www.ccdonline.ca
An intervener in the case of *R. v. Latimer,* the Council of Canadians represents persons with disabilities in Canada.

The DisAbled Women's Network Ontario
http://dawn.thot.net/index.html
The DisAbled Women's Network (DAWN) Ontario is a province-wide feminist organization for women with all types of disabilities. It supports the principle that women with disabilities have the right to direct their own lives.

Questions for Discussion

1. Natural law is the opposite of positivism and all other categories outside natural law and positivism are redundant. Discuss.
2. A young child suddenly begins to suffer life-threatening seizures. His mother bundles him into the family car and drives quickly to the hospital, speeding through a school zone at 20 kilometres over the 30-kilometre per hour limit. A police officer stops her car,

quickly understands what is going on, and gives her a police escort to the hospital. But he also insists on giving her a ticket for speeding—a minimum fine of $100. How would the different theories of law view the imposition of this $100 fine? Discuss.

Would it make any difference to your answer if

a. the police officer did not offer an escort to the hospital, but simply wrote out the ticket and then allowed the mother and child to travel on to the hospital—within the designated speed limit?

b. the mother survived on social assistance payments?

c. the mother's driver's licence had expired one week before this incident?

Discuss, given the competing perspectives of law presented in this chapter.

3. The British historian E.P. Thompson observed that a system of law represents "an unqualified human good." Do you agree or disagree? Why?

Further Reading

Baer, J.A. *Our Lives Before the Law: Constructing a Feminist Jurisprudence.* Princeton: Princeton University Press, 1999.

> This book has been described by one reviewer as a "clear and broad-based introduction" to feminist theories of jurisprudence. Baer's writing is quite accessible and critical, and allows students to understand a range of viewpoints within feminist scholarship.

Donovan, J. *Feminist Theory: The Intellectual Traditions.* 3d ed. New York: Continuum, 2000.

> This book has a useful compilation of the history and range of the traditions of feminist theory, considering liberal, Marxist, existential, and radical conceptions of feminist thought.

Hart, H.L.A. *The Concept of Law.* Oxford: Clarendon Press, 1961.

> This book is a complex examination of positivist views of law. Hart's analysis allows the reader to see the moral judgments that underlie a positivist analysis.

Heilbroner, R. *Marxism: For and Against.* New York: Norton and Company, 1980.

> This is a relatively accessible analysis of a Marxist view of society, one that explains both the strengths and the weaknesses of this framework for analysis.

Woodcock, G. *Anarchism: A History of Libertarian Ideas and Movements*. London, U.K.: Penguin, 1986.

> This history is a useful primer from a major scholar of anarchism. Often described as one of British Columbia's intellectual treasures, Woodcock was a theorist who managed to capture the interest of popular culture with his writings.

Notes

1. J. Austin, *The Province of Jurisprudence Determined* (London, U.K.: Wiedenfeld and Nicolson, 1955), 361.
2. H.L.A. Hart, "Positivism and the Separation of Law and Morals," in *Philosophy of Law*, 2d ed., edited by J. Feinberg and H. Gross (Belmont, CA: Wadsworth Publishing, 1980), 50. Reprinted from *Harvard Law Review* 71 (1958): 593H.
3. ——, *The Concept of Law* (Oxford: Oxford University Press, 1961), 197–8.
4. Ibid., 207.
5. Ibid.
6. D. Black, *The Behavior of Law* (New York: Academy Press, 1976), 110.
7. ——, "The Boundaries of Legal Sociology," *Yale Law Journal* 81 (1972): 1097.
8. D. Lloyd, *The Idea of Law* (Harmondsworth, U.K.: Penguin Books, 1973), 111.
9. G. Gall, *The Canadian Legal System,* 3d ed. (Toronto: Carswell, 1990), 11.
10. R. Cotterrell, *The Politics of Jurisprudence: A Critical Introduction to Legal Philosophy* (London, U.K.: Butterworths, 1989), 124.
11. D. Lloyd and M.D.A. Freeman, *Introduction to Jurisprudence*, 5th ed. (London, U.K.: Stevens, 1985), 92.
12. K.N. Llewellyn, "Some Realism About Realism," in *Jurisprudence: Realism in Theory and Practice* (Chicago: University of Chicago Press, 1962), 42–76.
13. ——, *The Common Law Tradition: Deciding Appeals* (Boston: Little, Brown, 1960), 510.
14. R. Heilbroner, *Marxism: For and Against* (New York: Norton and Company, 1980), 173.
15. These numbers have been culled from Statistics Canada, Income and Housing Section, 1990, and A.B. Fisher, "The New Debate over the Very Rich," *Fortune*, June 29, 1992, 42–54.

16. M. Kelman, *A Guide to Critical Legal Studies* (Cambridge, MA: Harvard University Press, 1987), 1.
17. Gall, *The Canadian Legal System*, 17.
18. Kelman, *A Guide to Critical Legal Studies*, 294–5.
19. C. MacKinnon, *Feminism Unqualified: Discourses on Life and Law* 16 (1987).
20. L.A. Obiara and R. Perry, "Feminist Legal Theory," *International Encyclopedia of the Social Sciences,* Vol. 8 (Oxford: Elsevier, 2001).
21. D. Friedman, *The Machinery of Freedom*, 2d ed. (Lasalle, IL: Open Court, 1989).
22. *Criminal Code*, R.S.C. 1985, c. C-46, s. 229(a)(i).
23. [2001] 1 S.C.R. 3.
24. See E.P. Thompson, *Whigs and Hunters: The Origin of the Black Act* (New York: Pantheon Books, 1975). Thompson writes, on page 265, of law as a "human good": "To deny or belittle this good," he suggests, is "a desperate error of intellectual abstraction. More than this, it is a self-fulfilling error, which encourages us to give up the struggle against bad laws and class-bound procedures, and to disarm ourselves before power. It is to throw away a whole inheritance of struggle about law, and within the forms of law, whose continuity can never be fractured without bringing men and women into immediate danger."

References

Becker, H. *Outsiders*. New York: Free Press, 1973.
Black, D. "The Boundaries of Legal Sociology." *Yale Law Journal* 81 (1972): 1086–1100.
——. *The Behavior of Law*. New York: Academic Press, 1976.
Boyd, N. *The Social Dimensions of Law*. Scarborough: Prentice-Hall, 1986.
——. *The Last Dance: Murder in Canada*. Scarborough: Prentice-Hall, 1988.
Cain, M., and A. Hunt. *Marx and Engels on Law*. London, U.K.: Academic Press, 1979.
Chambliss, W., and R. Seidman. *Law, Order and Power*. 2d ed. Reading, MA: Addison-Wesley, 1982.
Cheffins, R., and R. Tucker. *The Constitutional Process in Canada*. Toronto: McGraw-Hill Ryerson, 1986.
Claydon, J., and D. Galloway. *Law and Legality*. Toronto: Butterworths, 1979.

Coral, S.C., and J.C. Smith. *Law and Its Presuppositions: Actions, Agents and Rules*. Boston: Routledge and Kegan Paul, 1986.

Cotterrell, R. *The Politics of Jurisprudence: A Critical Introduction to Legal Philosophy*. London, U.K.: Butterworths, 1989.

Dworkin, R.M. *Law's Empire*. Cambridge, MA: Harvard University Press, Belknap Press, 1986.

Evan, W., ed. *The Sociology of Law*. New York: Free Press, 1980.

Feinberg, J., and H. Gross. *Philosophy of Law*. 2d ed. Belmont, CA: Wadsworth, 1980.

Gall, G. *The Canadian Legal System*. 3d ed. Toronto: Carswell, 1990.

Hart, H.L.A. *The Concept of Law*. Oxford: Oxford University Press, 1961.

Heilbroner, R. *Marxism: For and Against*. New York: Norton and Company, 1980.

James, P.S. *Introduction to English Law*. 11th ed. London, U.K.: Butterworths, 1985.

Kelman, M. *A Guide to Critical Legal Studies*. Cambridge, MA: Harvard University Press, 1987.

Kolmar, W.K. and Bartkowski, F. *Feminist Theory, Second Edition: A Reader*. Boston: McGraw Hill, 2005.

Llewellyn, K. *The Common Law Tradition: Deciding Appeals*. Boston: Little, Brown, 1960.

——. *Jurisprudence: Realism in Theory and Practice*. Chicago: University of Chicago Press, 1962.

Lloyd, D. *The Idea of Law*. Harmondsworth, U.K.: Penguin Books, 1973.

Lloyd, D., and M.D.A. Freeman. *Introduction to Jurisprudence*. 5th ed. London, U.K.: Stevens, 1985.

MacKinnon, C. *Feminism Unmodified: Discourses on Life and Law*. Cambridge, MA: Harvard University Press, 1987

Pfohl, S.J. *Images of Deviance and Social Control*. New York: McGraw-Hill, 1985.

Phillips, O.H. *A First Book of English Law*. 8th ed. London, U.K.: Sweet and Maxwell, 1988.

Pound, R. *Social Control Through Law*. New Haven: Yale University Press, 1942.

Rawls, J. *A Theory of Justice*. Cambridge, MA: Harvard University Press, Belknap Press, 1971.

Salmond, Sir J.W. *Salmond on Jurisprudence*. 12th ed. London, U.K.: Sweet and Maxwell, 1966.

Thompson, E.P. *Whigs and Hunters: The Origin of the Black Act*. New York: Pantheon Books, 1975.

——. *The Poverty of Theory and Other Essays*. London, U.K.: Monthly Review Press, 1978.

Twining, W.L. *Legal Theory and Common Law*. New York: Basil Blackwell, 1986.

Unger, R.M. *The Critical Legal Studies Movement*. Cambridge, MA: Harvard University Press, 1986.

Waddams, S.M. *Introduction to the Study of Law*. 4th ed. Scarborough: Carswell, 1992.

Walker, R.J., and M.G. Walker. *The English Legal System*. 6th ed. London, U.K.: Butterworths, 1985.

CHAPTER 2

The Sources of Canadian Law:
An Archaeology of Statutes
and Judicial Decisions

Canada's present legal system derives from various European systems brought to this continent in the 17th and 18th centuries by explorers and colonists. Although the indigenous peoples whom the Europeans encountered here each had their own system of laws and social controls, over the years the laws of the encroaching immigrant cultures began to prevail. After the English defeat of the French at Quebec in 1759, the country fell almost exclusively under English law. Other than in Quebec, where the civil law was codified on the model of the French Code Napoléon, Canada's criminal and private law has its basis in English common and statutory law.

(Justice Canada, 2005 [http://canada.justice.gc.ca/en/
dept/pub/ just/CSJ_page7.html])

Early Sources: Rethinking the Plains of Abraham

The **Magna Carta** of 1215 is significant for bringing the English their first true shift from monarchy to democracy. In clauses 60 to 63 of the *Magna Carta*, King John provided a legal concession by ceding to a council of 25 barons the opportunity to change certain of his decisions. Royal powers were no longer absolute. As legal historian Margaret Ogilvie noted, the *Magna Carta* was, however, far from a statement of democratic nationhood:

> *Magna Carta* was a feudal charter, a restatement of classical feudalism, and as such, benefited primarily the baronial interests. Those few clauses relating to freemen or villeins (feudal tenants), or merchants, reflected the status of those social segments; no magnanimous grants of important liberties were made. That the barons sought a written guarantee of established feudal usages was significant in itself; the Great Charter was a description of the past, not a prescription for the future.[1]

It was not until 1666 that **feudalism**—the political and economic system that granted nobility and land in exchange for the labour and military service of serfs or vassals on the land—was abolished in England. By this time, both the French and the British had established themselves in what were to become, respectively, Quebec and Ontario.

In 1627, Cardinal Richelieu established in law, at arm's length from France, the Company of New France, granting the land in part of what is now Quebec in perpetuity on the basis of a system of feudal tenure. By 1660, there was a governor and an elected council. In the 1670s, when the Company of New France was unable to defend itself against the Native peoples of the area, it surrendered its charter to France's King Louis XIV. From this time until the Battle of the Plains of Abraham in 1759, Canada became, in legal terms, the territory of two competing nations: Britain and France. Aboriginal claims were in the process of being restructured and extinguished.

The Battle of the Plains of Abraham took place on September 13, 1759. It would be the wellspring of significant future legal pronouncements: the **Royal Proclamation of 1763**, the *British North America Act, 1867*, and the *Constitution Act, 1982*. The battle was one event of the Seven Years' War (1756–1763), which ended with Britain establishing itself as the dominant naval and colonial power within Europe. British General James Wolfe and his 4 500 men surprised General Louis-Joseph Montcalm and his equally large French contingent by sailing past the fortified settlement of Quebec and climbing up the cliffs several kilometres above the city. Hundreds of men died in a bloody exchange of rifle power, and the better-trained and -organized English ultimately prevailed. The French retreated up the St. Lawrence River. In 1760, they tried to recapture the city but failed, and in 1761, the British were able to capture Montreal.

The British Parliament set out a legal structure for its new colony in the Royal Proclamation of 1763. The proclamation provided for a governor and council to administer Quebec until conditions permitted an elected assembly; the introduction of English laws and courts; and a guarantee of Aboriginal self-government. It was hoped that American settlers would flood into Quebec, ultimately assimilating the French. This vision of cultural conquest did not materialize, however, and in 1774 the British Parliament passed the ***Quebec Act***, providing, among other things, for the right of Roman Catholics to participate in government and for the use of French civil law.

The ***Constitution Act of 1791*** divided Quebec into Upper and Lower Canada. While ultimate legislative authority was retained by the

British Parliament, the 1791 act created legislative and executive branches of government in each of the Canadas, modelled to some extent on the emerging British parliamentary form. The executive branch of government, to mirror the Cabinet, was composed of a lieutenant governor and a council appointed by him. The legislative branch of government had two houses: a Legislative Council, not unlike the House of Lords, appointed by the British Parliament; and a Legislative Assembly, to which landowners in Upper or Lower Canada could be elected.

The 1791 *Constitution Act* was, again, far from a model of representative democracy. The executive branch of government was not responsible to the Legislative Assembly of either Upper or Lower Canada, but to Britain and British interests. In Lower Canada, the Executive Council was dominated by the English-speaking minority, and dubbed the "Château Clique" by Louis-Joseph Papineau and his *patriotes*. Papineau argued for the economic independence of Quebec and its annexation by the United States. The control of Quebec's commerce by appointed British interests ultimately led to armed rebellion in Quebec.

In Upper Canada, too, rebellions broke out against the legality of British rule, specifically, against the Family Compact, which represented British interests. William Lyon Mackenzie and a group of 800 rebels seeking independence from Britain marched south on Toronto's Yonge Street in 1837, armed with rifles, staves, and pitchforks. Like the rebels of Lower Canada, they were easily defeated by British troops. The rebellions led to the appointment of Lord Durham, whose task was to propose some resolution for the disputes in the colonies. Durham's 1839 report advocated union and self-government for Upper and Lower Canada, with Britain continuing to be responsible for the management of public lands and the emerging country's foreign interests. The 1840 *Act of Union* created the United Province of Canada, with Kingston as the capital. Both Upper and Lower Canada were granted an elected assembly and an appointed Upper House. By the 1850s, the Province of Canada was essentially a self-governing nation-state.

During the next 20 years, there was a series of political discussions about the integration of all British colonies north of the United States. The British in North America feared American expansion, and could also envision the economic advantages of sharing regional resources. Canada, in legal terms, was conceived in this period, emerging on July 1, 1867, as a result of the union of Upper and Lower Canada, Nova Scotia, and New Brunswick. Other provinces soon joined Confederation: Manitoba in 1870,

British Columbia in 1871, and Prince Edward Island in 1873. Alberta and Saskatchewan joined in 1905, and Newfoundland, in 1949.

The form of union sought by participants in the conception of Canada was a federal, rather than unitary, system of government. The distinctiveness of each province was a central aspect of the original legal design. Legal historian Ogilvie noted the following of Canada's original form:

> A legislative union and unitary form of government was impossible, and a federation at least permitted some local self-government which would hopefully guarantee the continuation of regional identities. Even so, the compromise was not adopted without a fight in each province.[2]

The *British North America Act, 1867* is Canada's original and defining source of law, setting out in sections 91 and 92 the respective powers of federal and provincial governmeonts, and more generally, a strategy for legal governance of the country. (See Chapter 4.) From 1867 to the present, provincial and federal governments have enacted thousands of statutes regulating family organization, labour relations, income taxation, contracts, behaviour defined as deviant, and acts of negligence, among other matters. And the monarchy, though no longer retaining decision-making power of any kind, remains a part of the Canadian legal tradition, for better or worse, embodied in the office of the Governor General of Canada.

The Conceptual Divisions of Law

In the contemporary Canadian state, we can make two conceptual classifications of law: **domestic law**, the law of a single nation-state, and **international law**, law that is, ideally, common to all nation-states. International law is typically mediated by the United Nations and involves the governance or accommodation of nations in relation to global treaties, conventions, and customs. All forms of Canadian domestic law can be further classified as public or private, and as **substantive** or **procedural**. For example, the section of the *Criminal Code* that prohibits first degree murder (section 231) is substantive law. Sections 645 and 646 of the *Code*, dealing with trial procedures and the taking of evidence at trial, are, on the other hand, procedural law.

The distinctions commonly made between private and public law and substantive and procedural law do have limitations. Procedural law is also substantive in that the procedural mechanism is often set out within specific statutes, as noted above with the example of the *Criminal Code*. Additionally, private agreements have public-interest issues embedded within them; private law affects the public interest, and public law affects private interests. Law professor Gerald Gall suggests the following classification:

Public Law	Private Law	
Constitutional law	Contracts	Torts
Criminal law	Real estate	Company law
Administrative law	Property	The law of agency
Taxation law	Family law	Patent law
	Wills and trusts	

Based on Figure 2.7 in Gerald Gall, *The Canadian Legal System*, 5th ed. (Toronto: Carswell, 2004), 29. Reprinted by permission of Carswell, a division of Thomson Canada Limited.

As Gall notes, the classification of **private** or **public law** is dependent on the issue of public as opposed to private interest. If the area of law is primarily concerned with the definition and regulation of individual matters, the law will be classified as private. If the area of law is primarily of collective interest, it is appropriately classified as public law. Constitutional and criminal law are therefore defined as public law, the former concerned with the construction and regulation of political life, the latter concerned with the collective definition of intolerable behaviours. On the other hand, the law of contract between individuals or corporations and the law of tort (the remedy of individual or corporate wrongs or wrongdoing) are defined as matters of essentially private interest, theoretically regulating not so much the economic interests of the collective but economic relations between individuals and their legal creations.

In the case of family law, Gall's classification as private law appears more problematic. There is a strong collective interest in the legal definition of "family" relationships and in the responsibilities that flow from these relationships, particularly when children are involved. Likewise, in the case of the law of wills and trusts and the law of property, it is not clear that we are primarily concerned with private interests. The rules governing the passage of wealth from one generation to the next and both personal and real property and their acquisition define the collective character of a nation—economically, socially, and politically.

All classifications or divisions of law are to some degree arbitrary: "[O]ne must appreciate the integrated nature of the law and the legal system, and thus not fall prey to an element of artificiality which befalls an attempt at categorization."[3] We must add a corollary here. The classifications of law into domestic and international, substantive and procedural, private and public do have some meaning, even if the meaning, like law itself, is subject to qualification and caveat.

Canada's Legal History: The Social, Political, and Economic Context

The enactment of all forms of law in Canada spans a little more than 135 years, but the history of law spans over 4 000 years. In the seventeenth century B.C.E., Hammurabi, the sixth king of the first dynasty of Babylonia, constructed a code of 282 case laws and had it inscribed on a slab of rock in the temple of the god Marduk. Hammurabi's Code dealt with economic issues and family, criminal, and civil law in Babylon. Confucius, writing in China some 2 600 years ago, developed a system of philosophical and ethical teachings that substantially influenced the development of Chinese law. Confucius stressed decorum, virtue, and love for one's fellow human beings. Muhammad, born in Mecca over 1 000 years later, was inspired to develop the Islamic faith, which influenced and continues to influence the law in Muslim nations.

The Sources of Canadian Law

If we are to speak and write of the sources of Canadian law, we need to be sensitive to this lengthy global history and to the many religious and ideological constructions of law that have emerged during the past 4 000 years. Some, such as Confucianism and Islam, have had relatively little direct effect on the development of Canada's legal system. Others, such as Christianity and Judaism, have had profound influence. In nation-specific terms, Canadian law has been most substantially influenced by the British, French, and U.S. legal systems.

British law professor Philip James has proposed that, in order to understand the sources of law in society, we need to think of these influences as either principal or subsidiary.[4] He cites two sources as principal: legislation and case law (written judicial decisions), and two influences as subsidiary: custom and books of authority. These four sources of law will be discussed in detail later in this chapter.

Historically, law has also been distinguished as either written or unwritten, with legislation defined as written law, and case law, custom, and books of authority as unwritten law. As James has noted, the distinction between written and unwritten law is not particularly helpful. Judicial decisions amount to written law, but because they do not take the form of a statute, they have typically been classified as unwritten. Custom, particularly in commerce, may also have the essential structure and importance of written law, and yet be classified as unwritten law.

The sources of Canadian law are to be found in both legislation and judicial decisions from 1867 to the present, as well as in the great body of British common law that was in existence before 1867 and was received into Canadian law upon Confederation. Specifically, Canada is given its legal identity by the **British North America Act, 1867** and the *Constitution Act, 1982*, with its entrenched *Canadian Charter of Rights and Freedoms*. (See Chapter 4.) Debate about the essential structure of Canadian law continues in the early years of the twenty-first century, with the separatist Bloc Québécois currently holding the majority of federal seats from the Province of Quebec, and with the propositions of the Meech Lake and Charlottetown Accords unable to win political support during the 1990s.

At the heart of the continuing disputes about Canada's legal identity is the centrality of Quebec and Québécois culture within Canada, and the political and legal reality of both French and English as the founding cultures of the country. But there is more to the dispute: an argument for recognition of the Aboriginal peoples of Canada, men and women displaced during the past 300 years by the aggressive policies of French and English colonization, as the first founders of the nation. There is also the 1982 *Charter,* a moral covenant of the country's values, which is adjudicated by a politically appointed judiciary.

STATUTE LAW

Statutory or enacted law is generally accorded dominance as a source of the legal form because of the long-standing tradition of British parliamentary supremacy. Parliament is said to be supreme in that it represents the will of the people, after democratic debate and resolution. The other sources of law—judicial decisions, custom, and books of authority—cannot have the same direct accountability to a democratic system of representative government.

But there is also a sense in which Parliament cannot be supreme. All statutes must be applied, and in the process, they must often be interpreted, giving judicial decision makers a measure of control over the meaning and operation of law. Philip James has provided an illustration of the power exerted by the judiciary over the operation of **statute law**: Suppose that Old King Cole, who is an absolute despot, commands that all "dogs" in his kingdom are to be killed. Suppose that Jack Sprat has an Alsatian wolfhound, and applies to the court for a decree that it shall be spared, alleging that it is a "hound" and the royal command is concerned only with "dogs." The court will have to decide whether the word "dogs" is to be taken to embrace "hounds"; whichever way it decides, it will influence the practical application of the King's command.[5] In all circumstances, such judicial interventions provide a sharper focus for the understanding of statute law, and in some circumstances, they may serve to reconstruct the operation and meaning of the statute in question.

The sources of statute law in Canada are the House of Commons and the legislative assemblies of the provinces and territories. These parliaments collectively produce hundreds of statutes every year, often with regulations attached. In the early twenty-first century, the average Canadian citizen can be aware only of the most basic operations of the law, and in complex matters of either public or private law, must purchase specialized legal advice.

The legislative process for the creation of a statute is similar for the federal, provincial, and territorial governments. The government of the day introduces a bill into either the House of Commons or the Legislative Assembly and gives it what is called its "first reading." It is then passed to second reading without debate. At this point, many bills simply die on the order paper. The government often decides not to proceed, perhaps for reasons related to Cabinet and caucus priorities.

If there *is* a second reading of the legislation, the minister responsible for the proposed law sets out the purpose of the legislation. This is followed by a full debate. After debate, the bill is typically sent to a committee of the House or Assembly composed of both government and Opposition members.

Next come further debate and, possibly, public hearings. For example, in making changes to criminal law, a committee of the House of Commons will often travel across Canada in order to receive public input from a wide range of Canadians. When the bill comes back to the House or Assembly for its third reading, it may contain one or several proposed amendments. At third reading, if the government still wishes to proceed and has sufficient support, the bill is passed. For federal legislation, this process must be repeated in the Senate before the bill is submitted to the governor general for approval. Provincial or territorial legislation passed on third reading is submitted to the lieutenant governor of the province or territory for approval. The submission for approval to the governor general or lieutenant governor is a formality, a monarchical remnant dating to the time when English barons had to submit their legislation for the approval of the king or queen. The governor general and the lieutenant governors are the monarch's representatives in Canada.

Statutes of the various governments are published every year, and can be found in the libraries of Canada's courts and most other libraries. This annual legislative production is typically cited in reference catalogues as *Statutes of Canada, 2000; Statutes of Ontario, 2000*; and so on. There are also occasional compilations of all federal and provincial statutes, to a given date. The most recent compilation of all federal statutes is *Revised Statutes of Canada, 1985,* a set of more than 15 volumes of legislation.

CASE LAW

Case law is the law established by decisions in specific court cases. Subsequent courts will turn to these decisions, known as judicial precedents, when attempting to make judgments about similar issues. The importance of a judicial precedent depends upon the hierarchical placement of the court issuing the decision. If the Supreme Court of Canada issues a judgment defining obscenity, pursuant to section 163(8) of the *Criminal Code*, the decision will potentially affect all Canadian courts. If the same decision emanates from a provincial court judge, it will have no determinative influence on the prosecution of obscenity in the province, or in other jurisdictions. (See Chapter 5.)

The continuing interpretation of statute law by the courts renders the legal system dynamic, with new cases permitting and requiring new rules. An open system of interpretation is, in theory, a kind of legislative democracy, adjudicated by the courts in concert with legislators. Ideally, the rules come to reflect the litigants' realities, not the more abstract designs of a legislator.

There are at least two problems with judicial precedents as sources of law. First is the danger that, in trying to mesh current situations with preexisting case law, the courts and counsel may make illogical distinctions. Judicial decisions must be set against a complex backdrop of precedents; in trying to fit the current case into this framework, both lawyers and the judiciary may lose contact with the intention of the legislators. For litigator and advocate alike, the object of statutory interpretation is to distinguish one's case from damaging precedents, from facts that would seem to bind the court to make a finding contrary to the interest of one's client.

The second problem has to do with the ability of a court, particularly the Supreme Court of Canada, to reverse itself. The logic of a system of binding precedent is that the court of last resort binds itself and all other courts in the country by its decisions. Yet the Supreme Court must occasionally depart from its past decisions, weighing the value of new evidence or responding to new conceptions of a problem. The need to reverse earlier judgments presents a difficulty for those who argue that judges do not make law, but only interpret statutes. In reversing previous decisions, the judiciary is exercising, at the least, a quasi-legislative power; it cannot be said simply to be building a binding system of precedent.

Reporting Case Law

The decisions of the judiciary are published or "reported" in a variety of sources. However, not all judicial decisions are reported. *Supreme Court Reports* carry all important judgments from the Supreme Court of Canada. *Dominion Law Reports* carry significant judgments from the Supreme Court of Canada, provincial courts of appeal, and some county courts. There are also reporting services for specific regions of the country: *Ontario Reports* and *Western Weekly Reports* are two prominent examples. Finally, some reporting services cater to specific areas of legal practice; examples include *Canadian Criminal Cases* and *Reports of Family Law.*

The editors of these reporters (as they are called) make decisions about which cases to report, typically selecting judicial decisions made in superior courts—those with the power to bind other courts to their findings. They then write what is called a headnote, and place it before each judicial decision. A headnote is a summary of the facts of the case, the issues in dispute, and the reason for the court's decision. The reason for the decision is termed the *ratio decidendi*—the judge's determination of law, in relation to the particular set of facts. The court may also issue what are termed *obiter dicta*—literally, "statements, by the way"—legal pronouncements on issues not directly relevant to the present case. *Obiter dicta* may, nonetheless, carry substantial weight in future cases that are at least somewhat related to the present case.

When searching for judicial decisions, you will be attempting to locate various reporting services: *Supreme Court Reports, Canadian Criminal Cases,* and so on. Judicial decisions are cited in a manner allowing for easy access. For example, the citation *R. v. Gunn and Ponak* (1971), 5 C.C.C. (2d) 503 (B.C.C.A.) tells you that this was a criminal case against the accused Gunn and Ponak, decided in 1971; it can be found in Volume 5 of *Canadian Criminal Cases,* 2nd edition; and it was a decision of the British Columbia Court of Appeal. In criminal cases, the abbreviation "R." refers to *Rex* or *Regina*—the king or queen of England. This designation is, again, a remnant from the British system of prosecution, in which the monarch is said to be acting in the interest of the state against the criminal accused. In the United States, criminal prosecutions are commenced in the name of "the people," as in *People v. Aguilar,* 35 Cal. Rptr. 516 (1963).

CUSTOM

Most forms of law originally derived from **custom**, from the practices and patterns of behaviour through which society had come to order itself. As Philip James has observed, this was particularly true in Britain, where centuries of commercial practice, for example, were ultimately shaped into legislative form in the *Sale of Goods Act* of 1893. But in contemporary Canada, custom did not have as significant an effect as a form of law in most areas of conduct. Law was typically imported from Britain and had already incorporated custom, whether in the realm of commerce or in the designation of deviant behaviour.

One notable exception to the preeminence in Canada of law over custom is constitutional law, where Supreme Court decisions have typically given considerable prominence to the role of custom or "convention" in federal–provincial disputes over constitutional change. The Supreme Court's decision in 1981 on the patriation of the Canadian Constitution is probably the best example. In *Manitoba (A.G.) v. Canada (A.G.) (Patriation Reference),*[6] the Supreme Court held that there was a constitutional convention requiring the federal government to have the consent of the provinces before amending the *British North America Act.* Although the Supreme Court indicated that the federal government required no such consent as a matter of law, its emphasis on convention served to push the constitutional reform initiative back into the political arena.

BOOKS OF AUTHORITY

From the time of Hammurabi to the present, there have been scholars of law who have written authoritative texts or commentaries summarizing various forms of law and applicable principles. Within the British parliamentary tradition, Coke and Blackstone are two prominent authors of books of authority. Coke wrote *Institutes* in the seventeenth century; Blackstone's *Commentaries* followed in the next century. Both works survive as useful documents for the present era.

During the past three decades, the application of books of authority to judicial decisions has increased in both breadth and volume. The courts seek guidance from the contributions of outstanding early scholars, as well as from living academics and writers of treatises who contribute to a developing legal and socio-legal literature. The courts also seek expertise from "expert witnesses" who give opinions in their specialized area of knowledge in court.

Consider, for example, the Supreme Court of Canada's decision in *Rabey v. R.* in July 1980.[7] Rabey was a young university student who brutally assaulted a young woman who had rejected him. He was acquitted at trial on the ground that he experienced "non-insane automatism" at the time of the attack. In determining the validity of this acquittal, the Supreme Court considered several books of authority. The justices referred, with approval, to lawyer M.E. Schiffer's text *Mental Disorder and the Criminal Trial Process* (1976), as well as to British jurist Glanville Williams's 1978 treatise *Textbook of Criminal Law.* The Court also mentioned being helped by several articles published in a number of law journals: S.M. Beck's article on voluntary conduct in *Criminal Law Quarterly;* Professor J.L.J. Edwards's article on automatism in *Modern Law Review;* and G.A. Martin's article on insanity, again in *Criminal Law Quarterly.*

In other areas of law besides criminal—constitutional, family, and labour relations—courts are increasingly using books of authority to assist them in the construction of judicial precedent. The growth of the social importance of law and the increasing complexity of statutory and regulatory law have led to the production of a wide array of treatises and articles. In turn, and for similar reasons, the judiciary has been prompted to consult these books of authority to a greater extent than at any other time in Canadian history.

This development seems likely to continue. Since the entrenchment of the *Charter* as a constitutional document, the courts have been looking for both empirical and theoretical guidance with respect to the meaning to be given to such complex rights as freedom of religion, freedom from cruel and unusual punishment, and freedom of expression. While books of authority have only subsidiary power as sources of law, they have become an important part of the process of lawmaking, providing the Canadian legal system with a more comprehensive knowledge of itself. Similarly, courts will continue to hear from experts in a wide range of disciplines: medicine, engineering, criminology, and anthropology, among others.

Further Sources of Law

We have now considered four sources of law: the principal sources, statute and case law; and the subsidiary sources, custom and books of authority. But there is more to law and to understanding its sources than these essentially written forms of law. They are typically the outcomes of the legal process; they cannot provide a full understanding of the process itself.

Consider, for example, the task of tracking the current murder provisions in the *Criminal Code* retrospectively, in order to determine the source of such law in Canada. We find the statute law defining murder and manslaughter in the current *Code* and trace the statute back, noting the years of amendments. In the case of the murder provisions, we find a considerable number of amendments from 1961 to the present, but very few between 1892, the date of Canada's first *Criminal Code,* and 1961. We see, in 1961, Canada's original legal definitions of "murder" and "manslaughter" transformed into legal definitions of "capital murder," "non-capital murder," and "manslaughter"; then, in 1976, into "first degree murder," "second degree murder," and "manslaughter."

This exercise provides us with a statutory paper trail, a sequence of statute law over time. The exercise can be repeated with any form of law. It is a necessary part of understanding the growth of a particular kind of legislation from its inception to the present. At the same time, it is important to look to judicial decisions relating to these various statutes: to construct a historical weave of statute and case law, looking to the relationship between legislative amendments and judicial decisions.

The history of judicial decisions will also give us a history of books of authority as further sources of law; there may, in addition, be some circumstances when custom or convention becomes preeminent. What we ultimately arrive at is a history of law over time, with law and judicial decisions and books of authority often in conflict. We can see clearly enough the changes in statutes over time, and the various issues litigated by the judiciary in response to these statutes. We can see custom or convention in specific circumstances, and the occasional influence of books of authority. What we do not see, after engaging in this exercise, are critical connecting threads. We don't have an organizing description of events or sources, a narrative that attempts to make objective sense of the intentions and consequences of law in historical context.

For example, as an entirely technical task, it may be sufficient simply to cite the various sources of law that apply to first degree murder, second degree murder, and manslaughter, documenting statutory change, case law, and the relevance of custom and books of authority. But this analysis would not be sufficient; the debates of the House of Commons and many other sources (newspapers, commission hearings, polls of public opinion) reveal that legislation regarding homicide has virtually always been focused on the question of penalty for the crime, and, more specifically, on the appropriateness of capital punishment. The 1976 legislation abolishing capital punishment and simultaneously increasing minimum terms of imprisonment cannot be fully understood without a thorough documentation of social, political, and historical developments in Canada from the early years of the twentieth century to 1976. And, of course, debates continue with respect to the form and substance of existing legislation.

In virtually any form of lawmaking, law represents power: the power to compel certain kinds of conduct, to support certain world-views and simultaneously to reject others. Law is the prize that various political actors seek within a terrain of social, political, and economic conflict. In the face of social consensus, there is little need for statutory enactments or judicial decisions, the enforcement of custom or the application of books of authority. Law is invariably constructed as a response to conflict or, specifically, to a given social problem; it is a means of controlling certain kinds of activities or behaviours. Changes to the *Income Tax Act* benefit certain taxpayers and disentitle others. Changes to the *Criminal Code* increase or decrease penalties, supporting certain interests and rejecting others. Changes to the constitutional law of Canada benefit certain provinces and constituencies, and correspondingly place limitations on the powers of other provinces and constituencies.

There is, however, considerable support for the idea that law reflects consensus, at least in certain contexts. In order to maintain law and legal order, it is necessary to build a consensus with respect to the moral and social legitimacy of law. A predominant ideology or at least clusters of predominant ideologies are constructed and maintained over time. Hegemony—the ongoing maintenance of a predominant ideology—is the linchpin of legal control.

Any organizing description of the sources of law must take into account this backdrop of conflict and consensus. The legal formalist or legal positivist will argue that the morality, politics, or economics underlying the law is unimportant; what count are the validity of the legal form and the ability to accurately document the contributing sources of law.

But the limitation of this technical conception of law and the sources of law is that it views law as separate from the social world from which it is created; it asserts that reference to statute law, judicial decisions, custom, and books of authority will provide a fully sufficient account of the legal sources of law. What follows is a more thorough accounting of the sources of law, within one specific context, looking beyond statute law, judicial decisions, custom, and books of authority to gain a more complete understanding of the process of law's creation.

The Criminalization of Drugs: Taking Account of the Complexities of Sources of Law

The history of Canada's criminalization of certain mind-active drugs, to take just one example, demonstrates that the sources of data noted above are *not* sufficient. Law can be fully comprehended only by documenting and analyzing the social, political, and economic contexts that gave it life and continue to influence its existence.

> On June 6, 1998, a surprising letter was delivered to Kofi Annan, secretary general of the United Nations. "We believe," the letter declared, "that the global war on drugs is now causing more harm than drug abuse itself." The letter was signed by statesmen, politicians, academics, and other public figures. Former U.N. secretary general Javier Perez de Cuellar signed. So did George Shultz, the former American secretary of state, and Jocelyn Elders, the former American surgeon general. Nobel laureates such as Milton Friedman and Argentina's Adolfo Perez Esquivel added their names. . . .
>
> The drug policies the world has been following for decades are a destructive failure, they said. Trying to stamp out drug abuse by banning drugs has only created an illegal industry worth $400 billion U.S. . . . The letter continued, "This industry has empowered organized criminals, corrupted governments at all levels, eroded internal security, stimulated violence, and distorted both economic markets and moral values." And it concluded that these were the consequences "not of drug use per se, but of decades of failed and futile drug war policies."
>
> (Dan Gardner, *Ottawa Citizen*, September 5, 2000.
> Reprinted by permission of the *Ottawa Citizen*.)

The criminalization of certain drugs began in Canada in 1908, when *An Act to prohibit the importation, manufacture, and sale of opium for other than medicinal purposes* was passed by the federal government of Wilfrid Laurier. The act provided penalties of up to three years' imprisonment for the importation, manufacture, or sale of the drug, a fine of not less than $50, and a six months' grace period during which opium merchants could sell their remaining stocks.

What circumstances gave rise to narcotics law? Or, put differently, what are its sources? Canadian narcotics legislation is unusual in the realm of criminal law in that its genesis cannot be traced, at least entirely, to late-nineteenth-century England or to other jurisdictions of that era. It is a twentieth-century development, originating in both Canada and other Western nations in the early years of that century.

The Original 1908 Statute

As noted above, the original statute was titled *An Act to prohibit the importation, manufacture and sale of opium for other than medicinal purposes.* The legislation was introduced into the House of Commons by the minister of labour, and was strongly supported by all parties in the House. But the statute itself gives no suggestion as to how and why it was introduced and quickly passed into law. Why was the legislation introduced by the minister of labour? Why was it strongly supported by all parties? We will need other information if we are to comprehend more fully the meaning to be attributed to legal sources: the intentions and consequences of lawmaking.

As noted above in our brief discussion of homicide, the first important information source is **Hansard**, the recorded proceedings of debates in the House of Commons. Hansard gives some idea of the intentions of legislators at the time a bill is introduced and debated; and though Hansard may not be used for the purpose of statutory interpretation (as you will learn in Chapter 3), it is, nonetheless, a valuable aid to understanding the sources of law. Many other kinds of information are also likely to be useful in this exercise: the archival papers of those involved in the passage of law, particularly the papers of government ministers; the newspapers of the day; the work of historians; the reports of relevant commissions; and other relevant government documents.

When we examine these sources to reach an understanding of the genesis of Canadian narcotics legislation, we find there does not seem to have been significant public clamour for this law. In fact, in British Columbia, the cities of Vancouver, Victoria, and New Westminster had licensed smoking-opium factories as legitimate businesses for almost 40 years. The major local newspapers, the *Vancouver Province* and the *Victoria Times-Colonist*, carried advertising for the sale of opium daily, and there were few expressions of concern about the distribution or use of the drug.

In 1885, when testifying before a commission on Chinese immigration, Sir Matthew Begbie, the chief justice of British Columbia, made the following comments, which were endorsed by other members of the court:

> I altogether disbelieve in any widespread mischief here from opium. . . . Opium, as generally used here, is probably as harmless as tobacco, which is also extensively used in British Columbia. . . . Neither opium nor tobacco extend in their evil effects beyond the individual. They are not nearly so dangerous to the public peace as whiskey. . . . All the evils arising from opium in British Columbia in a year do not, probably, equal the damage, trouble, and expense occasioned to individuals and to the state by whiskey in a single month, or perhaps in some single night.[8]

The opium factories sold a black-tar opium to whites and Chinese in about equal numbers; the opium users would smoke the drug, typically as a recreation. But this was not the only opium business in the province; opiated tonics, elixirs, and analgesics—the products of a white patent medicine industry—were sold to a predominantly white population. Other drugs were, of course, also in use in the province during this time. Alcohol was consumed at saloons and privately. Tobacco was smoked privately and publicly.

The smoking-opium businesses were owned and operated by Chinese. Asians had been encouraged to come to Canada in the 1870s to assist in building the Canadian Pacific Railway and the industrial infrastructure of western Canada. Some brought smoking-opium with them. By 1900, western Canada's labour shortage gave way to a labour surplus; and the Chinese, willing to work for half the wages of white workers, were vilified. The Asiatic Exclusion League was formed, and the local newspapers caricatured the recent immigrants in almost daily racist cartoons. On September 7, 1907, anti-Asian sentiment reached a fever pitch when a crowd of 10 000 angry white workers stormed through the Asian section of Vancouver, assaulting the inhabitants and damaging and destroying property.

In response to this racially and economically motivated violence, the federal government appointed a young bureaucrat, William Lyon Mackenzie King, the deputy minister of labour, to settle Chinese claims for damages resulting from the riot. In the course of the hearings, Mackenzie King received two claims from opium manufacturers. After also receiving a deputation from a local Chinese scholar, merchants, and clergy opposed to the drug, Mackenzie King told the assembled commission, "My own opinion is that it should be made impossible to manufacture this drug in any part of the Dominion. We will get some good out of this riot yet."[9]

In a report to Parliament, King spoke of the "dire" consequences of smoking-opium and urged the prohibition of its sale, importation, and manufacture. Opiated tonics, elixirs, analgesics, and cocaine-laced mixtures—the products of the white patent medicine industry—were not to be affected by the law; they would continue to be regulated by the *Patent or Proprietary Medicine Act.*

Thus, we see that the prohibition of opium originated in a racially motivated labour confrontation on the west coast of Canada. The legislation was intended to "get some good" out of an anti-Asian riot, and only secondarily to prevent the harms of opiate use and dependence. There was no presentation of any sound empirical analysis of harm caused by the distribution and use of the drug. Alcohol and tobacco were not to be considered drugs, in the political and economic sense that smoking-opium was a drug. Even the opiated tonic, containing the same product as smoking-opium, was not conceptualized as a drug, and, therefore, not subject to criminal prohibition.

Can we understand the statute law of 1908 without reference to this social history? Or, to put it more conservatively, does a consideration of the specifics of legislative history enrich or diminish our comprehension of the sources of law and legal process?

At the least, the original 1908 statute provides evidence of law as arising from political expediency: "We will get some good out of this riot yet." What is less clear is the intent of the legislation. Although the statute was designed to resolve a labour conflict, it was also premised on the harm that was said to flow from the use and distribution of smoking-opium. But it is not at all certain that Mackenzie King, the architect of the legislation, believed in this supposition of harm. His 1907 diaries contain the following comments about an upcoming visit to India, and the Indian trade in opium:

> I would learn the part that opium played in the life of the people. Some persons, for example, were of the opinion that opium was used by many of the Sikhs in the same way that Lord Morley was using the cigar which he smoked; that it did not appear to harm them in that climate when used in moderation; that if taken from them, it might lead to other drugs being used. . . . Lord Morley would give me the names of one or two gentlemen to whom I could speak freely. . . . [T]hey would give me a true statement of conditions, not to be given, for example, to the people in North Waterloo [King's constituency], but which I might impart privately to Sir Wilfrid. I would be informed on the real conditions so that the Government of Canada might be made fully aware of them.[10]

Mackenzie King's diary notations only complicate our understanding of the intentions of the 1908 statute: the people of Canada are to be given one view of a social problem and the purpose of the law, while the government of Canada (the prime minister and, presumably, his Cabinet) is to be provided with the "truth."

How are we to understand the legislation, in light of this admission? The legal positivist would respond that all the scrutiny is irrelevant. The law was validly enacted, and it continues to stand as a valid source of our current *Controlled Drugs and Substances Act*. Still, given this background knowledge, it is difficult to argue that a full understanding of the origins or sources of law can be obtained from relevant statutes, **case law** (cited legal decisions—i.e., judicially made law), customs over time, and **books of authority** (influential and comprehensive texts). As we continue to document other sources of Canadian narcotics legislation from 1908 to the present, this difficulty in limiting the scope of our inquiry does not disappear.

The Opium and Drug Act of 1911

In 1911, two key changes were made to the 1908 legislation. One provided that cocaine be added to the list of prohibited drugs; the second made possession of either smoking-opium or cocaine an offence punishable by imprisonment. The new statute, the *Opium and Drug Act*, premised the possession offence on police experiences with the original legislation. When moving a second reading of the proposed law, Mackenzie King had noted, "The police have found that the present legislation is not drastic enough, or broad enough, to give them the powers of seizure and confiscation which they regard as necessary. One of the objects of the present Bill is to make more drastic the regulations in that regard."

King was speaking specifically of the new possession offence and another section of the act that provided penalties for being in a "house, room, or place" where opium was smoked. These changes in law were a product of difficulties in police enforcement against consensual transactions of importation, manufacture, and sale. Hence, possession was criminalized, not because of informed debate about the possible evils of opiate or cocaine use, but because effective enforcement required this weapon in the statutory arsenal: evidence of distribution offences had proven to be difficult to obtain.

Commons debate of the 1911 legislation was highlighted by opposition to one section of the bill: a proposal that the federal Cabinet be given a procedural power to add prohibited drugs to the schedule to the act without debate in Parliament. This prompted a significant exchange between Mackenzie King and the Opposition. "We might pass this Act just as it is," one member began, "and the Governor in Council will still be free to add tobacco to that schedule. The Governor in Council are taking a power without any limit." King shot back: "Cigarettes and tobacco have not yet been considered a drug. In naming the three drugs, cocaine, morphine, and opium, Parliament makes it plain that it is legislating against what are known as habit-forming drugs."

We know today that this defence of tobacco is invalid—another indication, perhaps, of the contradictory theoretical foundation on which both the 1908 and the 1911 statutes were premised.

The Opium and Narcotic Drug Act of 1922

In 1922, amendments to the *Opium and Narcotic Drug Act* provided for a minimum term of six months' imprisonment upon conviction for possession; the amendments also provided for whipping of the convicted, at the discretion of the trial judge, and the deportation of immigrants convicted of drug offences. Section 7 of the 1922 legislation enabled a police officer "with reasonable cause to suspect, to search, without warrant, any premises other than a dwelling house."

The 1922 amendments were influenced by Judge Emily Murphy's book *The Black Candle*, serialized in *Maclean's* magazine in 1921. Murphy advocated increased penalties for both use and distribution, and expanded powers of search and seizure for police. Her book depicted a drug trade monopolized by Blacks and Asians, a conspiracy against the "bright-browed races of the world":

> [T]he Chinese pedlars taunted him with their superiority at being able to sell the dope without using it, and by telling him how the yellow race would rule the world. They were too wise, they urged, to attempt to win in battle, but would win by wits; would strike at the white race through "dope," and when the time was ripe, would command the world. . . . Some of the Negroes coming into Canada— and they are no fiddle-faddle fellows either—have similar ideas, and one of their greatest writers has boasted how ultimately they will control the white men.[11]

It is appropriate to consider *The Black Candle* a book of authority with respect to the development of Canadian narcotics legislation. Emily Murphy was a judge of the Family Court in Edmonton, and a leading suffragette; her views, though often racist and typically uninformed, had a profound impact on both statute and case law during the 1920s.

In 1923, marijuana was added to the schedule of prohibited drugs, with the consent of all parties and with no debate. By 1929, penalties for the distribution and sale of opiates, cocaine, or marijuana had risen from a maximum of six months' to seven years' imprisonment. Antinarcotics police had also been given relatively sweeping powers of search and seizure through the legal mechanism of writs of assistance, which allowed the holder to enter any dwelling without a search warrant if the person believed that "narcotics" might be on the premises.

There was very little case law during the 1920s relating to the *Opium and Narcotic Drug Act*. The cases that were decided, however, strongly supported the thinking of Emily Murphy and the general philosophy of the statute law; the judiciary endorsed exceptional prosecutorial powers and increased penalties for those convicted. In *R. v. Venegratsky*, which was a Crown appeal against a six-month term for trafficking, the Manitoba Court of Appeal increased the sentence to three years, noting, "The narcotic problem in Canada is a very acute one. . . . The government is evidently alarmed and determined to stamp out this illegal traffic. . . . In an effort to effect such a laudable object, it is entitled to every assistance the Court can legitimately give it."[12]

In the case of *R. v. Sung Lung*,[13] a Quebec court indicated that, unlike for other *Criminal Code* offences, there was no **mens rea** requirement in cases of possession of opium. (See Chapter 10 for an in-depth discussion of the concept of *mens rea*.) In other words, in order for a criminal conviction to be valid, it was not necessary that there be any "evil intent." Specifically, the court decided that it was not necessary for the accused to be proven to have knowledge of possession of opium. "If such a defence could be admitted," the judge wrote, "it would be very easy to evade the law and as this law must be, in the public welfare and interest, strictly interpreted, I find the defendant guilty."[14]

From the 1930s until the early 1960s, there was very little legislation or case law in relation to narcotics in Canada. Any amendments substantially increased both the penalties for all offences and the powers of search and seizure provisions. Within both statute and case law, we find the gradual transformation of drug use "from a status of private indulgence to a status of public evil."[15] The "war on drugs" was already in full flight.

The Narcotic Control Act of 1961

In 1961, the Conservative government of John Diefenbaker passed the *Narcotic Control Act*, a statute that remained for more than 35 years until May 1997, when it was replaced by the *Controlled Drugs and Substances Act*.[16] (The *Controlled Drugs and Substances Act* is essentially an amalgamation of the *Food and Drugs Act* and *Narcotic Control Act*, with a few revisions). The *Narcotic Control Act* set terms of life imprisonment for importation or "trafficking" in "narcotics," principally the opiates, cocaine, and marijuana. But within a few years of its implementation, the number of Canadians using illegal drugs increased substantially. In the mid-1960s, there were about 1 000 narcotics convictions annually; by the mid-1970s, the figure had grown to more than 40 000. More than 90 percent of the increase could be tied to marijuana distribution and consumption.

In response to this increase, a significant change in the punitive direction of the law was made in 1969. The *Narcotic Control Act* was amended to provide for the possibility of summary conviction procedure in cases of narcotic possession. Prior to the amendment, prosecutors were required to proceed by indictment in all cases of possession; the move to a hybrid form of prosecution was a sign that the government was prepared to punish possessors less severely, particularly in marijuana cases.

Millions of Canadians, particularly the young, continued to challenge the legitimacy of the *Narcotic Control Act*. Drugs were intrinsic to the counterculture advocacy of sex, drugs, and rock-and-roll; the peaceful practice of hedonistic pursuits; and a retreat from materialism and war. The response of the federal government to their challenge of authority was the LeDain Commission, an inquiry into the "non-medical" use of drugs, chaired by Osgoode Hall Law School dean Gerald LeDain. The commission was to gather research findings, hold public hearings, and interview medical and law enforcement experts in order to recommend how the law might be changed to respond more usefully to the growing use of illegal drugs.

In 1972 and 1973, the commission submitted its reports to the government. The five commissioners—prominent physicians, lawyers, and academics—advocated the abolition of the criminal offence of possession of marijuana, as well as a general philosophical shift on the drug problem from a strict model of criminal enforcement toward the "wise exercise of freedom of choice." However, its recommendations were never acted upon directly by the government.

Nevertheless, in 1973 some relevant amendments were made to the *Criminal Code*, providing for two new criminal sanctions: absolute and conditional discharges. The amendments provided that offenders convicted of a wide range of offences could now be granted "absolute" or "conditional" discharges rather than be fined, placed on probation, or imprisoned. Their significance lay in the fact that those convicted of these offences could now claim, for purposes of employment, that they had never been convicted of a criminal offence. An absolute discharge involves no penalty other than courtroom appearance and a finding of guilt. A conditional discharge involves the completion of a condition, typically probation or community service, prior to discharge. The amendments were immediately incorporated into the sentencing of those convicted of narcotic possession, most notably in marijuana cases. By the late 1970s, about 20 percent of those convicted of marijuana possession received a discharge.

The *Narcotic Control Act* of 1961 was not the subject of much legislative debate and statutory enactment. The primary source of law in relation to illegal drugs since 1961 has been the judiciary, setting new norms for sentence length, striking down procedural provisions in conflict with the *Charter,* and drawing distinctions between marijuana and other "narcotics." For the past twenty years, case or common law has been the predominant source of law controlling illegal drugs.

In 1986, in *R. v. Oakes,*[17] for example, the Supreme Court of Canada decided unanimously that the reverse onus provision in section 8 of the *Narcotic Control Act* was unconstitutional, a violation of section 11(d) of the *Charter* and its presumption of innocence. The reverse onus section of the act dealt with procedure in cases of possession for the purpose of trafficking; it had required that an individual convicted of narcotic possession must then prove, on a balance of probabilities, that he or she was not trafficking the drug. The section's reversal of the presumption of innocence had been justified by the perceived need to take extraordinary statutory measures against the trade in narcotics.

The courts have also drawn relatively consistent distinctions between marijuana and other narcotics in matters of sentencing. As early as 1970, the Ontario Court of Appeal made the following remarks in the case of *R. v. Johnston and Tremayne,* a case of conspiracy to import marijuana: "The maximum sentence ... [in this case] is life imprisonment. Thus, the framers of the Act regarded, and presumably still do regard, both offences as very grave, although I must confess at once that the Court takes a different view of the use or importation of marijuana as compared with the more serious drugs embraced by the Act, such as heroin."[18] Other cases since that time have generally endorsed these sentiments. Similarly, the *Controlled Drugs and Substances Act* of 1997 now places marijuana in a separate category.

Most significantly, perhaps, the penalties prescribed by the judiciary have changed over time, despite the absence of statutory change. In the late 1960s, about 50 percent of all convicted marijuana users were sent to jail for their crimes. Notwithstanding this judicial "get tough" policy, the numbers of Canadians charged with the offence continued to rise.[19] Between 1966 and 1975, in response to a 4 000 percent increase in convictions, the judiciary moderated penalties for marijuana, fining most users, imprisoning about 5 percent, and generally giving the remainder either absolute or conditional discharges. It was not only marijuana possession, however, that was affected by this shift in judicial perceptions of appropriate punishment. While almost 90 percent of heroin and cocaine users were jailed in the 1960s, by the mid-1970s, fewer than half were imprisoned. These patterns of sentencing continue to this day.

The sources of our current prohibition of certain drugs are a complex interplay of statutory change and case law. Judges have generally acted to moderate the philosophy and penalties of the 1961 and 1997 statutes, having had to adjust their conceptions of the drug problem in light of the cultural changes of the late 1960s and the greater medical and social knowledge on drug use and abuse now available. Today, Emily Murphy's *Black Candle* is no longer regarded as a book of authority; it has been displaced by texts offering technically and empirically based analysis.[20] And yet the heart of the law—a criminal prohibition of certain drugs—remains.

Controlling Cannabis Cultivation: The Continuing Evolution of Law

As we enter the last half of the first decade of the twenty-first century, we are facing an evolving set of issues with respect to the use and distribution of cannabis. Although marijuana distribution was originally an import–export business, with the product coming from Thailand, Colombia, Lebanon, and Mexico, it emerged during the late 1990s as a burgeoning industry of domestic production. The "grow-ops," large-scale indoor cultivation projects, have become widespread, and the judiciary have been reluctant to impose substantial terms of imprisonment in response, given both the greater social acceptance of such drug use by adults, and the need to limit the use of imprisonment to acts that have a clear and identifiable social harm.

At the same time the growers belong to a very large, unregulated, untaxed, and highly lucrative industry. In some segments, theft of electricity by growers is relatively common. Less common in some sectors, but nevertheless very much a concern, is the presence of violent "ripoffs" and weapons to protect some of the "grows." In November 2004, the Liberal government of Paul Martin introduced Bill C-17, legislation that would allow individual adults to possess up to 15 grams of cannabis, and grow up to three marijuana plants, without the possibility of being charged and taken to court. The behaviours would still be prohibited in law, but they would not be prosecuted in Canadian courtrooms. At the same time Bill C-17 proposed increasing the maximum penalty for cultivation of cannabis from 7 to 14 years' imprisonment, an indication that the government was trying to respond to public concerns about some of the problematic features of the industry of marijuana cultivation.

Conclusion: The Evolution of Substantive and Procedural Law

As we come close to the 100th anniversary of prohibition in Canada (July of 2008) the contradictions that flow from the criminalization of certain drugs—and the simultaneous promotion of other arguably more harmful drugs (alcohol and tobacco)—have not disappeared from the political stage. And more important for our purposes in this chapter, it remains clear that an understanding of the continuing evolution of substantive and procedural law depends upon more than even the most detailed examination of statute law, case law, custom, and books of authority.

Web Links

Parliament of Canada
http://www.parl.gc.ca/
This is the home page of Canada's Parliament, which comprises the House of Commons and the Senate. This site contains the debates of both houses, information about senators and members of Parliament, as well as links to House committees and to other sites concerning the parliamentary process.

World History of Democracy
http://www.unipissing.ca/department/history/muhlberger/histdem/index.htm
Hosted by Nipissing University, North Bay, Ontario, this website contains an impressive number of links to primary writings on the historical roots of democracy. The site also contains scholarly research, essays, and original works devoted to the world history of democracy.

The Avalon Project at the Yale Law School: Documents in Law, History and Diplomacy
http://www.yale.edu/lawweb/avalon/avalon.htm
The Avalon Project mounts documents relevant to the fields of law, history, economics, politics, diplomacy, and government, as well as providing links from those documents to their supporting material.

Documents are listed from pre–eighteenth century, such as the Code of Hammurabi and *Magna Carta*, through to the twenty-first century.

British History
http://britannia.com/history/
This website, which is part of the main Britannia site, is a portal to extensive information about Britain's history.

National Library of Canada
http://www.nlc-bnc.ca/
The National Library of Canada has developed a website containing interesting information on Canada's history. There are links to historical documents.

Questions for Discussion

1. Three cultures—Native Canadians, the French, and the British—exercised legal powers in Canada before and after the legally defining moment of Confederation. Discuss the validity of this contention.
2. What are the distinctive characteristics of statute law, case law, custom, and books of authority?
3. The prohibition of certain drugs appears to have been developed for reasons related to race, cultural difference, and a labour crisis within the North American economy. Are the justifications for such law similar or different today?

Further Reading

Giffen, P.J. et al. *Panic and Indifference: The Politics of Canada's Drug Laws*. Ottawa: Canadian Centre on Substance Abuse, 1991.
> This book attempts an explanation of the social origins of Canadian drug legislation, complementing the analysis presented within this chapter and pointing to the complexity of a comprehensive understanding of the origins of law.

Ogilvie, M.H. *Historical Introduction to Legal Studies*. Toronto: Carswell, 1982.
> This is a comprehensive analysis of the historical sources of Canadian law, an indispensable resource for those interested in the origins of the Canadian legal system.

Thompson, E.P. *Whigs and Hunters: The Origins of the Black Act*. London, U.K.: Allen Lane, 1975.

> This is a masterful analysis of a specific instance of the origins and consequences of law, undertaken by the British historian E.P. Thompson. The book chronicles the complexity of law's sources; it also has much to say about the importance of law as a mechanism for both asserting and denying social, economic, and political justice.

Notes

1. M.H. Ogilvie, *Historical Introduction to Legal Studies* (Toronto: Carswell, 1982).
2. Ibid., 362.
3. G. Gall, *The Canadian Legal System*, 3d ed. (Toronto: Carswell, 1990), 28.
4. P.S. James, *Introduction to Law*, 11th ed. (London, U.K.: Butterworths, 1985).
5. James, *Introduction to Law*, 9.
6. [1981] 1 S.C.R. 753.
7. *Rabey v. R.* (1981), 54 C.C.C. (2d) 1, aff'd 37 C.C.C. (2d) 461, 79 D.L.R. (3d) 414 (S.C.C.).
8. "Report of the Commissioners Appointed to Inquire into the Subject of Chinese Immigration into the Province of British Columbia," *Sessional Papers*, no. 54A, 1885: 74–5.
9. *Vancouver Province*, June 3, 1908, 1.
10. *King Diaries*, Mission to the Orient, 1907–1909. Ottawa: National Archives of Canada (NA), 85–6.
11. E. Murphy, *The Black Candle* (Toronto: Thomas Allen, 1922), 188–9.
12. *R. v. Venegratsky* (1928), 49 C.C.C. 298 (Man. C.A.).
13. (1923), 39 C.C.C. 187 (Que. Dist. Ct.).
14. Ibid., at 189.
15. Mel Green, "A History of Canadian Narcotics Legislation: The Formative Years," *University of Toronto Faculty of Law Review* (1979): 42–79.
16. R.S.C. 1996, c. 19.
17. (1986), 24 C.C.C. (3d) 321, 50 C.R. (3d) 1, [1986] 1 S.C.R. 103.
18. *R. v. Johnston and Tremayne*, [1970] 4 C.C.C. 64 (Ont. C.A.).

19. See P.G. Erickson, *Cannabis Criminals* (Aurora, ON: Canada Law Book, 1980). This volume offers a most authoritative description of the legislation on narcotics.
20. B. MacFarlane, *Drug Offences in Canada*, 2d ed. (Aurora, ON: Canada Law Book, 1986).

References

Boyd, N. "The Origins of Canadian Narcotics Legislation: The Process of Criminalization in Historical Context." *Dalhousie Law Journal* 8 (1984): 102–36.

Erickson, P.G. *Cannabis Criminals*. Aurora, ON: Canada Law Book, 1980.

Gall, G. *The Canadian Legal System*. 3d ed. Toronto: Carswell, 1990.

Green, M. "A History of Canadian Narcotics Legislation: The Formative Years." *University of Toronto Faculty of Law Review* (1979): 42–79.

James, P.S. *Introduction to English Law*. 11th ed. London, U.K.: Butterworths, 1985.

LeDain, G. *Final Report of the Commission of Inquiry into the Non-Medical Use of Drugs*. Ottawa: Information Canada, 1973.

MacFarlane, B. *Drug Offences in Canada*. 2d ed. Aurora, ON: Canada Law Book, 1986.

Murphy, E. *The Black Candle*. Toronto: Thomas Allen, 1922.

Ogilvie, M.H. *Historical Introduction to Legal Studies*. Toronto: Carswell, 1982.

Phillips, O.H. *A First Book of English Law*. 8th ed. London, U.K.: Sweet and Maxwell, 1988.

Sim, R.S., and D.M. Scott. *"A" Level English Law*. 3d ed. London, U.K.: Butterworths, 1970.

Walker, R.J., and M.G. Walker. *The English Legal System*. 6th ed. London, U.K.: Butterworths, 1985.

CHAPTER 3

Interpreting Ambiguous Statutes: Rules and Principles and Their Application

In late August of 1989 Bernhard Hasselwander applied to the registrar of firearms in Guelph, Ontario, to register his Mini-Uzi submachine gun as a restricted weapon. After examining the gun, the registrar determined that it was not a restricted weapon, but rather one that was prohibited. The registrar seized the gun and applied to the Ontario Provincial Court for a declaration that the seized Mini-Uzi be forfeited, and disposed of.

At the provincial court hearing, after listening to a police firearms expert, a collector of weapons, and Mr. Hasselwander, the judge concluded that although the manufacturer had produced the gun as a semi-automatic weapon, capable of registration, there was ample evidence that the trigger mechanism could be easily replaced, converting it to a prohibited weapon. As a consequence, the judge ordered the destruction of the gun.

This judgment was ultimately appealed to the Ontario Court of Appeal, where the majority argued that the case turned on key wording of the definition of a prohibited weapon, "that it is capable of firing bullets in rapid succession." The majority concluded that the word "capable" means capable in its present condition, rather than any capability that might be achieved by alteration of the weapon. Accordingly, the Ontario Court of Appeal set aside the order for destruction of the gun. From the Ontario Court of Appeal the case went to the Supreme Court of Canada; the court of last resort rendered a 3–2 judgment, allowing the appeal by the Crown, and permitting the destruction of the weapon.

The judgments of the minority and majority are instructive, as they hinge upon different understandings of the key variables to be employed in the task of statutory interpretation. The judgment of the minority, authored by Justice Major, is excerpted below, and followed by an excerpt from the judgment of the majority, authored by Justice Cory.[1]

Major, J. (dissenting): This appeal turns on the interpretation of "capable" in para. (c) of the definition of "prohibited weapon" in s. 84(1) of the Code. Unless noted otherwise, all subsequent references to legislation are to s. 84(1) of the Code. The appellant seeks a broad interpretation that would include firearms with the potential to be made fully automatic with relative ease, submitting that such an interpretation underscores the policy underlying firearms control legislation.

The respondent submits that Parliament must be taken to have chosen the word "capable" deliberately and seeks a narrow interpretation restricting "capable" to present firing ability. "Capable" is used in the Code in defining "firearm," "prohibited weapon" and "restricted weapon." But the Code also uses terms which more clearly encompass future ability, such as "adapted," "designed," "altered" and "intended."

In the present case, the definitions of both "prohibited weapon" and "restricted weapon" depend on the definition of "firearm." If a particular object is not a "firearm" we need not take the further step of classifying it as "restricted" or "prohibited." "Firearm" is defined as any barrelled weapon from which any shot, bullet or other missile can be discharged and that is *capable* of causing serious bodily injury or death to a person, and includes any frame or receiver of such a barrelled weapon and anything that can be *adapted* for use as a firearm. [Emphasis added.]

The determination of what is a "firearm" involves both a test of capability (of causing serious bodily injury or death) and of adaptability (for use as a firearm). *R. v. Covin*, [1983] 1 S.C.R. 725, sets out the criteria to be used in determining when an object qualifies as a firearm.

The definition of "prohibited weapon" uses both "capable" and "adapted," however, not in the same paragraph:

"prohibited weapon" means

(c) any firearm, not being a restricted weapon described in paragraph (c) of the definition of that expression in this subsection, that is capable of firing bullets in rapid succession during one pressure of the trigger,

(d) any firearm adapted from a rifle or shotgun, whether by sawing, cutting or other alteration or modification, that, *as so adapted*, has a barrel that is less than 457 mm in length or that is less than 660 mm in overall length. . . . [Emphasis added.]

Whether or not a "firearm" is prohibited on the basis of rapid firing ability depends on capability. In contrast, prohibition on the basis of reduced barrel length depends on actual adaptation. Submissions that "capable" includes future ability or potential are weakened by the express reference to adaptation of a firearm in para. (d), in the definition of "prohibited weapon."

"Capable" is also used in the definition of "restricted weapon":
"restricted weapon" means

> (a) any firearm, not being a prohibited weapon, designed, altered or intended to be aimed and fired by the action of one hand,
>
> (b) any firearm that
>> (i) is not a prohibited weapon, has a barrel that is less than 470 mm in length and is capable of discharging a centre-fire ammunition in a semi-automatic manner, or
>> (ii) is designed or adapted to be fired when reduced to a length of less than 660 mm by folding, telescoping or otherwise, or
>
> (c) any firearm that is *designed, altered or intended* to fire bullets in rapid succession during one pressure of the trigger and that, on January 1, 1978, was registered as a restricted weapon and formed part of a gun collection in Canada of a genuine gun collector. . . . [Emphasis added.]

"Capable" is used in isolation from terms such as "adapted," "altered," "designed," and "intended"—terms which more clearly refer to future ability. This limits "capable" to present ability. Curiously, the only time rapid firing ability is referred to in association with the phrase "designed, altered or intended" is in para. (c) in the definition of "restricted weapon" (the grandfathering provision).

The recent amendment of the definition of "prohibited weapon" (S.C. 1991, c. 40, s. 2) has not clarified the meaning of "capable."

"prohibited weapon" means

> (c) any firearm, not being a restricted weapon described in paragraph (c) or (c.1) of the definition of that expression in this subsection, that is capable of, or *assembled or designed and manufactured with the capability of, firing projectiles* in rapid succession during one pressure of the trigger, *whether or not it has been altered to fire only one projectile* with one such pressure. . . . [Emphasis added.]

The effect of the amendment is that there are now two categories of weapons classed as "prohibited" under para. (c): (i) firearms capable of firing projectiles in rapid succession during one pressure of the trigger (ii) firearms assembled or designed and manufactured with the capability of firing in rapid succession during one pressure of the trigger regardless of whether they have been so altered.

The respondent submits that the second category includes only firearms that were originally fully automatic but now downgraded to fire a single shot at a time. Such weapons are clearly prohibited by that amendment. In contrast, the appellant submits that the second category also covers semi-automatic firearms that may be upgraded to full automation. However, a broad interpretation of "capable" in the first category, the only category in the unamended definition, catches all convertible weapons, both converted fully automatics and convertible semi-automatics. The amendment is redundant unless "capable" is restricted to present firing ability.

In *R. v. Zeolkowski*, [1989] 1 S.C.R. 1378, this Court recognized the policy behind firearms control legislation. See Sopinka J. at p. 1383:

While firearms have been regulated in some form in Canada since 1892, the amendments of 1977 were intended as a more comprehensive approach to protecting the public from firearm misuse (Hawley, Canadian Firearms Law (1988), at p. 2). In my opinion, Lane Co. Ct. J. accurately stated the purpose of legislation in R. v. Anderson (1981), 59 C.C.C. (2d) 439, at p. 447:

> *The recognized intent of s. 98 as a whole is to remove, or to prevent the acquisition of firearms from those members of the population who have committed offences, or who it may be reasonably anticipated may commit an offence.*

A narrow interpretation of "capable" does not thwart the concern for public protection. Those weapons that would have been classified as prohibited under a broad interpretation of "capable" in para. (c), are still highly controlled under the Code as "restricted weapons." An applicant for a "restricted" weapons certificate must demonstrate to the local registrar of firearms that the weapon's intended use falls within narrow categories set out in s. 109(3). If Parliament wishes to prohibit semi-automatic firearms which are easily converted to fully automatic firing it is open for Parliament to do so.

A broad interpretation of "capable" may be acceptable within in rem proceedings such as the present case, where the forfeiting of the firearm is the only penalty. However, the definition of "prohibited weapon" also applies in other circumstances. Section 90 of the Code provides for various possession offences of "prohibited weapons" punishable by imprisonment up to ten years. Section 95 makes trade in "prohibited weapons" punishable by up to ten years imprisonment. The definition of "prohibited weapon" is used in the *Export and Import Permits Act*, R.S.C., 1985, c. E-19, the violation of which carries both monetary and penal sanctions.

A "prohibited weapons" conviction carries serious consequences for the accused. Any test based on capability extending to future alterations, which may be beyond an accused's knowledge or skill, introduces an undesirable level of uncertainty. All persons are presumed to know the law. That being so it is incumbent on Parliament to ensure clarity in drafting penal statutes.

I would dismiss the appeal.

The majority judgment of La Forest, Gonthier and Cory JJ. was delivered by

Cory J.: I have read with great interest the excellent reasons of Justice Major. Unfortunately I cannot agree with them.

On this appeal it must be decided whether the Mini-Uzi submachine gun which is the subject of this case should be classified as a prohibited weapon. The decision requires a consideration of the balance which must be struck between the protection of the public from the potential scourge of killing from the use of automatic weapons and the rights of the individual who, through possession of a prohibited weapon, can become liable either to a conviction for an indictable offence which, at the time, carried the potential of imprisonment for five years or to a conviction on a summary conviction offence.

III—Analysis

In 1989, s. 84(1) of the Criminal Code included, among other things, the following definition of a "prohibited weapon":

>(c)   any firearm, not being a restricted weapon described in paragraph (c) of the definition of that expression in this subsection, that is capable of firing bullets in rapid succession during one pressure of the trigger. . . .

The same section defined a "firearm" as

>any barrelled weapon from which any shot, bullet or other missile can be discharged and that is capable of causing serious bodily injury or death to a person, and includes any

frame or receiver of such a barrelled weapon and anything that can be adapted for use as a firearm;

Section 102(3) of the Criminal Code provides the authority for the seizure of prohibited weapons. It reads as follows:

> (3) Where any restricted weapon, firearm or prohibited weapon that was seized pursuant to subsection (1) is not returned as and when provided by subsection (2), a peace officer shall forthwith take it before a provincial court judge who may, after affording the person from whom it was seized or the owner thereof, if known, an opportunity to establish that he is lawfully entitled to the possession thereof, declare it to be forfeited to Her Majesty, whereupon it shall be disposed of as the Attorney General directs.

Section 90(1)(a) and (b) made it an offence to possess a prohibited weapon. At the time that section provided:

> 90.(1) Every one who has in his possession a prohibited weapon
>
> (a) is guilty of an indictable offence and liable to imprisonment for a term not exceeding five years; or
>
> (b) is guilty of an offence punishable on summary conviction.
>
> (2) Every one who is an occupant of a motor vehicle in which he knows there is a prohibited weapon
>
> (a) is guilty of an indictable offence and liable to imprisonment for a term not exceeding five years; or
>
> (b) is guilty of an offence punishable on summary conviction.
>
> (3) Subsection (1) does not apply to a person who comes into possession of a prohibited weapon by operation of law and thereafter, with reasonable despatch, lawfully disposes thereof.
>
> (4) Subsection (2) does not apply to an occupant of a motor vehicle in which there is a prohibited weapon where, by virtue of subsection (3) or section 92, subsection (1) does not apply to the person who is in possession of that weapon.

1. The Approach that should be Taken to the Interpretation of the Definition of "Prohibited Weapon"

We are dealing here with the *Criminal Code*. In days gone by it was a fundamental principle of statutory interpretation that penal enactments should be strictly construed so that any uncertainty as to the meaning or the scope of the law would be resolved in favour of the accused. See, for example, *Cité de Montréal v. Bélec*, [1927] S.C.R. 535, and *Winnipeg Film Society v. Webster*, [1964] S.C.R. 280. This rule has been modified and indeed transformed over the last fifty years. In his book, The Interpretation of Legislation in Canada (2nd ed. 1991), Pierre-André Côté provides a helpful historical analysis of this rule. On pages 397–98, the following appears:

Historically, the rule of strict construction drew its justification from a time when courts had to temper extremely severe penal legislation. Maxwell mentions that a person who cut down a cherry tree in an orchard, or who was seen in the presence of gypsies for a period of one month, could be sentenced to death (Maxwell on the Interpretation of Statutes, 12th ed., London: Sweet & Maxwell, 1969, p. 238). Strict construction of penal statutes often meant interpretation in favorem vitae. The nineteenth century witnessed a relaxation of penal legislation, and the death penalty ceased being the standard punishment for serious crimes. The reinforced presumption was relegated to a subsidiary one (Livingston Hall, "Strict or Liberal Construction of Penal Statutes", (1935) 48 Harv. L. Rev. 748, 752. Concerning interpretation of penal statutes, see: André Jodouin, "L'interprétation par le juge des lois pénales", (1978) 13 R.J.T. 49; Stephen Kloepfer, "The Status of Strict Construction in Canadian Criminal Law", (1983) 15 Ottawa L.R. 533).

As early as the beginning of this [20th] century, Justice Lyman Duff, at that time a member of the Supreme Court of British Columbia, observed that "the rule of strict construction, as applied to penal statutes, has been much relaxed (in recent years)" (*McGregor v. Canadian Consolidated Mines Ltd.* (1906), 12 B.C.R. 116 (S.C.), 117).

The rule of strict construction of penal statutes appears to conflict with s. 12 of the *Interpretation Act*, R.S.C., 1985, c. I-21. That section provides that:

> Every enactment is deemed remedial, and shall be given such fair, large and liberal construction and interpretation as best ensures the attainment of its objects.

The apparent conflict between a strict construction of a penal statute and the remedial interpretation required by s. 12 of the *Interpretation Act* was resolved by according the rule of strict construction of penal statutes a subsidiary role. In *Bélanger v. The Queen*, [1970] S.C.R. 567, Cartwright C.J. harmonized these opposing principles. In so doing he cited with approval the following words of Maxwell (*The Interpretation of Statutes* (7th ed. 1929), p. 244) at p. 573:

Where an equivocal word or ambiguous sentence leaves a reasonable doubt of its meaning which the canons of interpretation fail to solve, the benefit of the doubt should be given to the subject and against the Legislature which has failed to explain itself.

More recently, Martin J.A., writing for the Ontario Court of Appeal in *R. v. Goulis* (1981), 125 D.L.R. (3d) 137, employed this approach in interpreting the meaning of a word in the Criminal Code. He stated at pp. 141-42:

This Court has on many occasions applied the well-known rule of statutory construction that if a penal provision is reasonably capable of two interpretations, that interpretation which is the more favourable to the accused must be adopted: see, for example, R. v. Cheetham (1980), 53 C.C.C. (2d) 109, 17 C.R. (3d) 1; R. v. Negridge (1980), 54 C.C.C. (2d) 304, 17 C.R. (3d) 14, 6 M.V.R. 255. I do not think, however, that this principle always requires a word which has two accepted meanings to be given the more restrictive meaning. Where a word used in a statute has two accepted meanings, then either or both meanings may apply. The Court is first required to endeavour to determine the sense in which Parliament used the word from the context in which it appears. It is only in the case of an ambiguity which still exists after the full context is considered, where it is uncertain in which sense Parliament used the word, that the above rule of statutory construction requires the interpretation which is the more favourable to the defendant to be adopted. Thus, the rule of strict construction becomes applicable only when attempts at the neutral interpretation suggested by s. 12 of the Interpretation Act still leave reasonable doubt as to the meaning or scope of the text of the statute. As Professor Côté has pointed out, this means that even with penal statutes, the real intention of the legislature must be sought, and the meaning compatible with its goals applied. (See, for example, R. v. Johnston (1977), 37 C.R.N.S. 234 (N.W.T.C.A.), aff'd [1978] 2 S.C.R. 391; R. v. Philips Electronics Ltd. (1980), 116 D.L.R. (3d) 298 (Ont. C.A.), aff'd [1981] 2 S.C.R. 264; R. v. Leroux, [1974] C.A. 151, and R. v. Nittolo, [1978] C.A. 146.)

In my view, any uncertainty as to whether the word "capable" means either "immediately capable" or "readily capable," is resolved as soon as the word is interpreted in light of the purpose and goals of the prohibited weapons provisions of the *Code*. Therefore, there is no need to resort to the rule of strict construction in this case.

2. The Purpose and Goals of the Provisions Pertaining to Prohibited Weapons

Let us consider for a moment the nature of automatic weapons, that is to say, those weapons that are capable of firing rounds in rapid succession during one pressure of the trigger. These guns are designed to kill and maim a large number of people rapidly and effectively. They serve no other purpose. They are not designed for hunting any animal but man. They are not designed to test the skill and accuracy of a marksman. Their sole function is to kill people. These weapons are of no value for the hunter, or the marksman. They should then be used only by the Armed Forces and, in some circumstances, by the police forces. There can be no doubt that they pose such a threat that they constitute a real and present danger to all Canadians. There is good reason to prohibit their use in light of the threat which they pose and the limited use to which they can be put. Their prohibition ensures a safer society.

The American authorities should not be considered in this case. Canadians unlike Americans do not have a constitutional right to bear arms. Indeed, most Canadians prefer the peace of mind and sense of security derived from the knowledge that the possession of automatic weapons is prohibited.

This Court, in *R. v. Covin*, [1983] 1 S.C.R. 725, determined that a purposive approach should be taken in interpreting the definition of "firearm." In that case, the issue was whether a pellet gun from which several essential parts were missing could be considered a firearm within the meaning of s. 83 (now s. 85) and s. 82 (now s. 84) of the *Criminal Code*. The definition of "firearm" in s. 84(1) includes "anything that can be adapted for use as a firearm." In deciding whether the instrument in question fell within the definition of a "firearm," Lamer J., as he then was, employed the purposive approach to determine the acceptable amount of adaptation required in order for something to be considered a firearm. At page 729 of that case Lamer J. stated:

In my view the acceptable amount of adaptation and the time required therefore for something to still remain within the definition is dependent upon the nature of the offence where the definition is involved. The purpose of each section should be identified and the amount, nature and the time span for adaptation determined so as to support Parliament's endeavour when enacting that given section.

It is equally appropriate to utilize the purposive approach in order to determine the meaning of the phrase "capable of firing bullets in rapid succession during one pressure of the trigger."

3. The Appropriate Interpretation of the Definition of Prohibited Weapon

What then, should "capable" mean as it is used in the s. 84(1) definition of prohibited weapon? It should not be restricted to the narrow meaning of immediately capable. Such a definition would mean that the simple removal of a part which could be replaced in seconds would take the weapon outside the definition. This surely could not have been the intention of Parliament. If it were, the danger from automatic weapons would continue to exist just as strongly as it did before the prohibition was enacted.

The word "capable" as it is defined in the *Oxford English Dictionary* (2nd ed. 1989) includes an aspect of potential capability for conversion. It is defined as:

4. Able or fit to receive and be affected by; open to, susceptible . . .
5. Having the needful capacity, power, or fitness for (some specified purpose or activity).

From this, it is clear that "capable" does in fact include a potential for conversion. It is then fair and reasonable to interpret the definition of "prohibited weapon" as including a gun that has the potential to be readily converted to a fully automatic weapon.

It is the proper role of the court to define the meaning of "capable" as it is used in the definition of "prohibited weapon" in s. 84(1). In my view, it should mean capable of conversion to an automatic weapon in a relatively short period of time with relative ease. There can be no doubt that on the findings of the Provincial Court judge, which are well supported by the evidence, this weapon comes within that definition.

Nor can it be a valid defence that a collector such as Mr. Hasselwander would never convert the weapon. Collectors are attractive targets for thieves who are seeking these weapons with every intention of using them or selling them to others who wish to make use of them. Members of the community are entitled to protection from the use of automatic weapons. This can be accomplished by giving the word "capable" given the definition set out above.

Major J. notes that a conviction for possession of a prohibited weapon under s. 90 of the Criminal Code may now result in imprisonment for a term of up to ten years. (In 1989, the maximum term of imprisonment was five years.) In his view, the potential of imprisonment requires a strict construction of the statute. With respect, I disagree. Automatic weapons or those which may be easily and quickly converted to automatic status have such potential for killing and indeed, mass killing, that their possession may properly bring consequences of imprisonment. It is because of their lethal potential that the definition of "prohibited weapon" requires a reasonable interpretation based upon the wording of the section and the aim or purpose of the legislation. Furthermore, s. 90 permits the Crown to proceed by way of indictment or summary conviction. Therefore, an individual who is found to be in possession of a weapon which he may not have realized was prohibited may be charged with a summary offence and thus, if convicted, be eligible for an absolute discharge. Thus, I do not think that a strict interpretation of para. (c) of the definition of "prohibited weapon," as it stood at the time of the trial, was appropriate.

Nor can I agree with Justice Major's contention that the latest amendment to the section indicates that the word "capable" should be given a narrow or strict interpretation. Rather, it should be viewed as a response to the perceived need to remove any doubt as to the meaning of the word.

The reasoning in other cases support the position that I have taken. Thus, I am in agreement with the reasons of Hart J.A. in *R. v. Haines* (1981), 45 N.S.R. (2d) 428, at p. 436, where he stated:

The offences charged here against the appellant were the possession of prohibited weapons. In my opinion the determination of whether or not a particular thing is a "prohibited weapon" is to be determined by applying the facts to the definition contained in s. 82 [now s. 84] of the Criminal Code. If a firearm is partially or completely dismantled but can be rendered "capable of firing bullets" by the simple reassembly of its parts or the making of some minor alterations to its works, I would think it could be found as a fact that it was a prohibited weapon. If, on the other hand, it was in such a condition that it could not be made operable because of lack of all parts or because of physical changes made to its structure which would be difficult to repair that it may cease to be in fact a "weapon". There would have to be at the same time and place the necessary ingredients for an operable firearm together with the ability to place it in operable form.

In *R. v. Ferguson* (1985), 20 C.C.C. (3d) 256, the Ontario Court of Appeal considered whether a sawed-off shotgun constituted a prohibited weapon. Although that required the court to interpret a different definition from the one under consideration in the case at bar, nevertheless, I think that the approach taken by the Court of Appeal in resolving the ambiguity in that case is apposite. There the weapon was not operable since it was missing its "firing unit", without which it could not discharge a bullet. However, Lacourcière J.A. stated (at p. 262):

Possession is a continuing offence. The evil that this section was designed to prevent and the purpose of the section was obviously to suppress the possession of devices, knives or firearms which constitute a particular danger to the public, for example, silencers, switch-knives or, in the present case, under s. 82(1)(d), a sawed-off rifle which can be easily concealed because of its reduced length. Because of the nature of the continuing offence of possession of a prohibited weapon under s. 88(1) and having regard to the purpose of the subsection, we are all satisfied that the acceptable amount of adaptation and the time-span required to render the gun operable is longer than that required for a s. 83 offence, where the adaptation has to be made on the scene in order to support the charge of using a firearm during the commission or attempted commission of an indictable offence or during the flight thereafter.

The expert evidence was that the firing mechanism was easily obtainable and could be inserted in 30 seconds to one minute. In view of that evidence we are satisfied that the inoperable gun in this case could be adapted for use as a firearm from which bullets capable of causing serious bodily injury or death could be discharged and that being a "firearm" it was a "prohibited weapon" as defined in s. 82(1)(d).

He observed that it would be contrary to the purpose of the legislation if, by removing a portion of the weapon, a person could render his or her weapon inoperable and thereby avoid conviction.

Thus it appears that in the majority of the decided cases the courts have properly considered the purpose of the legislation. That purpose is to protect the public from these dangerous weapons that are designed specifically to kill or maim people. Where a weapon can be quickly and readily converted to automatic status, then that weapon must fall within the definition of "prohibited weapon." To come to any other conclusion would undermine the very purpose of the legislation.

The Hasselwander case illustrates the complexity of statutory interpretation. Who or what are we to consult about legislative meaning or intent? There are essentially two models of statutory interpretation: one derives from British traditions; the other, from European and U.S. traditions. In the former, a statute is interpreted literally; phrases and clauses are closely examined in order to extract their precise meanings. It is assumed that the law's intent has been fully formulated within the language of the statute, and, accordingly, there is usually no need to go beyond the wording. The European and U.S. traditions of statutory interpretation require a somewhat different focus for analysis. In order to determine the full intent of the legislature, any source that may assist in determining intent may be consulted: parliamentary or legislative debates, commission reports, and the statements of those responsible for the legislation. Within this latter framework of interpretation, there is at least a difference in emphasis: it is assumed that the words of a statute are not always sufficient to allow the judiciary or the practising lawyer to understand the meaning that attaches to ambiguous language.

In many instances, statutory interpretation is aided by definition sections written into specific statutes. For example, section 2 of the *Criminal Code* of Canada provides definitions of dozens of words and expressions found within the *Code*. "Highway" is defined, for instance, as "a road to which the public has the right of access, and includes bridges over which or tunnels through which a road passes." "Motor vehicle" is defined as "a vehicle that is drawn, propelled, or driven by any means other than muscular power, but does not include railway equipment." And "weapon" is defined as "(a) anything used or intended for use in causing death or injury to persons, whether designed for that purpose or not, or (b) anything used or intended for use for the purpose of threatening or intimidating any person." The intention of such definitions is to limit ambiguity from the outset and to lessen the need for legal debate about the meaning to be ascribed to key words within the particular statute.

There also exist federal and provincial interpretation acts, which apply to all statutes within their respective sphere. They contain definitions of certain words that are to have the same meaning across federal or provincial legislation and regulation, together with general rules to be employed in the reading of statutes. For example, the preamble to a statute is always to be read as a part of that statute. (The preamble is designed to set out the point or gist of the legislation.) The use of the male gender within legislation is always to be read as including the female gender.

Statutory Interpretation: Rules and Principles

Statutory interpretation in Canada has historically rested on the British tradition of narrow interpretation of legislative intent, developed by the English judiciary from the sixteenth century forward. Three rules and three grammatical principles exist to aid the construction of statutes. The rules have an elegant simplicity: (1) read the statute literally; (2) read it in context; and (3) read it in accordance with its intentions. The grammatical principles are still expressed in the traditional Latin: (1) *expressio unius est exclusio alterius*; (2) *ejusdem generis*; and (3) *noscitur a sociis*. Like the rules, they stress the importance of context and implication in the interpretation of ambiguous language. In most respects, statutory interpretation flows from a relatively straightforward and logical set of premises.

The rules and principles are simple but not simplistic, and provide a consistent method for analysis. As Ruth Sullivan has noted in a recent article in the *Canadian Bar Review*, "To resolve statutory interpretation disputes, judges must analyze and integrate a variety of factors, including textual meaning, legislative purpose, acceptable consequences, and presumptions of intent. The attention paid to the factors and the amount of emphasis each receives depend on the circumstances of the case—the type of legislation, the subject matter and audience, how precise the language is, the lapse of time since enactment, and the like. On this approach, judges have considerable discretion, but this discretion is structured and constrained by a principle-based practice of decision-making."[2] In other words, the principles are guidelines, to be used as dictated by the specifics of individual cases. The variables cited by Sullivan—the type of legislation, the lapse of time since enactment, and the audience to which the law applies—can all be relevant to the obviously complex task of statutory interpretation.

The Three Rules of Interpretation

THE PLAIN MEANING RULE: READ THE STATUTE LITERALLY

There is an appealing simplicity to the **plain meaning rule**, which demands that the words of a statute be read in accordance with their literal, grammatical sense. The courts are, as a consequence, not entitled to read a statute loosely or to impose their own construction upon the statute, even if a literal reading would appear to lead to an incorrect or incongruous result. The courts cannot assume that the legislature has made either errors or omissions. Consider, for example, a statute that prohibits dogs from a city park unless they are on a leash. It cannot be assumed or inferred that the statute was also designed, by implication, to apply to cats.

THE GOLDEN RULE: READ THE STATUTE IN CONTEXT

The second of the three rules is essentially a softening of the first. In 1857, in the case *Grey v. Pearson,* Lord Wensleydale wrote, "In construing statutes, the grammatical and ordinary sense of the words is to be adhered to . . . [but if there is] some absurdity or some repugnancy or inconsistency with the rest [of the statute] . . . the grammatical and ordinary sense of words may be modified so as to avoid that absurdity and inconsistency, but not further."[3] Thus, the **golden rule** proposes that words cannot always be read literally and that when inconsistency, absurdity, or repugnancy arises as a result of the wording of a statute, the inconsistency, absurdity, or repugnancy must be remedied. (A "repugnancy" within the law is not to be understood as something distasteful or horribly unpleasant, but as an anomaly or incompatibility.)

THE RULE IN HEYDON'S CASE: READ THE STATUTE IN ACCORDANCE WITH ITS INTENTIONS

The **rule in Heydon's case** has remained at the heart of statutory interpretation since it was first set out in England in 1584. "For the sure and true interpretation of all statutes," the court wrote, "four things are to be . . . considered." The first is the state of the common law before the statute; the second, the mischief for which the common law did not provide; the third, the remedy that Parliament has used to address the problem; and the fourth, "the true reason of the remedy."

The rule in Heydon's case, often referred to as the "mischief" rule, sets out a process for understanding legislative intent. (The word "mischief" is not meant here in its contemporary context of "troublesome but not malicious conduct." Rather, it refers to the defect or limitation in legal control that the statute was intended to correct.) The best-known application of this third rule is found in the Scottish case of *Gorris v. Scott* (1874). The plaintiff, Gorris, sued the defendant, Scott, to recover damages from the loss of his sheep. They were swept into the sea from Scott's boat during a storm. Scott had not provided pens for the animals, as required by law. However, the court held that Gorris was not entitled to recover damages for his loss because the law requiring pens was designed to prevent the spread of contagious disease, and not to prevent losses overboard. Since the law was not designed to control this form of mischief, the claim did not fall within the "mischief" of the act.

The Three Grammatical Principles of Construction

EXPRESSIO UNIUS EST EXCLUSIO ALTERIUS

This Latin maxim literally means "the expression of one is the exclusion of the other." It can be understood to mean that the expression of one thing or class of things excludes another thing or class of things. If an act of Parliament imposes a new property tax on the owners of "houses, outbuildings, apartments, and condominiums," it is to be assumed that the owners of land with no buildings on it are not to be taxed. The express mention of structures that sit on land and the corresponding omission of land itself suggest that the tax is meant to apply to building structures, not land. That is, the express mention of one category (in this case, buildings) excludes some other category (in this case, land).

Another example of *expressio unius est exclusio alterius* might be found in an invitation posted in a university residence inviting all graduates to attend a reception at the home of the university president. At the bottom of the invitation is the statement: Your Thesis Must Be Presented at the Door. Initially, the invitation appears a little ambiguous. Are all graduates of university programs welcome at the president's home—all those who have received diplomas, B.A. degrees, B.Sc. degrees, or postgraduate degrees? Or is the invitation extended only to those who have completed theses as part of their academic programs, typically, master's and doctoral graduates?

The answer here appears to be that the express mention of the thesis excludes certain graduates. "Graduate" is to be defined in this context only as the graduate of a program with a thesis requirement. Hence, diploma and baccalaureate students are to be excluded.

EJUSDEM GENERIS

This Latin expression is literally translated as "of the same kind." It again emphasizes the importance of context in statutory interpretation. The *ejusdem generis* principle dictates that ambiguous phrases or clauses will derive their meanings from the specific context in which they appear.

Suppose, for example, that a statute prohibited citizens from carrying "knives, rifles, pistols, clubs, brass knuckles, or any other such implements on their person." If an individual was found to be carrying a machine gun, it seems likely that it would be interpreted to be a prohibited "implement." If, on the other hand, an individual was found to be carrying a garden spade, it seems unlikely that it would be covered by the statute. In ordinary English usage, a garden spade is an implement, as is a machine gun. But given the specific words and context of this statute, carrying a machine gun appears to be a prohibited act; carrying a garden spade would not fall within the same category. Hence, a garden spade could not be defined as "any other such implement."

NOSCITUR A SOCIIS

Noscitur a sociis means "it is to be known by its associates." This principle is a variation on *ejusdem generis.* It states that a general word followed by specific words will be defined by the context of those specific words. Thus, *noscitur a sociis* is essentially the mirror image of *ejusdem generis.* Instead of an ambiguous phrase taking its meaning from a series of specific words, an ambiguous word takes its meaning from the specific phrases that follow it.

For example, if a statute requires that citizens obtain a licence to operate any "vehicle, automobile, motorcycle, truck, or machinery of a similar kind," the general word "vehicle" is interpreted in light of the specific words that follow. An automobile, motorcycle, and truck all share the characteristic of being driven by an engine rather than muscular power. It therefore seems likely that a bicycle would not be defined as a vehicle, within the meaning of this particular section of the statute.

The *noscitur a sociis* and *ejusdem generis* principles are functionally equivalent; both require general, ambiguous language to take its meaning from the specific descriptive context in which it appears. Whether the ambiguous language follows or precedes more specific language is ultimately of no consequence.

Illustrations of Statutory Interpretation: Applying the Rules and Principles

The three rules and grammatical principles are intended to facilitate the task of statutory interpretation. When judges encounter an ambiguous word or phrase, they, at least in theory, first resort to the plain-meaning rule, then the golden rule, and finally the rule in Heydon's case. When interpreting grammatical or verbal context, they turn to the three principles couched in the Latin phrases: *expressio unius est exclusio alterius*, *ejusdem generis*, and *noscitur a sociis*. But it is also appropriate to note that the ultimate task of statutory interpretation is to determine the intention of the legislature in circumstances that are, by definition, ambiguous. In this context the skillful practitioner of statutory interpretation will not proceed in a strictly linear fashion, but will analyze the text of the statute, will look to its purpose, and will examine how different consequences might flow from different interpretive choices—the interpreter will be examining the policies that underlie different analyses, and looking at the various impacts of these policy choices.

There are times when the common-sense meanings of language are displaced by the language of a given statute. If, for example, the law says that marijuana is a narcotic, it is not a legally useful response to say that science rejects such a classification. In law, words ultimately mean only what the law decides they mean. While a legal system cannot jettison everyday meanings of language and continue to be seen as legitimate, there is nonetheless, at least at times, a Humpty-Dumpty character to statutory interpretation.

The Persons Case of 1927

Consider the famous Persons case of 1927.[4] In the late summer of that year, five women requested that the federal Cabinet refer section 24 of the *British North America Act, 1867* to Canada's Supreme Court for interpretation. The section reads:

> 24. The Governor General shall from time to time, in the Queen's name, by instrument under the Great Seal of Canada, summon qualified persons to the Senate; and, subject to the provisions of this Act, every person so summoned shall become and be a member of the Senate and a senator.

Specifically, the women asked the Court to determine whether women were "qualified persons" and, hence, appropriate for appointment to the Senate.

The Supreme Court concluded that women were not "persons" and hence were not eligible for such appointment. The British Privy Council, on appeal from the five women, overturned the Supreme Court of Canada and declared that women were indeed persons and therefore eligible. From our vantage point, this all seems slightly absurd: women are clearly persons. In 1927, however, the word "person," in the context of political representation, meant men.

If the political and social context of law is placed to one side, there is ultimately little magic or mystery in the rules and principles of statutory interpretation. The rules state that we are to read statutes literally; to adjust their literal meanings if—and only if—absolutely necessary; and to determine the purpose or the "mischief" at which a given statute is directed. The principles of grammatical context hold that we are to assume that each word has a meaning; that in setting out inclusive categories, statutes can simultaneously be exclusive; and that ambiguous words can be made unambiguous by relating them to a specific context.

There are limitations on the kinds of information that Canadian courts may use in determining legislative intent. The major difference between the Canadian and U.S. methods of interpretation lies in the way in which certain kinds of legislative history are incorporated into legal decision making. In Canada, as in Britain, the political process that created the legislation is not subject to scrutiny. Hansard, the record of the House of Commons debates, cannot be cited in support of understanding legislative intent. Additionally, it may not always be acceptable to introduce the transcript of a minister's speech, the report of a parliamentary committee, or the transcript of a royal commission. It has often been argued that no certainty or clarity in understanding can be derived from consulting such documents, given their range of arguments. The conflicting social history that gives life to law is taken to be irrelevant as well. At the same time, however, the evolution of the law itself—the history of amendment and of other legal sources—is admissible as an aid to interpretation.

The accepted means of establishing legislative history are, then, tracing amendments to their source and consulting relevant case law. (A preamble may be consulted, since it is read as part of the statute.) But there are also signs that we are moving away from a narrow conception of the role of legislative history in the determination of legislative intent. The *Charter,* in place since April 1982, requires a greater awareness of the social, political, and economic contexts in which law is constructed and mediated. The terminology—"freedom of expression," "fair hearing," "cruel and unusual punishment," and so on—requires theoretical and empirical analysis of the law's intentions and consequences if it is to be applied in a meaningful way.

In the context of the *Charter*, the rules and principles of interpretation become less significant. The task of the judiciary is not only to reconcile ambiguities in language, but also to determine whether legislation is consistent with the broad general principles stated in the *Charter*—the putative values of the nation. In this respect, Canada is moving closer to the U.S. model of an activist judiciary; the acceptability of federal and provincial legislation is assessed against a judicially constructed benchmark of rights and freedoms.

The *Fisher v. Bell* Case of 1960

Despite these developments in statutory interpretation, the rules and principles continue to have some merit. As you read about *Fisher v. Bell*, ask yourself how the rules and principles clarify the case. Specifically, does the plain meaning or literal rule apply? Is the *expressio unius est exclusio alterius* principle applicable?

In England in 1960, Lord Chief Justice Parker and his colleagues were faced with a surprisingly difficult problem in the case of *Fisher v. Bell*.[5] Fisher, a chief inspector of police, had charged Bell, the owner of a shop in Bristol, with violating the *Restriction of Offensive Weapons Act*. Fisher had seen a knife in Bell's window with a sign behind it: Ejector knife—4 shillings. The relevant section of the act was as follows:

> Any person who manufactures, sells, or hires or offers for sale or hire, or lends or gives to any other person—(a) any knife which has a blade which opens automatically by hand pressure applied to a button, spring, or other device in or attached to the handle of the knife, sometimes known as a "flick knife" . . . shall be guilty of an offence.

Lord Parker concluded that no offence had been committed:

> The knife is there inviting people to buy it, and in ordinary language, it is for sale; but any statute must be looked at in the light of the general law of the country, for Parliament must be taken to know the general law. It is clear that, according to the ordinary law of contract, the display of an article with a price on it in a shop window is merely an invitation to treat. It is in no sense an offer for sale, the acceptance of which constitutes a contract. . . . [I]n many statutes and orders which prohibit selling and offering for sale of goods, it is very common . . . to insert the words "offering or exposing for sale," "exposing for sale" being clearly words which would cover the display of goods in a shop window.[6]

Lord Parker's reasoning was that because the words "exposing for sale" were not found in the statute, the act of advertising the ejector knife did not contravene the relevant provision of the *Restriction of Offensive Weapons Act*.

Those of us who are surprised at this finding might have applied the plain-meaning rule, which would have led us to a more common-sense conclusion: by placing a knife in a window with a tag advertising a specific price, the proprietor was offering it for sale, and hence contravening the literal meaning of the statute. Application of the golden rule to this set of facts would appear to yield a similar interpretation; there is no inconsistency or repugnancy within the section in question. Finally, the rule in Heydon's case would give the same result. The mischief targeted by the legislation is any form of commerce in flick or ejector knives. The proprietor of the store was clearly involved in this commerce.

The grammatical principles of construction have varying application. The *ejusdem generis* principle is not applicable since no ambiguous word or words are set out against the backdrop of a more specific context. The *expressio unius est exclusio alterius* principle will, however, help us understand—if not agree with—Lord Parker's decision. This judgment suggested that the express mention of "offering for sale" must be seen as simultaneously excluding "exposing for sale." In the absence of specific mention of "exposing for sale," he was forced to assume that the act was designed to control only offers for sale, not exposures for sale.

Further to this case, the language of the law of contract makes an important distinction between exposing a commodity for sale and offering it for sale. By placing a price on an item in a store, a proprietor is providing a customer with what is termed "an invitation to treat." There is no guarantee that there will be more than one knife for sale at the quoted price, and indeed no guarantee that the knife displayed is available for purchase. It is when the customer brings the knife to the counter that there is an offer for sale (or purchase); when money or credit is exchanged, there is an acceptance of the offer and a binding contract.

These facts leave us with a number of questions. Was the mischief targeted by the legislation the act of "exposing for sale," "offering for sale," or both? Should we assume that the British Parliament's failure to add the words "exposing for sale" to the act was intentional? Was the statute designed to permit the advertising and placement of flick knives in retail outlets and simultaneously to prohibit any offers that customers might make to purchase the product?

The *R. v. Sparrow* Case, or When Is a Horse a Bird?

At this point, you may be developing a feel for the application of the rules and principles of statutory interpretation. What meaning can you derive from the decision in *R. v. Sparrow*,[7] a fictitious case involving a breach of the fictitious *Small Birds Act*?

Blue, J.: This is an appeal by the Crown by way of a stated case from a decision of the magistrate, acquitting the accused of a charge under the *Small Birds Act*, R.S.O., 1960, c. 724, s. 2. The facts are not in dispute. John Sparrow was riding his pony through Queen's Park on January 2, 1965. Being impoverished, and having been forced to pledge his saddle, he substituted a downy pillow in lieu of the said saddle. On this particular day, the accused's misfortune was further heightened by the circumstance of his pony breaking its right foreleg. In accord with veterinary practice, the accused then shot the pony to relieve it of its awkwardness.

The accused was thereupon charged with having breached the *Small Birds Act*, section 2 of which states:

2. Anyone maiming, injuring, or killing small birds is guilty of an offence and subject to a fine not in excess of two hundred dollars.

The learned magistrate acquitted the accused, holding, in fact, that he had killed his horse and not a small bird. With respect, I cannot agree.

In light of the definition section, my course is quite clear. Section 1 defines "bird" as "a two-legged animal covered with feathers." There can be no doubt that this case is covered by this section.

Counsel for the accused made several ingenious arguments to which, in fairness, I must address myself. He submitted that the evidence of the expert clearly concluded that the animal in question was a pony and not a bird, but this is not the issue. We are not interested in whether the animal in question is a bird or not in fact, but whether it is one in law. . . .

Counsel also contended that the neighing noise emitted by the animal could not possibly be produced by a bird. With respect, the sounds emitted by an animal are irrelevant to its nature, for a bird is no less a bird because it is silent.

Counsel for the accused also argued that since there was evidence that the accused had ridden the animal, this pointed to the fact that it could not be a bird but was actually a pony. Obviously, this avoids the issue. The issue is not whether the animal was ridden or not, but whether it was shot or not, for to ride a pony or a bird is no offence at all. I believe counsel now sees his mistake.

Counsel contends that the iron shoes found on the animal decisively disqualify it from being a bird. I must inform counsel, however, that how an animal dresses is of no concern to this court.

Counsel relied on the decision in *Re Chickadee*, where he contends that in similar circumstances, the accused was acquitted. However, this is a horse of a different colour. A close reading of that case indicates that the animal in question there was not a small bird, but, in fact, a midget of a much larger species. Therefore, that case is inapplicable to our facts. . . . It remains then to state my reason for judgment which, simply, is as follows: Different things may take on the same meaning for different purposes. For the purpose of the *Small Birds Act*, all two-legged feather-covered animals are birds. This, of course, does not imply that only two-legged animals qualify, for the legislative intent is to make two legs merely the minimum requirement. That statute therefore contemplated multi-legged animals with feathers as well. Counsel submits that having regard to the purpose of the statute, only small animals "naturally covered" with feathers could have been contemplated. However, had this been the intention of the legislature, I am certain that the phrase "naturally covered" would have been expressly inserted just as "Long" was inserted in the *Longshoreman's Act*.

Therefore, a horse with feathers on its back must be deemed for the purposes of this act to be a bird, and, *a fortiori*, a pony with feathers on its back is a small bird.

Counsel posed the following rhetorical question: If the pillow had been removed prior to the shooting, would the animal still have been a bird? To this, let me answer rhetorically: Is a bird any less of a bird without its feathers?

The case *R. v. Sparrow* is, of course, a parody of statutory interpretation. But the satirical decision makes some useful points and raises questions about wresting certainty from the ambiguity of legal language. Note, for example, the court's comment, "We are not interested in whether the animal in question is a bird or not in fact, but whether it is one in law."

Let us apply the rules and principles of statutory interpretation to *R. v. Sparrow*. The key issue in dispute is whether a pony with a downy pillow saddle can be properly defined as a "small bird," pursuant to the *Small Birds Act*. The relevant section is that which defines a bird as "a two-legged animal covered with feathers."

If we apply the plain-meaning, or literal, rule, the pony in question would not appear to be a target of this definition. The pony, although it may have been covered with feathers, is not a two-legged animal. And the legislation does not provide for other possibilities: a one-legged animal or an animal with more than two legs. Counsel's argument in response is that the definition "does not imply that only two-legged animals qualify, for the legislative intent is to make two legs merely the minimum requirement." But can this argument be successful? If the intent was to make two legs the minimum requirement for defining small birds, would this not have been spelled out within the legislation? In this instance, the act would define a small bird as "an animal with two or more legs, covered with feathers." An application of the literal rule suggests that if the pony covered with feathers had two legs, it might well be defined as a small bird. But given the animal's four legs, it is difficult to argue that it would fall within this category.

The golden rule does not appear to apply to the case because there is no inconsistency or repugnancy within the words of the statute. Application of the rule in Heydon's case suggests that the mischief intended to be corrected by the legislation is the killing of small birds, and since the pony covered with feathers cannot be defined as a small bird, the intent of the legislation is not consistent with controlling the shooting of this pony, albeit a pony covered with feathers.

The grammatical principles of interpretation also suggest that the pony covered with feathers cannot be considered to be a small bird. While the *ejusdem generis* and *noscitur a sociis* maxims do not apply to the facts of the case, the principle of *expressio unius est exclusio alterius* does have relevance. In expressly mentioning two-legged animals in the definition of small birds, the legislators exclude all other possibilites, whether with fewer or more than two legs.

What of Blue, J.'s parting comment: Is a bird any less of a bird without its feathers? The answer is, of course, that a bird without feathers is not a bird at all, at least as defined by the *Small Birds Act*. Without the downy pillow saddle on the pony's back, this legal conundrum would never have arisen. But consider the effect on statutory interpretation if the *Small Birds Act* defined "bird" as "an animal with one or more legs, covered with feathers." Would Sparrow have been properly convicted of killing a small bird? And what of the argument that if one looks to the mischief targeted by the legislation, "only small animals 'naturally covered' with feathers could have been contemplated"? The court rebutted it by pointing out that if this had been the intention of the legislature, the words "naturally covered" would have been used in the statute. This assertion is similar to the one made in *Fisher v. Bell*: if "exposing [a knife] for sale" was to be an offence, the statute would have used these words to describe the prohibited behaviour.

In both *Fisher v. Bell* and *R. v. Sparrow,* the courts are wrestling with the intention conveyed by certain words. Does "offering for sale" include "exposing for sale"? Does the word "covered" mean only "naturally covered"? What, in short, is the legislative intent—the rule in Heydon's case?

In difficult cases, where legislative intention is a matter of debate, competing values are the focus of the court's attention. Which is more important—to stop the commerce in flick knives or to protect the commercial right to expose a commodity for sale? How expansive should the legal definition of "small bird" be? Should we limit the definition, thereby prosecuting a smaller number of animal killers, or should we protect more animals by seeking the most logically permissible expansion of the term?

At this point, the interpretation of law is no longer a technical task, but a matter of empirical and political reconstruction. The meaning to be applied to a rule has changed. The philosopher Ludwig Wittgenstein has described this conundrum:

> A rule stands there like a signpost. Does the signpost leave no doubt open about the way I have to go? Does it show which direction I am to take when I have passed it? . . . Where is it said which way I am to follow it; whether in the direction of its finger, or in the opposite one? And if there were not a single signpost, but a chain of adjacent ones or of chalk marks on the ground, is there only one way of interpreting them? So I can say, the signpost does after all leave no room for doubt. Or rather: it sometimes leaves room for doubt and sometimes not.[8]

The Case of *Re Elsom and Elsom,* 1983

What of Wittgenstein and his signposts in *Re Elsom and Elsom*? Does the law regarding business assets leave no "room for doubt"? The case concerns the distinction in family law between a "business asset" and a "family asset." The two terms are of interest during divorce proceedings. A family asset is to be divided equally between husband and wife; a business asset is an asset earned outside the context of the marriage and is accordingly to be claimed in its entirety by either the husband or the wife. As you read the excerpt from the decision, ask yourself how the rules and principles of statutory interpretation would apply; specifically, how they would relate to the terms "business asset" and "family asset."

> MacFarlane, J.A.: The question raised by this appeal is whether, under s. 46 of the *Family Relations Act,* R.S.B.C. 1979, c. 120, an asset, which otherwise would be a business asset, is to be regarded as a family asset upon the finding that a spouse has performed, entirely adequately, the duties of a wife and mother, or whether the spouse must prove that there have been savings through effective management of a household or child-rearing responsibilities and that there is a direct causal connection between those savings and the acquisition or operation of the business asset.

The question was before this court recently in *Blockberger v. Blockberger* [unreported]. The trial judge had held that there was no causal connection between the effective management of the household by the wife and the acquisition by Blockberger of his shares in two companies. The trial judge said that it was not to be assumed that an indirect contribution had been made to the business asset merely because the non-owning spouse had been an effective wife and mother. Mr. Justice Hutcheon, with whom Chief Justice Nemetz and Mr. Justice Carrothers agreed, held that "the finding that the wife was a model wife and mother leads, in this case, to a finding that the wife did contribute indirectly to the husband's business career and thus to the operation of the printing business. *Prima facie,* she is entitled to 50 percent in the shares he holds." In doing so, he referred to *Tratch v. Tratch* (1981), 30 B.C.L.R. 98; *McDougall v. McDougall* (1982), 39 B.C.L.R. 88 at p. 94, 29 R.F.L. (2d) 274 (B.C.S.C.); *Vance v. Vance* (1981), 128 D.L.R. (3d) 109, at p. 113–114 . . .

The most recent of these cases is *McDougall v. McDougall*, a decision of Locke, J. The judgement contains a useful review of the two different lines of authority that have been developed in British Columbia with regard to the interpretation of s. 46:

Excluded business assets

> 46. (1) Where property is owned by one spouse to the exclusion of the other and is used primarily for business purposes and where the spouse who does not own the property made no direct or indirect contribution to the acquisition of the property by the other spouse or to the operation of the business, the property is not a family asset.

One line of authority has now been cited with approval by this court in *Blockberger*. That line of authority holds that effective management of the household or child-rearing responsibilities will not be inquired into too closely, and savings will be presumed. The other line of authority holds that the wife must prove that her contribution had some connection, albeit in only a general way, with the property in which she seeks an interest. . . .

The meaning of s. 46 may, in my opinion, be summarized in this way. A business asset in the name of one spouse is not a family asset unless the other spouse makes a direct or indirect contribution to it. If the spouse has been effective as a wife and mother, it is to be inferred that savings have accrued to the benefit of her husband because he has not had to arrange for and pay someone else to provide those services. Those savings are assumed to have advanced the business interests of the husband because more time and money may be devoted to the business. In that sense, there is a nexus between the role of an effective wife and mother, and the acquisition or operation of the husband's business.

But there will be cases where there is, in fact, no such connection. Such cases may be rare. One such case was *Simpkins v. Simpkins* (1982), 41 B.C.L.R. 75, [1983] 2 W.W.R. 361, 32 R.F.L. (2d) 1, where, with money provided by his father, a husband acquired shares in a company only a few months before separation from his wife. The court held that there was no connection between the wife's activities and that particular acquisition. The wife's activities therefore did not constitute an indirect contribution under s. 46. *Laxton v. Laxton* (1982), 41 B.C.L.R. 194, 31 R.F.L. (2d) 337, was another unique case where it was held that a "windfall" was not a family asset. The profit was the result of a real estate "flip." The venture was organized by another person through a company incorporated for that purpose, and it was financed by a bank. Neither the personal assets of the husband nor any family assets were at risk, and the venture was completed without any appreciable expenditure of the husband's time. *Samuels v. Samuels* (1981), 30 B.C.L.R. 186, 22 R.F.L. (2d) 402, was a case where the asset was a farm in Saskatchewan, inherited by the husband but managed entirely by the husband's brother. The "savings" by the wife did not contribute to the acquisition or operation of the business. I do not think it unreasonable that where such an unusual situation exists, the onus should be on the owner of the business asset to rebut the usual inference that a wife and mother had made an indirect contribution to the business asset. . . .

In this case, the business assets were shares held in the name of the husband in several related companies incorporated to carry out a real estate development. The lands had been acquired by the husband before the marriage and it was conceded that the wife had not made any contribution to such acquisition. The judge held that the wife made an indirect contribution to the operation of the business because she had "entirely, adequately performed the duties of wife and mother during the time of the marriage." The relationship had lasted for eleven years. The judge also held that the wife had performed some "girl Friday" services including answering the telephone, bookkeeping, bank deposits, and delivering messages. The judge cited *Vance,* and in particular, this passage:

With great respect, I incline to the view that by effectively managing the household or child rearing, the wife relieves the husband of a concern that would otherwise be his. That is not to say that he would himself necessarily assume those roles, but he would be burdened with the responsibility of ensuring that somehow they were discharged. . . .

In the instant case, with the husband shuttling back and forth between England and Canada throughout the whole of the marriage, I cannot see how, particularly after the child arrived, she did not relieve him of "concern" at one place or another. Prima facie, her share is 50 percent.

I pause to say that one of the companies in which the husband (in the present case) held shares was an English company.

The appellant submits that the wife did not, in fact, make any contribution to the operation of the business in this case. But the situation here is not much different than the usual case. The wife relieved her husband of responsibilities in respect of the home and the child. She supported him in all that he did. The appellant was described by the trial judge as a man "who was prepared to spend his almost every waking hour to see his plans come to fruition, but only in one way: under his own tight, personal, and detailed control." The companies in which he held virtually all the shares were operating during the course of the marriage. They included landholding companies, and others incorporated for tax reasons, or to carry out ancillary activities, such as farming, landscaping, and management. All required continual guidance by the appellant. He was free to devote himself to these enterprises, while his wife undertook the responsibilities of wife and mother. It was open to the judge to infer a nexus, and to reject the contentions of the appellant that there was no nexus. . . .

The first ground taken by the appellant must fail.[9]

If we apply either the plain-meaning rule or the golden rule to the *Elsom* case, we focus on the words "direct or indirect contribution to the acquisition of the property . . . or to the operation of the business." What is intended or meant by "a direct or an indirect contribution"? *The Oxford Reference Dictionary* tells us that to contribute is "to give jointly with others." It adds that "to contribute" is defined as "to help to bring about."

The rule in Heydon's case leads to the conclusion that the purpose of the legislation in this instance is to create a distinction between a family asset, to be equally shared, and a business asset, not to be shared.

Section 46 proposes that in some circumstances assets are not to be equally divided in the event of divorce. Justice MacFarlane, in writing the decision in *Re Elsom*, set out a test for determining the applicability of the section:

> If the spouse has been effective as a wife and mother, it is to be inferred that savings have accrued to the benefit of her husband because he has not had to arrange for and pay someone else to provide those services. Those savings are assumed to have advanced the business interests of the husband because more time and money may be devoted to the business.[10]

This statement suggests that if a wife is judged to be an effective wife and mother, she will be entitled to an equal division of all assets attained or developed by either spouse during the course of the marriage. What remains unclear is a definitive interpretation of "effective wife and mother." The grammatical principles of construction do not appear to apply to the *Elsom* case. There is no ambiguity within general words or phrases linked to specific words or phrases *(ejusdem generis)*, there is no ambiguity within specific words or phrases *(noscitur a sociis)*, and there is no express mention of one thing or class of things that implies the exclusion of another *(expressio unius est exclusio alterius)*.

The task of statutory interpretation in *Re Elsom* therefore hinges on the rule in Heydon's case. What is the intention of the law that makes a distinction between a business asset and a family asset? Is it, as Justice MacFarlane suggested, the creation of an exception to a general rule of equally divided assets, an exception that is to be used only in extreme cases?

Little guidance is given as to how to determine when there has been an absence of a direct or an indirect contribution by the spouse. The judge referred to a number of precedents: *Simpkins v. Simpkins*, *Samuels v. Samuels*, and *Laxton v. Laxton*. But the precedents cannot always point a clear direction for future cases, just as the rules and principles of statutory interpretation cannot always give an unequivocal vision of the future path of the law.

The *R. v. Luxton* Case

In cases in which one argument can be as compelling as another, how are we to decide? Consider the Supreme Court of Canada's decision in *R. v. Luxton*.[11] In this case, counsel for Luxton asked the Court to rule that the current penalty for first degree murder, a minimum of 25 years' imprisonment before parole eligibility, constitutes cruel and unusual punishment, as defined by the *Charter.* Section 12 of the *Charter* reads as follows:

> 12. Everyone has the right not to be subjected to any cruel and unusual treatment or punishment.

The relevant part of the *Luxton* judgment, written by Chief Justice Lamer and supported by all seven members of the Court, states:

> In my view, the combination of ss. 214(5)(e) and 669 [the first degree murder provisions] does not constitute cruel and unusual punishment. These sections provide for punishment of the most serious crime in our criminal law, that of first-degree murder. This is a crime that carries with it the most serious level of moral blameworthiness, namely, subjective foresight of death. The penalty is severe and deservedly so. The minimum 25 years to be served before eligibility for parole reflects society's condemnation of a person who has exploited a position of power and dominance to the gravest extent possible by murdering the person that he or she is forcibly confining [as in the *Luxton* case]. The punishment is not excessive and clearly does not outrage our standards of decency. In my view, it is within the purview of Parliament, in order to meet the objectives of a rational system of sentencing, to treat our most serious crime with an appropriate degree of certainty and severity. I reiterate that, even in the case of first-degree murder, Parliament has been sensitive to the particular circumstances of each offender through various provisions, allowing for the royal prerogative of mercy, the availability of escorted absences from custody for humanitarian and rehabilitative purposes, and for early parole: see s. 672 (now s. 745), 674 (now s. 747) and 686 (now s. 751) of the *Criminal Code*. In *Smith, supra,* at p.137, I quoted with approval the following statement by Borins, District Court Judge, in *R. v. Guiller* (1985) 48 C.R. (3d) 226 (Ontario District Court):
>
> *It is not for the Court to pass on the wisdom of Parliament with respect to the gravity of various offences and the range of penalties which may be imposed upon those found guilty of committing the offences. Parliament has broad discretion in proscribing conduct as criminal and in determining proper punishment. While the final judgement as to whether a punishment exceeds constitutional limits set by the Charter is properly a judicial function, the Court should be reluctant to interfere with the considered views of Parliament and then only in the*

> *clearest cases where the punishment prescribed is so excessive when compared with the punishment prescribed for other offences as to outrage standards of decency.*
>
> Therefore, I conclude that in the case at bar, the impugned provisions in combination do not represent cruel and unusual punishment within the meaning of s. 12 of the *Charter*.[12]

How, then, are to we to define the expression, "cruel and unusual treatment or punishment"? If we apply the plain-meaning rule or the golden rule, we encounter some difficulties. First, a literal reading suggests that treatment or punishment must be both cruel and unusual in order to be objectionable. This interpretation is strengthened by the grammatical principle of *expressio unius est exclusio alterius,* inasmuch as the express use of the word "and" within the definition implies the exclusion of "or." But the ultimate difficulty is that there is no literal or easily reconcilable understanding of the wording. There is, instead, an inherent subjectivity in defining the boundaries of acceptable treatment or punishment: one person's remedy may be another person's torment. If we look to the rule in Heydon's case, we find that the purpose of the *Charter* and its protective and liberating terminology was both to set out and to protect the rights that all Canadians are to enjoy.

The Supreme Court, writing in *Luxton*, clearly indicated reluctance to be activist in interpreting section 12. The Court quoted Ontario County Court Judge Borins with approval:

> It is not for the Court to pass on the wisdom of Parliament with respect to the gravity of various offences and the range of penalties which may be imposed upon those found guilty of committing . . . offences. . . . [T]he Court should be reluctant to interfere . . . only in the clearest cases where the punishment prescribed is so excessive . . . as to outrage standards of decency.[13]

It may seem surprising that the Court is saying that a judicial definition of cruel and unusual punishment can stem only from a perceived outrage of decency, in response to the actions of the state. This interpretation is also consistent with a requirement that treatment or punishment must be not only cruel but also unusual in order to be a violation of human rights. The precise meaning that flows from the prohibition in section 12 of the *Charter* is the subject of a number of precedents, attempts to determine the validity of allegations about penalties or treatments that "outrage standards of decency." They include *Smith v. R.,*[14] *Steele v. Mountain Institution,*[15] and *Olson v. R.*[16]

Conclusion: Precedent—The Guiding Hand of Statutory Interpretation

Mention of precedents brings us to the final element in statutory interpretation. To this point in the chapter, we have been considering the rules and principles of statutory interpretation and their application to examples from various fields of law. We have seen that while the rules and principles can be extremely helpful in clarifying ambiguity, they can also conflict, and they offer no easy resolution of difficult cases. Rather, members of the judiciary are required to create law from among competing claims. Remember the importance of precedent in giving a real-world application to the rarefied rhetoric of statute. Decisions of the Supreme Court of Canada bind all courts in the country to their interpretation of a specific configuration of fact and law; decisions of provincial or territorial Courts of Appeal bind all courts within the given province.

The hierarchical development of case law over time is what takes statute law from a statement of general principles to a statement of negotiated realities. The Latin term ***stare decisis*** is applied to the development of case law within a context of hierarchy. Literally translated, *stare decisis* means "to stand by decided things"; specifically, to stand by the decisions of higher courts. (Refer to Figure 3.1.)

As sections and subsections of statutes are continually litigated, the room for alternative explanations of ambiguity decreases. The advantage of the system of *stare decisis,* of building on precedent, is that it provides greater predictability of outcome and greater certainty concerning the application of law. A disadvantage of rigid adherence to precedent is that illogical distinctions will be made in order to stay within pronouncements from the Courts of Appeal and the Supreme Court of Canada. Another drawback is that the law may take on an absurdly tautological character over time. Cruel and unusual punishment, for example, is whatever it is said to be—within a specific historical context. Finally, the system of precedent, taken to its logical conclusion, raises the question of whether the Supreme Court of Canada—the nine men and women who bind all other courts to their decisions—can reverse itself. Are the justices bound by their own decisions, able to change their interpretation of law only after the House of Commons has amended the statute in question? The best answer to this question is that reversals of previous decisions must be rare if the country's court of last resort is to have legitimacy. But such reversals are permissible in rare circumstances.[17]

Figure 3.1

The Operation of *Stare Decisis* in Canadian Courts

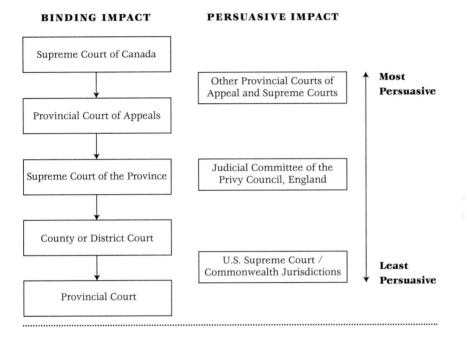

BINDING IMPACT

PERSUASIVE IMPACT

Supreme Court of Canada

Provincial Court of Appeals

Supreme Court of the Province

County or District Court

Provincial Court

Other Provincial Courts of Appeal and Supreme Courts

Judicial Committee of the Privy Council, England

U.S. Supreme Court / Commonwealth Jurisdictions

Most Persuasive

Least Persuasive

The late Bora Laskin once noted during his tenure as chief justice:

> It is worth remembering that for a final court, consistency in decisions is merely a convenience and not a necessity. No one expects the Supreme Court to break out in a rash of reversals of previous decisions, even if it should formally dissociate itself from *stare decisis*. ... In my view, such dissociation, whether formally expressed or not, is imperative if the Court is to develop a personality of its own.[18]

And so it is with statutory interpretation, and with all lawyers and all courts. In complex cases, where the rules and principles are contradictory or not clearly applicable, lawyers and judges must wrestle with their own beliefs and values in the process of construction of the law. In those brief moments, law is transformed from a technical task into an essentially political, economic, and social exercise. In the process, it is necessarily reconstructed, for better or for worse.

Web Links

W W W

Ontario e-Laws: Ontario Statutes and Regulations

http://www.e-laws.gov.on.ca/

Maintained by the Ontario government, this site provides a search engine to locate and read the statutes of Ontario, such as the *Family Law Act.*

Supreme Court of Canada Decisions

http://www.lexum.umontreal.ca/csc-scc/en/index.html

Decisions of the Supreme Court of Canada, currently going back to 1985, are provided on this website.

Legal Drafting

http://aix1.uottawa.ca/~ resulliv/legdr/index.html

This website, which is maintained at the Faculty of Law at the University of Ottawa, is being developed as an international resource for legal and legislative drafters and those who interpret legal texts.

The Persons Case

http://www.famous5.org

This website is devoted to information about the "Persons Case." It contains biographies of the five women who initiated the case, highlights of the case, and a bibliography of material about the women's struggle for legal personality.

Canadian Legal Information Institute

http://www.canlii.org/index_en.html

This website was designed by LexUM at the Centre de recherche en droit public at the University of Montreal for the Federation of Law Societies of Canada. This site provides easy links to all federal, provincial, and territorial statutes that are available online, as well as to all online case law released directly from courts in Canada.

Questions for Discussion

1. What are the greatest strengths and the greatest limitations of the rules and principles of statutory interpretation?
2. What impact does the *Canadian Charter of Rights and Freedoms* have on the process of statutory interpretation?
3. Consider the opposing interpretations of the word "capable" in *R. v. Hasselwander*. Which is more compelling and why?

Further Reading

Dworkin, R. "Hard Cases." *Harvard Law Review* 88 (1975): 1057.

> A very interesting legal and philosophical analysis of the hard cases that the judiciary is called upon to determine—an article that meshes nicely with the more legalistic interpretation of Willis in his 1938 article in the *Canadian Bar Review.*

R. v. Seaboyer; R. v. Gayme, [1991] 2 S.C.R. 577, 7 C.R. (4th) 117, 66 C.C.C. (3d) 321.

> This Supreme Court of Canada decision provides direction to legislatures as to the way a statute could be rewritten; see the comments of McLachlin, J. (as she then was). The Supreme Court's decision provides insight into the interpretation of ambiguous statutes.

Sullivan, R. "Statutory Interpretation in a New Nutshell." *Canadian Bar Review* 51, 82 (2003).

> This is a very useful and likely groundbreaking reworking of the classic *Canadian Bar Review* article by Willis. Sullivan restores lustre to the task of statutory interpretation by going beyond questions of text and legislative intent, and into the domain of a thoughtfully articulated "pragmatism." He develops a conceptual model of three quite different variants of statutory interpretation: textualism, intentionalism, and pragmatism.

Willis, J. "Statute Interpretation in a Nutshell." *Canadian Bar Review* 16 (1938).

> This is a classic article on the subject of statutory interpretation. Through the use of very straightforward examples, Willis helps students to understand the operation of the rules and principles of statutory interpretation.

Notes

1. *R. v. Hasselwander,* [1993] 2 S.C.R. 398.
2. R. Sullivan, "Statutory Interpretation in a New Nutshell," *Canadian Bar Review* 51, 82 (2003).
3. *Grey v. Pearson* (1857), 6 H.L.C. 61.
4. *Edwards v. Canada (A.G.)* (The Persons Case), [1930] A.C. 124, [1929] 3 W.W.R. 479, [1930] 1 D.L.R. 98 (P.C.).
5. (1960), 3 All E.R. 731, [1961] 1 Q.B. 394.

6. Ibid., at 399.
7. *R. v. Sparrow* was written by H. Pomerantz and S. Breslin. It has been modified and edited for the purposes of illustration.
8. L. Wittgenstein, *Philosophical Investigations* (London, U.K.: Academic Press, 1958), 80.
9. *Re Elsom and Elsom* (1983), 3 D.L.R. (4th) 500 at 501–504.
10. Ibid., at 500.
11. [1990] 2 S.C.R. 711, 58 C.C.C. (3d) 449.
12. Ibid., at 724–725.
13. Ibid., at 725.
14. (1987), 34 C.C.C. (3d) 97, [1987] 1 S.C.R. 1045, 58 C.R. (3d) 193.
15. (1990), 60 C.C.C. (3d) 1, 80 C.R. (3d) 257, [1990] 6 W.W.R. 673 (S.C.C.).
16. (1987), 38 C.C.C. (3d) 534, 62 O.R. (2d) 321, 32 O.A.C. 287 (C.A.), aff'd 47 C.C.C. (3d) 491, [1989] 1 S.C.R. 296, 68 O.R. (2d) 256.
17. See, for example, *Bell v. R.,* [1979] 2 S.C.R., 212, 9 M.P.L.R. 103, or *Paquette v. R.,* [1977] 2 S.C.R. 189, 39 C.R.N.S. 257, 30 C.C.C. (2d) 417, 70 D.L.R. (3d) 129, 11 N.R. 451.
18. *R. v. Gwillen* (1985), 48 C.R. (3d) 226.

References

....

Allen, C.K. *Law in the Making.* 4th ed. Oxford: Clarendon Press, 1946.

Beaupré, M. *Interpreting Bilingual Legislation.* 2d ed. Toronto: Carswell, 1946.

Bennion, F.A.R. *Statutory Interpretation.* London, U.K.: Butterworths, 1984.

Cross, R. *Statutory Interpretation.* 2d ed. London, U.K.: Butterworths, 1987.

Driedger, E.A. *The Composition of Legislation, Legislative Forms and Precedents.* 2d ed. Ottawa: Department of Justice, 1976.

———. "Statutes: The Mischievous Literal Golden Rule." *Canadian Bar Review* 59 (1981): 780.

———. *The Construction of Statutes.* 2d ed. Toronto: Butterworths, 1983.

Dworkin, R. "Hard Cases." *Harvard Law Review* 88 (1975): 1057.

Edwards v. Canada (A.G.) (The Persons Case), [1930] A.C. 124, [1929] 3 W.W.R. 479, [1930] 1 D.L.R. 98 (P.C.).

Fisher v. Bell (1960), 3 All E.R. 731, [1961] 1 Q.B. 394.

Frankfurter, F. "Some Reflections on the Reading of Statutes." *Colorado Law Review* 47 (1947): 527.

Gall, G. *The Canadian Legal System.* 3d ed. Toronto: Carswell, 1990, Chapters 10 and 11.

MacAdam, A.I., and T.M. Smith. *Statutes: Rules and Examples*. Sydney, Aus.: Butterworths, 1985.

Pearce, D.C. *Statutory Interpretation in Australia*. 2d ed. Sydney, Aus.: Butterworths, 1981.

Pigeon, L.P. *Redaction et Interpretation des Lois/Drafting and Interpreting Legislation*. Toronto: Carswell, 1988.

Russell, P.H. "Overcoming Legal Formalism: The Treatment of the Constitution, the Courts and Judicial Behaviour in Canadian Political Science." *Canadian Journal of Law and Society* 1 (1986): 5–33.

Smith, J.A.C. "The Interpretation of Statutes." *Manitoba Law Journal* 4 (1970): 212.

Statsky, W.P. *Legislative Analysis and Drafting.* 2d ed. New York: West Publishing, 1984.

Sullivan, R. "Statutory Interpretation in a New Nutshell." *Canadian Bar Review* 51, 82 (2003).

Vaughn, F. "The Canadian Courts and Policy Making: The Case of Justice Emmett Hall." *Saskatchewan Law Review* (1974): 357.

Willis, J. "Statute Interpretation in a Nutshell." *Canadian Bar Review* 16 (1938): 1.

Wittgenstein, L. *Philosophical Investigations*. London, U.K.: Academic Press, 1958.

PART 2

Building Blocks of the Canadian Legal System

CHAPTER 4

The Constitution of Canada: The British North America Act, 1867, the Constitution Act, 1982, and the Future of Federalism

We shall like to remember, when Confederation has stood the test of time, how beautiful was the day when it began.

(Editorial, *Le Journal des Trois-Rivières*, 1867)

On an August morning six years ago the appellant and a companion, both Mi'kmaq Indians, slipped their small outboard motorboat into the coastal waters of Pomquet Harbour, Antigonish County, Nova Scotia, to fish for eels. They landed 463 pounds, which they sold for $787.10, and for which the appellant was arrested and prosecuted.

On an earlier August morning, some 235 years previously, the Reverend John Seycombe of Chester, Nova Scotia, a missionary and some-time dining companion of the Governor, noted with satisfaction in his diary, "Two Indian squaws brought seal skins and eels to sell." That transaction was apparently completed without arrest or other incident. The thread of continuity between these events, it seems, is that the Mi'kmaq people have sustained themselves in part by harvesting and trading fish (including eels) since Europeans first visited the coasts of what is now Nova Scotia in the 16th century. The appellant says that they are entitled to continue to do so now by virtue of a treaty right agreed to by the British Crown in 1760. As noted by my colleague, Justice McLachlin, the appellant is guilty as charged unless his activities were protected by an existing aboriginal or treaty right. No reliance was placed on any aboriginal right; the appellant chooses to rest his case entirely on the Mi'kmaq treaties of 1760–61.

The trial judge ([1996] N.S.J. No. 246 (QL) (Prov. Ct.)) accepted as applicable the terms of a Treaty of Peace and Friendship signed on March 10, 1760, at Halifax. The parties disagree about the existence of alleged oral terms, as well as the implications of the "trade clause" written into that document. From this distance, across more than two centuries, events are necessarily seen as "through a glass, darkly." The parties were negotiating in March 1760 in the shadow of the great military and political turmoil following the fall of the French fortresses at Louisbourg, Cape Breton (June 1758), and Quebec (September 1759). The Mi'kmaq signatories had been allies of the French King, and Montreal would continue to be part of New France until it subsequently fell in June 1760. The British had almost completed the process of expelling the Acadians from southern Nova Scotia. Both the Treaty of Paris, ending hostilities, and the Royal Proclamation of 1763 were still three years in the future. Only six years prior to the signing of the treaties, the British Governor of Nova Scotia had issued a Proclamation (May 14, 1756) offering rewards for the killing and capturing of Mi'kmaq throughout Nova Scotia, which then included New Brunswick. The treaties were entered into in a period where the British were attempting to expand and secure their control over their northern possessions. The subtext of the Mi'kmaq treaties was reconciliation and mutual advantage.

I would allow this appeal because nothing less would uphold the honour and integrity of the Crown in its dealings with the Mi'kmaq people to secure their peace and friendship, as best the content of those treaty promises can now be ascertained. In reaching this conclusion, I recognize that if the present dispute had arisen out of a modern commercial transaction between two parties of relatively equal bargaining power, or if, as held by the courts below, the short document prepared at Halifax under the direction of Governor Charles Lawrence on March 10, 1760, was to be taken as being the "entire agreement" between the parties, it would have to be concluded that the Mi'kmaq had inadequately protected their interests. However, the courts have not applied strict rules of interpretation to treaty relationships. In R. v. Denny (1990), 55 C.C.C. (3d) 322, and earlier decisions cited therein, the Nova Scotia Court of Appeal has affirmed the Mi'kmaq aboriginal right to fish for food. The appellant says the treaty allows him to fish for trade. In my view, the 1760 treaty does affirm the right of the Mi'kmaq people to continue to provide for their own sustenance by taking the products of their hunting, fishing and other gathering activities, and trading for what in 1760 was termed "necessaries." This right was always subject to regulation. The Crown does not suggest that the regulations in question accommodate the treaty right. The Crown's case is that no such treaty right exists. Further, no argument was made that the treaty right was extinguished prior to 1982, and no justification was offered by the Crown for the several prohibitions at issue in this case. Accordingly, in my view, the appellant is entitled to an acquittal.

(Justice Binnie, Supreme Court of Canada, *R. v. Marshall,* 1999, 3. S.C.R. 456)

The section of the *Constitution Act* that governs the decision in Marshall is set out below:

> **35.** (1) The existing aboriginal and treaty rights of the aboriginal peoples of Canada are hereby recognized and affirmed.
>
> (2) In this Act, "aboriginal peoples of Canada" includes the Indian, Inuit and Métis peoples of Canada.
>
> (3) For greater certainty, in subsection (1) "treaty rights" includes rights that now exist by way of land claims agreements or may be so acquired.
>
> (4) Notwithstanding any other provision of this Act, the aboriginal and treaty rights referred to in subsection (1) are guaranteed equally to male and female persons.

As Binnie notes, section 35(3) must be given an expansive interpretation, with treaty rights viewed as flowing from the 1760 treaty. In attempting to understand the breadth of this document, the courts must necessarily look beyond the agreement itself, to its social, economic, and political backdrop, to the agreement at the time that it was enacted (the historical record), to practices that have evolved over time, and to the guarantee provided in section 35 of the *Constitution Act*. Since the Marshall decision in 1999, the interpretation of section 35 and its embedded treaty rights has, however, been somewhat muddied. In a 2005 decision, *R. v. Marshall, R. v. Bernard* (S.C.C. 43), the court was faced with convictions of the M'ikmaq for cutting trees on Crown lands in Nova Scotia. The M'ikmaq argued that their cutting and sale of the trees was protected by existing treaty rights, but the Supreme Court rejected this argument, indicating that, while trading rights were protected by the treaty (as in the right, established in 1999, to trade in eels), the right to engage in commercial use of the timber resource was not anticipated and consequently not protected by the 1760 treaty, nor by the royal proclamation of 1763.

For as long as Canada has been a nation, Canadians have debated the utility and value of our legal structure. Which First Nations' rights should have been entrenched in the Constitution? Do the provinces have too much or too little power? Should the Senate be reformed or abolished? What should be the process for constitutional amendment? Should judges have the power to determine whether law has violated individual or collective rights?

These questions flow from constitutional law, specifically from the **British North America Act, 1867**,[1] the **Constitution Act, 1982**,[2] and the **Canadian Charter of Rights and Freedoms**[3] contained in the latter.

Constitutional law has been described as a "mirror reflecting the national soul,"[4] and as a means to "protect the values of a nation."[5] Within Canada's Constitution, we find the rules that define the powers of respective governments and, correspondingly, the rights of citizens.

Canada is, most significantly, a federal state—a number of governments within a common overarching organization. Each government has retained certain exclusive powers; each has also ceded to a central government other exclusive powers, most notably those related to income taxation, defence, and external affairs. Tension between the powers of Canada's central government and the powers of provincial governments is a significant source of our country's strength—and of its weakness.

Constitutional law is different from other forms of statute law in that it cannot be changed by the mere passage of new law through the House of Commons and the Senate. Constitutional law is "entrenched" legislation, which can be changed only by a specific amending formula.

The British North America Act, 1867

In order to understand the importance and contemporary relevance of entrenched legislation and its amending formula, it is necessary to turn to the *British North America Act, 1867*. This act, passed by the British Parliament for the colony of Canada, first united the provinces of Canada. **Sections 91 and 92** set out, respectively, the powers of the federal and provincial governments. Section 91 also gives the federal government a residual power to legislate in relation to matters that appear not to fall under any specific provincial or federal jurisdiction; it is to be invoked in order to affirm "the peace, order, and good government" of the country. As we will see later in this chapter, the specific powers of sections 91 and 92 remain in force today. The act also provided for a national **bicameral Parliament** comprising an elected House of Commons and an appointed Senate. The House of Commons was to be based on the principle of representation by population; the Senate, on the principle of representation by region.

The 1867 statute that defined the new country of Canada was legislation, passed by Britain, not by Canada. Although Britain rarely intervened in Canada's internal affairs, two events nearly 60 years later raised concerns about whether the country was still, in some respects, a colony. When Mackenzie King's Liberal minority government lost a vote of confidence in 1926, he asked Lord Byng, the governor general, to dissolve

Parliament and call a general election. Surprisingly, the governor general, the monarch's representative in Canada, chose to exercise his discretionary authority and refused the prime minister's request for dissolution. He asked the Conservative leader, Arthur Meighen, to form a government. When Meighen's minority government was defeated in the House of Commons less than a week later, Lord Byng acceded to Meighen's request for the dissolution of Parliament and the calling of a general election. In the resulting election, Mackenzie King's Liberals won a majority, successfully exploiting Canadian independence as a campaign issue.

The other critical development of 1926 was the British Privy Council's decision in the case of *Nadan v. R.*[6] The Privy Council struck down an 1888 Canadian statute that had sought to abolish appeals to the Privy Council in criminal cases. It did so on the ground that Canada's abolition of the Privy Council's overview exceeded the colony's legislative powers; specifically, it was in direct conflict with the *British North America Act, 1867.*

The net effect of these two events was that Canada and other dominions of the British Empire lobbied the British government for their autonomy and for a mechanism that would remove their continuing colonial status. A 1930 conference of the dominions resulted in the declaration that "no law hereafter made by the Parliament of the United Kingdom shall extend to any dominion otherwise than at the request and consent of that dominion." In 1931, this declaration was reproduced as a preamble to the British government's Statute of Westminster. This change effectively precluded British intervention into the affairs of Canada's central and provincial governments. But the 1867 statute that set out Canada's Constitution remained a British statute. There was no established mechanism for amending this constitutional document— that is, for taking a British statute and reformulating it as a Canadian one, in both letter and spirit.

The *Constitution Act, 1982*

In 1967, constitutional scholar W.R. Lederman argued that there was a need to patriate the Canadian Constitution, "to make into law a set of amending procedures that can be carried out in Canada entirely by Canadian governments, legislative bodies, or electorates, acting severally or in combinations of some kind."[7] With the passage of the *Constitution Act, 1982,* **patriation** was accomplished.

The *Constitution Act, 1982* embodies two significant additions to Canadian constitutional law. The first is a formula to be applied in order to make future amendments to Canada's constitutional structure. The second is legislation in the mould of the U.S. *Bill of Rights*—the *Canadian Charter of Rights and Freedoms*, which is designed to be used by the courts to protect the rights accorded by the *Charter* to Canadian citizens.

The Amending Formula of the *Constitution Act, 1982*

Until the passage of the *Constitution Act, 1982*, there was no amending formula for the *British North America Act, 1867*. As mentioned, the *British North America Act, 1867* was unlike other federal or provincial statutes—it was a constitutional document and, as such, subject to a form of amendment different from that for other kinds of law. The 1964 Fulton–Favreau formula recommended unanimous consent of the federal and provincial governments for most significant amendments. The Victoria Charter of 1970 proposed less than unanimity among provincial governments, but gave veto powers to Quebec and Ontario on the ground that each had at least 25 percent of the country's population. The Trudeau government's amending-formula proposal of the early 1980s was based substantially on the Victoria Charter. It was strongly opposed by most provinces, largely because of the Ontario and Quebec veto. What ultimately emerged in 1982 as the amending formula for the Canadian Constitution was an elaborate compromise.

The **amending formula** created by the *Constitution Act, 1982* sets out three types of amendments. Section 38 of the act, the "general amending procedure," states that an amendment requires support from the House of Commons and the Senate, as well as from two-thirds of the provinces, provided that these provinces constitute at least 50 percent of the population of Canada.

> 38. (1)   An amendment to the Constitution of Canada may be
> made by proclamation issued by the Governor General
> under the Great Seal of Canada where so authorized by
>> (a)   resolutions of the Senate and the House of
>> Commons; and
>> (b)   resolutions of the legislative assemblies of at
>> least two-thirds of the provinces that have, in the
>> aggregate, according to the then latest general
>> census, at least 50 percent of the population of
>> all the provinces.

The so-called seven-fifty formula dictates that at least seven provinces must approve constitutional reform; given current populations, one of those provinces must be Ontario or Quebec. Significantly, however, no province has a veto over constitutional change. But section 38(3) softens the effect of the general amending formula by giving individual provinces, to a maximum of three, the power to "opt out" of constitutional amendments. If one, two, or three provinces with a cumulative population of no more than 50 percent of the total find a constitutional change unacceptable, they may declare that it will not apply within their jurisdictions.

The second type of amendment to constitutional law requires the unanimity of the federal government and all provincial governments. (The Northwest Territories, Yukon, and Nunavut fall under federal government jurisdiction until they become designated as provincial governments.) It is found in section 41 of the *Constitution Act, 1982*:

> 41.   An amendment to the Constitution of Canada in relation to the following matters may be made by proclamation issued by the Governor General under the Great Seal of Canada only where authorized by resolutions of the Senate and House of Commons and of the legislative assembly of each province:
>
> (a)   the office of the Queen, the Governor General and the Lieutenant-Governor of a province;
>
> (b)   the right of a province to a number of members in the House of Commons not less than the number of Senators by which the province is entitled to be represented at the time this Part comes into force;
>
> (c)   subject to section 43, the use of the English or the French language;
>
> (d)   the composition of the Supreme Court of Canada;
>
> (e)   an amendment to this Part.

Any of the matters named can be the subject of a constitutional amendment only if there is agreement from the federal government and every provincial government; in other words, every province has a veto. These issues—the monarchy, provincial representation in the House of Commons, the use of English or French, and the structure of the Supreme Court—are thought to be of such national significance that the unanimous consent of all governments is required.

Note that section 41 of the *Constitution Act, 1982* makes changes to the monarchical traditions of Canadian government a rather difficult task. Any legislation to eliminate the office of the queen, the governor general, or the lieutenant governor must have the consent of all federal and provincial governments. In Australia, in 1997 the federal government initiated a discussion about severing all political ties to the monarchy. In 1999 the Australian public voted to retain the queen as the titular head of state.

The third kind of constitutional amendment affects only certain provinces, as set out in section 43. For example, a number of language provisions in the *British North America Act, 1867* relate only to Manitoba, New Brunswick, and Quebec. These provisions can be changed with the consent of the federal government and the province affected; unaffected provinces have no say in the matter.

> 43. An amendment to the Constitution of Canada in relation to any provision that applies to one or more, but not all provinces, including
>
> (a) any alteration to boundaries between provinces, and
>
> (b) any amendment to any provision that relates to the use of the English or French language within a province,
>
> may be made by proclamation issued by the Governor General under the Great Seal of Canada only where so authorized by resolutions of the Senate and House of Commons and of the legislative assembly of each province to which the amendment applies.

Consider, in relation to this section of the amending formula, the *Constitution Act, 1999* (Nunavut).[8] This legislation increased the number of senators from 104 to 105 and provided that Yukon Territory, the Northwest Territories, and Nunavut "are entitled to be represented in the Senate by one member each." The purpose of this constitutional amendment was to strengthen Nunavut's capacity to achieve political autonomy in the inaugural days of its newly established government. Because the representation of senators in other provinces is unaffected by this change, section 41 of the *Constitution Act, 1982* is not applicable.

The *Canadian Charter of Rights and Freedoms*

The *Canadian Charter of Rights and Freedoms* (the *Charter*), which is entrenched in the *Constitution Act, 1982,* was the second significant addition to Canadian constitutional law. Its passage signalled a controversial shift in power from the legislative to the judicial branches of government. It became the task of judges to determine whether the legislation of either the federal or the provincial governments offends the core values of the *Charter*, and by implication, the nation. Debates about whether judges interpret law or make law have become irrelevant; the *Charter* requires judges to set aside legislation that contravenes a protected right. However, it is not an easy matter to determine what is meant, in practice, by "cruel and unusual punishment," "freedom of religion," or various other terms now subject to judicial definition.

THE *CANADIAN BILL OF RIGHTS* OF 1960

The *Charter* was not the first Canadian law to deal with the rights of citizens. In 1960, the Conservative government of John Diefenbaker enacted the ***Canadian Bill of Rights***[9] to protect the civil rights of Canadians. The *Bill of Rights* was not an entrenched constitutional document but a federal statute; it therefore applied only to federal laws and regulations.

The Canadian Bill of Rights

The Parliament of Canada, affirming that the Canadian Nation is founded upon principles that acknowledge the supremacy of God, the dignity and worth of the human person, and the position of the family in a society of free men and free institutions;

Affirming also that men and institutions remain free only when freedom is founded upon respect for moral and spiritual values and the rule of law;

And being desirous of enshrining these principles and the human rights and fundamental freedoms derived from them, in a *Bill of Rights* which shall reflect the respect of Parliament for its constitutional authority and which shall ensure the protection of these rights and freedoms in Canada:

Therefore Her Majesty, by and with the advice and consent of the Senate and House of Commons of Canada, enacts as follows:

1. It is hereby recognized and declared that in Canada, there have existed and shall continue to exist without discrimination by reason of race, national origin, colour, religion, or sex, the following human rights and fundamental freedoms, namely,

   (a) the right of the individual to life, liberty, security of the person, and enjoyment of property, and the right not to be deprived thereof except by due process of law;

   (b) the right of the individual to equality before the law and the protection of the law;

   (c) freedom of religion;

   (d) freedom of speech;

   (e) freedom of assembly and association; and

   (f) freedom of the press.

2. *Every law of Canada shall, unless it is expressly declared by an Act of the Parliament of Canada that it shall operate notwithstanding the Canadian Bill of Rights, be so construed and applied as not to abrogate, abridge, or infringe or to authorize the abrogation, abridgement, or infringement of any of the rights or freedoms herein recognized and declared, and in particular, no law of Canada shall be construed or applied so as to*

    (a) authorize or effect the arbitrary detention, imprisonment, or exile of any person;

    (b) impose or authorize the imposition of cruel and unusual treatment or punishment;

    (c) deprive a person who has been arrested or detained

        (i) of the right to be informed promptly of the reason for his arrest or detention,

        (ii) of the right to retain and instruct counsel without delay, or

        (iii) of the remedy by way of habeas corpus for the determination of the validity of his detention and for his release if the detention is not lawful;

    (d) authorize a court, tribunal, commission, board, or other authority to compel a person to give evidence if he is denied counsel, protection against self-crimination, or other constitutional safeguards;

    (e) deprive a person of the right to a fair hearing in accordance with the principles of fundamental justice for the determination of his rights and obligations;

    (f) deprive a person charged with a criminal offence of the right to be presumed innocent until proved guilty according to law in a fair and public hearing by an independent and impartial tribunal, or of the right to reasonable bail without just cause; or

    (g) deprive a person of the right to the assistance of an interpreter in any proceedings in which he is involved or in which he is a party or a witness, before a court, commission, board, or other tribunal, if he does not understand or speak the language in which such proceedings are conducted.

From the outset, some lawyers, judges, and politicians were disturbed by the possibility that the new law might be used to undermine the concept of **parliamentary supremacy** that lies at the heart of our version of democracy. The doctrine that Parliament is the supreme lawmaker has a corollary—namely, that no body or person has the legal right to override or set aside the law of Parliament.[10] Canada's British-based system of law is in marked contrast to the U.S. system, which cedes the legal protection of certain core rights to the courts.

Supporters of parliamentary supremacy feared that the *Bill of Rights* would move Canada closer to the U.S. model, in which the judiciary acts as a check on the possibility of abuse of legislative power. How, they asked, could an appointed judge, unaccountable to the voting public, be involved in making law or in interpreting the acceptability of a federal statute?

The counter argument to the concept of parliamentary supremacy is based on two points. First, there is a core of values to which all Canadians subscribe, enunciated in the *Bill of Rights*, and later, in the *Charter*. This core must be protected at all times, irrespective of the whims of legislators. Second, in view of the ongoing process of interpreting ambiguous law, Canadian judges were already involved in lawmaking before the *Bill of Rights* was enacted. Hence, it is probably overstatement to suggest that only the legislatures have ever had the exclusive right to create law.

Key sections of the *Bill of Rights* were first tested in 1969 in the case of *R. v. Drybones*.[11] Joseph Drybones, a Canadian Native, had been found intoxicated off a reserve, contrary to section 94(b) of the *Indian Act*. His counsel argued that this section of the act contravened the *Bill of Rights*, discriminating against Drybones on the basis of race. Section 1(b) of the *Bill of Rights* prohibits discrimination on the basis of race and guarantees "the right of the individual to equality before the law." The *Indian Act* created an offence for which only Native Canadians could be charged and convicted.

The Crown argued that the *Bill of Rights* was a "canon of construction," a guide for legislators in the drafting of legislation and for the judiciary in the interpretation of federal statutes. It was, therefore, never intended to give courts the power to render inoperative those federal laws that ran afoul of the *Bill*'s enumerated rights and freedoms.

Nevertheless, the Supreme Court determined in a 6–3 judgment that section 94(b) of the *Indian Act* was no longer enforceable. The Court noted in its decision that section 2 of the *Bill of Rights* provides that federal legislation not conforming to the *Bill* must clearly state its nonconformity in the specific legislation: "It must be expressly declared by an Act of the Parliament of Canada that it shall operate notwithstanding the *Canadian Bill of Rights*." In the absence of this express declaration, the relevant section of the *Indian Act* was inoperative.

The Supreme Court's decision in *Drybones* was greeted enthusiastically by civil libertarians as a sign that Canada's judiciary was prepared to use the new law in an activist manner to protect the rights of Canadians. The doctrine of parliamentary supremacy was being re-shaped, they felt, bringing Canada closer to the U.S. model of providing judicial checks and balances upon the powers of the legislature.

But the jubilation was relatively short-lived. In 1974, the nine male justices of the Supreme Court brought down a decision in *Canada (A.G.) v. Lavell*.[12] The case involved another challenge to a section of the *Indian Act*, which provided that female band members who married non-status Indians would have their names (and those of the children of the marriage) struck from the Indian register. Male band members who married non-status Indians would not have their names so treated, and would therefore continue to enjoy the advantages accruing to status Indians. The argument advanced by Jeannette Lavell was that she was being discriminated against on the basis of gender, in much the same manner that Joseph Drybones had been discriminated against on the basis of race. As both race and gender are prohibited grounds for discrimination under section 1 of the *Bill of Rights*, section 12(1)(b) of the *Indian Act* should have been declared inoperative. The Supreme Court held in a 5–4 decision, however, that there was no violation of the principle of equality before the law. The majority of the Court argued that the *Indian Act* provides a framework for the internal administration of life upon reserves, and cannot be changed by the broad general language of the *Bill of Rights*.

Many academics, civil libertarians, and Canadian citizens saw the decision in *Lavell* as contradicting the *Drybones* decision. The fact that *Drybones* concerned a matter off the reserves and that *Lavell* concerned a matter internal to reserves was not seen to be the point, although some members of the Supreme Court found it a crucial distinction. The net effect of the Court's decision in *Lavell* was that the role of the *Bill of Rights* was now unclear. Was this legislation ultimately to be powerless against parliamentary supremacy?

ENTRENCHING THE RIGHTS OF CANADIANS: THE *CONSTITUTION ACT* AND THE *CHARTER*

The *Constitution Act, 1982* provided an answer to the above question. During the 1970s and early 1980s, debate continued among politicians, judges, academics, and other Canadians about the appropriate role of the judiciary with respect to the protection of individual rights. In the political arena, the premier of Manitoba, Sterling Lyon, led the advocates of parliamentary supremacy against Prime Minister Pierre Trudeau, who argued for an activist judiciary and a *Charter* that would be entrenched in the Constitution.

With the proclamation of the *Constitution Act, 1982*, Canada departed from strict adherence to the doctrine of parliamentary supremacy. Although weakened by opting-out provisions, the *Charter* nonetheless demanded—and continues to demand—that both federal and provincial laws be tested against the values it enshrines. If specific legislation is found to provide inadequate protection of *Charter* rights, then the legislation, or the relevant section or sub-section, is effectively terminated. The *Charter* is now clearly preeminent, as well as constitutional in its form.

The "Limitations" Clause of the Charter

Section 1 of the *Charter* is typically referred to as the "**limitations clause**" and is modelled on a number of European codes of civil rights. Unlike the *Bill of Rights*, the *Charter* makes explicit the reality that no right is absolute. The *Charter*, for example, guarantees the right of freedom of expression, but this does not extend to a right to yell "Fire!" in a crowded theatre without cause or to libel another citizen.

> ### Guarantee of Rights and Freedoms
>
> *1. The Canadian Charter of Rights and Freedoms guarantees the rights and freedoms set out in it subject only to such reasonable limits prescribed by law as can be demonstrably justified in a free and democratic society.*

Section 1 sets out a two-part test to determine whether federal or provincial law can override a constitutional guarantee of protection within the *Charter*. First, the federal or provincial statute's limits on rights must be reasonable and prescribed by law. Second, the limits must be established, to the satisfaction of the presiding judge, to be demonstrably justified in a free and democratic society. In 1986, the Supreme Court of Canada expressed these criteria in more specific terms. In *R. v. Oakes*, Chief Justice Dickson wrote:

> To establish that a limit is reasonable and demonstrably justified in a free and democratic society, two central criteria must be satisfied. *First, the objective . . . must be of sufficient importance* to warrant overriding a constitutionally protected right or freedom. . . . *Second . . .* the party invoking s. 1 must show that the means chosen are reasonable and demonstrably justified. This involves *a form of proportionality test. . . .* There are, in my view, three important components. . . . First, the measures adopted must be carefully designed to achieve the objective in question. They must not be arbitrary, unfair, or based on irrational considerations. . . . Second, the means . . . should impair as little as possible the right or freedom in question. . . . Third, there must be a proportionality between the effects of the measures and the objective which has been identified as of sufficient importance.[13] [Author's emphasis.]

In the ***Oakes* case**, the accused was charged with possession of a narcotic for the purpose of trafficking. He argued that section 8 of the *Narcotic Control Act* was unconstitutional. Section 8 required a two-stage trial on charges of possession for the purpose of trafficking. First, the prosecutor had to establish possession. Once convicted of possession, the accused had then to convince the judge or jury that he or she was not likely to be in possession of the narcotic for the purpose of trafficking. The argument against section 8 was that it undermined the presumption of innocence in criminal cases and, as a result, the right to a fair trial (guaranteed in section 11[d] of the *Charter*). The Supreme Court agreed with this argument, suggesting that although the objective of prohibiting narcotics was "sufficiently important," section 8 ultimately failed the test of proportionality. As Chief Justice Dickson noted, there is no "rational connection" between the fact of possession of an illegal drug, and the "presumed fact" of possession for the purpose of trafficking.

The Supreme Court's decision in *R. v. Oakes* does not suggest, however, that Canadian courts will generally entertain wide-ranging debate about the boundaries of section 1 of the *Charter*. In fact, the judiciary has spent relatively little time questioning the collision of federal and provincial legislation and the core values set out in the *Charter*. Whether existing legislation threatens individual rights to freedom of expression, the sanction against cruel and unusual punishment, or collective rights to freedom of association, are issues too broad to be usefully placed on the agenda of the courts. Unlike legislatures, courts are not well equipped to debate and resolve broad philosophical issues; they *are* better equipped than legislatures, however, to resolve such issues as they arise within specific contexts. This is not true, however, of all jurisdictions. The German Supreme Constitutional Court has an exceptionally far-reaching competency in reviewing legislation; in contrast, the approach of Canada's judiciary could be seen as rather deferential.

Debates within the courts are usually quite circumscribed. In the *Oakes* case, there was a judicial insistence upon the right to be presumed innocent; the protection of this right was not seen to hamper the "sufficient importance" of apprehending and convicting narcotics users and distributors. In the event, neither police nor prosecutors have suggested that the removal of the reverse onus provisions in section 8 of the *Narcotic Control Act* has hampered their ability to act against illegal drug distributors.

The limitations clause ultimately presents two significant but not insurmountable obstacles to those who would use the *Charter* to advance social change. First, there are few circumstances for which no relevant precedents exist; the absence of precedents would permit existing government policies to be effectively challenged. Second, and perhaps more important, the cost of taking a claim of this kind to a provincial court of appeal or the Supreme Court of Canada is prohibitive for most individuals.

There is, nonetheless, a relatively recent example of a successful section 1 challenge in *Halpern v. R.* 225 D.L.R. (4th) 529 (2003). The applicants in this case challenged the constitutionality of legislation prohibiting same-sex marriage. The judgment of the Ontario Court of Appeal, excerpted below, was not appealed by the Government of Canada, and legislation has recently been passed (in June 2005) that legalizes same-sex marriages (civil unions):

> The Attorney-General of Canada submits that marriage, as a core foundational unit, benefits society at large in that it has proven itself to be one of the most durable institutions for the organization of society. Marriage has always been understood as a special kind of monogamous opposite-sex union, with spiritual, social, economic and contractual dimensions, for the purposes of uniting the opposite sexes, encouraging the birth and raising of children of the marriage, and companionship.
>
> No one is disputing that marriage is a fundamental societal institution. Similarly, it is accepted that, with limited exceptions, marriage has been understood to be a monogamous opposite-sex union. What needs to be determined, however, is whether there is a valid objective to maintaining marriage as an exclusively heterosexual institution. Stating that marriage is heterosexual because it always has been heterosexual is merely an explanation for the opposite-sex requirement of marriage; it is not an objective that is capable of justifying the infringement of a Charter guarantee.
>
> We now turn to the more specific purposes of marriage advanced by the AGC: (i) uniting the opposite sexes; (ii) encouraging the birth and raising of children of the marriage; and (iii) companionship.
>
> The first purpose, which results in favouring one form of relationship over another, suggests that uniting two persons of the same sex is of lesser importance. The words of Dickson C.J.C. in Oakes at 136 are instructive in this regard:
>
> The Court must be guided by the values and principles essential to a free and democratic society which I believe embody, to name but a few, respect for the inherent dignity of the human person, commitment to social justice and equality, accommodation of a wide variety of beliefs, respect for cultural and group identity, and faith in social and political institutions which enhance the participation of

individuals and groups in society. The underlying values and principles of a free and democratic society are the genesis of the rights and freedoms guaranteed by the Charter and the ultimate standard against which a limit on a right or freedom must be shown, despite its effect, to be reasonable and demonstrably justified.

Accordingly, a purpose that demeans the dignity of same-sex couples is contrary to the values of a free and democratic society and cannot be considered to be pressing and substantial. A law cannot be justified on the very basis upon which it is being attacked: Big M Drug Mart at 352.

The second purpose of marriage, as advanced by the AGC, is encouraging the birth and raising of children. Clearly, encouraging procreation and childrearing is a laudable goal that is properly regarded as pressing and substantial. However, the Attorney-General of Canada must demonstrate that the objective of maintaining marriage as an exclusively heterosexual institution is pressing and substantial: see Vriend at 554–57.

We fail to see how the encouragement of procreation and childrearing is a pressing and substantial objective of maintaining marriage as an exclusively heterosexual institution. Heterosexual married couples will not stop having or raising children because same-sex couples are permitted to marry. Moreover, an increasing percentage of children are being born to and raised by same-sex couples.

The Attorney-General of Canada submits that the union of two persons of the opposite sex is the only union that can "naturally" procreate. In terms of that biological reality, same-sex couples are different from opposite-sex couples. In our view, however, "natural" procreation is not a sufficiently pressing and substantial objective to justify infringing the equality rights of same-sex couples. As previously stated, same-sex couples can have children by other means, such as adoption, surrogacy and donor insemination. A law that aims to encourage only "natural" procreation ignores the fact that same-sex couples are capable of having children.

Similarly, a law that restricts marriage to opposite-sex couples, on the basis that a fundamental purpose of marriage is the raising of children, suggests that same-sex couples are not equally capable of childrearing. The AGC has put forward no evidence to support such a proposition. Neither is the AGC advocating such a view; rather, it takes the position that social science research is not capable of establishing the proposition one way or another. In the absence of cogent evidence, it is our view that the objective is based on a stereotypical assumption that is not acceptable in a free and democratic society that prides itself on promoting equality and respect for all persons.

The third purpose of marriage advanced by the AGC is companionship. We consider companionship to be a laudable goal of marriage. However, encouraging companionship cannot be considered a pressing and substantial objective of the omission of the impugned law. Encouraging companionship between only persons of the opposite sex perpetuates the view that persons in same-sex relationships are not equally capable of providing companionship and forming lasting and loving relationships.

Accordingly, it is our view that the AGC has not demonstrated any pressing and substantial objective for excluding same-sex couples from the institution of marriage. For that reason, we conclude that the violation of the Couples' rights under s. 15(1) of the Charter cannot be saved under s. 1 of the Charter.

Fundamental Freedoms

Section 2 of the *Charter* sets out the fundamental freedoms that Canadians are said to possess.

Fundamental Freedoms

2. *Everyone has the following fundamental freedoms:*
   - (a) *freedom of conscience and religion;*
   - (b) *freedom of thought, belief, opinion and expression, including freedom of the press and other media of communication;*
   - (c) *freedom of peaceful assembly; and*
   - (d) *freedom of association.*

The list shows similarities to the *Bill of Rights*, as well as some noteworthy differences. The *Bill*'s conception of freedom of religion has been expanded to encompass both "freedom of conscience" and "freedom of religion." "Freedom of expression" has also been extended to cover more possibilities: "thought, belief, opinion and expression." And "freedom of assembly" has been more carefully restated as "freedom of peaceful assembly."

Even before the *Bill of Rights* and the *Charter* existed, Canadian courts tried cases in which certain statutes were alleged to violate fundamental freedoms. In the absence of legislation specifically related to rights and freedoms, the Supreme Court of Canada based its decisions on either the exclusivity of federal powers or the "peace, order, and good government" clause in section 91 of the *British North America Act*.

For example, in 1938, the Supreme Court was faced with the Alberta Press Bill. The government of Alberta had introduced legislation that compelled newspapers in the province to print the government's reply to any press criticism of it or its policies. The Supreme Court effectively killed the legislation, holding that the Press Bill was beyond the jurisdiction of the province: free political discussion is so vital to the life of a country that its control must be an exclusively federal power.[14] The Court did not accept the province's technical argument that the legislation could be justified as flowing from exclusive provincial jurisdictions: section 92(13), "property and civil rights," or section 92(16), "matters of a merely local or private nature," as specified in the *British North America Act*.

In 1953, in *Saumur v. City of Quebec*, the Supreme Court had to respond to a Quebec City bylaw that made the permission of the chief of police necessary before pamphlets could be distributed on city streets.[15] The purpose of the bylaw was to prevent the dissemination of certain kinds of materials—specifically, religious tracts published by the Jehovah's Witnesses. The Court again struck down the offending legislation, holding that it interfered with the federal power to legislate in relation to free speech.

Since the enactment of the *Charter*, Canadian courts have heard a range of cases concerning free expression and freedom of assembly and association. In *R. v. Butler*,[16] the accused challenged the constitutionality of obscenity provisions within the *Criminal Code*, specifically section 163(8):

> 163.(8)   For the purposes of this Act, any publication a dominant characteristic of which is the undue exploitation of sex, or of sex and any one or more of the following subjects, namely, crime, horror, cruelty, and violence, shall be deemed to be obscene.

Butler was the operator of a sex shop selling materials that emphasized explicit sex and depicted violence. The Supreme Court held that while the obscenity provisions in the *Criminal Code* do offend section 2(b) of the *Charter* and its guarantee of freedom of expression, these controls can be justified by section 1, the limitations clause. Justice Sopinka, writing for the majority of the Court, noted that while explicit sex in itself might well be justified, material that portrays explicit sex with violence or explicit sex that places women and occasionally men "in positions of subordination, servile submission, or humiliation" cannot be justified. Justice Sopinka further noted that these kinds of pornography are "perceived by public opinion to be harmful to society, particularly to women."

Debate about the legitimacy of pornography will continue, and it seems likely that the Supreme Court will be asked to rule again on the appropriate ambit of the criminal law. In the 1990s, free expression for pornographers is seen to collide with other rights; specifically, the right of women to equal treatment, as guaranteed by section 15 of the *Charter*. Constitutional scholar Peter Hogg has commented on this shift: "[T]he advancement of the value of equality does constitute a far more important objective than the protection of conventional morality, and greatly strengthens the argument that can be made for s. 1 justification."[17] It should be noted, in relation to this issue of equality rights, that LEAF, the Women's Legal Education and Action Fund, was a key intervener in the *Butler* decision, discussed above. The argument advanced by LEAF in *Butler* was not one premised on the immorality of the pornography industry, but rather one premised on the damage that certain kinds of pornography impose on the equality rights of women.

In another case centring on freedom of expression, *RJR-MacDonald v. Canada (A.G.)*, the Quebec Superior Court was asked to rule on the constitutionality of the federal prohibition against the advertising of tobacco and tobacco products.[18] The court held that since the federal government was unable to prove a cause-and-effect relationship between a ban on advertising and a reduction in smoking, the legislation's limitation on freedom of expression could not be justified. Tobacco is a legal product, and a prohibition of the right to promote it contravenes section 2(b) of the *Charter*.

The federal government appealed this ruling, and the Quebec Court of Appeal reversed the judgment of the Superior Court.[19] A further appeal resulted ultimately in the Supreme Court of Canada deciding that the federal prohibition of tobacco advertising does contravene s. 2(b) of the *Charter* and that the limitation on freedom of expression imposed by that legislation cannot be justified under section 1.[20]

Voting and Mobility Rights

The following sections of the *Charter* spell out the basic rights of Canadian citizens with respect to voting, electoral representation, and social mobility. Sections 3 to 5 essentially maintain previous constitutional practice, but section 6 asserts a new right: occupational mobility across Canadian provinces, subject to "reasonable residency requirements" and the operation of "discriminatory" laws aimed at the amelioration of social and economic disadvantage within specific provinces.

Democratic Rights

3. *Every citizen of Canada has the right to vote in an election of members of the House of Commons or of a legislative assembly and to be qualified for membership therein.*

4. *(1) No House of Commons and no legislative assembly shall continue for longer than five years from the date fixed for the return of the writs at a general election of its members.*

   (2) In time of real or apprehended war, invasion or insurrection, a House of Commons may be continued by Parliament and a legislative assembly may be continued by the legislature beyond five years if such continuation is not opposed by the votes of more than one-third of the members of the House of Commons or the legislative assembly, as the case may be.

5. *There shall be a sitting of Parliament and of each legislature at least once every twelve months.*

Mobility Rights

6. *(1) Every citizen of Canada has the right to enter, remain in and leave Canada.*

   (2) Every citizen of Canada and every person who has the status of a permanent resident of Canada has the right

      (a) to move to and take up residence in any province; and

      (b) to pursue the gaining of a livelihood in any province.

   (3) The rights specified in subsection (2) are subject to

      (a) any laws or practices of general application in force in a province other than those that discriminate among persons primarily on the basis of province of present or previous residence; and

      (b) any laws providing for reasonable residency requirements as a qualification for the receipt of publicly provided social services.

   (4) Subsections (2) and (3) do not preclude any law, program or activity that has as its object the amelioration in a province of conditions of individuals in that province who are socially or economically disadvantaged if the rate of employment in that province is below the rate of employment in Canada.

Legal Rights

The following *Charter* sections focus on the legal rights of accused persons within the criminal justice system.

Legal Rights

7. Everyone has the right to life, liberty and security of the person and the right not to be deprived thereof except in accordance with the principles of fundamental justice.

8. Everyone has the right to be secure against unreasonable search or seizure.

9. Everyone has the right not to be arbitrarily detained or imprisoned.

10. Everyone has the right on arrest or detention
    (a) to be informed promptly of the reasons therefor;
    (b) to retain and instruct counsel without delay and to be informed of that right; and
    (c) to have the validity of the detention determined by way of habeas corpus and to be released if the detention is not lawful.

11. Any person charged with an offence has the right
    (a) to be informed without unreasonable delay of the specific offence;
    (b) to be tried within a reasonable time;
    (c) not to be compelled to be a witness in proceedings against that person in respect of the offence;
    (d) to be presumed innocent until proven guilty according to law in a fair and public hearing by an independent and impartial tribunal;
    (e) not to be denied reasonable bail without just cause;
    (f) except in the case of an offence under military law tried before a military tribunal, to the benefit of trial by jury where the maximum punishment for the offence is imprisonment for five years or a more severe punishment;
    (g) not to be found guilty on account of any act or omission unless, at the time of the act or omission, it constituted an offence under Canadian or international law or was criminal according to the general principles of law recognized by the community of nations;
    (h) if finally acquitted of the offence, not to be tried for it again and, if finally found guilty and punished for the offence, not to be tried or punished for it again; and
    (i) if found guilty of the offence and if the punishment for the offence has been varied between the time of commission and the time of sentencing, to the benefit of the lesser punishment.

12. Everyone has the right not to be subjected to any cruel and unusual treatment or punishment.

13. A witness who testifies in any proceedings has the right not to have any incriminating evidence so given used to incriminate that witness in any other proceedings, except in a prosecution for perjury or for the giving of contradictory evidence.

14. A party or witness in any proceedings who does not understand or speak the language in which the proceedings are conducted or who is deaf has the right to the assistance of an interpreter.

R. v. Morgentaler, perhaps the most significant legal case since the passage of the *Charter*, was based on section 7 and its protection of "life, liberty and security of the person."[21] Dr. Henry Morgentaler's challenge to state control over abortion was ultimately upheld by the Supreme Court of Canada when a majority of the justices found that the *Criminal Code*'s restrictions on abortion were contrary to the *Charter*. Specifically, the Court held that the requirement that abortions be approved by a therapeutic abortion committee created delays in treatment, delays that jeopardized the life, liberty, and security of the women subject to them.

The Supreme Court's interpretation of "life, liberty and security of the person" went beyond the narrow view that would simply have required protection of the physical health of the mother. The majority of the Court held that a woman's inability to control the termination of her pregnancy constituted an unjustifiable loss of "life, liberty and security of the person."

Section 7 of the *Charter* has also been used to protect the right of an accused not to make any statement when charged with a criminal offence. In *R. v. Hebert*, the accused exercised his right to retain counsel and told police that he did not wish to make any statement after being arrested.[22] He was then placed in custody with an undercover police officer to whom he unwittingly made an incriminating statement. The issue for the Supreme Court of Canada was whether this statement was admissible in court. Seven members of the Court unanimously held that the statement was not admissible; the police officer had been employed to elicit an incriminating response from the accused—that is, to subvert the accused's constitutional right to remain silent in the face of police questioning.

During the past decade, Canadian courts have been grappling with the *Charter*'s insistence under section 11(b) that "any person charged with an offence has the right to be tried within a reasonable time." The meaning of "within a reasonable time" has been the subject of nearly a dozen cases decided by the Supreme Court. Since 1989, the Court has held that the reasonableness of a delay can be inferred from the following factors: the length of the delay before trial, the reasons for the delay, any waivers made by the accused with respect to the delay, and any prejudice visited upon the accused by the delay. Unfortunately, this naming of factors has not brought about much consistency in the determination of what is "reasonable." In one 1989 decision, a delay of five years was considered reasonable; another Supreme Court decision in the same year found a delay of 16 months unreasonable.[23]

The most significant case with regard to reasonableness has probably been *R. v. Askov* in 1990.[24] The accused in *Askov* were charged with serious offences involving weapons and alleged threats of bodily harm. Thirty-four months elapsed between the original charges and the trial. The Supreme Court held that the jurisdiction in which the accused were charged (Ontario's Peel District) was one in which unreasonable delays were commonplace and that the accused could not be held responsible for these delays. The charges against Askov and his associates were therefore dismissed. Justice Cory, writing for a unanimous Supreme Court, argued that "a period of delay in a range of some six to eight months between committal and trial might be deemed to be the outside limit of what is reasonable."

The consequences of the *Askov* decision have been remarkable. Tens of thousands of charges, particularly in Ontario, have been withdrawn or stayed on the ground of delay. Although subsequent decisions by the Supreme Court have moderated Justice Cory's definition of six to eight months as an "outside limit," the Court has made clear that it will not tolerate "systemic" delays resulting from a lack of government resources. In *R. v. Morin*, the Court noted, "The government has a constitutional obligation to commit sufficient resources to prevent unreasonable delay, which distinguishes this obligation from many others that compete for funds with the administration of justice."[25]

Another provision of the *Charter* designed to protect the rights of the accused is section 12. The constitutional prohibition against cruel and unusual punishment was used in 1987 to strike down a section of the *Narcotic Control Act* that required a minimum term of seven years' imprisonment upon conviction for importing any amount of a narcotic, principally heroin, cocaine, or marijuana. In *R. v. Smith*, the Court held that, in some circumstances, the penalty of seven years' imprisonment could be seen to be "grossly disproportionate" to the offence committed.[26] Consider the example of a young person entering Canada with a couple of marijuana cigarettes. Would a seven-year sentence for such importation constitute cruel and unusual punishment? The Supreme Court answered this question in the affirmative.

In the case of *R. v. Luxton*,[27] however, the Court's response was much less sympathetic, as it was in *R. v. Latimer*, discussed in Chapter 1. The *Luxton* case challenged the *Criminal Code*'s minimum term of imprisonment for 25 years upon conviction for first degree murder. In 1976, when capital punishment was abolished in Canada, Parliament raised the minimum terms of imprisonment upon conviction for both first degree and second degree murder. These increases in the time to be served were a tradeoff given by the government to those who favoured the death penalty in order to accomplish its goal of abolition.

There is no decisive evidence to support the contention that increased terms have a greater corrective efficacy than shorter terms. Nevertheless, Chief Justice Lamer, writing in *Luxton* for a unanimous Supreme Court of Canada, simply asserted that such "punishment is not excessive and clearly does not outrage our standards of decency." Constitutional scholar Peter Hogg, however, has found this logic less than compelling:

> [I]n my opinion, the mandatory sentence of 25 years without parole is so severe that it cannot meet the standard. Two of the three categories of first-degree murder do not include any element of premeditation, and therefore would encompass a wide range of moral turpitude. For example, it is not "far-fetched" to postulate a hypothetical offender—one who killed in panic, perhaps, or one who was merely an accomplice of the killer, perhaps—for whom the 25 years without parole would be grossly disproportionate. And yet the Court in *Luxton* did not test the sentence by reference to any hypothetical cases, or otherwise explain why the punishment was not grossly disproportionate.[28]

Equality Rights

The "equality" section of the *Charter* has expanded the protections set out in the *Bill of Rights* of 1960.

Equality Rights

15. *(1) Every individual is equal before and under the law and has the right to the equal protection and equal benefit of the law without discrimination and, in particular, without discrimination based on race, national or ethnic origin, colour, religion, sex, age or mental or physical disability.*

    (2) Subsection (1) does not preclude any law, program or activity that has as its object amelioration of conditions of disadvantaged individuals or groups including those that are disadvantaged because of race, national or ethnic origin, colour, religion, sex, age or mental or physical disability.

Section 15(1) of the *Charter* prohibits discrimination based on two new categories: mental and physical disability. As noted above, the Supreme Court of Canada's "equality" decisions during the 1970s appeared inconsistent: Joseph Drybones was determined to have suffered unequal treatment on the basis of race but, in strikingly similar circumstances, Jeannette Lavell was said not to have suffered unequal treatment on the basis of gender.

Much of the difficulty in responding to allegations of unequal treatment, whether under the *Bill of Rights* or the *Charter*, is that inequality in itself is not considered to be an evil. There are many circumstances in which unequal treatment is not only justifiable but preferable and to be expected. Canadians who have not attained the age of majority are treated differently from those who have, most notably in relation to the right to vote, to drive an automobile, and to enter into contractual agreements; Canadians over 65 are treated differently from those under 65. The government responds to those convicted of criminal offences differently from those who have not been so convicted, and so on.

It is on the justification for unequal treatment that we must focus when looking at the protection offered by section 15. In addition to setting out prohibited grounds for discrimination—race, sex, age, and so forth—the section provides for an open-ended bar to unequal treatment, indicating that other forms of discrimination than those specifically set out may ultimately be determined to be constitutionally prohibited.

In *Andrews v. Law Society of British Columbia* (hereinafter *Andrews*) the Supreme Court was faced with Andrews's claim that the requirement of Canadian citizenship for the practice of law in British Columbia constitutes a denial of equality before the law. The Supreme Court held that the B.C. statute requiring lawyers to be Canadian citizens did create a lack of equality before the law, and the majority of the court held that this inequality could not be justified by section 1 of the *Charter*. Justice La Forest compared citizenship to such personal characteristics as race, age, and mental or physical disability: "The characteristic of citizenship is one typically not within the control of the individual and, in this sense, is immutable. Citizenship is, at least temporarily, a characteristic of personhood not alterable by conscious action and in some cases, not alterable except on the basis of unacceptable costs."[29]

Language Rights

Sections 16 to 23 of the *Charter* are essentially self-explanatory. They are concerned with the protection of minority-language rights.

Official Languages of Canada

16. *(1) English and French are the official languages of Canada and have equality of status and equal rights and privileges as to their use in all institutions of the Parliament and government of Canada.*

    (2) English and French are the official languages of New Brunswick and have equality of status and equal rights and privileges as to their use in all institutions of the legislature and government of New Brunswick.

    (3) Nothing in this Charter limits the authority of Parliament or a legislature to advance the equality of status or use of English and French.

17. *(1) Everyone has the right to use English or French in any debates and other proceedings of Parliament.*

    (2) Everyone has the right to use English or French in any debates and other proceedings of the legislature of New Brunswick.

18. *(1) The statutes, records and journals of Parliament shall be printed and published in English and French and both language versions are equally authoritative.*

    (2) The statutes, records and journals of the legislature of New Brunswick shall be printed and published in English and French and both language versions are equally authoritative.

19. *(1) Either English or French may be used by any person in, or in any pleading in or process issuing from, any court established by Parliament.*

    (2) Either English or French may be used by any person in, or in any pleading in or process issuing from, any court of New Brunswick.

20. *(1) Any member of the public in Canada has the right to communicate with, and to receive available services from, any head or central office of an institution of the Parliament or government of Canada in English or French, and has the same right with respect to any other office of any such institution where*

    (a) there is a significant demand for communications with and services from that office in such language; or

    (b) due to the nature of the office, it is reasonable that communications with and services from that office be available in both English and French.

    (2) Any member of the public in New Brunswick has the right to communicate with, and to receive available services from, any office of an institution of the legislature or government of New Brunswick in English or French.

21. *Nothing in sections 16 to 20 abrogates or derogates from any right, privilege, or obligation with respect to the English and French languages, or either of them, that exists or is continued by virtue of any other provision of the Constitution of Canada.*

22. *Nothing in sections 16 to 20 abrogates or derogates from any legal or customary right or privilege acquired or enjoyed either before or after the coming into force of this Charter with respect to any language that is not English or French.*

Minority Language Educational Rights

23. *(1) Citizens of Canada*

   (a) *whose first language learned and still understood is that of the English or French linguistic minority population of the province in which they reside, or*

   (b) *who have received their primary school instruction in Canada in English or French and reside in a province where the language in which they received that instruction is the language of the English or French linguistic minority population of the province, have the right to have their children receive primary and secondary school instruction in that language in that province.*

(2) Citizens of Canada of whom any child has received or is receiving primary or secondary school instruction in English or French in Canada, have the right to have all their children receive primary and secondary school instruction in the same language.

(3) The right of citizens of Canada under subsections (1) and (2) to have their children receive primary and secondary school instruction in the language of the English or French linguistic minority population of a province

   (a) *applies wherever in the province the number of children of citizens who have such a right is sufficient to warrant the provision to them out of public funds of minority language instruction; and*

   (b) *includes, where the number of those children so warrants, the right to have them receive that instruction in minority language educational facilities provided out of public funds.*

Remedies Under the Charter

Section 24 of the *Charter* is the enforcement mechanism that gives courts the power to exclude evidence if "the admission of it in the proceedings would bring the administration of justice into disrepute."

Enforcement

24. (1) *Anyone whose rights or freedoms, as guaranteed by this Charter, have been infringed or denied may apply to a court of competent jurisdiction to obtain such remedy as the court considers appropriate and just in the circumstances.*

(2) *Where, in proceedings under subsection (1), a court concludes that evidence was obtained in a manner that infringed or denied any rights or freedoms guaranteed by this Charter, the evidence shall be excluded if it is established that, having regard to all the circumstances, the admission of it in the proceedings would bring the administration of justice into disrepute.*

Police organizations have attacked section 24(2), claiming that it permits the guilty to go free. Civil libertarians have argued, in response, that an exclusionary rule is needed to deter police from misconduct.

Prior to the passage of the *Charter*, Canadian courts followed the British approach to illegally obtained evidence: the evidence was admissible if relevant to the issues in dispute. Police misconduct did not limit the courts' use of this information; the misconduct was properly the subject of a separate hearing. U.S. courts, on the other hand, have adopted an exclusionary approach to illegally obtained evidence: if police in the United States use means contrary to the U.S. *Bill of Rights* to obtain evidence, then the evidence—the so-called fruit of the poison tree—is inadmissible.

Section 24(2) of the *Charter* represents a compromise between the British and U.S. positions. It instructs Canadian courts to engage in a balancing test, excluding illegally obtained evidence only when its admission would "bring the administration of justice into disrepute." Evidence would be potentially inadmissible if gained by means of some searches for illegal drugs, weapons, and/or stolen property, as well as through questionable confessions.

The case law to date reveals that a balancing test is, in fact, emerging. Generally speaking, good-faith errors by the police will not lead to exclusion, but intentional violations of the *Charter* will. For example, in *R. v. Greffe*, police had no justifiable grounds for arresting the accused for a narcotics offence; they therefore arrested him for outstanding traffic tickets, conducted a rectal examination, and discovered heroin. The Supreme Court of Canada excluded the evidence of the heroin, arguing that the administration of justice would be brought into disrepute if Canadian courts were to permit the practice of rectal examination after arrest for outstanding traffic tickets, when no reasonable or probable grounds existed for believing that an accused had committed a criminal offence.[30]

On the other hand, in *R. v. Simmons*, the accused was searched at the airport before being informed of her right to retain a lawyer; illegal drugs were discovered taped to her body. The police officers who conducted the search were not aware that it was necessary to inform the accused of her right to retain counsel at this initial stage of their investigation; they believed that such "investigative detention" did not require accused persons to be advised of their right to counsel. The evidence of the illegal drugs was admitted.[31]

In *Collins v. R.*, Justice Lamer set out three issues to be considered in determining whether the administration of justice has been brought into disrepute: (1) the nature and significance of the evidence obtained; (2) the quality of the police conduct that permitted the evidence to be obtained; and (3) the consequences for the justice system as a whole if the evidence is excluded.[32] As we move through the early twenty-first century, it is becoming clear that Canada is charting its own course with respect to the exclusion of evidence, adopting neither extreme of the British and U.S. approaches.

Aboriginal Rights, Gender Equality, and the Opting-Out Provisions

The key sections within sections 25 to 34 relate to the application of the *Charter*.

General

25. The guarantee in this Charter of certain rights and freedoms shall not be construed so as to abrogate or derogate from any aboriginal, treaty or other rights or freedoms that pertain to the aboriginal peoples of Canada including

> *(a) any rights or freedoms that have been recognized by the Royal Proclamation of October 7, 1763; and*
>
> *(b) any rights or freedoms that now exist by way of land claims agreements or may be so acquired.*

26. The guarantee in this Charter of certain rights and freedoms shall not be construed as denying the existence of any other rights or freedoms that exist in Canada.

27. This Charter shall be interpreted in a manner consistent with the preservation and enhancement of the multicultural heritage of Canadians.

28. Notwithstanding anything in this Charter, the rights and freedoms referred to in it are guaranteed equally to male and female persons.

29. Nothing in this Charter abrogates or derogates from any rights or privileges guaranteed by or under the Constitution of Canada in respect of denominational, separate or dissentient schools.

30. *A reference in this Charter to a province or to the legislative assembly or legislature of a province shall be deemed to include a reference to the Yukon Territory and the Northwest Territories, or to the appropriate legislative authority thereof, as the case may be.*

31. *Nothing in this Charter extends the legislative powers of any body or authority.*

Application of Charter

32. *(1) This Charter applies*

    (a) to the Parliament and government of Canada in respect of all matters within the authority of Parliament including all matters relating to the Yukon Territory and Northwest Territories; and

    (b) to the legislature and government of each province in respect of all matters within the authority of the legislature of each province.

(2) Notwithstanding subsection (1), section 15 shall not have effect until three years after this section comes into force.

33. *(1) Parliament or the legislature of a province may expressly declare in an Act of Parliament or of the legislature, as the case may be, that the Act or a provision thereof shall operate notwithstanding a provision included in section 2 or sections 7 to 15 of this Charter.*

(2) An Act or a provision of an Act in respect of which a declaration made under this section is in effect shall have such operation as it would have but for the provision of this Charter referred to in the declaration.

(3) A declaration made under subsection (1) shall cease to have effect five years after it comes into force or on such earlier date as may be specified in the declaration.

(4) Parliament or the legislature of a province may re-enact a declaration made under subsection (1).

(5) Subsection (3) applies in respect of a re-enactment made under subsection (4).

Citation

34. *This Part may be cited as the Canadian Charter of Rights and Freedoms.*

Section 32 makes it clear that the *Charter*, unlike the *Bill of Rights*, applies to both federal and provincial legislation. Arguably, section 33 most critically weakens the impact of the *Charter*. Section 33(1) permits governments to opt out of *Charter* provisions simply by stating that a specific piece of legislation will operate "notwithstanding" the fundamental freedoms of section 2, the rights afforded accused persons by sections 7 to 14, or the equality rights of section 15. Although there is some limitation on using the so-called **notwithstanding clause** to opt out of *Charter* provisions (section 33[3] terminates the exception after five years have elapsed), there is no bar to reenacting the override every five years (section 33[4] permits reenactment of exceptions to the *Charter*).

Provincial governments have opted out of *Charter* provisions in a number of instances. The government of Quebec declared shortly after the enactment of the *Charter* that all laws of the province would operate notwithstanding sections 2 and 7 to 15 of the *Charter*. This legislation was ultimately thrown out by the Quebec Court of Appeal.[33] The Quebec government later successfully applied the notwithstanding clause to legislation that restricted the use of English on commercial signs. The government of Saskatchewan has applied the notwithstanding clause to legislation that prohibits strikes by public-sector workers in "essential services." Saskatchewan did so to ensure that the fundamental freedoms afforded by section 2 of the *Charter* would not apply to its labour legislation.

Strengths and Limitations of the Charter

The *Charter* has been subject to many criticisms, and has received as many plaudits. The original objection—that it diminishes the doctrine of parliamentary supremacy—has not disappeared. It is argued that the passage of the *Charter* as a constitutional document gave Canada's judges the power to make law, a power that should never be given to individuals who are not democratically elected and hence not accountable to the general public.

Police have also criticized the *Charter*, suggesting that its emphasis on legal rights, particularly in sections 7 to 14, has hampered their ability to enforce the law effectively. Many police organizations have suggested that the *Charter* makes it more difficult for them to detect, arrest, and successfully prosecute criminals.

Other opponents of the *Charter* have argued that its emphasis on the rights of private individuals tends to obscure and minimize the importance of collective rights, particularly in the economic sphere. Constitutional law scholar Andrew Petter has suggested that the focus on individual rights has combined with the substantial costs of litigation to yield a situation in which only the affluent can use this law to further their interests, with the net effect that the *Charter* can be used against the economically disadvantaged to uphold individual rights at the expense of the public good.[34] There is, in fact, nothing in the *Charter* about economic rights or economic equality.

Still other critics have pointed out that an entrenched Bill of Rights or Charter of Rights is no guarantee of the protection of civil liberties. Canada and Britain, in responding to crime, have shown less tendency to impose excessive punishments and infringe liberty than the United States, which has had an entrenched *Bill of Rights* for more than 200 years.

Finally, some critics have claimed that the *Charter* has taken political issues out of the hands of citizens and given them to the judiciary. Lawyers and judges—representatives of the affluent—conduct expensive litigation without accountability to the electorate, resolving conflicting interests, and, in the process, restructuring the nature of Canadian society. In the words of Osgoode Hall law professor Michael Mandel, the *Charter* has effectively permitted "the legalization of politics."[35]

Even those who find substantial merit in the *Charter*, and might be reluctant to accept any of these arguments, can find limitations in its present structure. Section 33 gives Parliament and the provinces the power to opt out of all significant *Charter* provisions and thereby, arguably, diminish its strength as a constitutional document.

The real test of the *Charter* is, however, to be found in the decisions that emanate from Canadian courts, as well as in the effect of these decisions on our social, political, and economic lives. In discussing the key sections of the *Charter* (the fundamental freedoms in s. 2, the rights afforded accused persons by ss. 7 to 14, and the equality provisions of s. 15) we have reviewed a number of the most significant decisions: *RJR-MacDonald*, *Morgentaler*, and *Andrews*. Consider also *M. v. H.* (discussed in Chapter 3), a key development in the interpretation of equality rights for same-sex couples. But what can we conclude from the judgments issued by Canadian courts in these and other cases? With respect to the four cases just named, it appears that our courts have been willing to protect the legal rights of corporations to advertise a drug that kills about 35 000 Canadians every year. They have also been willing to declare the century-old criminalization of a woman's control over her reproductive ability a violation of fundamental justice. And they have been willing to grant the right to practise law to individuals who are not citizens of Canada.

What we make of these decisions, and hundreds of others, will depend upon the political, economic, and social values we hold. For example, for some, the Supreme Court's decision in *Morgentaler* is an abomination; for others it is justice. Hogg has said that the *Charter* "protects the values of a nation"—but how do we define "the values of a nation"? One person's freedom of religion may involve the imposition of offensive or alien beliefs on another person. The right to be presumed innocent will be interpreted according to one's political values and, specifically, according to one's perceptions of crime and its control.

Ultimately, there are few values to which all Canadians subscribe. Although almost all of us believe in the rhetoric of terms such as "equality" and "freedom of speech," we diverge on the practical specifics of the law's application. What we intend as fundamental freedoms, rights for the accused, or equality before the law are matters of debate. The court is a forum in which a contest of values, albeit circumscribed, takes place. And to the victor goes the law.

Sections 91 and 92: The Distribution of Legislative Powers

As mentioned earlier on in the chapter, the original division of federal and provincial powers first set out in the *British North America Act, 1867* remains intact. Sections 91 and 92, though now part of the *Constitution Act, 1982*, are still central to the distribution of legislative responsibilities in Canada. The *British North America Act, 1867* was, under the *Constitution Act, 1982*, renamed the *Constitution Act, 1867*.[36]

Section 91 sets out the areas over which the federal government has jurisdiction.

> 91.   It shall be lawful for the Queen, by and with the Advice and Consent of the Senate and House of Commons, to make Laws for the Peace, Order, and good Government of Canada, in relation to all Matters not coming within the Classes of Subjects by this Act assigned exclusively to the Legislatures of the Provinces; and for greater Certainty, but not so as to restrict the Generality of the foregoing Terms of this Section, it is hereby declared that (notwithstanding anything in this Act) the exclusive Legislative Authority of the Parliament of Canada extends to all Matters coming within the Classes of Subjects next herein-after enumerated; that is to say, . . .
>
> 1A.   *The Public Debt and Property.*
> 2.   *The Regulation of Trade and Commerce.*
> 2A.   *Unemployment Insurance.*
> 3.   *The raising of money by any Mode or System of Taxation.*
> 4.   *The Borrowing of Money on the Public Credit.*
> 5.   *Postal Service.*
> 6.   *The Census and Statistics.*
> 7.   *Militia, Military and Naval Service, and Defence.*

8. *The fixing of and providing for the Salaries and Allowances of Civil and other Officers of the Government of Canada.*

9. *Beacons, Buoys, Lighthouses, and Sable Island.*

10. *Navigation and Shipping.*

11. *Quarantine and the Establishment and Maintenance of Marine Hospitals.*

12. *Sea Coast and Inland Fisheries.*

13. *Ferries between a Province and any British or Foreign Country, or between Two Provinces.*

14. *Currency and coinage.*

15. *Banking, incorporation of banks, and the Issue of Paper Money.*

16. *Savings Banks.*

17. *Weights and Measures.*

18. *Bills of Exchange and Promissory Notes.*

19. *Interest.*

20. *Legal Tender.*

21. *Bankruptcy and Insolvency.*

22. *Patents of Invention and Discovery.*

23. *Copyrights.*

24. *Indians, and Lands Reserved for the Indians.*

25. *Naturalization and Aliens.*

26. *Marriage and Divorce.*

27. *The Criminal Law, except the Constitution of Courts of Criminal Jurisdiction, but including the Procedure in Criminal Matters.*

28. *The Establishment, Maintenance, and Management of Penitentiaries.*

29. *Such classes of Subjects as are expressly excepted in the Enumeration of the Classes of Subjects by this Act assigned exclusively to the Legislatures of the Provinces.*

And any Matter coming within any of the Classes of Subjects enumerated in this Section shall not be deemed to come within the Class of Matters of a local or private Nature comprised in the Enumeration of the Classes of Subjects by this Act assigned exclusively to the Legislatures of the Provinces.

Section 92 catalogues the jurisdictional powers given to the provinces.

92.   In each Province the Legislature may exclusively make Laws in relation to Matters coming within the Classes of Subjects next herein-after enumerated; that is to say,

1. *The Amendment from Time to Time, notwithstanding anything in this Act, of the Constitution of the Province, except as regards the Office of the Lieutenant-Governor.*

2. *Direct Taxation within the Province in order to the raising of a Revenue for Provincial Purposes.*

3. *The borrowing of money on the sole Credit of the Province.*

4. *The Establishment and Tenure of Provincial Offices and the Appointment and Payment of Provincial Officers.*

5. *The Management and Sale of the Public Lands belonging to the Province and of the Timber and Wood thereon.*

6. *The Establishment, Maintenance, and Management of Public and Reformatory Prisons in and for the Province.*

7. *The Establishment, Maintenance, and Management of Hospitals, Asylums, Charities, and Eleemosynary Institutions in and for the Province, other than Marine Hospitals.*

8. *Municipal Institutions in the Province.*

9. *Shop, Saloon, Tavern, Auctioneer, and other Licences in order to the raising of a Revenue for Provincial, Local, or Municipal Purposes.*

10. *Local Works and Undertakings other than such as are of the following Classes:—*

    a. *Lines of Steam or other Ships, Railways, Canals, Telegraphs, and other Works and Undertakings connecting the Province with any other or others of the provinces, or extending beyond the Limits of the Province:*

    b. *Lines of Steam Ships between the Province and any British or Foreign Country:*

    c. *Such Works as, although wholly situate within the Province, are before or after their Execution declared by the Parliament of Canada to be for the general Advantage of Canada or for the Advantage of Two or more of the Provinces.*

11. *The Incorporation of Companies with Provincial Objects.*

12. *The Solemnization of Marriage in the Province.*

13. *Property and Civil Rights in the Province.*

14. *The Administration of Justice in the Province, including the Constitution, Maintenance, and Organization of Provincial Courts, both of Civil and of Criminal Jurisdiction, and including Procedure in Civil Matters in those Courts.*

15. *The Imposition of Punishment by Fine, Penalty, or Imprisonment for enforcing any Law of the Province made in relation to any Matter coming within any of the Classes of Subjects enumerated in this Section.*

16. *Generally all Matters of a merely local or private Nature in the Province.*

Questions of Jurisdiction: When Provincial and Federal Responsibilities Collide

Sections 91 and 92 have been subject to shifting interpretations since they were legislated into being in 1867. The language of these sections is not always sufficiently precise to permit a clear sense of whether provincial or federal jurisdiction is to prevail. Moreover, section 91 contains the "peace, order, and good government" clause, which gives the federal government residual power over areas of jurisdiction not expressly noted in either section 91 or section 92. For example, punishment of those who commit narcotics offences has been deemed to be a federal power. In the 1979 decision in *R. v. Hauser*, the Supreme Court of Canada held that narcotics law cannot be traced to the federal power to legislate criminal law and procedure under section 91(27) but to the justification of "peace, order, and good government" in the preamble of section 91.[37]

The residual power given to the federal government has meant that in perceived political, social, or economic emergencies, the federal government may act unilaterally in the interest of the country as a whole. Results of the use of residual federal power, in addition to narcotics control, include alcohol prohibition and runaway inflation.[38] (A separate federal statute, the *War Measures Act*, gives the federal government extraordinary powers in the event of war or a state of apprehended insurrection.)

The jurisdictions described within sections 91 and 92 have been the subject of many court battles, constitutional conferences, and elaborate delegations or interdelegations of federal and provincial power. The latter involve the granting of legal power by a federal or provincial government to a subordinate body in its own jurisdiction or to a subordinate body in another jurisdiction (federal or provincial) so that it may make law—pass statutes, bylaws, regulations, and so forth. An example of a potential source of conflict is section 91(2), which gives the federal government power to enact law in relation to "the regulation of trade and commerce." At what point does a commercial undertaking move from being an intraprovincial (hence, a provincially regulated) business to an interprovincial or extraprovincial business subject to federal control over "the regulation of trade and commerce"?

For some circumstances, the lack of precision in sections 91 and 92 has been clarified by the courts. The courts have determined that legislation is either "***intra vires***"—inside the jurisdiction—or "***ultra vires***"—outside the jurisdiction—of either the federal or the provincial government.

However, more productive solutions have typically been found in the delegation of a federal power to a provincial body or tribunal, and in what constititutional scholars, such as Hogg, have described as "co-operative federalism":

> The essence of co-operative federalism is a network of relationships between the executives of the central and regional governments. Through these relationships mechanisms are developed, especially fiscal mechanisms, which allow a continuous redistribution of powers and resources without recourse to the courts or the amending process. . . . Changes in the financial arrangements have naturally altered the balance of powers within the federation. Yet the federal–provincial financial arrangements since the Second World War have been worked out by the executives of the various governments, at first almost at the dictation of the federal government, latterly by intergovernmental negotiation leading to genuine agreements.[39]

An example of cooperative federalism can be seen in the equalization payments made by the federal government to the poorer of the Canadian provinces each fiscal year, theoretically in order to provide a minimum standard of public services throughout the country. Although these payments do not flow from the *British North America Act, 1867*— since they originated in 1957—they are now mandated by section 36(2) of the *Constitution Act, 1982*:

> 36.(2)   Parliament and the government of Canada are committed to the principle of making equalization payments to ensure that provincial governments have sufficient revenues to provide reasonably comparable levels of public services at reasonably comparable levels of taxation.

Clearly, however, this section of the *Act* offers only a vague commitment to a principle of provincial equality of access to public services. The form and amount of equalization payments have been the subject of debate in federal–provincial conferences for almost 40 years, and they will, in all likelihood, continue to be so.

Despite some contentious areas, there are significant and unchanging parameters of provincial and federal jurisdictions, which can be traced to sections 91 and 92 of the *British North America Act*. Section 91(27), for instance, gives the federal government the exclusive power to legislate in relation to criminal law. (In the United States, by contrast, each of the 50 states is responsible for creating its own criminal law and attendant penalties.) But note that section 92(13) gives each province the power to legislate in relation to "property and civil rights." If a province creates law that, for example, censors certain kinds of films—effectively legislating in relation to propriety[40]— is it intruding upon the power of the federal government to decide, through the *Criminal Code*, what is obscene and hence prohibited?

Section 92(14) gives the provinces power to control the administration of justice, the organization of the courts, and the procedure to be employed in civil matters. When one adds to this the provinces' power to appoint the judiciary for family, small claims, and criminal courts (given by section 96 of the *British North America Act*), it is evident that the regional governments have a strong voice in defining and dispensing justice. More than 90 percent of all litigation takes place in small claims courts, family courts, and provincial courts (criminal division); only 10 percent is heard in the federally controlled criminal and civil courts.

At this point, one can already see that much of Canada's legal structure flows from the *British North America Act, 1867*; the *Constitution Act, 1982* is a lesser source of jurisdictional distribution. The division of powers therefore exists for reasons that are largely historical. But is it cast in stone? It is possible to construct a different configuration of federal and provincial powers. Why is it necessary, for example, for the federal government to retain sole jurisdiction over the regulation of marriage and divorce, under section 91(26)? Should the federal government continue to dictate immigration and agriculture policy to the provinces, in the manner envisaged by section 95?

> 95.   In each Province the Legislature may make Laws in relation to Agriculture in the Province, and to Immigration into the Province; and it is hereby declared that the Parliament of Canada may from Time to Time make laws in relation to Agriculture in all or any of the Provinces, and to Immigration into all or any of the Provinces; and any Law of the Legislature of a Province relative to Agriculture or to Immigration shall have effect in and for the Province as long and as far only as it is not repugnant to any Act of the Parliament of Canada.

Should criminal law continue to be a national, rather than a provincial, concern? As is true of the other questions asked—about immigration, agriculture, and marriage and divorce—there is no "correct" answer, only grist for the mill of future constitutional discussions, arguments, and resolutions.

The Rejection of the *Constitution Act, 1982* by Quebec

Both the three types of amending formula described earlier in this chapter and the *Canadian Charter of Rights and Freedoms* were the product of thousands of hours of discussion, debate, and compromise. However, Quebec never approved the *Constitution Act, 1982*. In December 1981, the Quebec National Assembly passed a resolution rejecting the constitutional agreement reached by the federal government and the other provinces a month earlier. The Quebec government argued before the Supreme Court of Canada that the proposed constitutional amendments could not become law without Quebec's consent. The Supreme Court dismissed Quebec's arguments, noting that neither unanimity of governments nor the consent of the provinces was legally required for constitutional amendment. The Court added, however, that constitutional convention or custom requires that amendment by the federal government not proceed unilaterally.[41]

In April 1982, the new constitution became law, after passage through the House of Commons and the Senate, and its proclamation. But controversy about the *Constitution Act, 1982* has not diminished. The entrenchment of the *Charter* was strongly opposed (particularly by Alberta and Manitoba) during the negotiations that led to its introduction; and the arguments about its role and significance have not abated. Furthermore, the absence of Quebec from the 1982 agreement led to a flurry of constitutional proposals, none of which proved acceptable. The most serious efforts were led by Conservative Prime Minister Brian Mulroney, whose government came to power in 1984. Mulroney was determined to amend the Constitution to make it acceptable to Quebec. The Quebec Liberal government of Robert Bourassa, elected in 1985, was equally interested in a reconciliation with the rest of Canada. Both separatist and federalist politicians within Quebec generally felt that the *Constitution Act, 1982* had diminished the province's powers; if Quebec were to agree to the Constitution, concessions would have to be made by the rest of Canada.

The Wooing of Quebec: The Meech Lake and Charlottetown Accords

Packages of concessions ultimately surfaced in the form of the **Meech Lake Accord** and, later, the **Charlottetown Accord**.

THE MEECH LAKE ACCORD

In 1987, the Mulroney government's attempt to bring Quebec into the constitutional fold led to the Meech Lake Accord. The accord was an agreement reached by the federal government and provincial premiers at Meech Lake, Quebec, on June 3, 1987. In order for the accord to become law, it had to be ratified by the House of Commons, the Senate, and the legislatures of each province.

The Meech Lake Accord had essentially been initiated by the Quebec government in 1985. Premier Bourassa indicated at the time that Quebec would be willing to accept the *Constitution Act, 1982* if a number of conditions were met. Specifically, he called for the recognition of Quebec as a distinct society, a veto for Quebec on constitutional amendments, a provincial voice in appointments to the Supreme Court of Canada, and a greater role for the province in the development of immigration policy.

In general terms, the Meech Lake Accord met these conditions, designating Quebec as a "distinct society," and permitting some changes with respect to veto of constitutional amendments, Supreme Court appointments, and control over immigration. There were, however, a number of criticisms of the accord. Most telling, perhaps, was the argument that it had been negotiated in private by "eleven white men in suits": the fact that the future of the country was being decided behind closed doors by a small group of powerful insiders seriously compromised public support for the pact. There were other criticisms as well: Quebec was seen by some as no more deserving of distinct-society status than other provinces; Aboriginal Canadians, women, and people with disabilities had been excluded from the decision-making process. Ultimately, ratification of the accord did not succeed. The governments of Newfoundland, New Brunswick, and Manitoba changed between the negotiation period and the ratification deadline. The new premiers—Clyde Wells, Frank McKenna, and Gary Filmon—were, in varying degrees, unsupportive.

THE CHARLOTTETOWN ACCORD

After the collapse of the Meech Lake Accord, the Mulroney government made one more attempt to bring Quebec within the constitutional framework of the *Constitution Act, 1982*. The result—the Charlottetown Accord—was a very ambitious reworking of the Canadian Constitution, reached in Charlottetown on August 28, 1992, by the 10 premiers, the federal government, and Aboriginal and territorial leaders. All three then-existing major political parties—Conservatives, Liberals, and New Democrats—were represented in the agreement. The Charlottetown

Accord not only addressed the issue of Quebec's representation within the country's Constitution, but also proposed changes to the Senate, the composition of the House of Commons, Aboriginal rights, and the amending formula, among other matters.

The Canada Clause

2. *(1) The Constitution of Canada, including the Canadian Charter of Rights and Freedoms, shall be interpreted in a manner consistent with the following fundamental characteristics:*

    (a) Canada is a democracy committed to a parliamentary and federal system of government and to the rule of law;

    (b) the aboriginal peoples of Canada, being the first peoples to govern this land, have the right to promote their languages, cultures, and traditions and to ensure the integrity of their societies, and their governments constitute one of three orders of government in Canada;

    (c) Quebec constitutes within Canada a distinct society, which includes a French-speaking majority, a unique culture, and a civil law tradition;

    (d) Canadians and their governments are committed to the vitality and development of official language minority communities throughout Canada;

    (e) Canadians are committed to racial and ethnic equality in a society that includes citizens from many lands who have contributed, and continue to contribute, to the building of a strong Canada that reflects its cultural and racial diversity;

    (f) Canadians are committed to a respect for individual and collective human rights and freedoms of all people;

    (g) Canadians are committed to the equality of female and male persons; and

    (h) Canadians confirm the principle of the equality of the provinces at the same time as recognizing their diverse characteristics.

(2) The role of the legislature and Government of Quebec to preserve and promote the distinct society of Quebec is affirmed.

(3) Nothing in this section derogates from the powers, rights, or privileges of the Parliament or the Government of Canada, or of the legislatures or governments of the provinces, or of the legislative bodies or governments of the aboriginal peoples of Canada, including any powers, rights, or privileges relating to language.

(4) For greater certainty, nothing in this section abrogates or derogates from the aboriginal and treaty rights of the aboriginal peoples of Canada.

The Canada Clause contained several controversial sections. Some Canadians, notably former prime minister Pierre Trudeau, objected to the classification of Quebec as a distinct society. (Trudeau dismissed the notion as a meaningless concession to "blackmailers.") Their argument was that Quebec is not the only "distinct" province or region of Canada. For others, the recognition of Aboriginal government as one of "three orders of government" was problematic, either because it was too substantial a concession or because the political ramifications were unclear, the essential justice of the position notwithstanding.

Proposed Amendments to the Senate

21. (1) *The Senate shall consist of 62 senators[42] of whom*

    (a) *six shall be elected for each province, namely, Ontario, Quebec, Nova Scotia, New Brunswick, Manitoba, British Columbia, Prince Edward Island, Alberta, Saskatchewan, and Newfoundland;*

    (b) *one shall be elected for each territory, namely, the Yukon Territory and the Northwest Territories; and*

    (c) *[aboriginal representation]. . . .*

23. (1) *Subject to this Act, the Parliament of Canada may provide for all matters relating to the election of senators.*

(2) *Subject to this Act, the legislature of any province or the legislative authority of any territory may provide for*

    (a) *the indirect election of senators for the province or territory by the Legislative Assembly of that province or legislative authority of that territory, and all matters relating thereto;*

    (b) *any special measures to provide for equal representation of male and female persons; and*

    (c) *the determination of electoral districts and the boundaries thereof in relation to the election of senators.*

(3) *Where a law of Parliament and a law of a province or territory under paragraph (2) (a) or (b) conflict, the law of the province or territory prevails to the extent of the conflict.*

(4) *Where a law of Parliament and a law of a province or territory under paragraph (2) (c) conflict, the law of Parliament prevails to the extent of the conflict.*

(5) *No law made under this section in relation to the direct election of senators shall apply in respect of a general election of senators for which the writs are issued within six months after the law receives the Queen's assent.*

The amendments respecting the Senate represented major reform. The number of senators was to be cut to 62 from 104, and representation in the country's upper house was to be based, not on population, but on provincial status. Prince Edward Island, with a population of just over 100 000, was to have the same number of senators as Ontario, with a population of almost 10 million. The purpose of the change was to balance representation by population with representation by region. Some critics argued that the suggested changes to the Senate's structure went too far, ultimately undermining the principle of representation by population.

Section 23 of an amended Constitution Act would have provided for the election of senators, ending the present practice of appointment. Section 23(2)(b) would have permitted provinces to require an equal number of male and female senators. However, provinces could opt out of election and continue to appoint senators, since section 23(2) stated only that provinces "may provide" for the election of six senators. Quebec indicated, prior to the referendum, that it did not intend to hold Senate elections. The Senate would therefore be a hodgepodge: some senators would be elected, others would not; some provinces would insist upon gender equality, others would not. There was to be no consistent principle guiding Senate representation.

Other changes related to the powers of the Senate. Although the Charlottetown Accord would not have placed the Senate on an equal footing with the House of Commons, the upper chamber would possess expanded powers of legislative input, except in the crucial realms of revenue or expenditure bills, the taxation of natural resources, and bills affecting the French language or culture in Canada.

Proposed Amendments to House of Commons Representation

51A. (1) *In readjusting the number of members in the House of Commons, the Parliament of Canada shall be guided by the principles that the proportion of members of the House of Commons representing a province shall be based on the proportion of the population of Canada from that province.*

(2) *Notwithstanding anything in this Act,*

    (a) *a province shall always be entitled to a number of members in the House of Commons not fewer than the number of senators by which the province was entitled to be represented on April 17, 1982;*

    (b) *Quebec shall always be entitled to a number of members in the House of Commons that is no fewer than 25 percent of the total number of members in the House of Commons;*

(c) *except as a result of the application of paragraph (b), no province shall have fewer members in the House of Commons than any other province that had, at the then latest general census, a smaller population;*

(d) *in any readjustment of the number of members in the House of Commons, no province shall have its representation reduced by more than one member; and*

(e) *the Yukon Territory and the Northwest Territories shall always be entitled to a number of members in the House of Commons not fewer than the number of members to which they were entitled on the coming into force of this section, and this entitlement applies to any new province established from either of them.*

These amendments were among the most debated constitutional changes proposed by the Charlottetown Accord. Many critics particularly objected to Quebec's holding 25 percent of House of Commons seats in perpetuity, regardless of future population changes. Although demographers stressed that Quebec's share of Canada's population was unlikely to change by more than 1 percentage point over the next century, the principle of potentially unequal representation was strongly criticized. Opponents suggested that this was not an amendment of principle, but a political tradeoff not unlike those found in labour–management negotiations.

Proposed Amendments to Aboriginal Rights

35.1 (1) *The aboriginal peoples of Canada have the inherent right of self-government within Canada.*

(2) *The right referred to in subsection (1) shall be interpreted in a manner consistent with the recognition of the governments of the aboriginal peoples of Canada as constituting one of three orders of government in Canada.*

(3) *The exercise of the right referred to in subsection (1) includes the authority of duly constituted legislative bodies of the aboriginal peoples, each within its own jurisdiction,*

(a) *to safeguard and develop their languages, cultures, economies, identities, institutions, and traditions, and*

(b) *to develop, maintain, and strengthen their relationship with their lands, waters, and environment,*

so as to determine and control their development as peoples according to their own values and priorities and to ensure the integrity of their societies. . . .

35.2 *(1)   The government of Canada, the provincial and territorial governments, and the aboriginal peoples of Canada, including the Indian, Inuit, and Métis peoples of Canada, in the various regions and communities of Canada, shall negotiate in good faith the implementation of the right of self-government, including issues of*

   (a)   jurisdiction,

   (b)   lands and resources, and

   (c)   economic and fiscal arrangements,

with the objective of concluding agreements elaborating relationships between governments of aboriginal peoples and the government of Canada and provincial or territorial governments.

This statement of support for Native self-government was seen as a major accomplishment, taking Canada's First Peoples beyond the current "recognition and affirmation of aboriginal and treaty rights" within section 35 of the *Constitution Act, 1982*. Yet Canada's Aboriginal peoples were divided on the merits of the change. Some argued that section 35.2 committed the federal government and the provinces only to further negotiation to determine the nature and structure of Aboriginal self-government; in the absence of specifics, nothing of substance had been accomplished. On the other hand, the recognition of Aboriginal rule as one of three levels of government in Canada was a major breakthrough. Many who voted against the Charlottetown Accord were disappointed that this part of the agreement did not become a part of the Canadian Constitution.

The Amending Formula

41. *An amendment to the Constitution of Canada in relation to the following matters may be made by proclamation issued by the Governor General under the Great Seal of Canada only where authorized by resolutions of the Senate and House of Commons and of the Legislative Assembly of each province:*

   (a)   the office of the Queen, the Governor General, and the Lieutenant-Governor of a province;

   (b)   the powers of the Senate and the election of senators;

   (c)   the number of senators by which a province or territory is entitled to be represented in the Senate and the qualifications of senators set out in the Constitution Act, 1867;

   [(c.1)   the number of senators by which the aboriginal peoples of Canada are entitled to be represented in the Senate and the qualifications of such senators;]

   (d)   an amendment to section 51A of the Constitution Act, 1867;

   (e)   subject to section 43, the use of the English or the French language;

(f) subject to subsection 42 (1), the Supreme Court of Canada;

(g) an amendment to section 2 or 3 of the Constitution Act, 1871; and

(h) an amendment to this Part.

The proposed changes to the amending formula provoked substantial criticism. As in the case of the Meech Lake Accord, most significant parts of the Charlottetown Accord could be changed only with the unanimous consent of the federal and all provincial governments. Given the concerns raised by many of the proposed changes—the structure of Senate reform, a guarantee of 25 percent of Commons seats to Quebec, and uncertainty over both Aboriginal representation in the Senate and the form of Aboriginal self-government—the inflexible amending formula was a major stumbling block. Even its most ardent supporters acknowledged that the Charlottetown Accord was an imperfect compromise, and the amending formula would have cast that imperfect compromise in stone.

• • •

The Charlottetown Accord, unlike the Meech Lake Accord, was to be decided by a national referendum. It is probably not surprising that in October 1992, the voters of Canada rejected it by a margin of 55 to 45 percent. Although every government in the country had endorsed the accord, the Canadian people remained unconvinced. Former prime minister Pierre Trudeau had spoken out against the agreement, and a host of other politicians and interest groups had campaigned against its passage, albeit for often contradictory reasons.

In the end, the Charlottetown Accord probably failed because it tried to accomplish too much too quickly, lumping together the issues of Aboriginal rights, Senate reform, House of Commons representation, and distinct society status for Quebec. It did not help that its initiator, Prime Minister Brian Mulroney, together with his Conservative government, was both extremely unpopular and distrusted across the country.

Conclusion: The Future of Canadian Federalism

With the demise of the Charlottetown Accord, the future of Canadian federalism is unclear. There is widespread agreement among the federal and provincial governments to put constitutional reform on the back burner, although the emergence and continuance of strong showings by the Bloc Québécois in the federal elections of 1997, 2000, and 2004, and the exceptionally close referendum in Quebec in 1995, may require a rethinking of such sentiments. In the interim, the numerous questions raised by the Charlottetown Accord remain unanswered. Can the goal of Aboriginal self-government be accomplished? Can Quebec be accommodated within the *Constitution Act, 1982*, or is separation inevitable? Can the Senate be reformed into a decision-making body that genuinely provides a sober second look at legislation passed by the House of Commons? Can an amending formula be developed that embraces the bedrock character of constitutional law, yet permits future flexibility?

The answers to these questions will probably shape Canada's constitutional law in the twenty-first century. Our task, as students, teachers, and citizens, is twofold: to involve ourselves in the changes that will ultimately define our country, and to understand the origins and consequences of these changes.

Web Links

Constitution Acts: 1867 to 1982, Department of Justice
http://laws.justice.gc.ca/en/const/index.html
This website provides the full texts of the constitutional documents of Canada, including the *Canadian Charter of Rights and Freedoms*.

Library of Parliament, Parliamentary Research Branch
http://www.parl.gc.ca/information/library/PRBpubs/bp295-e.htm
This Web link is available through the Library of Parliament, which prepares research papers on matters of public interest. This particular article is entitled "Quebec's Constitutional Veto: The Legal and Historical Context."

Quebec's Politics on the Web
http://quebecpolitique.com
This website is dedicated to politics in Quebec and contains extensive information about Quebec's political history—for example, the province's political system and parties, its judicial system, all provincial elections since 1867, and the referendums.

Federal–Provincial Relations & National Unity, University of British Columbia Library
http://www.library.ubc.ca/poli/cpwebfed.html
This website, which is available through the University of British Columbia library, provides comprehensive access to the major political and constitutional documents in Canada's history.

Questions for Discussion

1. Should Canada's judges move toward a more restrictive interpretation of the *Canadian Charter of Rights and Freedoms*, thereby preserving the long-standing doctrine of parliamentary supremacy?

2. Is the amending formula set out in the *Constitution Act, 1982,* sufficient to meet the needs of the Canadian federation? Or is the formula set out in the Charlottetown Accord a preferable mechanism for constitutional change?

3. "The limitations clause (s. 1) and the provisions for opting out (s. 33) diminish the impact of the *Canadian Charter of Rights and Freedoms*; this is a constitutional document that claims to protect the rights of Canadians, but, in reality, can offer few if any guarantees." Discuss the validity of this statement.

Further Reading

Beaudoin, G.A., and E. Mendes. *The Canadian Charter of Rights and Freedoms.* 3d ed. Toronto: Carswell, 1996.

> This legal text provides a comprehensive look at the application of the *Charter*. The authors analyze and interpret a wide range of *Charter* decisions that have served to alter the Canadian legal landscape. Their book also provides insight into their expectations of future judicial decisions within this realm.

Hogg, P.W. *Constitutional Law of Canada.* 4th ed. Toronto: Carswell, 1997.

> This 1700-page tome is a remarkable and ongoing piece of work from Canada's foremost constitutional scholar. Dean Peter Hogg of Osgoode Hall Law School dissects constitutional law with a thorough and thoughtful analysis. There is no more comprehensive text available on the subject of Canadian constitutional law.

Mandel, M. *The Charter of Rights and the Legalization of Politics in Canada.* 2d ed. Toronto: Wall and Thompson, 1992.

> This is a well-researched and critical analysis of the emergence and continuation of the *Charter*. Professor Mandel suggests that the *Charter* has contributed to the decline of democracy in Canada, has promoted inequality, and has diminished collective rights in favour of a "fundamentally dishonest, authoritarian and above-all anti-democratic form."

Notes

1. 30–31 Vict., c. 3 (U.K.).
2. Being Schedule B to the *Canada Act 1982* (U.K.), 1982, c. 11.
3. Part I of the *Constitution Act, 1982*, being Schedule B to the *Canada Act 1982* (U.K.), 1982, c. 11.
4. R. Cheffins and R. Tucker, *The Constitutional Process in Canada*, 2d ed. (Toronto: McGraw-Hill Ryerson, 1976), 4.
5. P.W. Hogg, *Constitutional Law of Canada*, 3d ed. (Toronto: Carswell, 1992), 1.
6. [1926] A.C. 482 (P.C.).
7. W.R. Lederman, "The Process of Constitutional Amendment for Canada," *McGill Law Journal* 12 (1967): 377.
8. *Constitution Act, 1999* (Nunavut)—1998, c. 15, Part 2, s. 47.
9. S.C. 1960, c. 44, reprinted in R.S.C. 1985, App. III.
10. E.C.S. Wade, *Constitutional and Administrative Law* (Essex: Longman Group, 1985), 64.
11. [1970] 3 C.C.C. 355, 10 C.R.N.S. 334 (6:3).
12. (1973), 38 D.L. R. (3d) 481, [1974] S.C.R. 1439, 23 C.R.N.S. 197 (5:4).
13. *R. v. Oakes*, [1986] 1 S.C.R. 103 at 138–139.
14. *Re Alberta Statutes*, [1938] S.C.R. 100.
15. *Saumur v. City of Quebec*, [1953] 2 S.C.R. 299.
16. *Criminal Code*, R.S.C. 1985, c. C-46, s. 163(B), as cited in *R. v. Butler*, [1992] 1 S.C.R. 452.
17. Hogg, *Constitutional Law of Canada*, 977.
18. *RJR-MacDonald v. Canada (A.G.)* (1991), 82 D.L.R. (4th) 449 [hereinafter *MacDonald*].
19. *RJR-MacDonald v. Canada (A.G.)* (1993), 102 D.L.R. (4th) 289.
20. *RJR-MacDonald v. Canada* (A.G.), [1995] 3 S.C.R. 199.
21. *R. v. Morgentaler (No. 2)*, [1988] 1 S.C.R. 30.
22. *R. v. Hebert*, [1990] 2 S.C.R. 151.
23. See *R. v. Conway*, [1989] 1 S.C.R. 1659 and, alternatively, *R. v. Smith*, [1989] 2 S.C.R. 1120.
24. [1990] 2 S.C.R. 1199.
25. *R. v. Morin*, [1992] 1 S.C.R. 771 at 795.
26. *R. v. Smith*, [1987] 1 S.C.R. 1045.
27. [1990] 2 S.C.R. 711.
28. Hogg, *Constitutional Law of Canada*, 1135.
29. *Andrews v. Law Society of British Columbia*, [1989] 1 S.C.R. 143 at 195.

30. *R. v. Greffe* (1990), 55 C.C.C. (3d) 161, 75 C.R. (3d) 257, [1990] 1 S.C.R. 755.
31. *R. v. Simmons* (1988), 45 C.C.C. (3d) 296, [1988] 2 S.C.R. 495.
32. *Collins v. R.* (1987), 33 C.C.C. (3d) 1, [1987] 1 S.C.R. 265.
33. See also *Ford v. Quebec*, [1988] 2 S.C.R. 712.
34. A. Petter, "The Politics of the Charter," *Supreme Court Law Review* 8 (1986): 473–505; A. Hutchinson and A. Petter, "Private Rights/Public Wrongs: The Liberal Lie of the Charter," *University of Toronto Law Journal* 38 (1988): 278.
35. M. Mandel, *The Charter of Rights and the Legalization of Politics in Canada* (Toronto: Wall and Thompson, 1989).
36. 30–31 Vict., c. 3 (U.K.), reprinted in R.S.C. 1985, App. II, no. 5.
37. *R. v. Hauser*, [1979] 1 S.C.R. 984, [1979] 5 W.W.R. 1, 8 C.R. (3d) 89, 98 D.L.R. (3d) 193, 46 C.C.C. (2d) 481, 26 N.R. 541, 16 A.R. 91.
38. See, for example, *Reference re Anti-Inflation Act*, [1976] 2 S.C.R. 373, 68 D.L.R. (3d) 452, 9 N.R. 541.
39. Hogg, *Constitutional Law of Canada,* 131.
40. For a discussion of this issue see the Supreme Court of Canada's decision in *Re Nova Scotia Board of Censors and McNeil*, [1978] 2 S.C.R. 662, 84 D.L.R. (3d) 1.
41. *Patriation Reference (Re Resolution to Amend the Constitution)*, [1981] 1 S.C.R. 753.
42. The number of senators was to be subject to future decisions regarding the number of guaranteed Aboriginal seats. The amendment concerning Nunavut is a partial answer.

References

Abel, A.S. *Toward a Constitutional Charter for Canada*. Toronto: University of Toronto Press, 1980.

Bayefsky, A.F., and M.A. Eberts. *Equality Rights and the Canadian Charter of Rights and Freedoms*. Toronto: Carswell, 1985.

Berger, T. *Fragile Freedoms*. Toronto: Clarke Irwin, 1982.

Cheffins, R.I., and P.A. Johnson. *The Revised Canadian Constitution: Politics as Law*. Toronto: McGraw-Hill Ryerson, 1976.

Finkelstein, M. *The Right to Counsel*. Toronto: Butterworths, 1988.

Gibson, D. *The Law of the Charter: General Principles*. Calgary: Carswell, 1986.

Hogg, P.W. *Meech Lake Constitutional Accord Annotated*. Toronto: Carswell, 1988.

———. *Constitutional Law of Canada*. 3d ed. Toronto: Carswell, 1992.

Laskin, B. "The Canadian Constitution after the First Century, Part 1." *Canadian Bar Review* 45 (1967): 395.

———. *Laskin's Canadian Constitutional Law*. 5th ed. Revised by N. Finkelstein. Toronto: Carswell, 1986.

Lederman, W.R. "Unity and Diversity in Canadian Federalism: Ideals and Methods of Moderation." *Alberta Law Review* 14 (1976): 34.

———. *Continuing Canadian Constitutional Dilemmas*. Toronto: Butterworths, 1981.

Mackenzie, J.A. "Planning of the B.N.A. Act." *Ottawa Law Review* 6 (1974): 332.

McDonald, D.C. *Legal Rights in the Canadian Charter of Rights and Freedoms*. 2d ed. Calgary: Carswell, 1989.

McDonald, R. St. J., and J.P. Humphrey, eds. *The Practice of Freedom*. Toronto: Butterworths, 1979.

McWhinney, E. "The Supreme Court of Canada and the Constitutional Division of Powers." *Supreme Court Conference* 55 (1986).

Mandel, M. *The Charter of Rights and the Legalization of Politics in Canada*. Toronto: Wall and Thompson, 1989.

Marshall, G. *Parliamentary Sovereignty and the Commonwealth*. Oxford: Clarendon Press, 1957.

Milne, D.A. *The Canadian Constitution*. 2d ed. Toronto: James Lorimer, 1991.

Monahan, P. *Politics and the Constitution: The Charter, Federalism and the Supreme Court of Canada*. Toronto: Carswell, 1987.

———. *Meech Lake: The Inside Story*. Toronto: University of Toronto Press, 1991.

Morton, F.L., ed. *Law, Politics and the Judicial System in Canada*. Calgary: University of Calgary Press, 1984.

Morton, J.C., and S.C. Hutchison. *Presumption of Innocence*. Toronto: Carswell, 1987.

Petter, A. "The Politics of the Charter." *Supreme Court Law Review* 8 (1986): 473.

Russell, P.H. "Constitutional Reform of the Canadian Judiciary." *Alberta Law Review* 7 (1969): 103.

———. *The Judiciary in Canada: The Third Branch of Government*. Toronto: McGraw-Hill Ryerson, 1987.

Saywell, J., and G. Vegh. *Making the Law: The Courts and the Constitution*. Mississauga: Copp Clark Pitman, 1991.

Schmeiser, D.A. "The Case Against Entrenchment of a Canadian Bill of Rights." *Dalhousie Law Journal* 1 (1973): 15.

Scott, F.R. "Canadian Federalism: The Legal Perspective." *Alberta Law Review* 5 (1967): 262.

Strayer, B.L. *The Canadian Constitution and the Courts*. 3d ed. Toronto: Butterworths, 1988.

Swinton, K. *The Supreme Court and Canadian Federalism*. Toronto: Carswell, 1990.

Tarnopolsky, W. "Just Desserts or Cruel and Unusual Treatment or Punishment? Where Do We Look For Guidance?" *Ottawa Law Review* 10 (1978): 1.

Tarnopolsky, W., and G.-A. Beaudoin, eds. *Canadian Charter of Rights and Freedoms: Commentary*. Toronto: Carswell, 1982.

Trudeau, P.E. "Constitutional Reform and Individual Freedoms." *Western Ontario Law Review* 8 (1969): 1.

Weiler, J., and R.M. Elliot, eds. *Litigating the Values of a Nation: The Canadian Charter of Rights and Freedoms*. Calgary: Carswell, 1986.

Weiler, P.C. "The Supreme Court of Canada and Canadian Federalism." *Osgoode Hall Law Journal* 11 (1973): 225.

CHAPTER 5

Canada's Courts: The Processes of Dispute Resolution

The following story forms part of a growing backdrop for Simon Fraser University's Centre for Restorative Justice. The speaker, Doug Borch, points to a victim–offender reconciliation that had benefits for both parties, and, ultimately, for society as well. As you read through this chapter, you might ask yourself about the role of restorative justice as we move further into the twenty-first century. It is a process that insists that a crime is not only an offence against the state, but an offence involving individuals.

Afternoon All—I have a nice quick story to send us all off for the holidays. A young guy committed a number of break and enters, and along with his family, met with two of the families in a community conference. Among other things, it was revealed that the boy and his family have serious financial struggles. While doing follow-up calls with one of the homeowners today, our facilitator, Darrel, relates that the husband wants to buy a turkey for the young guy and his family. This will be done tomorrow so they have it for Christmas dinner.

Not only does this boy have a far greater understanding of the impact of his decisions on others, but the homeowners now see him as far more than "the little ^%*&" who took away their sense of security. And they are far more than victims in the police report. These folks have redefined the rather ugly beginning of their relationship, beyond that of simply "victim" and "offender," and added some meat (as it were) to notions of "community." It seems rather a side note at this point, but it will be interesting to hear the judge's response to this when the lad returns for sentencing in the new year.

(Doug Borch. M.S.W., Coordinator, Children & Youth Services,
Calgary, Alberta < www.sfu.ca/crj/dborch >)

The Structure of Canada's Court System

Imagine the following scenario. A man steals a bottle of wine from a liquor store. After he leaves the store, while in the parking lot, he removes the bottle from under his jacket. He is noticed by a police officer, who begins to walk toward him.

The thief wields the bottle of liquor as a weapon and brings it crashing down on the police officer's jaw. With the police officer lying on the ground, the thief jumps into his car and drives off at high speed. He has gone no more than a kilometre when he loses control of the vehicle and plunges into a crowd of schoolchildren waiting for a bus. One child is killed.

The man is apprehended at the scene and jailed overnight. The next morning in **provincial court**, he faces an array of criminal charges: theft under $5 000, assaulting a police officer, impaired driving (his blood alcohol level was 0.18), and criminal negligence causing death.

One of the first things that he will learn from his lawyer is that Canada's court system—our criminal courts, our superior courts, and our courts of appeal—each have different jurisdictions. The man in the prisoner's dock can make some choices about where he appears to respond to these charges. He can elect, in some circumstances, to have his case determined by a jury of his peers.

And so it is crucial to understand the jurisdiction of each of Canada's courts—to understand the ultimate flow of power from the provincial courts to the **superior courts of the province**, on to the provincial courts of appeal, and from there to the **Supreme Court of Canada**.

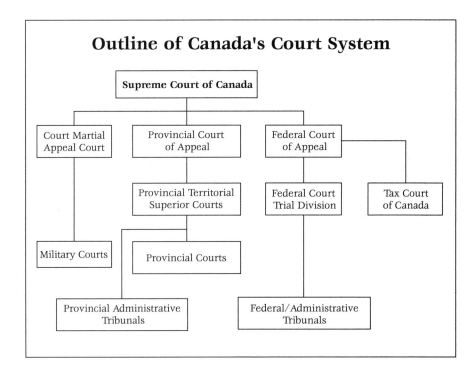

Outline of Canada's Court System

The diagram above sets out the flow of decision-making power within Canada's court system (www.canada.justice.ca). As you can see, the first decision-making bodies that an individual will encounter are either the provincial courts (criminal, family, and small claims), the military courts, provincial administrative tribunals (e.g., workers' compensation, human rights, labour relations, landlord–tenant relations) or federal administrative tribunals (e.g., parole, employment insurance, immigration). From these initial decision-making bodies, one can appeal to higher courts, typically to either the superior courts of the province, or the federal court, trial division, and then from there to provincial and federal courts of appeal, and finally to the Supreme Court of Canada.

The Provincial Courts

CRIMINAL DIVISION

- The Criminal Division of provincial court hears all summary conviction offences and all offences under provincial statutes, such as the *Motor Vehicle Act* and the *Liquor and Licensing Act*.
- The court hears all **indictable offences** under section 553 of the *Criminal Code.*[1] The primary difference between summary and indictable offences is that indictable offences typically have more serious consequences than summary offences. Section 553 of the *Criminal Code* states that "the jurisdiction of a provincial court judge to try an accused is absolute and does not depend on the consent of the accused where the accused is charged . . . with theft." Section 553 goes on to require that only thefts under $5 000 in value must be heard in provincial court. A few other offences are set out in section 553: keeping a gaming house, bookmaking, keeping a common bawdy house, and driving while disqualified are crimes that also fall within the absolute jurisdiction of the provincial court.
- The court may hear most indictable offences under the *Criminal Code* and the *Controlled Drugs and Substances Act*, except those listed under section 469 of the *Code*—essentially, murder, treason, piracy, sedition, and the bribing of the judiciary. Section 469 establishes an exclusive jurisdiction in the superior courts for the hearing of all charges of murder (and treason, piracy, and the others).
- The court hears all preliminary hearings when the accused elects to proceed with a preliminary hearing prior to a possible trial. Proposals have been put forward to eliminate more preliminary inquiries; an onus would be placed on an accused to demonstrate why a preliminary inquiry should be held before a trial; court backlogs and unnecessary costs could, arguably, be reduced.

Our man in the dock, charged with criminal negligence causing death, among other offences, could plead guilty to all his charges in provincial court. The charge of theft of the bottle of wine must be heard in provincial court since it is an offence under section 553 of the *Criminal Code*. But the accused could also elect to have his three indictable charges of impaired driving, criminal negligence causing death, and assaulting a police officer dealt with in provincial court.

In fact, only criminal negligence causing death is exclusively an indictable offence. The other two charges—impaired driving and assaulting a police officer—are classified as hybrid offences. With these hybrid offences, a prosecutor chooses to proceed either summarily or by indictment, depending upon the seriousness of the accused's specific actions. In this case, because of the loss of life and the conduct of the accused, the prosecutor would likely proceed by indictment in relation to impaired driving and assaulting a police officer.

Before turning to the superior courts of the provinces, the next step upward in the hierarchy of judicial decision making, we must first take a look at the other provincial courts. There are essentially two other kinds of provincial court: the youth and family courts, and the small claims courts. The youth and family courts, as the name implies, respond to the problems created by young offenders and attempt to resolve family disputes. The small claims courts are designed for citizens without lawyers; these courts allow the resolution of small financial disputes, up to a maximum of $10 000.

YOUTH AND FAMILY DIVISION

- The court in the Youth and Family Division hears matters arising out of disputes within families: separation, maintenance of children and spouses, custody, adoption, guardianship, child welfare, and divorce, where a unified family court system is in place.
- The court hears cases pursuant to the *Youth Criminal Justice Act,* as well as some criminal charges such as the assault or threatening of a spouse.
- The family court, with its emphasis on reconciliation and family harmony, is characterized by a greater informality and a less adversarial atmosphere than the Criminal Division.

SMALL CLAIMS DIVISION

- The Small Claims Division hears minor civil matters, outside the context of the family; in this court the average citizen can seek compensation without the assistance of a lawyer.

- The court is primarily concerned with the fields of contract and tort law, and is limited in its monetary jurisdiction—in most provinces, to amounts of less than $10 000.

The Superior Courts of the Provinces

TRIAL DIVISION

- The Trial Division of the provincial superior court hears indictable offences under section 469 (murder, piracy, bribery of the judiciary), as well as indictable offences by election of the accused. Trial can take place before a provincial court judge, a superior court judge sitting alone, or a superior court judge and jury.
- The court hears all civil cases within a given monetary jurisdiction— amounts larger than those permitted in either small claims court or county court.
- The court hears all libel and defamation actions.
- The court hears appeals from provincial court Criminal Division and Family Division, depending upon the jurisdiction in which the appeal is launched.
- The court hears divorces, except in those jurisdictions where unified family courts exist.

APPEAL DIVISION

- The court hears civil and family law appeals from the superior court (Trial Division), on questions of law, fact, and a mixture of law and fact.
- The court hears appeals of criminal cases from the superior court (Trial Division) on questions of law, fact, and a mixture of law and fact.

The Supreme Court of Canada

- The Supreme Court of Canada has been the court of last resort in the country since 1949. Composed of eight justices and one chief justice, the Court hears cases in panels of three, five, seven, or all nine members.
- The Court hears appeals in criminal cases from provincial courts of appeal when there has been dissent on a question of law in a three- or five-member decision. The Court also grants leave to hear appeals in criminal cases from provincial courts of appeal when there has been no dissent. Leave to appeal is a request for an appeal; the issue advanced in such circumstances must have public significance beyond the private interest of the party affected.

- The Court grants leave to hear appeals in civil cases if an issue of sufficient public importance is at stake.
- The Court hears references regarding constitutional matters, the division and sphere of powers for the federal and provincial governments, and any other matter of law that might be referred to it.
- Like provincial courts of appeal, the Supreme Court of Canada is a lawyer's court: lawyers typically appear before it to argue points of law, but the parties to a dispute do not appear.

The Federal Court of Canada

TRIAL DIVISION

- The Trial Division of the **Federal Court of Canada** has jurisdiction over civil matters—specifically, disputes created by actions of the federal government, its officers in the Armed Forces, and its employees.
- The court responds to disputes over trademarks, copyrights, patents of invention, and maritime law.
- The court may also hear appeals from citizenship courts and, with the consent of the parties, federal–provincial disputes.

APPEAL DIVISION

- The Appeal Division hears appeals from the Trial Division of the Federal Court of Canada.
- The division may hear appeals from decisions of federal boards, commissions, and tribunals, such as the Immigration Board, the Parole Board, and the Tax Appeal Board.

One final note about these different court jurisdictions. Provincial court judges—criminal court, family court, and small claims court judges—are all appointed by the provincial government. The judges sitting in the supreme courts of the provinces, the Federal Court, and the Supreme Court of Canada are federally appointed, on the advice of provincial bar associations.

The Courts, Law, and Social Control

Our man in the dock at the outset of this chapter would likely go to jail for his crimes, regardless of his lawyer and which court and which judge heard his case. More than 90 percent of those convicted of criminal offences plead guilty to all charges in the Criminal Division of provincial court. The overwhelming majority of those convicted do not appeal their conviction or sentence.

Canada's judges impose penalties, financial and otherwise; they require the fulfillment of contracts; order compensation for individual or corporate negligence; try to settle claims that arise between the federal and provincial governments; and perform numerous other tasks related to the resolution of disputes. It is against the complex and varied backdrop of public and private law that the courts try to reconcile competing interests within certain kinds of relationships: husband and wife, creditor and debtor, consumer and producer or distributor, the state and the deviant, one government and another.

In doing so, the courts set directions for social control in many areas of life. Sociologist Donald Black argues that all forms of law and all courts ultimately invoke one or more of four styles of social control: compensation, conciliation, punishment, or treatment. Criminal law, for example, is typically concerned with punishment and treatment, but can also provide compensation and conciliation. Family law is typically concerned with compensation and conciliation, but, on occasion, can impose punishment and/or treatment. The essential task of the court is to arrive at a productive and helpful blend of these ingredients, regardless of the specific context of private or public law.

Canadian Courts: Essential Characteristics

The Adversarial System

The most obvious characteristic of Canadian courts is that they bring down decisions within the context of an **adversarial system**. It has been assumed that "the truth" is most likely to emerge from a contest of two competing arguments. In Canada's courts, the strengths of one lawyer's claim are pitted against the strengths of the opposing claim, and, in the process of this "duel," the judge or **jury** is to arrive at a just decision or verdict. Accordingly, the adversarial system places its confidence in the counsel who appear before the court. The most common alternative to an adversarial system of justice is an **inquisitorial system**. This approach places greater expectations on judges, for they are required to ask relevant questions and to direct the investigation of the issues of a given case.

Law professor S.M. Waddams has noted of the adversarial system, "Procedural rules are designed to see that each party gets a fair hearing.

The role of the judge is not to discover what he may conceive to be 'the truth' but to act as an impartial arbiter. It is often said, without apology, that litigation is a game played according to rules of which the judge is umpire."[2] The adversarial system is therefore not ultimately concerned with finding "the" truth, but with choosing from among the truths presented by two competing advocates.

Herein lies a critical weakness of the adversarial system: counsel are equal neither in ability nor in cost. The strength and thoroughness of an individual's legal argument will depend, to a significant extent, upon the resources at his or her disposal. In other words, wealth can provide an individual—or a corporation—with particularly skilled counsel and meticulously researched, well-documented arguments, irrespective of the merits of the case. The response to this allegation concerning inequality is that all lawyers must meet the provincial law societies' minimum standards of competence in order to graduate from law school and enter the practice of law. The process provides the public with a minimum guarantee of competence.

Open Access to the Courts

Canadian courts are also characterized by openness and accessibility to the public. Any member of the public can enter virtually any courtroom in the country, and watch and listen to justice being dispensed. We have come a long way from the days of the **Star Chamber**, the British Privy Council's home from the fourteenth to the sixteenth centuries. The Star Chamber was an apartment in the royal palace where, protected from public scrutiny, the judiciary handed down often arbitrary judgments.

There is, however, one exception to the general rule of open courts. Under the *Youth Criminal Justice Act*, the proceedings of Canada's youth courts may be held *in camera* when, in the opinion of the judge, it is in the public interest to bar access. Section 132 of the *Youth Criminal Justice Act* states that the public may be excluded from all or part of the proceeding where "it would be in the interest of public morals, the maintenance of order, or the proper administration of justice to exclude any or all members of the public from the courtroom." In the early 1980s, a constitutional challenge to the validity of this exclusion was not successful. The Southam newspaper chain argued that the ban on access constituted a denial of the *Charter*'s guarantee of freedom of expression; the Ontario Court of Appeal ultimately rejected this argument.[3]

More recently, in the trial of serial rapist and killer Paul Bernardo, his own videotapes of his sex crimes were not made public in criminal court. Only the audio portion of the tapes was played in the courtroom;

there was no compelling reason for the public to watch these crimes taking place, particularly given the impact that such a presentation might have on the families and friends of Bernardo's young victims.

More common than a ban on access to Canadian courts is a ban on publication of their proceedings. The names of those convicted in youth court cannot, in most circumstances, be published. The rationale is that the stigma of arrest and conviction will be reduced, and that young offenders will be given an opportunity to change their behaviour without being publicly labelled as criminals. There are two exceptions to this publication ban. First, if a young person's trial is transferred to adult court, the defendant is treated as an adult offender and his or her name may be published. Second, a judge may permit the identification of a young person who is believed to have committed a crime and is at large when the judge is satisfied that "(a) there is reason to believe that the young person is dangerous to others; and (b) publication of the report is necessary to assist in apprehending the young person."[4]

In adult courts, counsel for the accused can (and usually does) request a ban on publication of the proceedings of a preliminary inquiry. The finding of the inquiry—the name of the accused, and whether there was sufficient evidence to commit the accused to trial—may be published, but specific evidence heard by the court cannot be published, since this might jeopardize the accused's right to receive a fair trial or the accused's standing within the community. The concern is that the press could communicate a misleading impression to potential judges or jurors, prior to a trial of the matter.

The preliminary hearing publication ban raises a fundamental question concerning the publication of the name of an accused prior to conviction. The right of the public to know who has been charged with criminal offences must be balanced against the presumption of innocence. By publishing the name of the accused, we run the risk that in the event of an acquittal, the individual will still be stigmatized by the initial charges. The public may be inclined to believe that a criminal charge is tantamount to a conviction, and ultimate acquittal may do little to alter this perception, particularly since acquittals seldom receive as much media attention as the laying of criminal charges. The contrary argument is that the public has the right to know—for its own safety and the safety of the community. A trial may take place months after initial charges have been laid, and the final disposition, after all appeals, may not take place until years later. In many senses, however, the issue is empirical: Is there evidence that public safety will be adversely affected by restricting publication of an accused's name until after a conviction has been handed down by the court that first hears the case?

There is one other context in which a limitation is placed on the open nature of courtroom proceedings. Section 486(1) of the *Criminal Code* states:

> Any proceedings against an accused shall be held in open court, but where the presiding judge, provincial court judge, or justice, as the case may be, is of the opinion that it is in the interest of public morals, the maintenance of order, or the proper administration of justice to exclude all or any members of the public from the court-room for all or part of the proceedings, he may so order.

The section, with its focus on the ambiguous concept of "public morals," is typically applied to sexual offences. Although Canadian courts have held that embarrassment of the complainant is not a sufficient reason to bar the public from the courtroom, the public *was* excluded in one definitive Ontario case after the court determined that the complainant would otherwise be too nervous to give her testimony.[5] Section 486(3) of the *Code* also provides Canadian judges with the power to direct that the identity of the complainant in a sexual offence or an offence of extortion "shall not be published in any document or broadcast in any way." The purpose of this ban on publication is to protect the privacy of the potential victim of a sexual offence or an extortion; this section has withstood constitutional challenge.

Finally, it is worth noting that, at present, only print journalists have full access to the proceedings of Canadian courts. Television cameras and tape recorders are generally not permitted to record the testimony of witnesses or the commentary of the judiciary, although Ontario typically permits audio recording devices, but not cameras or any visual recording apparatus. During the past decade, there has been substantial discussion about granting access to broadcast journalists; in the United States, such access has been commonplace for almost two decades. The trial of O.J. Simpson, conducted before a television audience of millions, high-lighted the differences between Canadian and U.S. approaches to media coverage of the trial process. In the aftermath of the Simpson trial, how-ever, many U.S. jurisdictions began rethinking the wisdom of permitting cameras in the courtroom; in 1996, the year after his acquittal on homi-cide charges, Simpson's civil trial for wrongful death was not televised.

Opponents of cameras in the courtroom have pointed to the often sensa-tionalistic tendencies of this visual medium. The rationale and complexity of court decisions may be ignored in favour of dramatic testimony or indi-vidual showmanship. It has also been suggested that by presenting only parts of a trial or of judicial commentary, the television camera will neces-sarily distort the full context of a case. In a worst-case scenario, a defendant may be judged more on physical attractiveness, race, gender, accent, eloquence—or his taste in ties—than on the specifics of the testimony.

The Supreme Court of Canada does permit television cameras in its courtroom (the Supreme Court is, of course, wholly concerned with matters of law and policy), and courts in Ontario will permit cameras if the judiciary and both counsel are supportive. But there is no access as a matter of right. To date, constitutional challenges to the restriction, on the ground of freedom of speech or freedom of expression, have been unsuccessful. The argument in favour of television coverage is that few Canadians attend courts; accordingly, few understand the structure of the court, the procedure employed, and the kinds of arguments typically made. A television camera can educate and inform the public, for example, about Canada's criminals and judges and why they do what they do or about family disintegration and the underlying social scripts. Print journalism conveys a sense of these issues and social problems, but broadcast journalism can add another layer of complexity to our understanding. There is some merit in the claim that a picture is worth a thousand words.

The Formality of the Courts

A third characteristic of Canadian courts is their air of formality. Justice is delivered by judges and justices who wear ritual garments and are elevated above the participants in the courtroom. Norwegian criminologist Nils Christie said of this display that the court's function is to appropriate the conflict of the citizens who appear before it. The conflict is appropriated through law enforcement and prosecution; it is reconstructed by the language and the drama of the courtroom.[6]

The atmosphere of formality in Canadian courts, like so much in Canadian law, harks back to British practice. The forms of address for those who sit in judgment reflect the level of court: Your Honour, Your Worship, My Lord. The use of these is more historical reflex than an accurate expression of the sentiments of counsel. In the United States, these vestiges of a monarchical past have been excised, though much of the formality of the court process has been retained.

It is imperative that a country's system of courts be worthy of its citizens' respect. Supporters of formality, such as law professor Gerald Gall, argue that it is therefore important that courtroom procedure be conducted within an "atmosphere of dignity and decorum":

> While some may argue that these formalities constitute a certain stuffiness, if not elitism, on the part of judges and lawyers, the counter-argument is more persuasive. This argument holds that by conforming to certain formalities, the court achieves the prestige it deserves, given the important function it exercises in society.[7]

The difficulty with Gall's argument is twofold. First, it equates manners with merit. More important, it does not adequately consider the attitudes and values of those subject to the rulings of Canadian courts, particularly those who do not share the educational, social, and economic backgrounds of an essentially upper-middle-class and overwhelmingly male judiciary. Consider, for example, the perception that many Aboriginal Canadians have of the court system:

> The general impression Dene people have of the court circuit is that a bunch of strangers, most of whom are non-Native people, have come to town. They see the court proceedings as very strict and formal, and for most of them, scary.
>
> I was always impressed with a Cree who is involved in the James Bay communities in the courts. He was asked by the translator to put his hand on the Bible and swear to tell the truth, the whole truth, and nothing but the truth. He replied: "I would never be able to tell the whole truth and nothing but the truth; all I would be able to do is tell you what I know."
>
> The psychology of the legal system is a very complex one, especially to Native people who are not bilingual. People who do not speak both languages are passive in the administration of justice. They know what the sentence is and how long they can go to jail, but they do not really know the intricacies of the legal system. The communication process should not be a one-way exchange. People should not be bystanders; they should be participants who know what is happening to them.[8]

It is not only Aboriginal Canadians who may be restricted in their dialogue with the courts. Legal representation is a costly enterprise, particularly if one wishes to pursue one's case through the court hierarchy. Most economically disadvantaged Canadians experience Canadian courts only in the context of criminal or family law; their tragedies and conflicts are determined and resolved for better or for worse. From their research interviews with more than 100 individuals charged with criminal offences, sociologists Richard Ericson and Patricia Baranek concluded:

> Given that the accused rarely speaks or is given the opportunity to speak, it is highly unlikely that a benevolent, well-meaning court would have any knowledge of the accused's comprehension. Rather than the court attempting to make the proceedings comprehensible, the onus is on the accused to inform the court that he does not understand. However, given the anxiety and stage fright that most

accused suffer, this is unlikely. . . . [E]ven when asked if they understand, accused are reluctant to say no because they feel powerless,
they don't want to appear incompetent, and/or they are too nervous
to say anything.

It might be assumed that it is the lawyer's role to ensure that
the accused comprehends the court's discourse. On the contrary,
the lawyer is usually left to "do the understanding" for the accused
and to order the accused in a way that does not encourage the
accused even to seek understanding, let alone acquire it.[9]

This is a harsh indictment of our court system, standing in marked contrast to Gall's claim that Canadian courts have "achieved the prestige
[they] deserve." Perhaps the differences between Gall's perceptions and
those of Ericson and Baranek are explained by considering the lens
through which these academics are observing "the ordering of justice."
From the point of view of the judiciary, judicial administrators, and
most lawyers, Canadian courts operate in an atmosphere of prestige,
dignity, and decorum that mirrors their nature. To those who are subject
to the courts' judgments but are not stakeholders in the system, the
atmosphere and the very nature of the courts might, if only occasionally, be described as elitist, arrogant, and self-congratulatory.

The Purposes of Canadian Courts and the Standards for Judgments

As mentioned earlier, the four styles of social control used by the courts
are compensation, conciliation, punishment, and treatment. No single
one of these purposes is common to all Canadian courts. Canada's civil
courts respond to disputes between a plaintiff and a respondent; the
plaintiff may be asserting rights in relation to a contract, a will, a failed
marriage, or the negligence of the respondent. In these circumstances,
the task of the court is to compensate the plaintiff or to seek some
means of conciliating the parties. The nature and form of the compensation or conciliation will vary according to the type of law before the
court. The outcome in civil cases depends upon a balance of probabilities: a plaintiff must establish that his or her claim is more probable
than not in order to be successful. In other words, the plaintiff's case
must be given a better than 50 percent likelihood of legitimacy. If the
respondent's defence or counterclaim is seen to be equally or more
valid, the plaintiff's action will be lost.

Criminal courts act on behalf of the state—that is, in the collective interests of all Canadians. In the realm of criminal law, punishment and treatment are preeminent. The court has two separate tasks: first, it must establish the guilt of the accused; second, it must prescribe an appropriate punishment or treatment. In prescribing treatments and/or punishments, criminal courts are guided by the principles of (1) general deterrence—deterring the general public from committing the crime—(2) specific deterrence—deterring the specific defendant from committing future crimes—and (3) rehabilitation—assistance to prepare the convicted person for community reintegration and ultimate abstinence from criminal activity.

The former chief justice of the Supreme Court of Canada, Antonio Lamer, suggested that courts fulfill two functions in Canadian society: they provide a **conflict resolution** service and perform a "dramatization function."[10] The dramatization function is held to be particularly applicable to criminal law, wherein the penalties serve dramatically to reaffirm societal values. It is not clear, however, that a core of commonly held values exists in all realms of the criminal law. While crimes against persons and against property are almost universally seen as offending societal values, there is substantial debate about so-called victimless crimes, including certain kinds of drug use, consensual sexual behaviours, and gambling. In these realms, it is more difficult to assert that criminal punishments reaffirm core values. What they reaffirm, instead, is a somewhat controversial status quo—a dominant majority typically asserts its world-view over a reluctant minority.

Even in the case of crimes against persons or property, it can be argued that there may be less consensus about the need to dramatize commonly held values than the former chief justice has suggested. While Canadians overwhelmingly reject and abhor violence, theft, and fraud, we have no consensus on the form that punishments should take in response, or—to use the language of the former chief justice—the form that the dramatization function should take.

In criminal courts, the judge or jury must be satisfied that an accused's guilt has been established beyond a reasonable doubt by the prosecuting lawyer. This standard is difficult to quantify. The judge or jury may be less than 100 percent certain of guilt—perhaps 90 to 95 percent certain—yet convict the accused. Convictions are probably assigned when levels of certainty of guilt are in the range of 90 or 95 percent. In other words, the balance that criminal courts strike between convicting the guilty and protecting the rights of the innocent is not absolute; there are likely to be occasional mistakes. Human beings are not infallible; consequently, a human system of criminal justice is not infallible.

The Case of David Milgaard: Responding to the Fallibility of the Courts

On the morning of January 31, 1969, Gail Miller left her rooming house in Saskatoon to take a bus to her job as a nurse's assistant at a local hospital. It was –42°C and visibility was poor because of ice crystals in the air. Gail Miller never arrived at work; shortly after dawn, her body was discovered in a back alley near her home. She had been raped and stabbed eleven times.

A little more than four months later, David Milgaard was arrested and charged with the murder of Gail Miller. Milgaard was a 16-year-old who had been driving through Saskatoon on the morning of the killing with two teenaged companions, Nichol John and Ron Wilson. The three teenagers were looking for their friend Albert "Shorty" Cadrain. After finding him several hours later, all four left the city about noon to buy marijuana in Alberta.

The prosecution argued at trial that shortly before 7:00 on the morning of the murder, the teenagers' car had become stuck in snow and ice. Milgaard was said to be away from the car for about 15 minutes, ostensibly looking for help. It was during this time that he is alleged to have found Miller, raped her, and stabbed her to death. He then returned to the car, and he and his companions continued to search for the home of Cadrain, obtaining a map at a motel within about 20 minutes of the killing. The motel manager testified at trial that Milgaard was polite and friendly in asking for directions. He did not see any blood on Milgaard or any indication that he had just participated in a struggle.

At trial, Milgaard's companions implicated him in the murder. Although Wilson, John, and Cadrain had all initially rejected suggestions that any one of them was responsible, they later provided damning testimony. Wilson and Cadrain testified that they had seen blood on Milgaard that morning, and John told police that she had seen Milgaard stab a woman, then drag her into an alley, ostensibly to rape her.

The jury convicted Milgaard of non-capital murder, and in January 1970, he was sentenced to life imprisonment. His appeals to the provincial court of appeal and the Supreme Court of Canada were unsuccessful. Throughout 22 years of imprisonment, Milgaard never ceased to maintain that he did not kill Gail Miller. In the late 1980s, with the assistance of Winnipeg lawyers Hersh Wolch and David Asper, Milgaard applied to the minister of justice, Kim Campbell, requesting that his case be reopened. A mistake had been made by the court, he argued.

Like all Canadians who have exhausted their appeals, he relied on section 690 of the *Criminal Code*:

> 690. The Minister of Justice may, upon an application for the mercy of the Crown by or on behalf of a person who has been convicted in proceedings by indictment . . .
>
>   (a)   direct, by order in writing, a new trial . . . before any court that he thinks proper, if after inquiry he is satisfied that in the circumstances a new trial or hearing, as the case may be, should be directed;
>
>   (b)   refer the matter at any time to the court of appeal for hearing and determination by that court as if it were an appeal by the convicted person . . . or
>
>   (c)   refer to the court of appeal at any time, for its opinion, any question on which he desires the assistance of that court, and the court shall furnish its opinion accordingly.

There was also new evidence in the *Milgaard* case. Wilson, who had testified that he had seen blood on Milgaard at trial, told private investigators that he had lied in order to "get the police off my back." He said that he and John had agreed to "sink" Milgaard in order to stop persistent police questioning. John's claim that she witnessed the stabbing had been revealed, even at trial, to be an impossibility. Her description required that there be knife cuts in Miller's dress; there were none, since the dress had been removed before Miller was stabbed. And Cadrain, the first to claim that he had seen blood on Milgaard, was found to be a highly unreliable witness. Within a year of the trial, he was committed to a psychiatric institution. In the early 1970s, he alleged that another individual had committed a crime. This allegation was found by police to be without foundation.

In 1990, an alternative scenario emerged for the morning of the murder. The defence learned of an unusual coincidence: a serial rapist by the name of Larry Fisher had been living in the basement of the Cadrain home at the time of the murder. In the months before the Miller murder, Fisher had abducted three women in Saskatoon, held knives to their throats, and raped them in back alleys. On other occasions, he had stabbed and beaten his rape victims; everything done to Miller, he had done to other women. Fisher was not a suspect at the time of the Miller murder, though Saskatoon police reported to the media immediately after the killing that they believed the crime was related to a number of unsolved rapes in the neighbourhood. Fisher was not apprehended for these rapes until months after David Milgaard's conviction.

The minister of justice, faced with this evidence, initially turned down Milgaard's application for a new trial. In a 12-page decision handed down in February 1991, Campbell claimed that Wilson's testimony was not credible, that Cadrain's was credible, and that there was no good evidence against Fisher. The following November, she changed her mind, after front-page stories about the case in *The Globe and Mail* and *The Toronto Star*. Campbell ordered a hearing before the Supreme Court of Canada. At the conclusion of that hearing, David Milgaard was set free after more than 23 years in jail.

The *Milgaard* case raises questions about the justice system and the manner in which it responds to its inevitable fallibility. What is the burden of proof that must be met by an accused in section 690 of the *Criminal Code*? Should an accused have to establish innocence on a balance of probabilities? Or beyond a reasonable doubt? The section gives no guidance as to the standard to be employed in those instances in which fallibility in the justice system is alleged.

The courts have made mistakes on other occasions as well. Donald Marshall was set free in the 1980s and financially compensated after being wrongfully convicted of a murder that another man ultimately confessed to. However, the issue is not that the Canadian justice system, like all other justice systems, makes mistakes. Rather, it is whether our justice system is equipped to respond fairly and effectively to allegations of wrongful conviction.

In its review of David Milgaard's conviction, the Supreme Court set out to answer three key questions: Can Milgaard establish his innocence beyond a reasonable doubt? Is it more likely than not that Milgaard is innocent? If a new trial were to be held today, would there be a similar result? The Supreme Court concluded that Milgaard's innocence could not be established either beyond a reasonable doubt or on a balance of probabilities. As regards the third question, the Court could not be sure that if a new trial were held, a conviction would be forthcoming. Accordingly, it decided that a new trial was in order. The Province of Saskatchewan decided not to proceed with a new trial, however, citing cost and compassion, and David Milgaard was set free in April 1992. He was not found to be either innocent or guilty; nor was he found to be deserving of any compensation.

It was not until the summer of 1997 that the Province of Saskatchewan changed its approach to the *Milgaard* case, apologizing to him for his wrongful conviction and offering compensation. DNA test results from London, England, had confirmed what many observers of the case had believed for years: there was no DNA match between Milgaard and Gail Miller; there was, however, a DNA match with Larry Fisher. Fisher is now in jail, after being convicted in 1999 of first degree murder.

For those who followed the *Milgaard* case, or the cases of Guy Paul Morin and Donald Marshall, questions remain, particularly about the way in which our justice system responds to claims of fallibility within its courts. With Milgaard, Saskatchewan convened an inquiry into his conviction; that inquiry should conclude with a report in late 2006. More generally, however, what should be the standard—the burden of proof—in circumstances in which allegations of wrongful conviction are made? What procedure should the minister of justice employ in evaluating claims like Milgaard's? And in what circumstances should compensation be contemplated?

There is one additional lesson from the *Milgaard* and *Morin* cases. We should probably be skeptical of human abilities in the realm of determination of guilt. In both the Morin and Milgaard cases, it was science—the technology of DNA testing—that set innocent men free; our system of justice was exposed as more fragile and fallible. In the context of an issue such as capital punishment, this fragility and fallibility is particularly critical, given our long-standing commitment to the notion that it is better to let a guilty man go free than to convict—and execute—an innocent man.

By a Jury of One's Peers

In Canada's criminal courts, the general public is involved in the determination of guilt, through the mechanism of the jury. There are also jury trials, albeit in more limited circumstances, in civil cases. In the United States, jury trials are common in both criminal and civil cases. In fact, it has been estimated that 80 percent of all the world's jury trials take place there. It is also permissible in the United States to speak to jurors after the trial about the jury's deliberation. In Canada, by contrast, section 649 of the *Criminal Code* makes disclosure of jury proceedings a summary conviction offence, punishable by a fine of up to $2 000 and imprisonment of up to six months. The Canadian position is that post-deliberation inquiries can serve only to impeach or undermine jury verdicts, thereby weakening the value of the jury to the justice system.

Considerable debate has taken place about the value of the jury to the court structure. Critics assert that the business of law is too complex to be left to "amateurs." The former dean of Harvard Law School, E.N. Griswold, once noted, "The jury trial is the apotheosis of the amateur. Why should anyone think that twelve persons brought in from the street, selected in various ways for their lack of general ability, should have any special capacity for deciding controversies?"[11] Similarly, the British legal scholar Glanville Williams remarked, "[I]t is an understatement to describe a jury . . . as a group of twelve men of average ignorance."[12] And the American jurist and academic Jerome Frank asserted, "While the jury can contribute nothing of value so far as the law is concerned, it has infinite capacity for mischief, for twelve men can easily misunderstand more law in a minute than the judge can explain in an hour."[13]

Those who defend the jury system maintain that the collective intelligence of 12 decision makers is almost always an improvement upon the fact-finding abilities of a single judge. And, as jury experts Hans and Vidmar have noted, juries will often apply standards of community fairness and equity to a case, whereas a judge, preoccupied with the technicalities of the law, would tend to ignore these essentially democratic principles:

> Newspapers recently carried an article about a woman who shot her common-law husband. For fifteen years, she had suffered physical abuse and threats of death from him. He threatened to kill her if she reported the assaults to the police. Finally, she purchased a gun. When her husband again attacked her in a drunken rage, she took the gun and shot him in the leg. Because of the premeditated nature of her act, a judge would have felt compelled to follow the letter of the law and find her guilty, but the jury acquitted her. In short, the jury differs from the judge on the values it brings to the case and on the freedom to apply those values.[14]

The *Morgentaler* case offers another illustration of the jury's imposition of democratic values upon the authority of the courts. The law respecting abortion was ultimately struck down by the Supreme Court of Canada in 1988; one of the catalysts for this legal change was the continued inability of prosecutors to obtain jury convictions,[15] although the case was ultimately decided on constitutional grounds.

The trial of O.J. Simpson in California also raised questions about the role of the jury in criminal and civil cases. Simpson, a Black male, was acquitted by a largely Black jury in October 1995, after a lengthy trial in which DNA evidence had clearly connected him to his two victims, Nicole Brown Simpson and Ronald Goldman. The jury heard, however, of the alleged racism of one white police officer and of claims that some members of the Los Angeles Police Department may have conspired to frame Simpson for these horrific crimes. The jury, with a legacy of oppression against Blacks in the United States as its backdrop, chose to exercise a reasonable doubt in favour of Simpson. A year later, the largely white civil jury that convened to hear a claim of wrongful death against Simpson was more inclined to believe the DNA evidence; it rendered a substantial financial judgment against the former football star.

In both these instances, juries imposed their own long-standing perceptions of justice, crime, and race in their verdicts.

The injection of community sentiments into the determination of guilt in criminal cases, or even into civil cases, raises questions about the limits that should be imposed upon the power of the jury. The many examples of juries in Canada, England, and the United States refusing to support unpopular laws ring alarm bells for those concerned about the dangers of juries displacing lawmakers. While a jury may well embrace progressive and democratic sentiments within its decisions, it is as likely to embody community prejudices that reaffirm racism, religious bigotry, sexism, and other kinds of bias and intolerance.

Recently, in some U.S. trials, the jury's role has moved away from the principle of community representation. U.S. law typically demands jurors to be "death-qualified"—that is, to serve on a jury in most states permitting capital punishment, a citizen must support the death penalty. In California, for example, jurors must be willing to vote for guilt or innocence, and, in the second stage of the trial, to vote for death. In one California study, researchers found that 21 percent of the population would not find an accused guilty if they knew that the death penalty could be imposed. A further 17 percent said that they could not vote for the death penalty, but would be willing to determine guilt in a capital case with an open mind. Thus, almost 40 percent of the state's population is excluded from jury trials in capital cases. Hans and Vidmar commented on these research findings:

> These figures tell us that a significant number of otherwise eligible jurors will automatically be excluded from capital-murder juries. . . . Women and blacks are more likely to be in both of these groups. So are Jews, atheists, and agnostics. So are poor people and Democrats. To put it the other way around, the typical juror in a capital-murder trial is more likely to be wealthier, a Protestant or a Catholic, a Republican, male, and white. In short, juries in death-penalty cases are not representative of the population, or similar to other juries.[16]

In a Canadian survey of jury responsibilities, psychologist Anthony Doob asked both the general public and the Canadian judiciary whether individual jurors should decide cases according to their own consciences, ignoring the law if doing so would produce a just result. More than 75 percent of the general public believed that jurors should have the right to nullify unfair laws, but fewer than 5 percent of Canadian judges were in favour of giving this power to citizens.[17]

Courtroom Delay: The Right to Be Tried "Within a Reasonable Time"

In Chapter 4, we discussed the *Askov* case as a significant development of the *Canadian Charter of Rights and Freedoms* focusing on the rights of the accused. For Canada's court system, *Askov* was even more significant, since it represented a call from the judiciary to government about the need for more court resources.

Askov and his associates did not initially appear to be the sort of accused who were likely to gain the sympathy of the court. They provided nightclubs with exotic dancers, and had been charged with possession of a prohibited weapon, possession of a weapon for a purpose dangerous to the public peace, pointing a firearm, and assault with a weapon. The three accused were at first denied bail. They remained in jail from November 1983 until May 1984. They were then released, pending the outcome of the trial, on a recognizance of $50 000 each. They were required to report to police on a regular basis, as well as to abstain from communicating with one another.

A preliminary hearing for the three men began in July 1984, but could not be completed because of a conflict in the court's timetable. The preliminary was finally completed in late September 1984, almost 10 months after the initial arrests. Because of a crowded court schedule, the first available date for the trial of the accused was in October 1985, almost two years after the arrests. When the date arrived, it became clear that there would not be sufficient time for the trial to be held during the fall sitting after all. Accordingly, the case was put over to September 1986—almost three years after the initial arrests. At that time, counsel for the accused argued that a stay of proceedings should be entered since the right of the accused to a fair trial within a reasonable time had been unfairly violated by courtroom delays. The presiding judge agreed, taking the position that the delay was not attributable to the accused, but the result of institutional problems. District Court Judge Bolan wrote: "I am satisfied that the reason for the delay was caused by the insufficient institutional resources in the Judicial District of Peel. . . . It is obvious that this jurisdiction lacks sufficient resources to meet the demands and administer the criminal justice system with minimal delay. This has caused a systemic delay in the administration of justice."[18]

Delays in Canadian courts had been a matter of judicial and political concern since the early 1980s. In 1986, Justice Thomas Zuber of the Ontario Court of Appeal was appointed to conduct a study of the Ontario court system in response to escalating court costs, together with increasingly lengthy delays in gaining access to the courts. Justice Zuber released his report in 1987, noting, among other things, that some districts were particularly slow in bringing cases to court for disposition, and that a "delay reduction strategy" was imperative. The Ontario government's response to Justice Zuber's report was to introduce such a strategy, which included pilot projects in six areas of the province identified as having the most serious problems of delay. The government also suggested funding for increased staff—13 judges, 24 Crown attorneys, and support staff—and improvements to existing facilities.

The decision handed down by Judge Bolan in *Askov* was taken to the Ontario Court of Appeal, which upheld the prosecutor's argument that the rights of the accused to trial within a reasonable time had not been infringed. The Court of Appeal found, first, that there was no misconduct on the part of the Crown with respect to the delay; second, that there was no objection made by any of the accused to the various adjournments; and third, that there was no evidence of prejudice to the accused as a consequence of the delay.

Askov and his associates appealed to the Supreme Court of Canada, which issued its decision in October 1990. The Court noted a number of factors to be taken into account when determining whether a court delay is sufficient to deprive an accused of the right to trial within a reasonable time: the length of the delay, the explanation for the delay (such as the conduct of the Crown, systemic or institutional delays, or the conduct of the accused), the accused's waiver of rights, and prejudice to the accused. On this basis, the Supreme Court rejected the Ontario Court of Appeal's claim that the accused in *Askov* had waived their right to trial within a reasonable time. Justice Cory wrote:

> [T]here was no explicit waiver of their rights by the appellants. . . . The term "waiver" indicates that a choice has been made between available options. When the entire record of the proceedings . . . is read, it becomes crystal clear that the appellants had no choice as to the date of the trial. . . . The silence of the appellants or their failure to raise an objection to a long delay is certainly not enough in the circumstances to infer waiver. Rather, the onus rests upon the Crown to demonstrate that the actions of the accused amounted to an agreement to the delay, or waiver of their right.[19]

The Supreme Court also noted that the delays in the judicial district of Peel were more substantial than in virtually all other districts in the country. This deviation from the norm became an important part of the decision: "The usual delays in Peel are more than four times as long as those of busy metropolitan districts in the Province of Quebec and the delay in this case, is more than eight times as long."[20]

The *Askov* case highlights a conflict between competing interests. On the one hand, the crimes that the accused were alleged to have committed were very serious; armed violence stands in stark opposition to the values of a civilized society. But the *Charter* enshrines the right to be tried within a reasonable time. Justice Cory commented on this conflict:

> Extortion and threatened armed violence tear at the basic fabric of society. To accede to such conduct would constitute a denial of the rule of law and an acceptance of a rule that unlawful might makes right. . . . There can be no doubt that it would be in the best interest of society to proceed with the trial of those who are charged with posing such a serious threat to the community. Yet, that trial can only be undertaken if the *Charter* right to trial within a reasonable time has not been infringed. In this case, that right has been grievously infringed and the sad result is that a stay of proceedings must be entered.[21]

Other cases heard since the *Askov* decision have clarified and refined the right to be tried within a reasonable time.[22]

Emerging Models of Conflict Resolution: Mediation and Restorative Justice

There has been an understandable frustration with the time and cost required for courtroom litigation of both civil and criminal disputes. In the realm of family law it is often fairly said that all parties lose when they proceed to contest their claims in the courtroom. And while the adversarial system of justice remains in place within family law, developments over the past two decades have at least modified the centrality of the adversarial approach to the breakdown of relationships.

Mediation involves the use of an independent third party whose task is to attempt to bring the parties to agreement. The goal of the mediator is not to impose a decision on the two litigants but to encourage them to come to a mutual agreement about the issues in dispute—matrimonial property, support, and/or custody of children. If mediation fails, the court process is the obvious fallback position. But there are many good reasons for engaging in mediation: it is usually much less expensive, the parties themselves can come to terms—rather than having terms imposed upon them, and an ongoing monitoring of the settlement can also be a part of the agreement (allowing for greater future flexibility, since the situations of the parties will inevitably change).

At the same time, however, no clear standards have been set out with respect to the qualifications required of a mediator. The mediator may or may not be a lawyer. In fact, many mediators have no legal training, but rely rather on their training and skills in social work, psychology, or psychiatry for their expertise; still others have no formal educational training. Given this backdrop, there is a significant risk for the consumer of these services. Law is, after all, the system that prescribes appropriate remedies for disputes, whether in the realm of family law, contract, or property. And those who trust their legal rights to individuals who have no legal training may well be doing themselves a great disservice. Perhaps the future of mediation can be found in what has been termed "collaborative divorce," a term that might seem, at first glance, to be an oxymoron. Collaborative divorce brings an interdisciplinary team of professionals to the task at hand: a lawyer with a specialty in family law, a psychologist or social worker, and a financial counsellor. Courses that canvass and detail this process of collaborative separation and divorce are now offered, for example, by provincial legal education societies.

Those who practise criminal law have also seen the emergence of alternative models to the judiciary's traditional sentencing paradigms of punishment and treatment. More specifically, section 718.2(e) of the *Criminal Code* states: "(e) [A]ll available sanctions other than imprisonment that are reasonable in the circumstances should be considered for all offenders, with particular attention to the circumstances of [A]boriginal offenders." This section directs the judiciary to hand down a sentence to the Aboriginal offender that is different from sentences for other offenders. In *R. v. Gladue*,[23] the Supreme Court held that because of systemic discrimination and markedly different circumstances, principles of **restorative justice** must be applied alongside or in place of the more traditional sentencing principles. The Court held that an Aboriginal offender's community will often understand the nature of a just penalty very differently from non-Aboriginal communities.

Both the *Gladue* decision and the legislation that spawned it (section 718.2(e) of the *Criminal Code*) have been subject to considerable public criticism, from both within and outside Aboriginal communities. It remains to be seen whether this different treatment will ultimately be perceived as just by the Aboriginal community, and/or by the larger national community of Canadians. In the interim, the decision does appear to prompt a number of empirical questions: Is crime committed by Aboriginals "different" in its origins and its consequences? Is there a consensus within Aboriginal communities to support this kind of restorative rather than punitive approach to the sentencing of offenders? And does the broader community view this response as a violation of equality provisions—or as an important initiative consistent with section 15(2) of the *Charter,* an approach that has both its intent and its consequences in the amelioration of the conditions of one category of especially disadvantaged Canadians? We can only await the verdict of the next few decades.

But regardless of the ultimate impact of *Gladue,* it is clear that restorative justice has emerged within the past decade as a significant development within the criminal justice systems of Canada and most other Western industrialized nation-states. The following question-and-answer posting from Justice Canada's website highlights the increasing importance of restorative justice (www.canada.justice.gc.ca):

> Restorative justice is one way to respond to a criminal act. Restorative justice puts the emphasis on the wrong done to a person as well as on the wrong done to the community. It recognizes that crime is both a violation of relationships between specific people and an offence against everyone—the state.
>
> Restorative justice programs involve the voluntary participation of the victim of the crime and the offender and ideally members of the community, in discussions. The goal is to "restore" the relationship, fix the damage that has been done and prevent further crimes from occurring.
>
> Restorative justice requires wrongdoers to recognize the harm they have caused, to accept responsibility for their actions and to be actively involved in improving the situation. Wrongdoers must make reparation to victims, themselves and the community.
>
> What are some examples of restorative justice programs?
>
> All restorative justice programs have some common elements. They seek healing, forgiveness and active community involvement. The programs can take place at different times after a crime has occurred—sometimes after charges have been laid; sometimes after an accused has been found guilty of an offence.
>
> Some examples of restorative justice programs include:
> * victim offender mediation;
> * family group conferencing;
> * sentencing circles;
> * consensus-based decision-making on the sentence; and
> * victim offender reconciliation panels.
>
> Good restorative justice programs have well-trained facilitators who are sensitive to the needs of victims and offenders, who know the

community in which the crime took place and who understand the dynamics of the criminal justice system.

How do victims of crime benefit from restorative justice programs?

The restorative justice process provides victims with the opportunity to express their feelings about the harm that has been done to them and to contribute their views about what is required to put things right. Some studies of restorative justice programs show that victims who are involved in the process are often more satisfied with the justice system and are more likely to receive restitution from the offender. Involvement can also help victims heal emotionally as well as lessen their fear of the offender and of being a victim of crime again.

However, restorative justice programs can be time-consuming and emotionally draining. For some crime victims, meeting the offender is difficult. The criminal justice system is working out ways to make sure that restorative justice programs give victims a voice in the process without pressuring them to participate or causing them more distress.

Does a victim of crime have to participate in restorative justice?

No. A victim's participation is voluntary. To help a victim decide whether or not to participate in a restorative justice program, the victim should be given complete information about the restorative justice process, possible outcomes, her or his role, the role of the offender and other process participants, as well as information about the criminal justice system options.

The fundamental principle is that restorative justice must not re-victimize the victim in any way. The process and the outcome should not cause further harm.

Whether or not a victim of crime participates in a restorative justice program, she or he is entitled to all the victims' services that are available in the community.

Are restorative justice programs in place across Canada?

There is a growing number of restorative justice initiatives under way across the country. More programs are being put in place all the time.

Will restorative justice programs replace other criminal justice system responses to criminal behaviour?

No. There will always be the need for a court process. Restorative justice can only take place when:

* an offender admits guilt, accepts responsibility for his or her actions and agrees to participate in the program;
* the victim of the crime freely agrees to participate in the program, without feeling pressured to do so; and
* trained facilitators are available in the community and a restorative justice program is in place.

Conclusion: Future Prospects for the Courts and Court Reform

Among other topics, this chapter has discussed two difficulties currently facing Canadian courts: first, delay in the administration of justice and, second, the legal response to the inevitable fallibility of judges and juries in making decisions. The resolution of the problem of delay appears to require certain changes in the jurisdictions most affected, including the construction of new facilities; the provision of more judges, Crown attorneys, and support staff; and the integration of existing court structures—for example, collapsing the county courts into the provincial superior courts (Trial Division).[24] The problem of the fallibility of the courts is more difficult, particularly in the case of criminal trials. The existing law, section 690 of the *Criminal Code*, does not specify what procedure is to be employed in such instances; and until governments can acknowledge the inevitability of mistakes, it seems unlikely that the necessary reforms will take place.

Various movements within the Canadian court system have taken shape within the last two decades. First, there is an increasing use of diversion for first-time offenders, particularly young offenders. The purpose of diversion—a community-based response—is twofold: to reserve the courts for the most serious cases and, by taking the offender out of the court process, to lessen the likelihood of stigmatization of the offender by the judicial process.

Related to the practice of diversion is the increasing involvement of the community within the justice system. This development can take the form of the community-service orders that flow from both youth and adult courts; lobby groups created as a reaction against specific crimes (Victims of Violence, Mothers Against Drunk Driving); or the development of alternative systems of dispute resolution, particularly within Aboriginal communities.

A third movement in the court system appears in the considerable amount of administrative law designed to enable boards, commissions, and tribunals to become alternatives to courts when specific expertise in decision making is deemed necessary. The National Parole Board, the Workers' Compensation Review Board, the Industrial Relations Council, and the Labour Relations Board are federal and provincial agencies that currently function as courts within specified spheres of expertise. They tend to be less formal and less rigorously structured than the court system.

Canada's court structure has its strengths—openness and accessibility—but it also has its weaknesses—delay and fallibility. There are many possibilities for improvement in making the courtroom more accessible and more democratic, and in the construction of a better legal mechanism for responding to allegations of judge and jury fallibility. The task ahead is to build on what we have accomplished, mindful that the open court, operating with public support, is the linchpin of any civilized nation-state.

Web Links

Department of Justice Canada: Publications
http://canada.justice.gc.ca/en/dept/pub/trib/index.html
This page of the website of the Department of Justice Canada provides details of Canada's court system. The site also offers extensive information on the Justice Department and its programs and services, including matters such as access to information, child access and custody, electronic commerce, youth justice, and victims of crime.

Justice Manitoba
http://www.gov.mb.ca/justice/index.shtml
This is the home page for Manitoba's Justice Department. It has links to matters of provincial jurisdiction such as family law, including information about domestic violence.

Manitoba Justice: Court Processes
http://www.gov.mb.ca/justice/court/index.html
A site accessed through Manitoba's Justice Department, this page provides an excellent resource for information on the court system in Manitoba.

Supreme Court of Canada
http://www.scc-csc.gc.ca/

This is the home page of the court of last resort in Canada. Its functions and mandate are explained on the website, which also contains links to judgments.

Federal Court of Canada
http://www.fct-cf.gc.ca/index_e.html

The website of the Federal Court of Canada provides details of the court's work: its functions and mandate; its judges, decisions, and publications. It is linked to the online Federal Court Reports, which can be accessed through a search engine.

Australian Law Reform Commission
http://www.alrc.gov.au/publications/index.htm

Canada and Australia share a similar juridical history because of their shared links to Britain and their implementation of a common-law system. Australians have been struggling with issues of law and justice reform, which are similar to some of the issues of concern in Canada. This website provides access to online publications of the Australian Law Reform Commission on diverse topics, such as judicial reform, children in the legal system, and matrimonial law review.

Law Commission of Canada
http://www.lcc.gc.ca/

The Law Commission of Canada is an independent federal law reform agency that advises Parliament on how to improve and modernize Canada's law. The website has links to, among others, the Access to Justice Network, which in turn has links to information about Alternative Dispute Resolution and websites devoted to this. The Law Commission's site itself has information on restorative justice and transformative justice.

Department of Justice Canada: Applications to the Minister of Justice for a Conviction Review Under Section 690 of the *Criminal Code*
http://www.justice.gc.ca/en/ps/ccr/report_04/ar2004-e.pdf

This link to the department's site publishes a guide for Canadians on applications to the minister of justice for a conviction review under section 690 of the *Criminal Code*.

The Continuing Legal Education Society of British Columbia
http://www.cle.bc.ca/CLE/default.htm

The website of the Continuing Legal Education Society of British Columbia offers up-to-date information on a variety of legal issues, as well as links to law faculties of universities in B.C. and decisions of B.C. courts.

Questions for Discussion

1. Is the jury, as Lord Devlin suggests, "the lamp that shows that freedom lives," or as Dean Griswold suggests, "twelve persons brought in from the street, selected in various ways for their lack of general ability"? What does the trial of O.J. Simpson tell us of the jury system?
2. The Supreme Court's decision in *Askov* has been criticized by police as an example of the way a literal insistence on *Charter* rights can hamper effective enforcement of the law. What are the strengths and weaknesses of this argument?
3. Does section 690 of the *Criminal Code* constitute an adequate government response to allegations of wrongful conviction? In your discussion, make particular reference to the *Milgaard* case.

Further Reading

Canadian Centre for Justice Statistics. *The Juristat Reader: A Statistical Overview of the Canadian Justice System, Unit 3:* Court Statistics. Toronto: Thompson Educational Publishing, 1999.

> This is an excellent empirical description of the work done by Canadian courts, highlighting the kinds and numbers of cases heard by various levels of court, the characteristics of the accused in criminal cases, dispositions, sentencing, and case processing. *The Juristat Reader* is a very useful complement to the statute and case law that governs Canada's courts.

Canada. Royal Commission on Aboriginal Peoples. *Final Report of the Royal Commission on Aboriginal Peoples.* 5 vols. Ottawa: Canada Communications Group, 1996.

> The final report of the Royal Commission on Aboriginal Peoples is a compilation that could be cited as critical further reading for a number of chapters in this text. The royal commission was given the task of developing recommendations on a wide range of issues, including the right of self-government, land claims, living conditions in Aboriginal communities, and programs to improve the lives of Aboriginal Canadians. The more than 400 recommendations have had and continue to have a significant impact on the development of Canadian law and policy.

Karp, C., and C. Rosner. *When Justice Fails: The David Milgaard Story.* Toronto: McClelland and Stewart, 1991.

This is a comprehensive analysis of the *Milgaard* case, a wrongful conviction that dramatically demonstrated the fallibility of a human justice system. The authors point to the factors that culminated in Milgaard's conviction, providing the reader with a good grasp of the variables that underlie such cases.

Notes

1. R.S.C. 1985, c. C-46.
2. S.M. Waddams, *Introduction to the Study of Law*, 4th ed. (Toronto: Carswell, 1992), 123.
3. *Re Southam Inc. and The Queen* (1984), 16 C.C.C. (3d) 262, 48 O.R. (2d) 678 (H.C.J.), aff'd 53 O.R. (2d) 663 (C.A.).
4. *Youth Criminal Justice Act,* R.S.C. 1985, c. Y-1, s. 38 (1.2).
5. See *R. v. Quesnel and Quesnel* (1979), 51 C.C.C. (2d) 270 (Ont. C.A.). For a more restrictive interpretation, see *R. v. Lefebvre* (1984), 17 C.C.C. (3d) 277 (Que. C.A.).
6. N. Christie, "Conflicts of Property," *British Journal of Criminology* 17 (1977): 1–15.
7. G. Gall, *The Canadian Legal System*, 3d ed. (Toronto: Carswell, 1990), 135.
8. C.T. Griffiths and D. Chunn, eds., *Circuit and Rural Court Justice in the North: A Resource Publication* (Burnaby, B.C.: The Northern Conference and Simon Fraser University, 1986), 1–6 to 1–7.
9. R. Ericson and P. Baranek, *The Ordering of Justice: A Study of Accused Persons as Dependants in the Criminal Process* (Toronto: University of Toronto Press, 1982), 186.
10. A. Lamer, "Are We Over-Judicialized?" Address delivered to the Canadian Institute for the Administration of Justice, February 1977. Cited in Gall, *The Canadian Legal System*, 137.
11. E.N. Griswold, cited in H. Kalven and H. Zeisel, *The American Jury* (Boston: Little, Brown, 1966).
12. G. Williams, *The Proof of Guilt*, (1963), cited in Kalven and Zeisel, ibid., 6.
13. G. Williams and J. Frank, cited in V. Hans and N. Vidmar, *Judging the Jury* (New York: Plenum Press, 1986), 114–5.
14. Hans and Vidmar, *Judging the Jury*, 116.

15. *R. v. Morgentaler, Smoling and Scott* (1988), 37 C.C.C. (3d) 449, 62 C.R. (3d) 1, [1988] 1 S.C.R. 30.

16. Hans and Vidmar, *Judging the Jury*, 232.

17. A.T. Doob, "The Canadian Trial Judges' View of the Criminal Jury Trial," in *Law Reform Commission of Canada, Background Studies on the Jury* (1979).

18. Bolan D.C.J., cited in *R. v. Askov* (1991), 59 C.C.C. (3d) 449, rev'g 37 C.C.C. (3d) 289, 60 C.R. (3d) 277, 33 C.R.R. 319 [hereinafter *Askov*].

19. *Askov*, 494–5.

20. Ibid., 490.

21. Ibid.

22. See, for example, *R. v. Bennett* (1991), 64 C.C.C. (3d) 449 and *R. v. Morin* (1992), 71 C.C.C. (3d) 1.

23. [1999] 1 S.C.R. 688

24. T.G. Zuber, *Report of the Ontario Courts Inquiry* (Toronto: Government of Ontario, 1987).

References

Beckton, C.F. *Law and the Media*. Toronto: Carswell, 1982.

E. Elliott and R.M. Gordon, *New Directions in Restorative Justice: Issues, practice, evaluation*, Willan Publishing, Portland, Oregon, 2005

Ericson, R., and P. Baranek. *The Ordering of Justice: A Study of Accused Persons as Dependants in the Criminal Process*. Toronto: University of Toronto Press, 1982.

Gall, G. *The Canadian Legal System*. 5th ed. Toronto: Carswell, 2004, Chapter 6.

Griffiths, C.T., and D. Chunn, eds. *Circuit and Rural Court Justice in the North: A Resource Publication*. Burnaby, B.C.: The Northern Conference and Simon Fraser University, 1986.

Hans, V., and N. Vidmar. *Judging the Jury*. New York: Plenum Press, 1986.

Henry, D.J. "Televised Court Proceedings: The Case for Implementation Today." *Advocates' Society Journal* 3 (1984): 19.

Kalven, H., and H. Zeisel. *The American Jury*. Boston: Little, Brown, 1966.

Karp, C., and C. Rosner. *When Justice Fails: The David Milgaard Story*. Toronto: McClelland and Stewart, 1991.

Kesterton, W.H. *The Law and the Press in Canada*. Carleton University Library Series. Toronto: McClelland and Stewart, 1976.

Lepofsky, D. *Open Justice: The Constitutional Right to Attend and Speak About Criminal Proceedings.* Toronto: Butterworths, 1985.

Marks, J.B. "An Overview of Alternative Dispute Resolution Techniques, Successes and Obstacles." *Antitrust Law Journal* 53 (1984): 283.

Mewett, A.W. "Television in the Courtroom." *Criminal Law Quarterly* 26 (1984): 385.

Pirie, A.J. "The Lawyer As Mediator: Professional Responsibility Problems or Profession Problem?" *Canadian Bar Review* 63 (1985): 378.

Robertson, S. *Courts and the Media.* Toronto: Butterworths, 1981.

Vidmar, N. "The Small Claims Court: A Reconceptualization of Disputes and an Empirical Investigation." *Law and Society Review* 18 (1984): 515.

Zuber, T.G. *Report of the Ontario Courts Inquiry.* Toronto: Government of Ontario, 1987.

CHAPTER 6

The Study of Law, Lawyers, and Judges: The Evolution of the Legal Profession

It is not possible to think usefully about legal education without thinking about law itself—the subject that is taught—about its complexity and polycentricity, its political and economic functions in the larger society, its social origins and cultural significance. . . . Nor is it possible to think about the architects, theorists, practitioners, critics, clienteles, benefactors, and beneficiaries of legal education without recalling that they are also embedded in the larger polity, society, economy, culture, professional ethos, and higher education system—all dynamic and conflicted systems. Nor finally, can we ignore the fact that the relationships amongst these actors constitute an internal political economy, which does much to define the character and strategies of the legal academy. That is why curriculum committees and faculty councils may propose, but cannot dispose. And that is why even what they propose is often the outcome not so much of reasoned debate as it is of contestation for control over scarce resources of time, money and prestige.

The assumptions engendered by Wall Street and its legal culture ultimately leach back into the legal academy, not only in the United States, where its influence has long been noted, but in Canada as well. Canadian law students—no less than their American counterparts—overtly or tacitly choose the legal education which they imagine will advance their future careers. As Wall Street firms, or Wall Street-influenced Canadian firms, come to dominate the Canadian legal scene, many law students will try to make themselves attractive to those firms. This will affect the way in which they prepare themselves for their careers: the courses they choose to take, the attitudes towards colleagues and clients they develop, the amount of debt they are prepared to accumulate, the alacrity with which they will take up offers of summer internships on Wall Street or seek opportunities to study in the U.S. and the balance they strike between their studies and other activities. Wall Street-influenced student attitudes will in turn reshape the "real" curriculum of Canadian legal education— the curriculum which students choose to pursue, rather than the one mandated by faculty policy.

(Harry Arthurs, "Poor Canadian Legal Education: So Near to Wall Street, So Far from God," *Osgoode Hall Law Journal* 381, 38 [2000])

Harry Arthurs, the former dean of Osgoode Hall Law School, makes two important points in these excerpts from a relatively recent article. He describes the context in which legal education takes place—the reality that the teaching of law cannot be divorced from the ever-changing political, social, and economic context that underpins everyday life. Arthurs also points to the teaching of law in a professional school—an accredited law faculty—as an exercise that is in part a critically driven intellectual analysis of legal process and in part participation in a training ground for an evolving role, a role that is largely shaped by developments outside the walls of the law school. In pointing to the influence of Wall Street and its globalization of legal practice in the last decade, Arthurs points to an emerging change not only in legal education, but in our conceptions of law and the realities of legal practice.

And it is perhaps because of these structural changes that one must not lose sight of the need to study and to think about law in a setting that does something more than deliver a range of career choices. More specifically, legal education must continue to be focused on critical inquiry, and in this respect, it may be that the teaching of law outside of law schools performs an especially useful function, whether this takes place in our high schools or in our universities. For example, the Department of Law at Carleton University points to this strength in describing its program:

> Carleton University offers the most comprehensive Bachelor of Arts in Law in the country. Our programs reflect the growing demand for legal studies outside the professional LL.B., placing law and legal issues within a social context. Our courses move beyond the study of legal rules, to examining what we know about the law and how it works in our society. (www.carleton.ca/cu/ed4life/brochures/law.html)

A Brief History of Legal Education in Canada

How are Canada's lawyers chosen? How are they educated? What do Canadians expect from them when they undertake legal practice? Some 50 years ago, no formal university education in law existed in Canada; law students apprenticed with practising lawyers, wrote a few examinations, and gradually earned their admission to the bar. The 1983 Arthurs report, *Law and Learning*, noted:

> [U]ntil after World War II, legal education consisted of practical training in law offices, supplemented by attendance on a part-time basis at lectures offered for the most part by practitioners, and by a

very few full-time law teachers. The content and direction of the curriculum were heavily influenced by the desire to impart knowledge quickly, with an emphasis upon "black letter" law and the rules of procedure. There was little time—and often less incentive—to reflect on matters of jurisprudence.[1]

In 1949, debate over legal education in the Province of Ontario led to a schism within Toronto's Osgoode Hall. On one side were legal academics who argued that academic views and values were not adequately dealt with by the law school curriculum. On the other side were law teachers supporting the existing curriculum, which was aimed at training practitioners—setting out statute and case law and the rules of procedure—with little attention to the more theoretical questions of jurisprudence; legal philosophy; or the social, economic, and political contexts of law. The debate was resolved when a number of full-time Osgoode faculty established a university-based study of law at the University of Toronto, creating a clear choice for lawyers-to-be between a broad academic approach and practical training.

During the 1950s and 1960s, the university-based model of legal education gained ascendance. Law was to be studied for three years at university **law schools** approved by provincial **law societies**. Typically, the three years would follow at least two years of undergraduate study in another discipline. A period of apprenticeship, or "**articling**," would follow the successful completion of courses in law, after which examinations, to be developed by provincial law societies, would admit successful candidates to the bar. Both the number and the size of law schools in Canada have expanded considerably since then. There were, for example, fewer than 50 law professors in Canadian law schools in 1950; in the late 1990s, there were more than 600. Furthermore, as the Arthurs report noted, there has been a substantial expansion of the traditional law school curriculum over the past 40 years:

> [A] growing emphasis on interdisciplinary work; a commitment to legal research and writing programs; the proliferation of new courses and seminars, including some in nontraditional areas such as poverty law; the teaching of legal skills; and new concepts of teaching such as clinical programs, intensive full-term programs in specific areas, and opportunities for individual, directed research.

Measures of Eligibility for Law School Admission

In the early twenty-first century, applicants to law school are selected on the basis of their grade point averages (GPA) and their scores on a U.S.-designed aptitude test, the Law School Admission Test, or **LSAT**. Canada's law schools typically combine the two measures in order to determine eligibility for admission, assigning a greater statistical weight to previous university performance than to LSAT scores.

There have been many criticisms of the adequacy of these measures. Some have suggested that these essentially academic indices are too narrow, that students should be interviewed to determine such social attributes as their community involvement, relevant employment, and so on. Academic excellence, in itself, is no guarantee that a person will be able or willing to serve the community as an advocate. Like doctors, dentists, engineers, and other professionals, lawyers are trained in specialized areas in order to fulfill a function intended to serve the public good. Most Canadian law schools admit a small number of "mature," First Nations, and "access" students, in addition to those admitted on the basis of traditional entrance requirements. Mature students are those who have demonstrated academic ability through a combination of the LSAT score and some academic coursework, but do not have the university degree that is typically required for entrance. Their work histories to date are set in the balance, however, and they are granted entrance to the law school because they have demonstrated this combination of academic promise and relevant work experience; the mature student brings a diversity of experience to the law school classroom.

The additional categories of Aboriginal and "access" applicants are also quite common in Canadian law schools. For example, Osgoode Hall Law School has both Aboriginal applicant and "access" applicant categories for admission, in addition to a mature student classification. The law school noted of its Aboriginal applicant category in 2005: "Osgoode Hall Law School is concerned that members of First Nations, Inuit and Métis do not have substantial representation in the legal profession, and accordingly encourage applications from these groups. The Admissions Committee's decision to admit an applicant ultimately depends on its judgment of the applicant's ability to complete law school."[2] In other words, although a certain number of spaces may be set aside for First Nations applicants, these spaces will not be occupied unless the law school is convinced that the student will be able to graduate and make a contribution to the practice of law.

Similarly, the law school noted of its access applicant category:

> [Our] aim is to recruit and admit individuals with good academic potential who have themselves confronted or who are from groups which have confronted identifiable social, educational and/or economic barriers to education in general, or legal education in particular. Applicants must submit a personal statement identifying and

> discussing those factors which they feel have influenced their access to education. Applicants may identify barriers of a systemic, enduring nature, or they may list several contributing factors.[3]

The law school noted that barriers may involve language, place of birth, economic background, a rural education, and physical handicaps or learning disabilities. Similar kinds of categories of access now exist at most Canadian law schools. For example, the University of Western Ontario has created a category for applicants with disabilities and another category for "applicants whose academic performance has been significantly affected by some proven disadvantage."

The non-traditional criteria used to admit student applicants appear to work well; as noted, these students appear to perform as well as those admitted through traditional criteria. In the United States, however, such "preferential" treatment is often viewed as reverse discrimination, denying equality before the law to applicants who are not First Nations, or, more typically in the U.S. situation, to applicants who are not Black.

One argument in favour of affirmative action is that First Nations peoples (and Blacks) have suffered both legal and non-legal oppression and colonization. Second, these groups are underrepresented within the legal profession, and affirmative action is a useful means of correcting the imbalance. Moreover, it encourages the assumption of leadership roles within the community. Finally, proponents of such measures note that, once admitted to law school, Black and First Nations students are evaluated by the same standards as all other students.

The *Canadian Charter of Rights and Freedoms* (unlike the U.S. *Bill of Rights*) states that affirmative-action programs are consistent with the protection of rights and freedoms. Section 15(2) states that the guarantees of equality within section 15(1) do not "preclude any law, program, or activity that has as its object the amelioration of conditions of disadvantaged individuals or groups including those that are disadvantaged because of race, national or ethnic origin, colour, religion, sex, age or mental or physical disability."

There have also been many criticisms of the use of the LSAT. Some critics argue that a U.S.-oriented aptitude test should not determine admissions to Canadian law schools. Others believe that the test is biased toward the language and orientation of a white middle-class culture; still others hold that it has no predictive abilities and that the cumulative weight of three years of university courses taken from a wide range of professors is all that is needed to determine eligibility. Indeed, supporters of the LSAT are not able to provide convincing evidence that test scores can adequately predict success in law school and within legal practice.

As imperfect as LSAT scores and grade point averages may be, it has been difficult to create alternative standards for admission that are either more useful to the law schools and Canada's communities or fairer to prospective applicants. Evaluation by interview is highly subjective, potentially biased by the attitudes, beliefs, and values of interviewers. A lottery system appears to produce law students at least marginally less capable than those admitted with traditional qualifications.

More recently, however, legal academics are focusing on the admissions process in Canadian law schools, suggesting that the underpinnings of admissions decisions have not been rigorously evaluated or debated. Dawna Tong and Wes Pue wrote in the *Osgoode Hall Law Journal* in 1999 about the cultural imposition of the LSAT, a U.S. aptitude test, and more pointedly, of the goals that underlie the admissions process itself. They noted:

> [T]he public interest requires a legal profession that is both "competent" and "diverse." A profession consisting entirely of extremely competent, hard-working, selfless, and ethical individuals who were all, nonetheless, exclusively drawn from a narrow social group would not be well placed to serve the public interest. It could understand nothing beyond its own narrow sectoral interests. The foundation of liberal democracy lies not in the denial of diversity but in finding creative ways of negotiating difference so as to make life-in-common possible, tolerable and just.[4]

Tong and Pue are wary, then, of admissions decisions that are based only on grade point average and LSAT scores. They imply that such an approach will compromise diversity and hence diminish the law's capacity for tolerance and justice.

Inside the Law Schools: Numbers and Curricula

In 1962, Canada graduated fewer than 1 000 lawyers; in the late 1990s, nearly 3 000 lawyers were graduating each year. During this period, the Canadian population grew by about 50 percent, while the number of lawyers increased by about 300 percent. The cumulative effect of these changes has been substantial: 10 000 lawyers were practising in Canada in 1962; today there are more than 60 000. In 1962, women formed less than 5 percent of each law school class; currently, they make up about 40 percent of law graduates.

The increased contribution of women to the legal profession has developed largely because of growing demands for gender equality. The disproportionate growth in the numbers of Canadian lawyers relative to many other occupations flows, at least in part, from the increased complexity of social life and the related need for regulation and dispute resolution. There has been a substantial rise in both the law and the litigation relating to such matters as labour relations, radio and television communications, welfare, unemployment insurance, workers' compensation, immigration, family relationships, and correctional administration. Furthermore, market surveys reveal that an increasing percentage of graduating law students do not intend to practise law as such; they have chosen a legal education in order to pursue an academic, government, or corporate/commercial career.

Law degrees are also useful for those who wish to pursue a career outside the practice of law. A small percentage of each graduating class goes on to complete a master's or a doctorate in law, typically embarking upon an academic career at the conclusion of this further degree. And many other students, contemplating a career in either business or government service, have found a law degree to be a useful springboard for such work.

There has been considerable debate over the past three decades about whether Canada's law schools are graduating a surplus of lawyers. Most agree that it is mainly enrollment increases that account for the 300 percent increase between 1960 and 2000. But, as legal historians David Stager and Harry Arthurs noted, the increase has not been linear:

> Law school enrolment in Canada more than doubled between 1964 and 1970; this represented an average annual increase of 12.4 percent. Between 1971 and 1976, enrolment increased at an annual average of 3.6 percent, and since the mid-1970s, enrolment has increased at an average yearly rate of only 1 percent. This virtual plateau appears to represent a return to long-run equilibrium in the lawyers' market. Moreover, the proportion of law graduates entering private practice in Canada has continued to decline because of increasing demand for lawyers in government and business, and lawyers finding employment in nonlegal fields.[5]

Not surprisingly, in the face of increased enrollments and increased diversity within the profession, the law school curriculum has also expanded. While the basics of the first-year LL.B. program have generally remained intact—torts, real property, personal property, criminal law, jurisprudence, constitutional law, and contracts—the second and third years now typically permit a wide range of courses and of approaches to law.

When deans of Canadian law schools were asked to rank the three most important goals of their programs, the value of training students for the practice of law was not seen to have overwhelming importance. Of almost equal importance were the tasks of "providing students with an understanding of the relationship of law and society," "developing interest in law as a scholarly discipline," and "developing critical reflection on legal practice."[6] These goals reflect a change in the understanding of the purpose and nature of legal education, as well as an effort to respond to public concerns about the nature of legal practice. Today's graduate in law is asked to understand not only the literal content of statute and case law, but also the social, political, and economic contexts in which such law develops.

The role of legal education continues to be the subject of considerable debate and disagreement, within both law schools and the legal profession. Many students complain that faculty members who emphasize an understanding of the relationship between law and society or critical reflection on legal practice are not adequately preparing them for the exigencies of the profession. They urge, together with some faculty, greater emphasis on the attainment of technical skills, on so-called black letter law. Their argument is that discussion of the values and principles that underlie specific forms of law is relevant only if it contributes directly to their effectiveness as advocates.

With the advent of the *Canadian Charter of Rights and Freedoms* (the *Charter*), this kind of argument has less persuasiveness. The *Charter* forces Canada's lawyers to litigate the values of the nation—to engage in debate about such principles as freedom of expression, cruel and unusual punishment, and so forth. Even if the *Charter* did not exist, however, it seems doubtful that a university education in law could now be justified by the attainment of technical skills. A university education in law was designed to supplement, not replace, apprenticeship. The pre-1949 structure of apprenticeship and the current structure of articling and bar admission examinations are systems designed to test the attainment of technical skills.

Thus, a university education in law is, at least in theory, designed to provide students with a broad base of understanding in the form of insight into the history, purpose, principles, and controversies within specific areas of the legal system. It is unclear, however, whether the refocused law school curriculum will change the trajectory of legal practice for most students. Lawyer Robert Kerry Wilkins argues:

> [W]e absorb the politics of aspiration while we practise refining the rhetoric of justice. The price of success in the program is learning to treat the one as the other. It is an exercise shot through with bogus necessity. The harm and dislocation many law students suffer have their origins in just such contortions. They change us, often in ways we had not noticed, do not understand, and may not like.[7]

At the conclusion of the LL.B. program, law school graduates typically apply for articles and register for the bar admission program in the province in which they intend to practise. Each province sets its own requirements with respect to the length of both the articling period and the bar admission examinations. In most provinces, a lawyer can be called to the bar after one year to eighteen months of articling and examinations. Transferring to practise in another province typically requires the writing of transfer examinations.

The Lawyer in Practice

The past three decades represent a significant evolution in the role of law and lawyers within our culture. As noted earlier, there are both more laws and more lawyers. It is perhaps to be expected, then, that there should also be more negative attitudes toward lawyers. Practitioners of law are the subject of any number of derisive jokes, caricatured as greedy and amoral, driven more by material considerations than by principles. In short, the profession does not always succeed in convincing the public that justice, rather than material gain, is the linchpin of legal practice. In the words of Wilkins:

> The power and prestige that lawyers as a group enjoy remain contingent . . . on certain unvoiced public assumptions about lawyers' roles in our culture: that the work they do is essential to the realization of justice, for example, and that it is beyond the competence of ordinary mortals acting alone. These assumptions (and others like them) underpin the correlation in people's minds between privilege and desert. Any serious erosion of them would invite inconvenient questions about the whole notion of legal professionalism: about the tasks and attitudes appropriate to it, and about its moral and functional legitimacy within a system dedicated, nominally at least, to marketing justice.[8]

Within public culture, there are other, more neutral, images of the Canadian lawyer: corporate technocrat, crusading litigator, general practitioner serving a small community, and so on. The most dominant of these is the image of the courtroom advocate. In fact, however, even lawyers who are litigators spend very little of their time in the courtroom, engaged in advocacy. A survey of lawyers in private practice in the United States revealed that almost two-thirds of their time was taken in drafting documents, interviews with clients, correspondence, library research, orally counselling clients, and office administration. Time in the courtroom amounted to about 5 percent of the legal practice.

From this list of tasks, we may conclude that Canada's lawyers have conflicting obligations. They must fulfill responsibilities to their clients, their professional societies, the criminal and civil courts, and their communities. Many of these obligations are common to lawyers in other countries, as well as to other professionals such as medical practitioners and accountants.

There is one essential distinction, however, between lawyers and other professionals. Lawyers, like physicians, can claim that communications between themselves and their clients are "privileged"—that is, any written or oral communication between lawyer and client may not be revealed to a court, board, or tribunal without the client's permission. The purpose of privilege is, in theory, to give clients the assurance that their interests will supersede those of the other participants within the justice system, notably the prosecutor, the police, and the judiciary. But some critics have suggested that the existence of solicitor–client privilege is not sufficient to ensure that clients' interests will indeed be paramount. Sociologists Richard Ericson and Patricia Baranek, after an empirical study of hundreds of accused within the criminal process, made the following observation:

> The accused does not typically have a relationship with his lawyer that would allow trust to be built up and used on either side to accept evidence at face value; furthermore, the accused and lawyer do not have the same stake in a future relationship. . . . The accused's trust in his lawyer is, thus, . . . a forced faith that his lawyer will act in his best interests. . . . [T]he accused has little choice but to accept matters on blind faith when his lawyer attempts out-of-court settlements with the police and Crown attorney. He is nearly always excluded from these transactions and therefore must rely on his lawyer's account of what happened and what it is possible to achieve.[9]

The provincial law societies are typically more demanding than clients in the structuring of their relationships with the lawyers within their jurisdictions. These professional societies establish the relevant standards and construct examinations for admission to the bar, set and collect annual fees from practising lawyers, administer government-funded systems of legal aid for the working poor and the indigent, arrange insurance for their membership, and discipline lawyers who fall short of their existing standards of professional conduct.

During the 1990s, the problem of gender bias in the legal profession emerged as a source of both concern and empirical scrutiny. A task force of the Canadian Bar Association produced a report on gender equality, "Touchstones for Change: Equality, Diversity and Accountability." This 1993 report set out more than 100 recommendations on topics ranging from barriers to entry into the profession and barriers to equality within the profession to problems encountered by women in private and government practices. Most pointedly, the report presented four critical findings resulting from studies of women in legal practice: (1) the vast majority of women surveyed reported both the perception and the experience of gender bias in the legal profession; (2) the vast majority of female lawyers face barriers to career advancement, and this is evidenced in the patterns of access to legal positions, areas of practice, partnership, and remuneration; (3) female lawyers with child-care responsibilities are discriminated against because of the lack of accommodation by the profession, resulting in lost income and reduced opportunities for advancement; and (4) more than one in three female lawyers have experienced sexual harassment in the form of unwanted sexual advances.[10]

Some empirical evidence of these dissatisfactions can be found in the percentage of women who leave the practice of law. Most recently, Kay and Brockman report that women are leaving the profession at higher rates than men. By 1990, for example, 22 percent of women called to the bar in British Columbia between 1974 and 1988 had left the profession, in contrast to 13 percent of men called to the bar during that time. But it would also be a mistake to portray the lot of women in law as one of a unidimensional gendered misery. A 1996 study of more than 1 500 Ontario lawyers revealed no significant differences in job satisfaction between men and women in the province, except with respect to issues of parental leave arrangements and job security.[11]

The Canadian Bar Association's *Code of Professional Conduct*

The professional conduct expected of Canada's lawyers has been a subject of considerable discussion. In 2004, after consultations with provincial law societies, the Canadian Bar Association published an updated *Code of Professional Conduct*, generally held to be reflective of established opinion within the legal profession.

RULES OF THE CANADIAN BAR ASSOCIATION

Code of Professional Conduct (2004)

1. *The lawyer must discharge with integrity all duties owed to clients, the court or tribunal, other members of the profession and the public.*

2. *(a) The lawyer owes the client a duty to be competent to perform any legal services undertaken on the client's behalf.*

   (b) The lawyer should serve the client in a conscientious, diligent and efficient manner so as to provide a quality of service at least equal to that which lawyers generally would expect of a competent lawyer in a like situation.

3. *The lawyer must be both honest and candid when advising clients.*

4. *(i) Maintaining Information in Confidence: The lawyer has a duty to hold in strict confidence all information concerning the business and affairs of the client acquired in the course of the professional relationship, and shall not divulge any such information except as expressly or impliedly authorized by the client, required by law or otherwise required by this Code.*

   (ii) Public Safety Exception: Where a lawyer believes upon reasonable grounds that there is an imminent risk to an identifiable person or group of death or serious bodily harm, including serious psychological harm that would substantially interfere with health or well-being, the lawyer shall disclose confidential information where it is necessary to do so in order to prevent the death or harm, but shall not disclose more information than is required. The lawyer who has reasonable grounds for believing that a dangerous situation is likely to develop at a court or tribunal facility shall inform the person having responsibility for security at the facility and give particulars, being careful not to disclose confidential information except as required by paragraph 2 of this Rule. Where possible the lawyer should suggest solutions to the anticipated problem such as:

      (a) the need for further security;

      (b) that judgment be reserved;

      (c) such other measure as may seem advisable.

   (iii) Disclosure Where Lawyer's Conduct in Issue: Disclosure may also be justified in order to establish or collect a fee, or to defend the lawyer or the lawyer's associates or employees against any allegation of malpractice or misconduct, but only to the extent necessary for such purposes.

5. *The lawyer shall not advise or represent both sides of a dispute and, except after adequate disclosure to and with the consent of the clients or prospective clients concerned, shall not act or continue to act in a matter when there is or is likely to be a conflicting interest.*

6. *(a) The lawyer should not enter into a business transaction with the client or knowingly give to or acquire from the client an ownership, security or other pecuniary interest unless:*

    (i) the transaction is a fair and reasonable one and its terms are fully disclosed to the client in writing in a manner that is reasonably understood by the client;

    (ii) the client is given a reasonable opportunity to seek independent legal advice about the transaction, the onus being on the lawyer to prove that the client's interests were protected by such independent advice; and

    (iii) the client consents in writing to the transaction.

    (b) The lawyer shall not enter into or continue a business transaction with the client if:

    (i) the client expects or might reasonably be assumed to expect that the lawyer is protecting the client's interests;

    (ii) there is a significant risk that the interests of the lawyer and the client may differ.

    (c) The lawyer shall not act for the client where the lawyer's duty to the client and the personal interests of the lawyer or an associate are in conflict.

    (d) The lawyer shall not prepare an instrument giving the lawyer or an associate a substantial gift from the client, including a testamentary gift.

    (e) The lawyer must comply with the terms of all professional liability insurance policies.

7. *The lawyer who engages in another profession, business or occupation concurrently with the practice of law must not allow such outside interest to jeopardize the lawyer's professional integrity, independence or competence.*

8. *The lawyer owes a duty to the client to observe all relevant laws and rules respecting the preservation and safekeeping of the client's property entrusted to the lawyer. Where there are no such laws or rules, or the lawyer is in any doubt, the lawyer should take the same care of such property as a careful and prudent owner would when dealing with property of like description.*

9. *When acting as an advocate, the lawyer must treat the tribunal with courtesy and respect and must represent the client resolutely, honourably and within the limits of the law.*

10. *The lawyer who holds public office should, in the discharge of official duties, adhere to standards of conduct as high as those that these rules require of a lawyer engaged in the practice of law.*

11. *The lawyer shall not*

    (a) *stipulate for, charge or accept any fee that is not fully disclosed, fair and reasonable;*

    (b) *appropriate any funds of the client held in trust or otherwise under the lawyer's control for or on account of fees without the express authority of the client, save as permitted by the rules of the governing body.*

12. *The lawyer owes a duty to the client not to withdraw services except for good cause and upon notice appropriate in the circumstances.*

13. *The lawyer should encourage public respect for and try to improve the administration of justice.*

14. *Lawyers should make legal services available to the public in an efficient and convenient manner that will command respect and confidence, and by means that are compatible with the integrity, independence and effectiveness of the profession*

15. *The lawyer should assist in maintaining the integrity of the profession and should participate in its activities.*

16. *The lawyer's conduct toward all persons with whom the lawyer comes into contact in practice should be characterized by courtesy and good faith.*

17. *The lawyer should assist in preventing the unauthorized practice of law.*

18. *The lawyer who engages in public appearances and public statements should do so in conformity with the principles of the Code.*

19. *The lawyer should observe the rules of professional conduct set out in the Code in the spirit as well as in the letter*

20. *The lawyer shall respect the requirements of human rights and constitutional laws in force in Canada, and in its provinces and territories. Except where differential treatment is permitted by law, the lawyer shall not discriminate with respect to partnership or professional employment of other lawyers, articled students or any other person, or in professional dealings with other members of the profession or any other person on grounds including, but not limited to, an individual's ancestry, colour, perceived race, nationality, national origin, ethnic background or origin, language, religion, creed or religious belief, religious association or activities, age, sex, gender, physical characteristics, pregnancy, sexual orientation, marital or family status, source of income, political belief, association or activity, physical or mental disability.*

21. *(i)* *A lawyer who acts as a mediator shall, at the outset of the mediation, ensure that the parties to it understand fully that:*

    (a) *the lawyer is not acting as a lawyer for either party but, as mediator, is acting to assist the parties to resolve the matters in issue, and*

    (b) *although communications pertaining to and arising out of the mediation process may be covered by some other common law, civil law, statutory or other privilege, they will not be covered by the solicitor-client privilege.*

    (ii) *A lawyer shall not act as a mediator if the lawyer or the lawyer's firm has acted or is acting in a matter that may reasonably be expected to become an issue during the mediation, except with the informed consent of all parties.*

22. *(a)* *The lawyer must exercise independent professional judgment in providing legal advice, services and representation to a client.*

    (b) *The lawyer must conduct himself or herself in a manner that respects, protects and advances the independence of the bar.*

(Reprinted by permission of the Canadian Bar Association.)

The 22 rules set out in the *Code of Professional Conduct* take the form of guidelines; they are not precise or specific in their instructions to practising lawyers. The code has no legal force within a given province until adopted by that jurisdiction's law society.

INFRINGEMENTS OF THE CODE OF PROFESSIONAL CONDUCT

When the *Code of Professional Conduct* states that the lawyer must discharge duties "owed to clients, the court, other members of the profession, and the public . . . with integrity," it is not clear about what kinds of behaviour are acceptable or unacceptable. Fortunately, in its discussion of the 22 rules, the Canadian Bar Association has given illustrations of the kinds of actions that are likely to infringe the code:

(a) committing any personally disgraceful or morally reprehensible offence that reflects upon the lawyer's integrity (whereof a conviction by a competent court would be *prima facie* evidence);

(b) committing, whether professionally or in the lawyer's personal capacity, any act of fraud or dishonesty, e.g. by knowingly making a false tax return or falsifying a document, even without fraudulent intent, and whether or not prosecuted therefor;

(c)   making untrue representations or concealing material facts from a client with dishonest or improper motives;

(d)   taking improper advantage of the youth, experience, lack of education or sophistication, ill health, or unbusinesslike habits of a client;

(e)   misappropriating or dealing dishonestly with the client's monies;

(f)   receiving monies from or on behalf of a client expressly for a specific purpose and failing, without the client's consent, to pay them over for that purpose;

(g)   knowingly assisting, enabling, or permitting any person to act fraudulently, dishonestly, or illegally toward the lawyer's client;

(h)   failing to be absolutely frank and candid in all dealings with the Court, fellow lawyers, and other parties to proceedings, subject always to not betraying the client's cause, abandoning the client's legal rights, or disclosing the client's confidences;

(i)   failing, when dealing with a person not legally represented, to disclose material facts, e.g. the existence of a mortgage on a property being sold, or supplying false information, whether the lawyer is professionally representing a client or is concerned personally;

(j)   failure to honour the lawyer's word when pledged even though, under technical rules, the absence of writing might afford a legal defence.

These 10 illustrations suggest that dishonesty and "morally reprehensible" conduct are at the heart of behaviour that would infringe the code. Significantly, the first illustration shows that conviction for a criminal offence does not, in itself, constitute an infringement. What is at issue is that the crime must be either "personally disgraceful" or "morally reprehensible" to infringe the code. We might, therefore, wonder what kinds of convictions might be seen to be "personally disgraceful" or "morally reprehensible."

This question reveals that the specificity of the code and its 10 illustrations are not as clear as its rhetoric might imply. First, we must remember that the legal profession is self-regulated, so we might expect its professional code of conduct to reflect primarily the interests of lawyers, not those of the general public. Second, what behaviours do the ambiguous illustrations actually prohibit?

It can be argued, concerning the first illustration, that conviction for any criminal offence is evidence of disrespect for the law and effectively compromises a lawyer's standing before the law society and the public. On the other hand, certain offences may be said to reflect only personal weakness or indulgence, and a criminal conviction for such crimes does not constitute conflict of interest for a defence counsel. For a prosecutor or judge, however, any criminal conviction represents conflict of interest. The prosecutor who seeks conviction and penalty and the judge who determines guilt and penalty cannot be seen as impartial if they have engaged in criminal acts outside the court that they respectively prosecute and sanction within the court. But another point of view argues that judges and prosecutors are drawn from a select, typically upper-middle-class segment of society. Hence, they are insulated from the classes of people who appear in criminal courts, and their lack of association with criminal conduct may be as much a badge of ignorance as it is a qualification for employment.

We are still left with the question of what kinds of crimes can be considered to be personally disgraceful or morally reprehensible. A property offence might be said to reveal a fundamental dishonesty, and an offence involving violence might be termed disgraceful or reprehensible. But what of the categories of vice—possession of an illegal drug or the noncriminal use of the services of a prostitute? Would a lawyer who helped to arrange an abortion for a teenager be taking improper advantage of the youth or ill health of a client (illustration [d])? Should a distinction be drawn between a handful of parking tickets and impaired driving?

Canada's provincial law societies have disciplined and reprimanded lawyers convicted of illegal drug possession, impaired driving, or using the services of prostitutes, but they have generally not disbarred them for such behaviours. In some instances, lawyers have been fined and suspended from practice for a period of time (typically less than one year); in others, they have received reprimands. Paradoxically, impaired driving convictions have typically been tolerated to a greater extent than drug possession convictions, perhaps because alcohol is the establishment drug of choice even though it usually presents a greater risk to others than some illegal substances. But lawyers who have acted dishonestly are most often disbarred. Within Canada and most other Western nations, lawyers have been disbarred for the misappropriation of trust funds, monies entrusted to them by members of the public. This and other violations of the lawyer–client relationship are dealt with by illustrations (b) to (j).

Illustration (h)—the requirement that lawyers be "absolutely frank and candid in all dealings with the Court, fellow lawyers, and other parties to proceedings"—raises a quite different issue from the betrayal of a client's economic interests. This illustration confronts the ethical problems surrounding the disclosure of information relevant to a case before the court. Specifically, it suggests that in matters of criminal law, there is an obligation on the part of the prosecutor to inform the defence fully of the evidence against the accused. In the instance of indictable offences, the Crown prosecutor is generally required to disclose to the accused all evidence relevant to the charge, regardless of whether this evidence will be used at trial and regardless of whether the evidence is inculpatory or exculpatory. In *R. v. Stinchcombe*,[12] a case that highlights the importance of disclosure, the Supreme Court of Canada determined that in the case of an unrepresented accused, a trial judge should not take a plea unless this accused has been informed of his right to disclosure by the Crown.

Allegations of nondisclosure by Crown counsel continue to be a major issue in many criminal cases. However, while nondisclosure in criminal cases is rarely found to be deserving of disbarment or reprimand, it is significant that the bar association's *Code of Professional Conduct* mandates disclosure as a professional responsibility.

By considering a number of recent cases of disciplinary action taken against five lawyers in Ontario in 2005,[13] we can examine more closely at least a few of the circumstances in which provincial law societies will take action against individual lawyers for their misconduct, and the range of penalties that they will impose. Note that forms of theft such as misappropriation of a client's trust funds—a violation of honesty—are treated much more harshly than criminal convictions for illegal drug possession or domestic conflict, where honesty is not at stake.

William Thomas Dyer, 57, of the City of Cambridge, was found guilty of professional misconduct for:

> between 1995 and 2003, misappropriating from his trust account monies totaling $6,300, more or less. . . .

The Hearing Panel ordered that:

> the Member is disbarred as a barrister and solicitor, his name is struck off the roll of solicitors, his membership in the Law Society is revoked, and he is prohibited from acting or practicing as a barrister or solicitor and from holding himself out as a barrister or solicitor. . . .

Victor Steven Savino, 58, of the City of Winnipeg in the Province of Manitoba was found guilty of conduct unbecoming a barrister and solicitor for:

> on March 9, 2004, before Mr. Justice R.D. Clarke in the Ontario Court of Justice at Thunder Bay, being found guilty of the following criminal offences:
>
> *[O]n or about the 24th day of March in the year 2002 at the City of Timmins in the Province of Ontario, he engaged in careless driving contrary to s. 130 of the Highway Traffic Act;*

> *on or about the 26th day of April in the year 2003 at the City and District of Thunder Bay in the Province of Ontario, while his ability to operate a motor vehicle was impaired by a drug, he did operate a 2001 GMC pickup truck . . .*
>
> *on or about the 26th day of April in the year 2003 at the City and District of Thunder Bay in the Province of Ontario, he did unlawfully possess a substance included in Schedule I to wit Rock Cocaine (benzoylmethylecgonine) contrary to s. 4(1) of the Controlled Drugs and Substances Act;*
>
> *on or about the 24th day of November in the year 2003 at the City of Kenora in the Province of Ontario, he did have in his possession a controlled substance to wit: crack cocaine, contrary to s.4(1) of the Controlled Drugs and Substances Act;*
>
> *on or about the 12th day of January in the year 2004 at the City of Kenora in the Province of Ontario he did, being at large on his own recognizance entered into before a justice, without lawful excuse, fail to attend court at Courtroom #140, 215 Water Street, Kenora, in accordance therewith, contrary to s. 145(2) of the Criminal Code of Canada;*
>
> *on or about the 27th day of February in the year 2004 at the City of Kenora in the Province of Ontario, he did, being at large on his own recognizance entered into before a justice and being bound to comply with a condition of that recognizance directed by the said justice, fail without lawful excuse to comply with that condition to wit: Report to Kenora Police Service and provide them with proof of being enrolled in a treatment program and advise them of the course of treatment and that he attended for the assessment, contrary to s.145 (3) of the Criminal Code of Canada. . . .*

The Hearing Panel ordered that:

> the Member shall be suspended for a definite period of six (6) months, such suspension to commence at the conclusion of the Member's administrative suspensions;
>
> the Member shall be suspended indefinitely thereafter until he produces medical evidence satisfactory to the Secretary of the Law Society confirming that he has been successfully treated for any drug or alcohol addictions. . . .

William Patrick Cody, 57, of the Town of Oakville, was found guilty of conduct unbecoming a barrister and solicitor for:

> on or about February 23, 2004, pleading guilty to and being found guilty of the following offence, that between the 28th day of July in the year 2000 and the 30th day of January in the year 2001, both

dates inclusive, at the Town of Oakville, he did steal a sum of money the property of CB of a value exceeding $5,000, contrary to section 334(a) of the *Criminal Code* of Canada.

The Hearing Panel ordered that:

the Member is disbarred.

Coulson Vernor Mills, 54, of the City of Toronto, was found guilty of conduct unbecoming a barrister and solicitor for:

on November 20, 2003, before Justice R. Bigelow in the Ontario Court of Justice at Toronto, being found guilty of the following criminal offence:

On or about the 7th day of November in the year 2002 in the City of Toronto in the Province of Ontario did unlawfully possess a controlled substance, to wit: cocaine, contrary to s. 4(1) of the *Controlled Drugs and Substances Act*.

The Hearing Panel ordered that:

- the Member shall be suspended for a period of 45 days.
- the suspension shall commence at the conclusion of the Member's administrative suspension, but run concurrently with any other undertakings that he may have given not to practice law in the interim.
- the Member shall abstain from the possession and use of non-medically prescribed drugs.
- the Member shall continue with his weekly attendance in the Continuing Care phase of the Cocaine Addiction Therapy Program until the end of July 2005, and will provide a letter to the Law Society from HV or her designate by August 15, 2005, attesting to his participation in and completion of this phase of the Program.
- between now and July 2005, the Member shall submit from time to time as directed by HV or her designate to random drug testing and arrange for HV or her designate to provide copies of test results to the Law Society, which must show that the Member has not been using any non-medically prescribed drugs.
- the Member shall continue in individual therapy on a monthly basis with LE or her designate until at least the end of July 2005, and provide a letter from LE or her designate by August 15, 2005, attesting to his participation in such therapy.

Barry Elliott Plant, 39, of the Town of Richmond, was found guilty of professional misconduct for:

> receiving cash funds from various clients, $15,000 of which more or less, he withheld and applied to his personal use as opposed to remitting to his firm for deposit to the firm's trust account in breach of By-Law 19 made pursuant to the *Law Society Act*.

The Hearing Panel ordered that:

- the Member is suspended for a period of six (6) months commencing April 6, 2005;
- if the Member chooses to resume the practice of law following his suspension, he shall be restricted for the first 18 months of practice, to practicing as either an employee or, alternatively, if he wishes to practice as a sole practitioner, it will be to a plan of supervision and under the supervision of another member of the Law Society, both the plan of supervision and supervisor having been approved by the Secretary prior to his return to practice;
- if the Member chooses the employment option, prior to commencing his employment and changing his status the Member must confirm his employment plans to the Law Society and arrange for his employer to confirm to the Law Society that the employer has reviewed the endorsed Notice of Application, the signed Agreed Statement of Facts and this Order. The Member shall also arrange for the employer to provide quarterly reports to the Secretary of the Law Society confirming that he remains in this employment arrangement;
- [if the Member] chooses the sole practitioner option, he must arrange for his supervisor to operate his trust account for a period of 18 months.
- the Member will not be permitted to receive any cash from his clients for a period of 18 months. Any and all cash payments from clients will have to be provided directly to the Member's supervisor or employer, as the case may be. The Member will only be permitted to receive cheques from clients that are made payable to his supervisor or employer in trust;
- with the exception of Legal Aid retainers, all clients must be given a written retainer by the Member that requires

> them to advance cash retainer and cash payments for legal fees and disbursements directly to the supervisor or employer, as the case may be. . . .

What conclusions are we to draw from these admittedly few cases? (Approximately 100 lawyers may be disciplined in Ontario in a given year.) Dishonesty in economic relationships between lawyer and client are most likely to be punished. Individual indulgences in legal or illegal drugs seem to be taken less seriously than the more fundamental issues of honesty and trust. With respect to the misappropriation of funds, however, it appears that there is room for discretion.

Disciplinary cases raise another issue. Who should be responsible for disciplining lawyers, making decisions to reprimand, fine, or disbar? Should the provincial law societies be more accessible to and controllable by public interest? Why are lawyers permitted to police themselves, with virtually no input from those outside the profession? If the practice of law must be in the public interest, it would seem to follow that the public should play a major role in helping the legal profession define the boundaries of unacceptable conduct for its membership.

THE CODE OF PROFESSIONAL CONDUCT AND THE COST OF LEGAL SERVICES

One other matter concerning the ethical responsibilities of Canada's lawyers requires some discussion. The issue of the fees charged to clients is covered in rule 11 of the *Code of Professional Conduct*: "[All fees should be] fully disclosed, fair, and reasonable." There is little guidance, however, as to what constitutes a "fair and reasonable" fee. The Canadian Bar Association's discussion of rule 11 notes only that the size of a lawyer's fee will depend upon

> the time and effort required and spent, the difficulty and importance of the matter, whether special service has been required and provided, the customary charges of other lawyers . . . in like matters and circumstances, in civil cases, the amount involved . . . in criminal cases, the exposure and risk to the client, the results obtained, tariffs or scales authorized by local law . . . the urgency and uncertainty of reward, and any relevant agreement between the lawyer and the client.

These criteria indicate that the economic value of the legal dispute, or, in criminal cases, the seriousness of the charge, will necessarily affect the value of the legal services provided.

The *Code of Professional Conduct* also makes it clear that the practice of charging contingency fees is an acceptable one, although some provinces prohibit it. When contingency fees are agreed upon by lawyer and client, the lawyer provides services on the basis that the client will be billed only if the action is successful. The amount charged will typically be a percentage of the total award, potentially providing a greater enrichment than the lawyer would have received if the legal tariff had been applied irrespective of the result in the case. In any event, the code dictates that the contingency fee must again be "fair and reasonable."

These principles aside, there are significant differences in the fees charged by Canada's lawyers for similar kinds of work. Some lawyers have reputations and abilities that can justify more substantial levies. This discrepancy raises the question of whether access to justice is dependent on the ability of individuals or corporations to pay for legal services.

It was mentioned earlier that, over the past three decades, the provision of legal services within Canada has changed markedly. For most of the twentieth century, the consumers of legal services were individuals with significant assets, businesses, governments, or the poor; the latter class of clients was typically involved only in litigation related to crime or accident. Since the 1960s, however, Canadian lawyers have increasingly become involved in serving corporate clients; in drawing from provincial legal-aid plans (particularly in relation to criminal law); and in servicing the needs of more complex kinds of government regulation and legislation in such areas as family law, administrative law, real property, and wills and estates.

The greater affluence of the Canadian population in the postwar era is a leading factor in the increased demand for legal services; the primary use of legal services has been to protect growing individual and corporate wealth. As Stager and Arthurs have observed, these changes have had the effect of creating considerable diversification within the practice of law, leading to substantially different structures for the delivery of legal services. The 1980s and 1990s witnessed the merger of individual law firms into a small number of multi-city international practices serving a wide range of corporate and government clients. Computer technology has also changed the nature of legal research, introducing economies of scale that can benefit all practitioners.

There have been fewer rewards for lawyers concerned with the rights of the disadvantaged or the legal problems of the middle class. Although legal-aid clinics and consumer and environmentally driven practices have become more common, their numbers and their economic well-being pale when placed alongside the rosy financial health of Canada's major corporate law firms. In the face of such discrepancies, could we imagine a system of universal insurance for the provision of all forms of legal assistance—a government-funded program along the lines of Medicare? Is "judicare" a logical next step in the construction of Canada's system of government services?

Medicare proceeds on the premise that all citizens are equally entitled to health care as a matter of right, regardless of wealth, disability, or social contribution—at the least, to a basic minimum of health care. It is not clear, however, that this premise would fairly apply to the provision of all legal services. While a citizen might be said to have a right to a lawyer when facing family separation, a criminal charge, deportation, or the consequences of an accident, it is not clear that there is a corresponding right to use legal services to facilitate and protect the accumulation of real property, stocks and bonds, and similar assets. Thus, if a system of judicare were to be constructed, it would have to take account of the diverse uses of legal services within Canadian society. As noted earlier, corporations, governments, and the wealthy are the major consumers of the product. Most working-class or middle-class Canadians will typically use a lawyer within a fairly restricted set of circumstances: to write a will, purchase a property, facilitate a family separation, or face a charge relating to the criminal law or the operation of a motor vehicle. For these restricted purposes, it may be reasonable to consider a private or government legal insurance program, financed by individual or taxpayer contributions.

Judicial Recruitment and Standards of Conduct

In November 1981, British Columbia Supreme Court Justice Thomas Berger criticized the federal government's abandonment of support for Aboriginal rights during the negotiations that led to the patriation of the Constitution. Berger told the press:

> Our leaders felt it was in the national interest to sacrifice the rights. They felt they were serving the greater good in reaching an agreement. It was mean-spirited. There are a million and more Natives in Canada: Indians, Inuit, and Métis, and for the most part, they are poor and powerless. They were the people who were sacrificed in this deal. That is the whole point of minority rights, that they should not be taken away for any reason.[14]

Berger's statement elicited a strong response from the prime minister, Pierre Trudeau; from Bora Laskin, then chief justice of the Supreme

Court; and, ultimately, from the **Canadian Judicial Council**. The council convened a committee to consider allegations that Justice Berger's comments were detrimental to the interests of an impartial judiciary. It concluded that the comments were "unwise, inappropriate, and indiscreet," but that they were not sufficient to justify his removal from the bench. The committee urged "members of the judiciary [to] avoid taking part in controversial political discussions except only in respect of matters that directly affect the operation of the Courts."[15] Justice Berger, dissatisfied with this restriction on his right to free expression, resigned from the bench. "I believe a judge has the right, a duty, in fact, to speak out on an appropriate occasion on questions of human rights and fundamental freedoms," he told the press.[16]

The so-called Berger affair highlights the issue of an impartial judiciary. As legal academic Paul Weiler has noted, there are essentially two competing models for judicial recruitment, one stressing the impartiality and neutrality of the judiciary and the other stressing the prospective judge's policy-making skills, political beliefs, and past practices. Weiler writes of the model of impartiality, currently in use within Canada:

> [T]he most necessary prerequisite for judicial office is legal training which must be accompanied by some degree of moral probity and respectability; the judge does not campaign for office on the basis of a policy program, but rather is selected for his legal ability, as adjudged primarily by his peers in the profession; once in office, the judge has tenure for life until retirement age, subject only to removal for misbehaviour: the latter ground for impeachment should never include substantive results in particular decisions.[17]

The competing model of judicial recruitment, found in the United States, dictates that a judge will not be impartial and that the political views of the prospective candidate will play a key role in determining eligibility to serve. Weiler notes:

> [T]he logic of the system demands that these (individuals) be evaluated in some manner other than an apolitical appointment process. Instead, judges should either be directly elected, or the various groups whose interests are affected by the judges' decisions should have some more formalized and legitimized form of participation in the making of the selection.[18]

Under both systems of recruitment, it appears that members of the judiciary bring certain political values to the courts, which inform the decisions they make. Legal academic Sidney Peck has found, for example, that justices of the Supreme Court of Canada show patterns of legal decision making that either support an extended interpretation of civil liberties or oppose such an extension.[19] The provincial governments have consistently pushed for input into Supreme Court appointments, knowing that prospective members of the Court will have markedly different views on the division of powers between the federal and provincial governments. The assumption is clear: these political views will find expression in action, specifically, within a wide range of constitutional decisions.

The assumption that the members of Canada's judiciary act as value-neutral, impartial arbiters is difficult to support in empirical terms. A claim of impartiality has rhetorical value, but it is probably more accurate to say that Canadian judges are simply able to act independently of political forces if appointed to their positions.

The question whether the judiciary, once appointed, should be able to express views on the law is at the heart of the "Berger affair." Research on the issue shows that judges do, in fact, bring their economic, social, and political values to the tasks they face on the bench. Moreover, as the esteemed sociologist John Porter once observed, many members of the judiciary in Canada were formerly political elite: Cabinet ministers, members of Parliament, and provincial representatives. "They constitute what must be one of the most curious of occupational systems, one in which a person whose political role is marked by partiality, irrationality, and opinion-expressing assumes a judicial role marked by impartiality, rational inquiry, and attention to fact."[20] Thus, there is an air of pretence in the assumption that the judiciary is or should be impartial. It is not clear that a judge's commitments—to specific human rights or provincial powers, for example—will limit judicial independence or create disrespect among the public toward the legal system. After all, the members of the judiciary are already chosen from a relatively restricted range of political, economic, and social opinion. Canada's federally appointed judges are chosen almost exclusively from the ranks of men and women who support the Conservative and Liberal parties. Those who seek judicial appointment typically support what may fairly be termed "status quo" or "mainstream" political views. The potential judicial appointee must, then, chart a careful course between the Scylla of reformist activism and the Charybdis of bureaucratic inertia.

In its report on Justice Berger, the committee of the Canadian Judicial Council argued that once appointed, he descended to the impropriety of reformist activism:

> It is apparent that some of the Native peoples are unhappy with section 35 of the *Canadian Charter of Rights and Freedoms*. If Justice Berger should be called on to interpret that section, for example,

> the meaning to be given to the word "existing" in the phrase, "the existing aboriginal and treaty rights of the aboriginal peoples of Canada," would the general public have confidence now in his impartiality?[21]

The potential flaw in the council's logic is that the question whether treaty rights exist is not only a legal question, but also a matter of political, economic, and social interpretation. The interpretation of which Aboriginal rights are existing and, correspondingly, which rights have been extinguished, is not ultimately a technical matter, but a moral issue about which judges, lawyers, and other citizens are likely to disagree. To the extent that we continue to ask those who sit in judgment within our legal system to refrain from the expression of political opinion, we continue to confuse the value of judicial independence with the pretence of judicial impartiality.

Conclusion: Law, Lawyers, and the Public Interest

The legal profession in Canada has been dramatically restructured since the Second World War, and particularly since the cultural changes of the late 1960s and early 1970s. The advent of more complex systems of criminal, family, environmental, and consumer law and regulation has increased the need for legal representation. Likewise, the growing complexity of corporate law and regulation has increased government and corporate investment in legal services.

Legal historians Stager and Arthurs argue that the legal profession in Canada is no longer a single profession but a collection of distinct groups of lawyers, lacking political, economic, or cultural cohesion:

> Lawyers who never practise in court are still capable of identifying with the profession's heroes who made their reputations as advocates, but office-bound lawyers will also develop a subculture that is largely foreign to the advocate. For example, the ritual surrounding the "closing" of certain formal transactions has no courtroom counterpart, and the terms used to describe clients, staff, and tasks vary between—and even within—the two types of practice. This accumulation of cultural differences and gradual dissolution of unifying cultural symbols are both the effects and causes of the diminishing cohesion of the profession.[22]

The road ahead for lawyers, judges, and the public is uncertain. For the most part, lawyers are, at least by their own standards, a relatively honest if highly privileged lot. In Ontario, from 1921 to the present, fewer than 1 percent of the province's lawyers have been disciplined in any given year; in fact, the average yearly rate of discipline is close to one-tenth of 1 percent of the profession. But can we demand more of the men and women who practise law, and of those who sit in judgment of others? Probably. But can we actually achieve greater public regulation of the legal industry? Or a greater professional commitment to the elusive Holy Grail of justice, as opposed to adherence to existing political, economic, and moral structures and conventions? The answers to these questions are likely to define the landscape of legal practice for generations to come.

Web Links

Canadian Law School
http://www.canadalawschools.org/
The excellent website created by the Council of Canadian Law Deans provides information for prospective law students. There are links to all Canadian law schools, to colleges and universities in Canada, as well as to the Law School Admission Council, which administers the LSAT.

Federation of Law Societies of Canada
http://www.flsc.ca/
Admission to the bar of each province is controlled by the provincial law societies. This is the website of the umbrella organization of 13 of the 14 law societies in Canada (the Law Society of Nunavut was not a member, as of printing time). The site provides information about admission to the profession generally, as well as links to member societies and their programs.

Canadian Judicial Council
http://www.cjc-ccm.gc.ca/article.asp?id=5
The Canadian Judicial Council's website provides details about the council and its work. One of its functions is the handling of complaints against federally appointed judges. The website has links to media releases and advisories concerning its investigations, as well as the reports and decisions of its committee. It also publishes frequently asked questions dealing with the procedure for making complaints against judges.

National Judicial Institute

http://www.nji.ca/

This is the website of the National Judicial Institute, an educational resource for Canada's federal, provincial, and territorial judges. Its programs reflect "Canada's cultural, racial, and linguistic diversity, as well as the changing demands on the judiciary."

Questions for Discussion

1. What kinds of attributes ought to be crucial for admission to law schools? Is the present system—LSAT and grade point average—the least unfair of possible alternatives?
2. Should a lawyer be disbarred if convicted of the offence of possession of marijuana? What about impaired driving, shoplifting, auto theft, robbery, or murder? Should the standard for disbarment depend on whether the person convicted is a defence counsel, Crown counsel, or judge?
3. Why has there been such a rapid increase in the number of lawyers over the past 30 years? Is social life more complex, requiring lawyers for a myriad of tasks? Or are Canadians more territorial and materialistic, and, accordingly, more litigious?

Further Reading

Canadian Bar Association. *Touchstones for Change: Equality, Diversity and Accountability*. Ottawa: Canadian Bar Association, 1993.

> This 300-page task force report looks at the legal profession in Canada and its difficulties in establishing both equality and diversity within the practice and administration of law. The report covers the issues of barriers to entry into the profession; women in the legal profession; barriers to equality; problems in private, government, and corporate practice, faculties of law, administrative tribunals, and the judiciary. The report concludes with more than 100 recommendations regarding equality and diversity.

Kay, F.M., and J. Brockman. "Barriers to Equality in the Canadian Legal Establishment." *Feminist Legal Studies* 8, 4 (2000): 169–98.

> This article chronicles current difficulties faced by women in achieving equality within the Canadian legal profession. The

authors canvass the historical exclusion of women from the legal profession, contemporary patterns of inequality, the gap in wages, departures from practice, and difficulties in accommodating family and the workplace.

Tong, D., and W. Wesley Pue. "The Best and the Brightest?: Canadian Law School Admissions." *Osgoode Hall Law Journal* 37, 4 (1999): 843–79. Tong and Pue examine the process of law school admission, questioning the relevance of the LSAT (law school admission test), and the reliance placed by admissions committees on the combination of grade point average and LSAT score. The authors discuss the goals of legal education and the values of diversity and social equity within the legal profession. The authors then query the extent to which current admissions policies are able to reflect these values of diversity and social equity.

Notes

1. H. Arthurs, *Law and Learning* (Ottawa: Supply and Services, 1984), 13.
2. Osgoode Hall Law School website (http://www.yorku.ca/osgoode/admissions/applying/aboriginalapps.html).
3. Osgoode Hall Law School website (http://www.yorku.ca/osgoode/admissions/applying/accessapps.html).
4. D. Tong and W. Wesley Pue, "The Best and the Brightest? Canadian Law School Admissions," *Osgoode Hall Law Journal* 37, 4 (1999): 843–79.
5. D.A.A. Stager and H.W. Arthurs, *Lawyers in Canada* (Toronto: University of Toronto Press, 1990), 318.
6. Ibid.
7. R.K. Wilkins, "The Person You're Supposed to Become: The Politics of the Law School Experience," *University of Toronto Faculty of Law Review* (1987): 45.
8. Ibid., 140.
9. R. Ericson and P. Baranek, *The Ordering of Justice: A Study of Accused Persons as Dependants in the Criminal Process* (Toronto: University of Toronto Press, 1982), 14.
10. Canadian Bar Association, *Touchstones for Change: Equality, Diversity and Accountability* (Ottawa: Canadian Bar Association, 1993), 74.
11. F.M. Kay and J. Brockman, "Barriers to Gender Equality in the Canadian Legal Establishment, *Feminist Legal Studies* 8 (2000): 169–198.

12. [1991] 3 S.C.R. 326, 68 C.C.C. (3d) 1.
13. The cases are excerpted from the Discipline Digest of the Law Society of Upper Canada (www.lsuc.on.ca/regulation/a/discipline).
14. T. Berger, cited in F.L. Morton, ed., *Law, Politics and the Judicial System in Canada* (Calgary: University of Calgary Press, 1984), 109.
15. "Report of the Committee of Investigation to the Canadian Judicial Council," in *Law, Politics and the Judicial System in Canada,* edited by Morton, ibid., 120.
16. Berger, in *Law, Politics and the Judicial System in Canada,* ibid., 109.
17. P. Weiler, "Two Models: Judicial Recruitment," *Canadian Bar Review* (1968): 406.
18. Ibid.
19. S.R. Peck, "Patterns in Judicial Decision Making Within the Supreme Court of Canada," *Osgoode Hall Law Journal* (1969): 323.
20. John Porter, *The Vertical Mosaic* (Toronto: University of Toronto Press, 1965), 415.
21. "Report of the Committee of Investigation to the Canadian Judicial Council," vol. III in *Law, Politics and the Judicial System in Canada,* edited by Morton.
22. Stager and Arthurs, *Lawyers in Canada.*

References

Arthurs, H.W. *Law and Learning.* Ottawa: Supply and Services, 1984.

——. "Poor Canadian Legal Education: So Near to Wall Street, So Far from God," *Osgoode Hall Law Journal* 381, 38 (2000).

Brockman, J. "Leaving the Practice of Law: The Wherefores and the Whys." *Alberta Law Review* 32, 1 (1994): 116–76.

Colvin, E. "The Executive and the Independence of the Judiciary." *Provincial Judges' Journal* 11 (1987): 229.

Dickson, B. "Legal Education." *Canadian Bar Review* 64 (1986): 374.

Erickson, P.G. "Legalistic and Traditional Role Expectations for Defence Counsel in Juvenile Court." *Canadian Journal of Criminology and Corrections* 17 (1975): 78.

Ericson, R., and P. Baranek. *The Ordering of Justice: A Study of Accused Persons as Dependants in the Criminal Process.* Toronto: University of Toronto Press, 1982.

Finlayson, G.D. "Self-government of the Legal Profession—Can it Continue?" *Advocates Society Journal* 4 (1985): 1.

Gall, G. *The Canadian Legal System*. 3d ed. Toronto: Carswell, 1990, Chapter 9.

Johnston, D.L. "Role of the Lawyer in Our Society." *Gazette* 13 (1979): 119.

Laskin, B. "The Lawyer's Responsibility in the Supervision of the Legal Order." *Gazette* 4 (1970): 210.

LeDain, G. "The Quest for Justice: The Role of the Profession." *University of New Brunswick Law Journal* 19 (1969): 18.

Martin, G.A. "The Role and the Responsibility of the Defence Advocate." *Criminal Law Quarterly* 12 (1970): 376.

Morton, F.L., ed. *Law, Politics and the Judicial Process in Canada*. Calgary: University of Calgary Press, 1989.

Peck, S.R. "Patterns in Judicial Decision Making Within the Supreme Court of Canada." *Osgoode Hall Law Journal* (1969): 323.

Pirie, A.J. "The Lawyer as Mediator: Professional Responsibility Problems or Profession Problems?" *Canadian Bar Review* 63 (1985): 378.

Stager, D.A.A., and H.W. Arthurs. *Lawyers in Canada.* Toronto: University of Toronto Press, 1990.

Starr, G., L. Fisher, and L. Katz. "By Choice, by Chance, by Birthright: The First Three Years of an Admissions Policy." In *Essays on Legal Education*, edited by N. Gold. Toronto: Butterworths, 1982.

Taman, L., and F. Zemans. "The Future of Legal Services." *Canadian Bar Review* 5 (1973): 32.

Tong, D., and W. Wesley Pue. "The Best and the Brightest? Canadian Law School Admissions." *Osgoode Hall Law Journal* 37, 4 (1999): 843–79.

Weiler, P. "Two Models: Judicial Recruitment." *Canadian Bar Review* (1968).

Wilkins, R.K. "The Person You're Supposed to Become: The Politics of the Law School Experience." *University of Toronto Faculty of Law Review* 45 (1987): 98.

PART 3

Substantive Law

CHAPTER 7

Torts of Intention and Negligence: Private Law, Public Interest

In summer time, village cricket is the delight of everyone. Nearly every village has its own cricket field where the young men play and old men watch. In the village of Lintz in County Durham, they have their own ground, where they have played these last 70 years. They tend it well. The wicket area is well rolled and mown. The outfield is kept short. It has a good clubhouse for the players and seats for the onlookers. The village team plays there on Saturdays and Sundays. They belong to a league, competing with the neighbouring villages. On other evenings after work, they practise while the light lasts. Yet now after these 70 years, a judge of the High Court has ordered that they must not play there any more. He has issued an injunction to stop them.

He has done it at the instance of a newcomer (the plaintiff) who is no lover of cricket. This newcomer has built, or has had built for him, a house on the edge of the cricket ground, which four years ago was a field where cattle grazed. The animals did not mind the cricket. But now this adjoining field has been turned into a housing estate. The newcomer bought one of the houses on the edge of the cricket ground. No doubt the open space was a selling point. Now he complains that when a batsman hits a six, the ball has been known to land in his garden or near his house. His wife has got so upset about it that they always go out at weekends. They do not go into the garden when cricket is being played. They say that this is intolerable. So they asked the judge to stop the cricket being played. And the judge, much against his will, has felt that he must order the cricket to be stopped with the consequence, I suppose, that the Lintz Cricket Club will disappear. The cricket ground will be turned to some other use. I expect for more houses or a factory. The young men will turn to other things instead of cricket. The whole village will be much the poorer. And all this because of a newcomer who has just bought a house there next to the cricket ground.

(Lord Denning, *Miller v. Jackson*)

The situation described above is in the realm of **torts**, the remedying of private wrongs. The word "tort" is derived from Latin *tortus*: "crooked" or "wrong." In the contemporary world, "tort" is defined by *The Oxford*

Reference Dictionary as "a breach of a legal duty, other than under contract, with liability for damages." In Anglo-Saxon England, there was no clear distinction between a crime and a tort. The offending individual within a given clan or group would be required to compensate the offended clan or group for damages, and to pay the king some sum of money for breaching the peace. With the centralization of political authority, taken first by the monarchy and later by elected governments, the separation between tort and crime became significant. From the eleventh century onward, tort and crime were distinguished in Britain.

Crime and Tort: Distinctions and Similarities

We now define a crime as a public wrong, an offence against the public interest. We define a tort as a private wrong, an offence against the private interest of an individual, corporation, or government. At first glance, however, tort and crime seem easily equated. If you are walking down the street and you are assaulted by a man with a baseball bat, the assault is both a crime and a tort. The man is liable to be charged by the police for his violation of the assault provisions of the *Criminal Code*. But you may also pursue a civil claim in tort for this assault, going to court to recover damages from the man for his intentional infliction of physical harm. The object of the tort system is to compensate victims of either intentional acts or negligent acts. There is no guilt in tort, only a testing of liability. Criminal law, on the other hand, does not exist to compensate victims of various prohibited acts, but to punish wrongdoers and, in so doing, protect the general community (i.e., the country).

The purposes and scope of criminal law are broader than those of tort law. Criminal law is designed to respond to infringements against the public interest; sanctions are imposed in order to deter specific offenders from further crime, as well as to deter the general public from the commission of prohibited acts. Criminal law is also designed to rehabilitate offenders, so that they may be usefully reintegrated into the community. Its final purpose, independent of the effectiveness of deterrence or rehabilitation, is to express moral condemnation of proscribed behaviours.

Perhaps the case that best illustrates the distinction between criminal law conviction and tort liability is that of O.J. Simpson, the former football star who was charged with the murder of his wife, Nicole Brown, and her friend, Ron Goldman. Simpson was found not guilty after a long criminal trial; but when the Goldman and Brown families went to civil court to claim damages from Simpson for the wrongful deaths of their children, they were successful. The criminal court jury concluded that the public offence of murder had not been proven beyond a reasonable doubt; but when the case was heard as a private matter (between Simpson and the families of his victims), a civil jury determined that it was more probable than not that Mr. Simpson was responsible for these deaths. On the basis of the jury's finding of tortious liability, substantial damages were ordered to be paid by Simpson to the Goldmans and the Browns.

Tort law exists only to compensate for private wrongs. An action may be brought in either **intentional tort**—in response to the intentional infliction of mental or physical harm to persons or property—or, more commonly, in **negligence**—in response to the failure of an individual or collectivity to conform to a standard of reasonable care. Negligence may be premised upon doing something that a **reasonable person** would not be expected to do, or upon a failure or omission to do something that a reasonable person would be expected to do. In *Miller v. Jackson*, the British case from which the quotation at the start of the chapter was taken, the **plaintiffs** alleged negligence on the part of the cricketers— that is, they claimed the cricketers were doing something that a reasonable person would not be expected to do.[1]

The standards of tort liability and criminal conviction are very different in another important respect. Tort liability is premised upon meeting a balance of probabilities test, whereas criminal conviction demands proof of the offence beyond a reasonable doubt. Hence, it is much less difficult to find liability in tort; the plaintiff has only to make a case that is more probable than not.

Finally, criminal law premises criminal conviction upon a coincidence of *mens rea* and *actus reus:* an evil mind and an evil act. In order to be found guilty of a crime, an accused must have both committed the evil act and possessed an evil intention. In other words, the accused must be aware of, or able to appreciate, his or her responsibility for the crime. For example, an accused in possession of either stolen property or an illegal drug must have knowledge of possession—an evil intention. A person who has committed the evil act of murder must be able to appreciate what he or she has done in order to be found criminally culpable. Without awareness of this kind, a verdict of not guilty by reason of insanity might result. In tort law, particularly in the realm of negligence, there is no requirement of *mens rea*—evil intention.

Despite these important differences between criminal and tort law, there are areas in which they coincide, as noted earlier. An assault may be both a crime and an intentional tort, thereby giving rise to both criminal court proceedings and a civil tort action against the aggressor in order to recover damages for the intentional infliction of physical harm. In practice, however, very few victims of assault commence tort actions against their attackers, typically because the defendant in such cases has virtually no financial resources. Justice as a private matter can be extracted only from the wealthy. In an attempt to remedy this defect, most provinces have created criminal injury compensation boards or tribunals; these agencies make financial awards, on behalf of the state, to victims of violent crime.

There is one other coincidence of tort law and criminal law: the **Criminal Code**[2] defines certain kinds of negligence as criminal. Sections 219 and 220 of the *Code* create offences of criminal negligence and criminal negligence causing death.

219. (1) Every one is criminally negligent who
    (a) in doing anything, or
    (b) in omitting to anything that it is his duty to do,
  shows wanton or reckless disregard for the lives or safety of other persons.
  (2) For the purposes of this section, "duty" means a duty imposed by law.
220. Every one who by criminal negligence causes death to another person is guilty of an indictable offence and is liable to imprisonment for life.

This overlap in the jurisdictions of tort and crime notwithstanding, the purposes of tort law remain both quite distinct from and more limited than those of criminal law. As stated previously, tort law exists primarily to compensate those who have been wronged either by the intentional infliction of harm or by acts of negligence. While it is often argued that a complementary function of tort law is to impose **punitive damages** in order to deter negligent conduct and the intentional infliction of harm, this is far from a universally accepted principle. According to this view, the court's adjudication and ultimate award to a wronged plaintiff can have what has been termed an "appeasement" or "denunciation" function, serving simultaneously to condemn publicly the conduct of the defendant and to vindicate the rights of the plaintiff.[3]

There are difficulties with the punitive-deterrence and appeasement or denunciation functions of tort law. First, an emphasis on punitive damages in tort would duplicate the existing imposition of sanctions by the criminal court system, potentially imposing two sets of punishment upon an accused. Second, because the overwhelming majority of tort actions are to be found in the realm of negligence, specifically, in the realm of non-criminal negligence, the goals of punishment and denunciation are more difficult to justify.

And now, what of the cricketers and their plight in *Miller v. Jackson?* Lord Denning concluded:

> This case is new. It should be approached on principles applicable to modern conditions. There is a contest here between the interest of the public at large and the interest of a private individual. The public interest lies in protecting the environment by preserving our playing fields in the face of mounting development, and by enabling our youth to enjoy all the benefits of outdoor games, such as cricket and football. The private interest lies in securing the privacy of his home and garden without intrusion or interference by anyone. In deciding between these two conflicting interests, it must be remembered that it is not a question of damages. If by a million-to-one chance a cricket ball does go out of the ground and causes damage, the cricket club will pay. There is no difficulty on that score. Nor is it a question of an injunction. And in our law, you will find it repeatedly affirmed that an injunction is a discretionary remedy. In a new situation like this, we have to think afresh as to how discretion should be exercised. On the one hand, Mrs. Miller is a very sensitive lady who has worked herself up into such a state that she exclaimed to the judge:
>
> *I just want to be allowed to live in peace. Have we got to wait until someone is killed before anything can be done?*
>
> If she feels like that about it, it is quite plain that, for peace in the future, one or other has to move. Either the cricket club has to move, but goodness knows where. I do not suppose for a moment there is any field in Lintz to which they could move. Or Mrs. Miller must move elsewhere. As between their conflicting interests, I am of opinion that the public interest should prevail over the private interest. The cricket club should not be driven out. In my opinion, the right exercise of discretion is to refuse an injunction; and, of course, to refuse damages in lieu of an injunction. Likewise as to the claim for past damages. The club was entitled to use this ground for cricket in the accustomed way. It was not a nuisance, nor was it negligence of them so to run it. Nor was the batsman negligent when he hit the ball for six. All were doing simply what they were entitled to do. So if the club had put it to the test, I would have dismissed the claim for damages also. But as the club very fairly says that they are willing to pay for any damage, I am content that there should be an award of 400 pounds to cover any past or future damage.

Lord Denning's decision is noteworthy in that it pits the private inter-ests of tort law against more general principles of public policy. Although decisions in tort involve the resolution of the competing claims of private interests (in this case, the Lintz Cricket Club and the Millers), they may also involve the imposition of an overriding public interest on the decision-making process.

How might Lord Denning's decision have changed with changes in circumstances? What if the Millers' suit against the cricket club had resulted from a ball hit through the window, crashing into the side of Mrs. Miller's face, breaking her jaw, and knocking out her teeth? Alternatively, what if a member of the Lintz Cricket Club had inten-tionally thrown a cricket ball through the window, frustrated with the Millers' opposition to the use of the cricket ground?

In the first instance of a claim in negligence, it is not clear, given Lord Denning's logic, that the outcome would have been any different. The severity of Mrs. Miller's injuries would have been acknowledged as regrettable, but Lord Denning's principle governing *Miller v. Jackson* would still hold: "As between their conflicting interests, I am of opinion that the public interest should prevail over the private interest. The cricket club should not be driven out. In my opinion, the right exercise of discretion is to refuse an injunction; and, of course, to refuse damages in lieu of an injunction."

What about the second hypothetical situation—what if injuries to Mrs. Miller had resulted from an intentional tort, such as a ball tossed through the window while she was walking in front of it? Could the Lintz Cricket Club continue to claim that there should be no liability? Might criminal charges be warranted?

Intentional Infliction of Mental or Physical Harm: The Scope of Liability

A wide range of circumstances exist—assault and battery, false imprisonment, malicious prosecution, and the intentional infliction of mental harm—where liability in tort can flow from intentional conduct. Two key questions arise in these cases: Is the standard for liability similar to the standard imposed in instances of negligence? Is it similar to the standard imposed for conviction in criminal cases?

The Standard in Intentional Conduct v. the Standard in Negligence

Consider, with respect to the first question above (Is the standard for liability similar to the standard imposed in instances of negligence?), the case of *Bettel v. Yim.*

Borins, County Court Judge: The events giving rise to this action took place on May 22, 1976, in a variety store owned and operated by the defendant, Ki Yim, situated in a small commercial plaza located in Metropolitan Toronto. . . .

The defendant testified that the plaintiff, together with six or seven other boys, entered the store and went to the area of the pinball machines. Some of the boys were playing with a toy football and toy guns and the defendant told them to leave his store. Half of the boys, including the plaintiff, left and went outside. The defendant saw the plaintiff lighting matches and throwing them into the store. On the first occasion, the plaintiff entered the store and retrieved a burning match. The second match that was thrown into the store burned itself out. Then the plaintiff re-entered the store, proceeded toward the pinball machines and said, "What's the smell?" The defendant smelled nothing, but after 20 or 30 seconds, he saw flames coming from the bag of charcoal and proceeded to remove the bag from the store, unassisted by the plaintiff, who remained inside. The defendant did not see who had thrown the match which started the fire.

As the defendant returned to the store, he saw the plaintiff walking toward the door. He grabbed the plaintiff by the arm as he did not want the plaintiff to leave. The plaintiff denied that he set the fire. The plaintiff did not try to leave. He stood where he was. Because the plaintiff denied setting the fire, the defendant grabbed him firmly by the collar with both hands and began shaking him. His purpose in doing so was to obtain a confession from the plaintiff before he called the police. The plaintiff's constant denials had made the defendant unhappy. He shook the plaintiff two or three times and then his head came down and struck the plaintiff's nose. He relaxed his hold on the plaintiff, who fell to the ground. The defendant obtained some kleenex for the plaintiff, who was bleeding from the nose, and helped him to his feet. The defendant then telephoned the police.

In explaining the incident, the defendant said: "I shook him maybe three times and my head and his nose accidentally hit; I didn't intend to hit him." In cross-examination, he stated that he did not mean to hit the plaintiff with his head and that is why he said it was an accident. . . .

The law

The plaintiff has framed his action in assault. Properly speaking, the action should have been framed in battery, which is the intentional infliction upon the body of another of a harmful or offensive contact. However, in Canada, it would appear that the distinction between assault and battery has been blurred and when one speaks of an assault, it may include a battery. . . . [Note to students: Assault has occurred when there is a reasonable apprehension of bodily harm; battery has occurred when bodily harm is actually inflicted.]

On the defendant's evidence, his act in grabbing the plaintiff with both his hands and shaking him constituted the intentional tort of battery. It is obvious that he desired to bring about an offensive or harmful contact with the plaintiff for the purpose of extracting a confession from him. Viewed as such, the defendant's own evidence proves, rather than disproves, the element of intent insofar as this aspect of his physical contact with the plaintiff is concerned. Indeed, the defendant's admitted purpose in grabbing and shaking the plaintiff does not fit into any of the accepted defences to the tort of battery—consent, self-defence, defence of property, necessity, and legal authority. . . .

That there is no liability for accidental harm is central to the submission of defence counsel who argues that the shaking of the plaintiff by the defendant and the striking of the plaintiff by the defendant's head must be regarded as separate and distinct incidents. While he concedes that the defendant intentionally grabbed and shook the plaintiff, he submits that the contact with the head was unintentional. I have, of course, accepted the defendant's evidence in this regard. This, in my view, gives rise to the important question: Can an intentional wrongdoer be held liable for consequences which he did not intend? Another way of stating the problem is to ask whether the doctrine of foreseeability as found in the law of negligence is applicable to the law of intentional torts. Should an intentional wrongdoer be liable only for the reasonably foreseeable consequences of his intentional application of force, or should he bear responsibility for all the consequences which flow from his intentional act? . . .

It is my respectful view that the weight of opinion is that the concept of foreseeability as defined by the law of negligence is a concept that ought not to be imported into the field of intentional torts. . . . In the law of intentional torts, it is the dignitary interest, the right of the plaintiff to insist that the defendant keep his hands to himself, that the law has for centuries sought to protect. In doing so, the morality of the defendant's conduct, characterized as "unlawful", has predominated the thinking of the Courts and is reflected in academic discussion. The logical test is whether the defendant was guilty of deliberate, intentional, and unlawful violence or threats of violence. If he was, and a more serious harm befalls the plaintiff than was intended by the defendant, the defendant, and not the innocent plaintiff, must bear the responsibility for the unintended result. If physical contact was intended, the fact that its magnitude exceeded all reasonable or intended expectations, should make no difference. To hold otherwise, in my opinion, would unduly narrow recovery where one deliberately invades the bodily interest of another with the result that the totally innocent plaintiff would be deprived of full recovery for the totality of the injuries suffered as a result of the deliberate invasion of his bodily interests.

To import negligence concepts into the field of intentional torts would be to ignore the essential difference between the intentional infliction of harm and the unintentional infliction of harm resulting from a failure to adhere to a reasonable standard of care, and would result in bonusing the deliberate wrongdoer who strikes the plaintiff more forcefully than intended.[4]

The decision of Judge Borins in this case draws a line between a standard to be employed with torts of negligence and a standard to be employed with intentional torts. His argument is that the concept of foreseeability, while integral to a tort of negligence, would unfairly diminish the prospects for a plaintiff's recovery in cases involving an intentional tort. With intentional torts, it is sufficient that the **defendant** intended harm, and it is no answer to claim that some amount of the damage was not foreseeable. In the *Bettel v. Yim* case, the fact that Yim did not intend to strike Bettel's nose with his head, or could not foresee that he would do so, does not limit his liability for the assault.

The Standard in Intentional Conduct v. the Standard in Criminal Offences

When the standard for **liability** for intentional torts is compared with that for criminal offences, one can see that liability attaches more easily to intentional torts than it does to criminal offences. Liability for intentional torts may be established where it could not be justified for either negligence or a criminal offence. Consider first the case of *Tillander v. Gosselin.*

Grant, J.: The infant plaintiff who was born on August 4, 1960, at all material times was under the care of her mother at the home of the child's parents in the Township of East Ferris, in the District of Nipissing. The infant defendant who was born on August 12, 1960, lived with his parents in the adjoining property. On July 24, 1963, the infant plaintiff's mother had placed her in a baby carriage in an enclosed area adjacent to their home. Although no other person saw what took place, it is evident the infant defendant had entered such enclosed area and removed the infant plaintiff from her carriage and dragged her over 100 feet on to the Gosselin property. In the course thereof, he had either let the infant fall or had struck her, as she sustained a diastatic fracture of the right parietal bone of the skull. . . .

The infant defendant at the time of this mishap was about one week less than 3 years of age. If he was capable of forming an intent to do what he did, his actions would amount to an assault. The question to be decided is, can an infant of that age be held responsible in damages in such circumstances?

The action is framed in trespass (a form of intentional tort). It cannot be said to be in negligence because the defendant had no right whatever to touch or remove the infant. . . .

[I]n an action for damages in trespass where the plaintiff proves that he has been injured by the direct act of the defendant, the onus falls upon the defendant to prove that his act was both unintentional and without negligence on his part. If he fails to do so, the plaintiff must succeed; but if he succeeds, he is entitled to judgement dismissing the claim. In this action, the defendant's tender age at the time of the alleged assault satisfies me that he cannot be cloaked with the mental ability of the ordinary reasonable man, and hence negligence cannot be imputed to him. That same condition satisfies me that he cannot be said to have acted deliberately and with intention when the injuries were inflicted upon the infant plaintiff.

I do not believe that one can describe the act of a normal 3-year-old child in doing injury to the baby plaintiff in this case as a voluntary act on his part. There is no evidence as to what instrument, if any, was used to inflict the injury. The infant plaintiff may have been struck by some object or she might have been dropped on a stone, but as indicated, the plaintiff's rights must be considered on the basis of an action for assault. The defendant child, however, would not have the mental ability at the age of 3 to appreciate or know the real nature of the act he was performing. A child of that age emulates or imitates the actions of those about him rather than making his own decisions. In the present case, there could be no genuine intent formulated in his mind to do harm to the child plaintiff or to perform whatever act he did that caused the injury.

For these reasons, the action must be dismissed.[5]

Consider, by contrast, the decision in *Tindale v. Tindale* brought down in 1950 by the Supreme Court of British Columbia.[6] In this case, a mother, suffering from delusions, attacked her daughter with an axe. Although the mother could not be found criminally responsible for her actions, she was found liable in tort. Justice Macfarlane concluded that "the child here is an innocent and unfortunate sufferer on whom no fault can possibly lie. . . . [T]he estate of the mother should be used, so far as it avails, to provide for the necessary medical expenses of the child . . . in her crippled condition."

In 1957, the Supreme Court (Queen's Bench) of Manitoba made a similar finding in *Phillips v. Soloway*. The defendant had attacked the plaintiff with a knife, cutting the plaintiff's eye so badly that the eyeball had to be removed. The chief justice of the Supreme Court of Manitoba found that the rules governing insanity within the *Criminal Code* are not applicable to tort law. He concluded that "it makes no difference whether the defendant was or was not capable of knowing that his act was wrong."[7]

How, then, are we to distinguish liability for intentional torts from liability in criminal law? In *Tillander v. Gosselin,* there is a similarity in application, but in *Tindale v. Tindale* and *Phillips v. Soloway*, liability in tort diverges from criminal liability. Perhaps the best response to this apparent inconsistency, albeit not an entirely satisfactory one, is to note that criminal conviction and sanction require a more substantial burden of proof than liability in tort. Proof of liability on a balance of probabilities dictates a lower threshold of responsibility for a given action; some minimal awareness of the wrong is sufficient. The consequences of liability in tort are primarily economic, less encompassing than the consequences of criminal conviction: imprisonment, moral denunciation, and social stigmatization. Tort law, primarily concerned with the compensation of victims, is accordingly less focused on the mental state of the defendant. In order to establish tort liability, it is not necessary that a tortfeasor possess *mens rea*, at least not in the manner prescribed by criminal law.

Defences to Intentional Tort

In the *Bettel v. Yim* case, the Court mentioned the defences to claims of damages from intentional torts: consent, self-defence, defence of property, necessity, and legal authority. Examples of these defences are relatively easy to imagine. A police officer's use of force might, if undertaken by a citizen, constitute a tortious act; the police officer could be said to have acted under legal authority. Similarly, a person might intrude upon or damage another person or another person's property in order to avoid a physically threatening event; the defence would be necessity.

Self-defence is almost self-explanatory. If one harms another in defence of oneself, no liability arises. However, the extent and appropriateness of the response to a threat may give rise to liability.

Consent to an intentional tort can also apply as a defence, either in relation to sexual contacts or in relation to sporting contests in which injuries and damages are sustained. Consent is especially important in the context of sexual assault. Unlike most other assaults, consent is relatively common in sexual interactions. While it is virtually unthinkable for individuals to consent to being punched, kicked, stabbed, or shot, consent to sexual contact is considerably more common than sexual contact without consent. In suits to recover damages for sexual assault, the most common defence is that the person, typically the woman, consented to sexual activity. Therefore, the factual issue of consent is usually central to allegations of sexual assault.

Similarly, contact sports permit assaults that would otherwise be actionable. In boxing, football, hockey, and the like, it is fair to say that the participants consent to some forms of assault; these normally tortious acts fall within the rules of the game. In boxing, for example, the object of the game is to punch one's opponent into unconsciousness. In football and hockey, assaults that leave an individual with a concussion or a broken leg can be well within the rules of the game. Nonetheless, some assaults in sport may be outside the rules, leading to criminal charges and/or claims in tort. The task of determining tortious liability in such circumstances is necessarily focused on the specifics of what a person consents to when he or she steps onto the football field or hockey rink or into the boxing ring. While it is clear that assault with a knife would fall outside the rules of all these sports and hence be actionable, liability for inflicting an injury immediately after the conclusion of the match or liability for using a hockey stick as a weapon during the course of the game is much less certain.

Negligence and the Standard of the Reasonable Person

We noted at the outset of this chapter that the most common form of claim in tort is a claim in negligence. Claims in negligence began to appear in England at the time of the Industrial Revolution, placing a duty of care upon citizens within certain relationships. In 1856, in the case of *Blyth v. Birmingham Water Works*, the Court of Exchequer defined negligence in the following manner: "Negligence is the omission to do something which a reasonable man, guided upon those considerations which ordinarily regulate the conduct of human affairs, would do, or doing something which a prudent and reasonable man would not do."[8] (The gender-specific nature of reasonableness is, of course, a reflection of the era in which this judgment was written. Women had yet to secure the right to vote; the question of their reasonableness in relation to negligence was moot.)

In 1932, in the landmark negligence case of *Donoghue v. Stevenson*, Lord Atkin further defined the concept.

> The rule that you are to love your neighbour becomes in law, you must not injure your neighbour, and the lawyer's question, Who is my neighbour? receives a restricted reply. You must take reasonable care to avoid acts or omissions which you can reasonably foresee would be likely to injure your neighbour. Who, then, in law is my neighbour? The answer seems to be persons who are so closely and directly affected by my act that I ought reasonably to have them in contemplation as being so affected when I am directing my mind to the acts or omissions which are called in question.[9]

Donoghue v. Stevenson was a landmark case because of its extension of the doctrine of negligence to the products of manufacturers. The plaintiff, Donoghue, brought an action to recover damages from the manufacturer of a bottle of ginger beer. In the process of consuming part of a bottle of the defendant's ginger beer, the plaintiff had discovered the decomposing remains of a snail. This discovery caused the plaintiff to suffer shock and severe gastroenteritis. She argued that the defendant manufacturer should have had a system of inspection sufficient to prevent snails and other contaminants from getting into ginger beer bottles. Britain's House of Lords allowed the plaintiff's appeal, supporting their decision with the following logic:

> Lord Atkin: The question is whether the manufacturer of an article of drink sold by him to a distributor in circumstances which prevent the distributor or the ultimate purchaser or consumer from discovering by inspection any defect is under any legal duty to the ultimate purchaser or consumer to take reasonable care that the article is free from defect likely to cause injury to health. . . .
>
> My Lords, if your Lordships accept the view that this pleading discloses a relevant cause of action, you will be affirming the proposition that by Scots and English law alike, a manufacturer of products, which he sells in such a form as to show that he intends them to reach the ultimate consumer in the form in which they left him with no reasonable possibility of intermediate examination, and with the knowledge that the absence of reasonable care in the preparation or putting up of the products will result in an injury to the consumer's life or property, owes a duty to the consumer to take that reasonable care.
>
> It is a proposition which I venture to say no one in Scotland or England who was not a lawyer would for one moment doubt. It will be an advantage to make it clear that the law in this matter, as in most others, is in accordance with sound common sense. I think that this appeal should be allowed.

> Lord Macmillan: . . . [A]s I have pointed out, it is not enough to prove the respondent to be careless in his process of manufacture. The question is, Does he owe a duty to take care, and to whom does he owe that duty?
>
> Now I have no hesitation in affirming that a person who for gain engages in the business of manufacturing articles of food and drink intended for consumption by members of the public in the form in which he issues them is under a duty to take care in the manufacture of these articles. That duty, in my opinion, he owes to those whom he intends to consume his products. He manufactures his commodities for human consumption; he intends and contemplates that they shall be consumed. . . .
>
> It must always be a question of circumstances whether the carelessness amounts to negligence, and whether the injury is not too remote from the carelessness. I can readily conceive that where a manufacturer has parted with his produce and it has passed into other hands, it may well be exposed to vicissitudes which may render it defective or noxious, for which the manufacturer could not

in any view be held to be to blame. It may be a good general rule to regard responsibility as ceasing when control ceases. So, also, where between the manufacturer and the user there is interposed a party who has the means and opportunity of examining the manufacturer's product before he reissues it to the actual user. But where, as in the present case, the article of consumption is so prepared as to be intended to reach the consumer in the condition in which it leaves the manufacturer, and the manufacturer takes steps to ensure this by sealing or otherwise closing the container so that the contents cannot be tampered with, I regard his control as remaining effective until the article reaches the consumer and the container is opened by him. The intervention of any exterior agency is intended to be excluded and was in fact in the present case excluded.

The test of product liability for negligence, as set out by Lord Atkin and Lord Macmillan, focuses on the extent to which the product in question can be altered after leaving the manufacturer. If it is possible that individuals other than the manufacturer could affect the form or safety of the product before it reaches the consumer, the manufacturer's liability may be limited or terminated.

In contemporary cases of product liability, the legal issues in dispute have been compounded. The courts must not only sort out responsibility for a plaintiff's loss, but also determine whether sufficient information has been provided to potential consumers, asking, in the specific case, whether adequate warnings and instructions were given to the plaintiff.

In the 1972 case of *Lambert v. Lastoplex Chemicals Co.*, for example, the Supreme Court of Canada was faced with a tort action against a chemical company. The case was premised on the failure of the chemical company to warn consumers about the safe use of its product. The plaintiff had been badly burned and his house damaged by an explosion of lacquer sealer manufactured by the defendant. Unlike a competitor, Lastoplex Chemicals had not warned consumers of the need for adequate ventilation to the outdoors when applying the lacquer sealer, or of the danger of explosion if the sealer was applied near a furnace. The Supreme Court had this to say of the law in such an instance:

> The applicable principle of law according to which the positions of the parties in this case should be assessed may be stated as follows. Where manufactured products are put on the market for ultimate purchase and use by the general public and carry danger (in this case, by reason of inflammability), although put to the use for which they were intended, the manufacturer, knowing of their hazardous nature, has a duty to specify the attendant dangers, which it must

be taken to appreciate in a detail not known to the ordinary
consumer or user. A general warning, as for example, that the
product is inflammable, will not suffice where the likelihood of fire
may be increased according to the surroundings in which it may
reasonably be expected that the product will be used. The required
explicitness of the warning will, of course, vary with the danger
likely to be encountered in the ordinary use of the product.[10]

Now consider the application of the principle in the more recent decision
in *Nicholson v. John Deere Ltd.*

Smith, J.: This is a products liability case. The product is a John
Deere garden and lawn riding mower purchased by the plaintiffs in
1976 at an auction and several times repaired by the defendant
Hutchinson Farm Supply Limited of Stouffville, Ontario. . . .

The plaintiffs claim damages for the loss of their home and contents destroyed in a fire which occurred on May 23, 1981. It is alleged
that the fire was caused by a known defect in the design of the unit. It
was said to be inherently dangerous and it is contended that there was
a failure to rectify the defect and/or to adequately warn of the dangers. The hazard and risk of potential fire arose out of close proximity
of the exposed positive battery post and the fuel tank. The action
against Hutchinson is for negligent servicing and failure to warn. . . .

About noon on the day in question, the female plaintiff went to
her garage situated on the side of the house but not attached to it.
With the garage door open, she proceeded to refill the fuel tank on
the tractor. The hood had to be lifted to gain access to the tank. She
was using a two-gallon plastic container. She removed the cap and
placed it on the flat tank surface. She started to pour gasoline into the
tank and, realizing that the cap had started to roll toward the adjacent
battery, she retrieved it. She then placed it back on the flat surface of
the tank. It began to roll again. Since the tank was nearly full, she let
the cap continue its journey down from the tank in the direction of
the battery, secure in her knowledge that it could easily be taken
from its place of rest after she had completed her refilling operation.

The cap, unfortunately, was equipped with a stick that had
belonged at the time of manufacture to a fuel-gauge assembly. . . .
The attached metal stick contributed to the cap's lack of stability
when resting on the tank.

The gas tank was situated immediately adjacent to the battery. Some part of the dipstick/gauge and cap combination, all
made of metal, bridged the gap between the uncovered positive battery terminal and the tank, causing a spark that ignited the gasoline

vapours that concentrated around the opening to the gas tank. Both by process of elimination of other possible causes and by way of inferences, what I have described is the most likely and therefore the probable scenario for the start of the blaze. The phenomenon is called arcing. No additional refining of the cause of the fire is required for the purpose of determining liability. . . .

I find that the placing of the metal cap and "dipstick" on top of the fuel tank in preparation for filling the tank was the natural act of an ordinary user. Mrs. Nicholson had done it many times before. She was brought up on a farm and she had been taught by her father how to fuel large tractors. She specifically remembered that she was not to pour fuel in the tank when the engine was hot and she was to add oil each time. She had received no further instructions. . . . She had no specific knowledge of arcing and in this she was a typical consumer. . . .

John Deere first manufactured lawn and garden tractors in 1963, following a feasibility study conducted the previous year. . . . It is of some interest and relevancy that John Deere learned of personal injury to a user in the summer of 1964 caused by fire due to arcing from the uncovered positive battery post in close proximity to the fuel tank. The 112 model (the Nicholsons') had not yet come on the market. There were a number of accidents that came to John Deere's attention involving several models, including 110 and 112, between 1973 and 1979, all apparently involving arcing and therefore due in a general way to the close proximity of the battery to the fuel tank. Also a number of fires occurred between 1977 and 1980 of which John Deere became aware. The precise cause of the fires was not ascertained by John Deere. The significant feature of the evidence of these fires is that they brought home to the manufacturer the knowledge, both before and after it manufactured the 112 model, not only of the general hazard, but of the fact that older units had replacement batteries and uncovered positive battery posts. . . .

It was in early 1980 that John Deere decided to manufacture the battery-cover safety kit and implement a program to advise users of models 110 and 112 lawn and garden tractors of the hazard associated with the risk of fire and explosion due to arcing by reason of uncovered positive battery posts. . . .

John Deere takes the position that the cover put in place at the manufacturing stage of the 112 model, the warnings in the owner's manual and on the decals along with the battery-cover safety kits, all combined, were quite sufficient to fully discharge its duty to the consumer. For reasons which I propose to outline, I think not. . . .

At a minimum, however, the manufacturer in this case, assuming that full knowledge, actual or imputed, of the serious potential risk of harm reached him only some years after his product was marketed, had a duty to devise a program that left nothing to chance. The decal on the tank could not be counted on and neither could the manual. The newspaper advertisements could not be relied upon to reach but a small portion of potential victims. And finally, the battery-cover kit program failed dismally to meet the high standard which the circumstances called for. All of John Deere's efforts brought home the problem to a mere 15 percent of owners. . . .

Liability of repairer

Mr. Hutchinson operated a John Deere dealership in the Stouffville area. . . . Hutchinson knew that the 112 model came equipped with battery-terminal covers. The plaintiff also suggests that the dealer was negligent in failing to carry out John Deere's program. I am of the view that while the repairer may have escaped liability on either one of the two grounds standing alone, he cannot be heard to say, as he in fact testified, that in this case his only duty was to specifically carry out the instructions of the owner. With full knowledge that an important safety device, namely, the terminal covers, was missing, a knowledge reinforced forcefully by the safety program put into place by the manufacturer, of which he had clear and detailed knowledge, he delivered back to his customer an admittedly dangerous piece of equipment. In my view, that amounted to actionable negligence. There will accordingly be a finding of negligence against this defendant as well.

Contributory negligence

The defendants submit that the plaintiffs were negligent in failing to maintain their tractor in a safe condition. They allege that the plaintiffs specifically modified or failed to correct the modifications to their tractor. They further submit that the plaintiffs were negligent in failing to take any steps to inform themselves about the safe operation of their tractor and that they were negligent in failing to take any steps to obtain and read the operator's manual so as to inform themselves about the safety components of their tractor and the safe operation thereof. . . .

I have considered all of these allegations and it is my view that it must be assumed that an average consumer could not reasonably be expected to be alert to the possibility of arcing and much less to the presence of invisible vapours surrounding the entry into the tank that could ignite as a result of arcing. . . . I have concluded that once it is found that a consumer cannot be expected to be alert to the danger of ignition as a result of arcing, it would not be appropriate to make of fuelling in a garage with an open door, an act of negligence. The evidence is that even experienced and knowledgeable users did precisely what Mrs. Nicholson did. A reasonable user who was given this safety instruction of not fuelling indoors would not think, in my view, of the danger arising out of arcing but would be directing his or her mind to some other method of ignition of the gasoline itself. I accordingly exonerate the plaintiffs of any liability for the damage suffered in this unfortunate fire.

Judgement for plaintiffs; reference of question of damages to property to referee.[11]

Defences to Negligence

The decision in *Nicholson* raises the issue of defences to claims of negligence: **contributory negligence**, accident, voluntary participation, and voluntary assumption of risk. Although not available in this instance, the defence of contributory negligence is often used to diminish or even eliminate the plaintiff's liability for damages. The defence is based on an argument that the plaintiff has either contributed to or created the negligence complained of.

A second defence is that the negligence complained of took place in the context of voluntary participation in a criminal or antisocial action. In *Tallow v. Tailfeathers*,[12] the plaintiffs were passengers in a stolen car driven by the defendant, who fell asleep at the wheel and hit a telephone pole. One of the passengers was killed, and the rest were injured. At no time did the plaintiffs object to the defendant's driving of the car, even though he had been drinking very heavily, was very tired, and was clearly travelling at an illegal speed at the time of the accident.

The court found that the plaintiffs had no claim in negligence, premising its decision on the Latin maxim ***ex turpi causa, non oritur actio***. This maxim was perhaps best explained by Lord Diplock in a 1964 British case:

All that rule means is that the courts will not enforce a right which would otherwise be enforceable if the right arises out of an act committed by the person asserting the right (or by someone who is regarded in law as his successor) which is regarded by the court as sufficiently antisocial to justify the court's refusing to enforce that right.[13]

In *Tallow v. Tailfeathers*, the Alberta Court of Appeal concluded:

> Here, as I have said, the appellants participated with their driver in
> the theft of the car and in its unlawful use in the course of which the
> accident occurred that has given rise to their claims. The driving of
> the car was a continuation of the theft and it was that driving and the
> manner of it that caused the accident. I agree with Dechene, J. that
> the appellants' claims arise *ex turpi* and should not be entertained by
> the Court.

A third defence to a claim of negligence is the assertion that the event
in question was simply an accident, which no reasonable person could
or ought to have foreseen. This defence is often expressed as the
defence of inevitable accident, set out in an 1892 British case by Lord
Esher: "In my opinion, a person relying on inevitable accident must
shew that something happened over which he had no control, and the
effect of which could not have been avoided by the greatest care and
skill."[14]

Consider the application of the defence of accident to *Blyth v.
Birmingham Water Works Co.*, a tort claim to recover damages for the
flooding of the plaintiff's premises. The defendant had installed a
fire plug in the vicinity; because of an exceptionally severe frost in
the winter of 1855, the fire plug was damaged, resulting in the
flooding complained of. The fire plug had worked adequately for
25 years.

> Alderson, B.: A reasonable man would act with reference to the
> average circumstances of the temperature in ordinary years. The
> defendants had provided against such frosts as experience would
> have led men, acting prudently, to provide against; and they are not
> guilty of negligence, because their precautions proved insufficient
> against the effects of the extreme severity of the frost of 1855, which
> penetrated to a greater depth than any which ordinarily occurs
> south of the polar regions. Such a state of circumstances constitutes
> a contingency against which no reasonable man can provide. The
> result was an accident, for which the defendants cannot be held
> liable.[15]

The final defence to negligence is voluntary assumption of risk. It can
be argued that, in some circumstances, plaintiffs have voluntarily
assumed the risks of a given activity, thereby nullifying any tort claim
that they might bring. This defence was successfully used in the British
Columbia case of *King v. Redlich*.

Carrothers, J.A.: The appellant was a 32-year-old postman. Both parties were regularly engaged on different teams in recreational hockey played on an unscheduled basis by men ranging in age from 30 to their early 40s, in the interests of keeping fit and enjoying a game played since childhood. They are whimsically known as Old Timers.

During the pregame warm-up, the respondent took a practice shot at the goal. The puck hit the goal post, ricocheted and struck the head of the appellant who was not wearing a helmet. The evidence is that the appellant would not have suffered the injuries he did had he been wearing a helmet.

The trial judge also found that the practice shot was taken at the moment that the appellant emerged from behind the goal and when hit was several feet away from the left side of the goal toward which the respondent aimed his practice shot.

The appellant suffered permanent brain damage which impaired his speech and word selection, although he was able to continue with his employment. The appellant's involvement in sports and social relationships was severely curtailed. Had the respondent been held liable at trial, general damages of $40 000 would have been awarded. . . .

In regard to the matter of liability, the trial judge held that the respondent was not negligent, the warm-up shot was normal, and within the reasonable expectations of the appellant. The trial judge found that warm-up shots are usual during pregame rehearsal and injury from a puck is not uncommon. The appellant was deemed to have accepted and assumed the risk of injury during warm-up. . . .

In dismissing the appellant's action, Spencer, J. said this:

Since it is an accepted part of the game for players to practise shots during the warm-up, and since on all the witnesses' evidence I find that injury from a flying puck is not uncommon, I am of the opinion that a player like the plaintiff must be deemed to accept and assume a risk of injury during the warm-up. While it may be a wrongful act for one player, during a warm-up, to shoot deliberately at another, knowing him to be unaware, it was not negligent for the defendant in this case to shoot at the goal, having allowed the plaintiff to skate from behind it and under circumstances where the puck deflected at random off the post and struck the plaintiff. The plaintiff's action must be dismissed.

In my view, that finding cannot be faulted on the facts. The appellant challenges this finding of absence of negligence on the part of the respondent on the law. The appellant argues that notwithstanding the lessened duty of care which prevails in recreational hockey during warm-up, any higher risk which is perceived or ought to be perceived by the prudent player about to take a practice shot automatically elevates the level of the duty of care so that by proceeding to take the practice shot without taking that extra care, the player is negligent; any higher risk here would be due to the presence of the appellant behind the goal.

While the time frame of the practice shot would only be a few seconds, I think it can be fairly said that the respondent perceived the higher risk because on noting the appellant behind the goal post, the respondent momentarily delayed his practice shot to allow the appellant to clear the goal. In so doing, he correspondingly increased the care, which he took by delaying his practice shot until the appellant was, in the respondent's judgement, out of immediate danger. The respondent then proceeded with his practice shot. The respondent did not foresee and could not be expected to foresee the ricochet which redirected the puck and caused the injury of the appellant.

In these circumstances, I would not interfere with the trial judge's finding of no negligence and would dismiss the appeal.[16]

Compensation for Torts of Intention and Negligence

Both intentional torts and torts of negligence are largely, perhaps overwhelmingly, concerned with compensation. This finding prompts the question whether tort law is the best means we can devise to compensate individuals for the negligence of others. Canadian legal scholars Solomon, Feldthusen, and Mills have noted:

> [T]he present system of tort law cannot be explained or justified as a mechanism of accident compensation. First, tort law provides compensation to a relatively small number of accident victims and then only in very limited circumstances. Second, the accident victim must make a substantial financial investment to initiate the process. Third, the plaintiff must prove fault, not need, and will only recover if he is fortunate enough to be injured by a tortfeasor with assets. Finally, it is generally accepted and clearly documented that tort law is an extremely inefficient mechanism for providing compensation.[17]

The purpose of tort law can therefore be said to be somewhat elusive. While access to the courts may provide compensatory redress for certain individuals or corporations, it is not clear that the broad social goal of compensation can be adequately met by the present structure of the law.

Automobile accidents and work-related accidents are significant areas in which tort law has not provided an efficient mechanism of compensation. In Canada and most other industrialized states, compensation plans have therefore displaced the use of claims in tort for such accidents. In the case of automobile accidents, no-fault compensation is provided by either private insurers or government agencies. The compensation displaces tort in virtually every circumstance, though a plaintiff may seek damages in the courts in the unusual event that his or her losses exceed awarded benefits. Thanks to workers' compensation boards and tribunals, injuries at work have also been largely removed from the scope of tort claims. Workers' compensation schemes, funded for the most part by employers, have been in place in Canada since just after the turn of the century. The boards and tribunals are public bodies created by statute; they provide less costly, more efficient and comprehensive compensation for accidents in the workplace than courtroom claims in tort. Unlike actions in tort, however, the plans do not provide for the possibility of compensation for pain and suffering.

The system of claims in tort works well in restricted circumstances when there is a coincidence of key features: in intentional torts, a defendant with the financial capacity to compensate; in torts of negligence, an action with a highly significant impact for which no system of insurance or other form of compensation exists. There are many examples of the latter kind of claim: individual claims for medical or legal malpractice; collective, or class-action, claims to recover damages for the consequences of the Dalkon shield and thalidomide; failure to screen blood products for the HIV virus; and defects in automobiles or other consumer products.

Consider, as an example, an intentional tort with a defendant who has the financial capacity to compensate. This recent decision of the Supreme Court of Canada in *John Doe v. Bennett*, 1 S.C.R. 436, excerpted below, also raises the interesting question of the vicarious liability of the Roman Catholic Church for a sexual assault:

> Over a period of almost two decades, Father Kevin Bennett, a Roman Catholic priest in Newfoundland in the Diocese of St. George's, sexually assaulted boys in his parishes. Two successive bishops failed to take steps to stop the abuse. Ultimately, in 1979, a victim revealed the abuse to the Archbishop of the neighbouring diocese, St. John's, who was also Metropolitan of the broader ecclesiastical province.

He referred the complaint to Bennett's Bishop but again nothing was done. The unnamed plaintiffs, 36 in number, suffered greatly as a consequence of the abuse. Now adults, they remain deeply wounded.

The plaintiff-respondents sued for the wrongs that had been done to them. They sued Father Bennett; the Roman Catholic Episcopal Corporation of St. George's ("St. George's"); the bishop of St. George's at the time the lawsuit was commenced, Raymond Lahey; the archbishop of St. John's at the time of the abuse, Alphonsus Penney; the archbishop of St. John's at the time the lawsuit was commenced, James MacDonald; the Roman Catholic Episcopal Corporation of St. John's ("St. John's"); and the Roman Catholic Church. Father Bennett's liability is not at issue before this Court. The main issue is the liability of St. George's.

The trial judge found Bennett directly liable; St. George's and Bishop Lahey vicariously liable, and Archbishop Penney liable in negligence. He dismissed the claims against Archbishop MacDonald, St. John's and the Roman Catholic Church ((2000), 190 Nfld. & P.E.I.R. 277).

The Court of Appeal set aside the findings of personal liability against Archbishop Penney and Bishop Lahey, and upheld the dismissal of the action against Archbishop MacDonald, St. John's and the Roman Catholic Church. The majority found St. George's directly but not vicariously liable ((2002), 218 D.L.R. (4th) 276, 2002 NFCA 47). St. George's appealed the finding of direct negligence to this Court, and argued in addition that the Roman Catholic Church was liable. The plaintiff-respondents replied that St. George's is not only directly, but also vicariously liable for Bennett's wrongs. The plaintiff-respondents also filed a cross-appeal asserting the liability of Lahey, MacDonald, Penney, St. John's and the Roman Catholic Church. However, they also asserted that the cross-appeal was conditional on the success of St. George's appeal from liability and need not be considered in the event St. George's appeal was dismissed.

The main issue on the appeal is whether St. George's is liable to the plaintiff-respondents and if so, on what basis. St. George's contends it is neither directly nor vicariously liable; the plaintiff-respondents assert they are liable on both grounds. St. George's also argues that the Roman Catholic Church is liable.

A. Direct Liability

All of the abuse took place in the diocese of St. George's. A Roman Catholic diocese is a territorial enterprise, composed of a number of parishes and administered by a bishop or archbishop. Dioceses are constituted by the Pope, who also appoints bishops and archbishops. A number of dioceses may form an ecclesiastical province. It is common for legislation to incorporate bishops and archbishops as episcopal corporations. I conclude that the episcopal corporation is the secular arm of the bishop or archbishop for all purposes. The office of bishop/archbishop, the enterprise of the diocese and the episcopal corporation are legally synonymous.

The argument for direct liability of St. George's is as follows:

(1) The bishops of St. George's in charge of Bennett (Bishops O'Reilly and McGrath successively) knew or ought to have known that Bennett was abusing the plaintiff-respondents and negligently did nothing to stop the assaults from continuing;

(2) The bishops (successively) constituted the corporation sole of St. George's under the relevant legislation and acted on its behalf;

(3) Therefore St. George's is directly liable for these acts and omissions.

St. George's concedes the first proposition (the negligence of Bishops O'Reilly and McGrath) and does not seriously dispute the second. Its only argument is that St. George's is not liable for the Bishops' negligence, because the corporation sole's activities and powers are confined to holding property and do not extend to the placement, direction and discipline of priests.

The narrow issue is therefore whether the corporation sole's activities and liability are confined to matters pertaining to its property. The courts below rejected this proposition. So would I. I base this conclusion on the legislation creating the corporation sole and on its function or purpose.

The purpose for which ecclesiastical corporations sole like St. George's are created is to serve as a point of legal interface between the Roman Catholic Church and the community at the diocesan level. The Church is at one and the same time a spiritual presence in the community and a secular actor in the community. The task of the corporation sole is to provide a bridge between the two spheres for the diocese. On a secular level, the Church interacts with members of the diocesan community in a host of ways. It carries on a variety of religious, educational and social activities. It makes contracts with employees. It transports parishioners. It sponsors charitable events. It purchases and sells goods and property. To do these things, it requires a legal personality. That personality is the corporation sole. To restrict the purpose of the corporation sole to the acquisition, holding and administration of property is to capture only a portion of the purpose it is intended to serve and to artificially truncate its functions.

The role of the corporation sole as a legal interface between the Church and the community is set forth in the legislation creating it, *An Act to Incorporate the Roman Catholic Bishop of St. George's*, S.N. 1913, c. 12. The Act, quite simply, incorporates the office of bishop, in all its aspects. It does not confine itself to the holding of property belonging to the diocese.

Section 1 of the Act states that "the Roman Catholic Bishops from time to time of the Diocese of St. George's . . . shall be a body corporate . . . for the purpose of holding lands and property, personal or otherwise." However, the language of other sections makes it clear the Corporation's powers are not confined to property. Section 3 provides:

The Corporation shall have perpetual succession and a corporate seal, with power to alter the same, and by the name of the Roman Catholic Episcopal Corporation of St. George's shall be capable in law of suing and being sued, pleading and being impleaded in all Courts and places whatsoever, and shall have power to take and to hold lands, and all other property whatsoever for ecclesiastical, charitable and educational purposes and uses of the Roman Catholic Church, and to lease, sell, convey and dispose of the same.

This section permits the Corporation to be sued on all matters, not just those relating to property. . . .

I would confirm the conclusion below that the Roman Catholic Episcopal Corporation of St. George's is directly liable for the wrongs to the plaintiff-respondents resulting from its bishops' failure to properly direct and discipline Father Bennett.

B. Vicarious Liability

The plaintiff–respondents also seek a finding that the Roman Catholic Episcopal Corporation of St. George's is vicariously liable for Father Bennett's assaults, as his employer. The doctrine of vicarious liability imputes liability to the employer or principal of a tortfeasor, not on the basis of the fault of the employer or principal, but on the ground that as the person responsible for the activity or enterprise in question, the employer or principal should be held responsible for loss to third parties that result from the activity or enterprise.

The trial judge found St. George's vicariously liable for the assaults committed by Father Bennett. The majority of the Court of Appeal, per Marshall J.A., reversed this finding, emphasizing that Bennett's actions violated the norms of the Church and the charitable, non-profit nature of the diocese's activities. The dissenting justice, Cameron J.A., held vicarious liability to be established. In my view, the majority of the Newfoundland and Labrador Court of Appeal erred on this point and the view of the dissent is to be preferred.

This Court considered the application of the doctrine of vicarious liability to the tort of assault of children in *Bazley v. Curry,* [1999] 2 S.C.R. 534, *Jacobi v. Griffiths,* [1999] 2 S.C.R. 570, and *K.L.B. v. British Columbia,* [2003] 2 S.C.R. 403, 2003 SCC 51. The decisions affirm the same test for vicarious liability.

In *Bazley,* the Court suggested that the imposition of vicarious liability may usefully be approached in two steps. First, a court should determine whether there are precedents which unambiguously determine whether the case should attract vicarious liability. "If prior cases do not clearly suggest a solution, the next step is to determine whether vicarious liability should be imposed in light of the broader policy rationales behind strict liability": *Bazley,* at para. 15; *Jacobi,* at para. 31. Vicarious liability is based on the rationale that the person who puts a risky enterprise into the community may fairly be held responsible when those risks emerge and cause loss or injury to members of the public. Effective compensation is a goal. Deterrence is also a consideration. The hope is that holding the employer or principal liable will encourage such persons to take steps to reduce the risk of harm in the future. Plaintiffs must show that the rationale behind the imposition of vicarious liability will be met on the facts in two respects. First, the relationship between the tortfeasor and the person against whom liability is sought must be sufficiently close. Second, the wrongful act must be sufficiently connected to the conduct authorized by the employer. This is necessary to ensure that the goals of fair and effective compensation and deterrence of future harm are met: *K.L.B., supra,* at para. 20.

In determining whether there is a sufficient connection in the case of intentional **torts**, factors to be considered include, but are not limited to the following (*Bazley, supra,* at para. 41):

> (a) the opportunity that the enterprise afforded the employee to abuse his or her power;
>
> (b) the extent to which the wrongful act may have furthered the employer's aims (and hence be more likely to have been committed by the employee);

(c) the extent to which the wrongful act was related to friction, confrontation or intimacy inherent in the employer's enterprise;

(d) the extent of power conferred on the employee in relation to the victim;

(e) the vulnerability of potential victims to wrongful exercise of the employee's power.

The employer's control over the employee's activities is one indication of whether the employee is acting on his or her employer's behalf: *K.L.B., supra,* at para. 22. At the heart of the inquiry lies the question of power and control by the employer: both that exercised over and that granted to the employee. Where this power and control can be identified, the imposition of vicarious liability will compensate fairly and effectively.

In *Bazley, supra,* vicarious liability was imposed on a non-profit association operating residential care facilities for children, in an action brought by a former resident for sexual assault by a child care counsellor. The Court unanimously rejected the argument that non-profit bodies should be protected from tort liability in the public interest. The relationship between the employer and employee was sufficiently close, while the wrongful act was a manifestation of risks inherent in the employer's enterprise.

In the companion case, *Jacobi, supra,* the majority of the Court found a non-profit Boys' and Girls' Club not vicariously liable for sexual assaults committed by its employee, the program director, some of them in the course of excursions relating to the children's sports activities. Applying the test set out in *Bazley, supra,* the majority found the required connection between the employer's enterprise and the wrong had not been established. In the view of the majority, the facts established a much weaker connection than in *Bazley*: the level of intimacy was much less; the job did not require the employee to be alone with the child; the offence occurred off-premises and outside working hours; and the employee had established his own "bait" of home attractions. These facts, the majority held, negated the required strong connection between the risks inherent in the employer's enterprise and the wrong. Whatever power Griffiths used, Binnie J. wrote, it was not conferred by the Club, nor was it characteristic of the type of enterprise the Club put into the community. A minority of three justices found vicarious liability to be established, notwithstanding these differences.

In my respectful opinion, the majority of the Court of Appeal erred in reading *Jacobi* as suggesting that its effect is that non-profit employers should not be held vicariously liable for sexual assaults by their employees. The unanimous opinion in *Bazley*, which also involved a non-profit employer, and both the majority and dissenting opinions in *Jacobi*, are all inconsistent with this conclusion. The majority reasons in *Jacobi* suggest that non-profit status may sometimes negatively impact on the policy rationales that underlie the imposition of vicarious liability; however, they do not state that non-profit employers should not be held vicariously liable; nor do they affirm the old doctrine of charitable immunity. In the result, the majority held (at para. 78) that

"fairness" to these non-profit organizations is entirely compatible with vicarious liability provided that a strong connection is established between the enterprise risk and the sexual assault. [Emphasis in original.]

The majority in *Jacobi* grounds its conclusion firmly in the factors relevant to the connection between the employer's creation of risk and the wrong complained of as expressed in *Bazley*, notably the absence of job-conferred power.

In the present case, the relevant precedents dealing with church-related activities do not clearly determine the issue, although they tend to support the imposition of vicarious liability on the episcopal corporation. In *McDonald v. Mombourquette* (1996), 152 N.S.R. (2d) 109 (leave to appeal refused, [1997] 2 S.C.R. xi), the Nova Scotia Court of Appeal reversed the trial judge's finding that the Roman Catholic & Episcopal Corporation of Antigonish was vicariously liable for sexual assaults committed by a priest on children in the parish. A key factor was that the priest had acted "totally contrary to the religious tenets which he has sworn to uphold" (para. 47). In *K. (W.) v. Pornbacher* (1997), 32 B.C.L.R. (3d) 360 (S.C.), the court declined to follow *Mombourquette* and held the Catholic Church, through its Bishop of Nelson, to be both negligent and vicariously liable for sexual assaults committed by a priest. The trial judge emphasized the job-conferred power of a priest over church youth. Although the case law does not provide a clear answer, the facts of *Pornbacher* (as well as *Mombourquette*) more closely resemble *Bazley* than *Jacobi*.

The relationship between the bishop and a priest in a diocese is not only spiritual, but temporal. The priest takes a vow of obedience to the bishop. The bishop exercises extensive control over the priest, including the power of assignment, the power to remove the priest from his post and the power to discipline him. It is akin to an employment relationship. The incidents of control far exceed those characterizing the relationship between foster parents and the government, discussed in *K.L.B.*, and, as will become evident below, the priest is reasonably perceived as an agent of the diocesan enterprise. The relationship between the bishop and the priest is sufficiently close. Applying the relevant test to the facts, it is also clear that the necessary connection between the employer-created or enhanced risk and the wrong complained of is established.

First, the bishop provided Bennett with the opportunity to abuse his power. As noted by the trial judge, at para. 26, "the vast majority of all the activities which [Bennett] organized and in which he was always accompanied by boys, were activities which he organized and controlled in his capacity as parish priest." Canon 528 of the *Code of Canon Law* directs a parish priest to "have a special care for the catholic education of children and young people," and involvement with children was clearly an expected role for a parish priest. As priest, Bennett directed altar boys, led a parish band, involved boys in renovation and construction projects, was active in the Boy Scout troop, and engaged boys in various fundraising and parochial activities. All of these opportunities came via his appointment and placement as parish priest by the bishop.

Second, Bennett's wrongful acts were strongly related to the psychological intimacy inherent in his role as priest. As explained by Cameron J.A., at para. 184: "The Church encourages psychological intimacy between a priest and the members of the parish. A priest may not have to bath children [as in *Bazley*] but he, like parents, teaches them right from wrong, he represents God and they are to accept his instructions in spiritual matters." This psychological intimacy encourages victims' submission to abuse and increases the opportunity to abuse, partly by satisfying parents "that their children [are] in good hands while in the care and control of their priest" (trial decision, at para. 21). A church member's personal identity is closely intertwined with his or her faith and its institutional expression, which may nurture trust in the institution's hierarchy from a young age, granting it considerable power.

Third, the bishop conferred an enormous degree of power on Bennett relative to his victims. The power imbalance was intensified in St. George's diocese due to a number of factors. The parishes in which Bennett worked were geographically isolated, impacting on the opportunities for, and extent and frequency of, the sexual assaults and contributing to their remaining unchecked for many years. The communities were entirely Roman Catholic and the devoutly religious inhabitants placed the Church at the centre of their daily lives. There were few other authority figures; the communities lacked municipal government, diverse business activities, secular organizations, police, courts or any other form of community leadership, leaving that role entirely to the parish priest. The only schools were denominational, and as such, were influenced by the priest, who served as the only local representative of the distant school board.

Bennett had enormous stature because of his position as parish priest, both to the boys and to their parents. The plaintiffs perceived him as a "god"—quite logically given his centrality in the community and the disparity in lifestyles between himself and his parishioners. As the school principal, Kerry Dwyer, testified, "It was like having a celebrity in the community that you had to treat properly. . . . [T]here were incidents where I found people believed that the priest could turn you into a goat." Or, as one victim stated, when he asked his father if he should sleep over at Bennett's house as Bennett had requested, "my dad said of course, he's the priest." While Bennett had a particularly forceful personality, the root of his power over his victims lay in his role as a priest, conferred by the bishop. The trial judge summed it up eloquently, at para. 28: "The awe in which Father Bennett was held by the community at large contributed to his ability to control his victims and thus to satisfy a prodigious appetite for constant sexual gratification."

In summary, the evidence overwhelmingly satisfies the tests affirmed in *Bazley, Jacobi* and *K.L.B.* The relationship between the diocesan enterprise and Bennett was sufficiently close. The enterprise substantially enhanced the risk which led to the wrongs the plaintiff-respondents suffered. It provided Bennett with great power in relation to vulnerable victims and with the opportunity to abuse that power. A strong and direct connection is established between the conduct of the enterprise and the wrongs done to the plaintiff-respondents. The majority of the Court of Appeal erred in failing to apply the right test. Had it performed the appropriate analysis, it would have found the Roman Catholic Episcopal Corporation of St. George's vicariously liable for Father Bennett's assaults on the plaintiff-respondents.

I conclude that the Roman Catholic Episcopal Corporation of St. George's is vicariously liable for the wrongs done to the plaintiff-respondents.

III. The Liability of the Roman Catholic Church

The appellant St. George's argues that the Roman Catholic Church should be found liable. The trial judge and the Court of Appeal unanimously rejected this proposition. I decline to deal with this argument on the record before us in this case.

The Roman Catholic Church is a religious organization operating in many countries of the world, including Canada. It possesses a hierarchical structure with the Pope at its apex, and works through diverse orders, groups and individuals. On the record before us, it is impossible to answer the questions as to procedure and remedies for recovery which the claim against the Church raises. The record does not provide the clear picture of the details of the Church's hierarchy or of the relationship between the Church and its constituent parts, necessary to delineate the boundaries of the institution, the nature of its legal status, and its potential liability. Nor does the record offer much assistance on the procedural questions that would need to be answered before the Church, as a global institution, could be found liable for the wrongs committed by Father Bennett in the diocese of St. George's. Although named as a party, the Church was not represented during the proceedings in this case, and issues relating to procedure and remedies for recovery were left unexplored.

Without suggesting that the full organizational structure of the Roman Catholic Church and its relations with its various constituent organizations must be apparent on the evidence before a finding of Church liability could be made, I am satisfied that the record before us is too weak to permit the Court in this case to responsibly embark on the important and difficult question of whether the Roman Catholic Church can be held liable in a case such as this.

For these reasons, I decline to deal with the appellant's second argument.[18]

Social concepts of private wrongs vary, not only from one individual to another, but also in relation to social change within a given society. The case of *John Doe v. Bennett* demonstrates, among other things, that the claims of victims of sexual abuse, in tort and elsewhere, are taken more seriously today than they were even a decade or two ago. Additionally, the ability to make a claim, the willingness of social institutions to consider such a claim, and the justifications for recovery have necessarily changed over time.

Conclusion: Tort Law as a Mix of Private and Public Interests

Tort law is clearly a mix of private and public interests. Should the collective interests of the Lintz Cricket Club supersede the private interests of the Millers? Can a drug-dependent woman be said to consent to sexual contact with a physician if she does so for the purpose of obtaining an illegal drug (*Norberg v. Wynrib*)?[19] Can a manufacturer who attempts unsuccessfully to warn consumers of a long-existing danger properly be labelled as negligent? Should a Roman Catholic diocese be held responsible for the actions of one of its priests? In each of these cases, the courts were concerned with more than a simple resolution of the private claims of the parties. The collective right to recreation, the fiduciary duty of a physician, the social responsibility of a church and the responsibility of a manufacturer are fundamentally issues of public interest. When the system of tort law fails—as it does with most forms of injury and accident, whether negligent or not—it is public interest that dictates the failure. And so it is true of torts, as of contract law, property law, wills and estates—in short, all forms of private law: it may be the realm of private wrongs, but it is the public interest that lies at the heart of the matter.

Web Links

Lord Denning: An Affectionate Remembrance
http://lawsnet.com/canarticles/oGradyonDenning.htm
This essay on this site is written by an Ottawa lawyer as a eulogy to the judge who many regarded as the most interesting of all times.

Faculty of Law, University of Cambridge
http://www.law.cam.ac.uk
One of the most comprehensive academic legal sites in the U.K. is located at the University of Cambridge. For excellent essays and materials on legal history as well as links to British cases and statutes, this site is a good resource.

Cornell University: The Legal Institute
http://www.law.cornell.edu/topics
Listed as a topical index, the materials on the Cornell University website include explanations of key legal principles in concise and clear language.

Lexum at the University of Montreal
http://www.lexum.umontreal.ca
This site offers an excellent topical index for substantive law in Canada.

Legal Portal
http://www.gahtan.com/links
Maintained by internationally known Canadian Internet and technology lawyer Alan Gahtan, this site offers good definitions and explanations of topical areas of law. It also has numerous links to other Web pages and search engines with similar material.

David Friedman, Santa Clara School of Law
http://www.best.com/~ddfr/index.shtml
A prodigious author and academic, David Friedman has an excellent topical website that links tort and crime from an economics perspective.

Questions for Discussion

1. What are the major differences between torts of negligence and intentional torts?
2. What are the strengths and weaknesses of the tort system as a mechanism of compensation? Is the awarding of punitive damages in order to deter negligent conduct an appropriate function for the resolution of claims in tort based on negligence?
3. In *John Doe v. Bennett*, which view of vicarious liability is more compelling—that of the Newfoundland Court of Appeal or the Supreme Court of Canada? Why?
4. Consider the following excerpt from *Gagnon v. Beaulieu*, [1977] 1 W.W.R. 702 (B.C.S.C.).

> Fulton, J.: The plaintiff was injured in a collision which took place on August 31, 1974 on Highway 401 near Chilliwack, British Columbia, when a 1972 Vega, owned and driven by the defendant Beaulieu and in which the plaintiff was riding as a front-seat passenger, ran into the rear end of a pickup truck which was stopped at a railroad crossing, waiting for a train to pass by. Liability of the defendant driver is admitted—the main issue in this connection is whether or not the plaintiff was wearing a seat belt, and, if not, whether this constituted negligence contributing to the nature and extent of his injuries.

The plaintiff suffered vertical lacerations of the right forehead and scalp, a deep horizontal laceration running across the right lower eyelid and upper right cheek and into the right temple. The cheek was fractured and crushed, and the right eye was damaged. . . . The defendant maintains that the plaintiff was not wearing a seat belt apparatus provided for the passenger, consisting of a lap belt and shoulder harness, and that if the plaintiff had been wearing this apparatus, he would not have suffered those head and facial injuries.

For the plaintiff it was contended that failure to wear a seat belt is not *per se* negligence and that it is not negligence in any circumstances if the person concerned is not convinced of the efficacy of seat belts and/or believes that the wearing of a seat belt, including particularly the shoulder strap, may in certain circumstances create the hazard of greater injury or damage than if it were not worn—that if, for instance, the car were to overturn, the wearer might be trapped between the seat and the roof. There was evidence that the plaintiff had this opinion. . . .

On the whole of the evidence, I am satisfied that the plaintiff knew or ought to have known that the wearing of the seat belt provided, including the shoulder harness, would reduce the possibility of his being injured in a collision, that at the time of this accident, he was not wearing the seat belt equipment provided and that, had he been wearing it, and particularly the shoulder harness, his injuries would have been less severe, if not prevented altogether. . . . Applying the law which I have held to be applicable to these circumstances in this province, I find it to have been established that the plaintiff was negligent and that his negligence contributed to the nature and extent of his injuries.

Is the finding of this trial judge with respect to the contributory negligence of the plaintiff too onerous a standard to impose—that the plaintiff "knew or ought to have known" that the seat belt would prevent injuries of the kind sustained? Discuss.

Further Reading

Fleming, J.G. *The Law of Torts.* 9th ed. Sydney, Aus.: LBC Information Services, 1998.

This is the ninth edition of Fleming's now classic work on the subject of tort law. This text of more than 800 pages is required reading for many Canadian and U.S. law school courses on torts.

Although the book emanates from Australia, it clearly canvasses both timeless principles and new developments.

Solomon, R., B. Feldthusen, and S. Mills. *Cases and Materials on the Law of Torts.* 2d ed. Toronto: Carswell, 1986.

This book provides a thorough analysis of the realm of torts, exploring intentional torts; torts of negligence; defences to intentional torts; defences to torts of negligence; issues of causation, remoteness, and assessment of damages; and the theories, criticisms, and alternatives to tort law as a mechanism of compensation. The authors provide a good coverage of Canadian tort law in this Carswell student edition.

Wigmore, J.H. *Select Cases on the Law of Torts, with Notes and a Summary of Principles.* Boston: Little, Brown, 1912.

This book by the celebrated jurist John Henry Wigmore sets out the foundations of tort liability. Although the case law is specific to a rather different era, the book provides an insight into current developments within tort law, and allows the reader to understand the historical context from which this area of law has emerged.

Notes

1. *Miller v. Jackson*, [1977] Q.B. 966, [1977] 3 All E.R. 338 at 366 (C.A.).
2. R.S.C. 1985, c. C-46.
3. R. Solomon, B. Feldthusen, and S. Mills, *Cases and Materials on the Law of Torts*, 2d ed. (Toronto: Carswell, 1986).
4. *Bettel v. Yim* (1978), 20 O.R. (2d) 617 at 632, 88 D.L.R. (3d) 543 at 558 (Ont. Co. Ct.).
5. *Tillander v. Gosselin*, [1967] 1 O.R. 203 at 203–210, 60 D.L.R. (2d) 18 at 18–25, aff'd 61 D.L.R. (2d) 192 (Ont. C.A.).
6. *Tindale v. Tindale*, [1950] 4 D.L.R. 363 (B.C.S.C.).
7. *Phillips v. Soloway* (1957), 4 D.L.R. (2d) 570 (Man. Q.B.).
8. *Blyth v. Birmingham Water Works* (1856), 11 Ex. 781 at 784, 156 E.R. 1047 at 1049 (Ex. Ct.).
9. *M'Alister (or Donoghue) v. Stevenson*, [1932] A.C. 562.
10. *Lambert v. Lastoplex Chemicals*, [1972] S.C.R. 569 at 574–575, 25 D.L.R. (3d) 121 at 125.
11. *Nicholson v. John Deere Ltd.* (1986), 34 D.L.R. (4th) 542 at 543–552.
12. [1973] 6 W.W.R. 732, 44 D.L.R. (3d) 55 (Alta. C.A.).
13. *Hardy v. Motor Insurers' Bureau*, [1964] 2 All E.R. 742 at 750.

14. *The Schwan* [1892], cited in *McIntosh v. Bell*, [1932] O.R. 179 at 179–189.
15. *Blyth v. Birmingham Water Works.*
16. *King v. Redlich* (1985), 24 D.L.R. (4th) 636 at 636–638, aff'g [1984] 6 W.W.R. 705, 30 C.C.L.T. 247 (B.C.C.A.).
17. Solomon, Feldthusen, and Mills, *Cases and Materials on the Law of Torts*, 23.
18. *John Doe v. Bennett* [2004], 1 S.C.R. 436.
19. *Norberg v. Wynrib* [1992] 2 S.C.R. 226, 92 D.L.R. (4th) 449 at 449–507.

References

Abel, E.L. "A Socialist Approach to Risk." *Modern Law Review* 41 (1982): 695.

Brown, R. "Deterrence and Accident Compensation Schemes." *University of Western Ontario Law Review* 17 (1978–79): 111.

England, P. "The System Builders: A Critical Appraisal of Modern American Tort Theory." *Journal of Legal Studies* 9 (1980): 27.

Galanter, M. "When Legal Worlds Collide: Reflections on Bhopal, the Good Lawyer, and the American Law School." *Journal of Legal Education* 36 (1986): 292.

Hutchinson, A., and J. Morgan. "The Canengusian Connection: The Kaleidoscope of Tort Theory." *Osgoode Hall Law Journal* 22 (1984): 69.

Ison, T. "The Infusion of Private Law in Public Administration." *Cahiers de Droit* 17 (1976): 799.

Linden, A., L. Klar, and B. Feldthusen. *Canadian Tort Law: Cases, Notes and Materials.* 12th ed. Toronto: Butterworths, 2004.

Ontario Law Reform Commission. *Report on Motor Vehicle Accident Compensation.* Toronto: Government Services, 1973.

Pierce, R. "Encouraging Safety: The Limits of Tort Law and Government Regulation." *Vanderbilt Law Review* 33 (1980): 1281.

Posner, R. "A Theory of Negligence." *Journal of Legal Studies* 1 (1972): 29.

Solomon, R., B. Feldthusen, and S. Mills. *Cases and Materials on The Law of Torts.* 2d ed. Toronto: Carswell, 1986.

Sugarman, S. "Doing Away with Tort Law." *California Law Review* 73 (1985): 555.

CHAPTER 8

The Changing Family and Family Law: Marriage, Divorce, Support, and Custody

It will come as no surprise to anybody to know that I support the traditional definition of marriage as a union of one man and one woman to the exclusion of all others, as expressed in our traditional common law.

> (Stephen Harper, Conservative Party Leader, Address in the House of Commons on Bill C-38, February 16, 2005)

The Senate rang with cheers on Wednesday night when the chamber gave final legislative approval to a bill making same-sex marriage legal right across the country. The eruption was very much in order. By becoming just the fourth nation in the world to allow homosexuals to wed, this country has burnished its image as a decent, tolerant nation. The prejudice against gays and lesbians is one of the oldest there is. For millennia, they have been shunned as deviants, freaks and outcasts. The same-sex-marriage bill signals that, officially at least, that long, dark era of ostracism is over. Homosexuals are at last considered full and equal members of the human family.

> (Editorial, "Canada's enlightened stand on gay marriage,"
> *The Globe and Mail*, July 21, 2005, A14)

In July 2005 Canada passed Bill C-38, an act that provides for same-sex marriage for civil purposes. Although many in the religious communities argued against the bill, it was clear from the outset that the standards of these communities would not be affected by the legislation; these religious organizations could continue to bar homosexual men and women from marriage within their churches, synagogues, or mosques. More specifically, Bill C-38 simply provides for the equality of heterosexual and homosexual men and women within civil unions, extending these existing rights in British Columbia and Ontario to all provinces and territories of Canada. The text of the legislation is excerpted below.

An Act respecting certain aspects of legal capacity for marriage for civil purposes

[Assented to 20th July, 2005]

Preamble

WHEREAS the Parliament of Canada is committed to upholding the Constitution of Canada, and section 15 of the *Canadian Charter of Rights and Freedoms* guarantees that every individual is equal before and under the law and has the right to equal protection and equal benefit of the law without discrimination;

WHEREAS the courts in a majority of the provinces and in one territory have recognized that the right to equality without discrimination requires that couples of the same sex and couples of the opposite sex have equal access to marriage for civil purposes;

WHEREAS the Supreme Court of Canada has recognized that many Canadian couples of the same sex have married in reliance on those court decisions;

WHEREAS only equal access to marriage for civil purposes would respect the right of couples of the same sex to equality without discrimination, and civil union, as an institution other than marriage, would not offer them that equal access and would violate their human dignity, in breach of the *Canadian Charter of Rights and Freedoms*;

WHEREAS the Supreme Court of Canada has determined that the Parliament of Canada has legislative jurisdiction over marriage but does not have the jurisdiction to establish an institution other than marriage for couples of the same sex;

WHEREAS everyone has the freedom of conscience and religion under section 2 of the *Canadian Charter of Rights and Freedoms*;

WHEREAS nothing in this Act affects the guarantee of freedom of conscience and religion and, in particular, the freedom of members of religious groups to hold and declare their religious beliefs and the freedom of officials of religious groups to refuse to perform marriages that are not in accordance with their religious beliefs;

WHEREAS it is not against the public interest to hold and publicly express diverse views on marriage;

WHEREAS, in light of those considerations, the Parliament of Canada's commitment to uphold the right to equality without discrimination precludes the use of section 33 of the *Canadian Charter of Rights and Freedoms* to deny the right of couples of the same sex to equal access to marriage for civil purposes;

WHEREAS marriage is a fundamental institution in Canadian society and the Parliament of Canada has a responsibility to support that institution because it strengthens commitment in relationships and represents the foundation of family life for many Canadians;

AND WHEREAS, in order to reflect values of tolerance, respect and equality consistent with the *Canadian Charter of Rights and Freedoms*, access to marriage for civil purposes should be extended by legislation to couples of the same sex;

NOW, THEREFORE, Her Majesty, by and with the advice and consent of the Senate and House of Commons of Canada, enacts as follows;

1. This Act may be cited as the Civil Marriage Act.

2. Marriage, for civil purposes, is the lawful union of two persons to the exclusion of all others.

3. It is recognized that officials of religious groups are free to refuse to perform marriages that are not in accordance with their religious beliefs.

3.1 For greater certainty, no person or organization shall be deprived of any benefit, or be subject to any obligation or sanction, under any law of the Parliament of Canada solely by reason of their exercise, in respect of marriage between persons of the same sex, of the freedom of conscience and religion guaranteed under the Canadian Charter of Rights and Freedoms or the expression of their beliefs in respect of marriage as the union of a man and woman to the exclusion of all others based on that guaranteed freedom.

4. For greater certainty, a marriage is not void or voidable by reason only that the spouses are of the same sex.

The Canadian family of 2006 is dramatically different from the Canadian family of the 1960s. In the early 2000s, nuclear families, single-parent families, and blended families are common, and the divorce rate is four times that of 1960. Same-sex marriage, within a civil context, is now a legal reality. Moreover, the prevalence of **common-law relations** has led to legal recognition of spousal obligations in the absence of marriage. Such changes have been summarized by sociologist John Conway:

> The growing diversity of family forms is self-evident. New "unorthodox" family forms—especially dual-earner and single-parent families—will become the orthodox family forms of the future as they characterize the experience of a growing majority of Canadians. Families are smaller and less stable, and family life is more episodic as we marry later, as divorce and separation rates grow, and as remarriage touches more and more of our lives. Many more Canadians are opting for single lifestyles, and fewer are

feeling it obligatory to have children. More women are choosing to have children as single mothers and to remain single for significant portions of their lives. Materially, people have more choices, and ideologically, people are more willing to exercise them.[1]

Social Change and the *Divorce Act* of 1968

At the turn of the century, **divorce** was a rarity in Canada, a complex and cumbersome legal process. In some provinces, a "parliamentary divorce" was the only option: a private member's bill had to pass first reading in both the Commons and the Senate; after second reading in the House of Commons, it could be heard by a special divorce committee. James Snell observed from his study of divorce in Canada between 1900 and 1940:

> Divorce in Canada was squarely founded on a belief in innocence and guilt, which meshed nicely with the moral pathology of divorce. The process itself, through mandatory confrontation, always and with impressive assurance assigned those attributes to the participating parties. Few divorces were granted through either the judicial or the legislative process, and the matter was not of particular concern in the dominion.[2]

Changes in social attitudes with respect to divorce began before the Second World War, but it was not until the 1960s that the law was made to reflect the new realities. The *Divorce Act* of 1968, the first federal divorce statute, took a first step toward "no fault" divorce, permitting dissolution of a **marriage** if the partners had lived "separate and apart" for a period of three or five years.

Some have argued that the increase in divorce during the late 1960s and early 1970s can be tied to the sexual liberation and feminist movements. The slogans "Make love, not war," "If it feels good, do it," and "Love the one you're with" epitomized the viewpoint of the era. Sexual activity, with or without emotional commitment, was set out as a valuable experience fulfilling both physical and social needs. In this social climate, the commitments of traditional marriage were effectively undermined. Feminist arguments in favour of gender equality were also in conflict with traditional cultural conceptions. The bride's solemn vow to honour and obey the groom epitomized a pre-feminist family power structure. Feminism helped to rewrite this cultural script. Conservatives and liberals have been arguing ever since, with conservatives insisting that feminism is to blame for the increased divorce rate, and liberals suggesting that divorce is not an evil in itself, and that less restrictive divorce laws have helped to give women a greater range of choices.

Behind these changes in attitude and conflicts in philosophy were a number of empirical developments. In the early 1960s, the birth control pill became widely available, allowing women in most Western industrial cultures a measure of the sexual freedom that men had traditionally enjoyed. The ability to engage in sexual relations with minimal risk of pregnancy created the material conditions in which an ideology of sexual liberation could flourish. More important, women's control over their fertility changed the economic and social structure of the family. At the same time, women were entering the labour force in unprecedented numbers for both material and ideological reasons. In 1966, 2.3 million women were in the labour force in Canada; by 1975, the number had reached more than 5.5 million; and in 2001, the figure had reached almost 7.5 million women. The number of married women in the labour force increased by almost 70 percent during the same period. Today, dual-earner families are the most common type of family.[3]

Jurisdiction over Family Law

The power to legislate in relation to marriage and divorce is given to the federal government in the *British North America Act, 1867*. The power to solemnize marriage is given to the provinces by section 92(12) of the same act, but the key jurisdictional section for the purpose of family law is section 92(13), which is concerned with "property and civil rights." It gives the provinces the right to legislate in relation to matrimonial property, the support of **spouses** and children, and custody; it also confers jurisdiction over the related matters of succession, adoption, and guardianship. Therefore, Canada has a divided jurisdiction in matters of family law. The *Divorce Act* is federally constructed and applied in federal courts, pursuant to petitions for divorce. But other family-related matters—custody, property, and support—are heard only in provincial courts if they are not determined in the context of a divorce action.

The Legal Definition of "Family"

This brings us to the question of what the term "family law" really means. *The Oxford Reference Dictionary* defines "family" as "the members of a household." But how, then, do we define what is meant by "household"? Is the legality of marriage a precondition for a household, and hence a family? Can same-sex couples constitute a household and, hence, a family? Do obligations with respect to property, support, and child custody arise in the absence of marriage? The clear answer to the last question is yes, the state is willing to intervene, in the absence of marriage, to confer familial obligations upon individual citizens. The law of contract, implied or express, gives rise to these commitments. The law remains unclear, however, about whether same-sex couples constitute a family.

In the face of conflicting definitions and beliefs about the nature of family and sexuality, some Canadians advocate a return to an allegedly more simple time when Father was the breadwinner and Mother stayed at home raising the children. As sociologist Roberta Hamilton has noted, feminists, wage-earning women, homosexuals, and lesbians—inasmuch as each represents a changing family form—have all become, in some circles, targets of disaffection. Hamilton suggests that the enduring and defining feature of the family over the past 2 000 years has been the contributions of women, most often made in difficult circumstances:

> Women have always had to support their families. In feudal society, they toiled without respite to support themselves and their children. In capitalist society, they have had to supplement their husbands' incomes through work done at home, through seeking waged work, and making whatever arrangements they could for their children. . . . Because of death, sickness, desertion, or unemployment, many have been sole supporters of their children. The particular contingencies of women's lives today emerged on the world stage with the transition to capitalism three hundred years ago.[4]

As mentioned above, the law of contract gives rise to such familial obligations as **child custody, child support**, and **spousal support**. The question then arises: Is family law different from the law of contract in any way? Is the family simply one more context in which two individuals enter into a legally enforceable contract, express or implied? If that is the case, marriage is simply a statement of benefits and obligations existing over time. In legal terms, its only significance is that it serves to simplify definition of the contractual relationship. Although marriage might be said to have originated within the context of either property or ecclesiastical law, it is, in the contemporary world, best situated within the realm of contract.

Despite this narrowly legalistic viewpoint, the family, broadly defined, remains an important structure in cultural and community life, providing guidance to the future generation. The restructuring of the Canadian family over the past few decades has produced dramatic increases in the numbers of children raised in poverty. While 10 percent of single-male-**parent** families live in poverty, more than 60 percent of single-female-parent families do so. These figures are not adequately explained by the principles of contract; nor do such principles explain the recent recognition of homosexual marriage, which is, rather, an extension of the definition of family. And in child-custody disputes, the legal matter of the best interests of the child is best seen in the context of nurturance and support, not in the law of contract. All in all, family law is, in both human and conceptual terms, quite distinct from an essentially economic bargain.

Grounds for Divorce under the *Divorce Act* of 1968

The *Divorce Act* of 1968 imposed uniform standards for divorce on all the provinces and territories. The grounds for petitioning for divorce were set out in sections 3 and 4. For the most part, a petitioner still had to rely upon the notion of fault. Section 3 granted a divorce on the grounds of adultery, sodomy, bestiality, rape, bigamy, and physical and mental cruelty. Section 4 granted divorce in the instance of imprisonment, addiction to drugs without prospect of rehabilitation, failure to consummate the marriage, and, most significantly, varying periods of living separate and apart.

Section 4(1)(e)(i) provided that a divorce could be granted after three years of **separation** if the petitioner had been "deserted" by the respondent. In order to prove desertion, the petitioner had to establish that there had been an intention to desert, proof of living separate and apart as well as proof of lack of consent to the separation, and no just cause for the separation. Section 4(1)(e)(ii) allowed a petition for divorce after living separate and apart for five years, with no requirement of establishing desertion.

Between 1968 and the early 1980s, the number of divorces granted in Canada continued to increase, from just under 30 000 in 1970 to more than 70 000 in 1982. Although marital offences of adultery and mental and physical cruelty continued as the most common grounds for divorce, almost one-third of petitions were granted on the new ground of separation.[5]

Pressure for the reform of divorce law continued to mount throughout the 1970s. Critics argued that the 1968 legislation was too restrictive. The three- and five-year periods of separation were assailed as impractical, and as serving to produce lengthy conflict between the parties. Critics also argued that the grounds for divorce remained tied to the outdated practice of assigning fault for marriage breakdown, further intensifying rather than diminishing the existing conflict between husband and wife.

The *Divorce Act* of 1985

In 1985, a new *Divorce Act* was enacted which remains in force today. In its introduction to the act, the Ministry of Justice noted:

> [S]hortening the separation period to one year from the present requirement of three years is designed to reduce the conflict between the spouses. At the same time, it is considered long enough to allow for second thought, and to avoid rash and hasty divorces, especially since the law will allow for periods of resumption of cohabitation for the purpose of reconciliation without interrupting the period of separation.[6]

Section 8 of the 1985 *Divorce Act* reads as follows:

8. (1)   A court of competent jurisdiction may, on application by either or both spouses, grant a divorce to the spouse or spouses on the ground that there has been a breakdown of their marriage.

   (2)   Breakdown of a marriage is established only if
      (a)   the spouses have lived separate and apart for at least one year immediately preceding the determination of the divorce proceeding and were living separate and apart at the commencement of the proceeding; or
      (b)   the spouse against whom the divorce proceeding is brought has, since celebration of the marriage,
         (i)   committed adultery, or
         (ii)   treated the other spouse with physical or mental cruelty of such a kind as to render intolerable the continued cohabitation of the spouses.

Grounds for Divorce under the *Divorce Act* of 1985

The Canadian Bar Association had urged the federal government to adopt a different form of legislation, one which focused on *whether* a marriage had broken down, not *why*. The association urged abandonment of any notion of fault as an element of marriage breakdown, proposing this wording for the legislation:

A petition for divorce on breakdown of marriage:

   (a)   shall be established if the husband and wife have lived separate and apart for a period of one year that immediately precedes, includes, or immediately follows the date of presentation of the petition;

(b) may be established on proof satisfactory to the Court
that a marriage has irretrievably broken down.[7]

But the Canadian Bar Association's recommendations were not accepted. Current law maintains a focus on fault, within section 8(2) of the act. Proof of wrongdoing—adultery or mental or physical cruelty—continues to be required in the case of petitions filed pursuant to section 8(2)(b), even though such petitions are now rare.

ADULTERY

Is it even useful to inquire about fault, if the goal of the act is simply to establish whether a marriage has broken down? Furthermore, as a technical matter, how is adultery to be proven? Consider the dilemma of *Shaw v. Shaw*.

> Dubinsky, J.: At the conclusion of the hearing in this case, I granted a decree nisi in the divorce petition by Mrs. Shaw on the ground of cruelty. I reserved my decision on the counter-petition by Mr. Shaw on the ground of adultery.
>
> Harold Bellefontaine, the corespondent named in the counter-petition, denied that he had committed adultery with Mrs. Shaw, the respondent by the counter-petition.
>
> I am on safe ground in saying that there is no direct evidence of any adulterous relationship between Mrs. Shaw and Mr. Bellefontaine. It follows, therefore, that if adultery is to be found herein on the part of the respondent (the respondent by the counter-petition), it must be inferred from the proven facts.
>
> Power on Divorce, 2nd ed., 1964, p. 425, states as follows:
>
> *Since it is almost never possible to adduce direct evidence of the act of adultery, its commission is permitted to be proven by evidence of acts or a course of conduct which convinces the court that it should infer that it did occur.*
>
> *The inference can be drawn although both parties deny their guilt. The drawing of the inference must always be with caution and evidence that creates only a suspicion of adultery is insufficient.*
>
> *It is now settled that the standard of proof required in a divorce action wherein no question of legitimacy arises is not that applicable to criminal cases, where the prosecution must prove guilt beyond a reasonable doubt, but is the standard required in civil actions where the preponderance of probabilities determines the issues. . . .*
>
> *It is impossible to lay down any general rule defining the circumstances which are sufficient in an action for divorce to justify a finding of*

adultery, except that the circumstances must be such as lead by fair and reasonable inference to that conclusion. Each case depends on its own particular facts. Evidence of familiarities between the parties and of facts showing opportunity for the commission of adultery raise a prima facie case that adultery has been committed, but the inference should always be drawn with extreme caution and it has been held should not be drawn unless there is proof of an inclination to commit adultery.

It would, in my opinion, be a reasonable and guarded inference from the facts that Mrs. Shaw and Mr. Bellefontaine, a married man with two children, were seeing so much of each other that the opportunities for her to commit adultery were present. However, Lord Atkin in *Ross v. Ellison (Ross)*, [1930] A.C. 1 at 23, points out:

That there were opportunities for committing adultery is nothing; **there must be circumstances amounting to proof that the opportunities would be used.** *(The boldface is mine.)*

. . . I would regard it as a sorry day if a married person could not have and enjoy the warm friendship of one of the opposite sex, without being stamped with the stigma of impropriety.

In two fairly recent cases, where the same sort of situation existed, I did draw the inference that adultery had been committed. In each of these cases, there was something which led me to find as I did. In the first case, there was evidence that on one occasion the respondent and corespondent, who were both present at a party, were found lying fully clothed on the bed of a darkened bedroom. This uncontradicted piece of evidence led me to conclude that they were there for an amorous purpose. This incident, coupled with other evidence, led me to infer that adultery had taken place between the respondent and corespondent.

In the other cases, there was introduced a letter which had been written by the respondent to the corespondent and which referred to the great love that existed between them, as well as other things. That letter, when added to other evidence which had been given, led me to infer that adultery had been committed.

In each of these two cases, I had in mind what Lord Buckmaster said in *Ross v. Ellison (Ross)*, supra, at p. 7:

Adultery is essentially an act which can rarely be proved by direct evidence. It is a matter of inference and circumstance. It is easy to suggest conditions which can leave no doubt that adultery has been committed, but the mere fact that people are thrown together in an environment which lends itself to the commission of the offence is not enough unless it can be shown by documents, e.g. letters and diaries, or antecedent conduct that the association of the parties was so intimate and their mutual passion so clear that adultery might reasonably be assumed as the result of an opportunity for its occurrence. (The boldface is mine.)

In short, keeping in mind the authorities quoted above and reviewing all the evidence given in the present case touching upon the allegation of adultery, I am not led to the conclusion that adultery was committed by Mrs. Shaw and Mr. Bellefontaine. Accordingly, I dismiss the counter-petition.[8]

Shaw v. Shaw illustrates the difficulty of proof of adultery and simultaneously leads to the question whether such proof is ultimately relevant to a finding of marriage breakdown. As the Canadian Bar Association has argued, perhaps the inquiry of the court ought to be directed to the simpler question of whether the marriage has broken down, not to the requirement of proof of specific acts that often accompany marriage breakdown.

MENTAL OR PHYSICAL CRUELTY

With the issues of mental or physical cruelty, the requirement of proof poses similar difficulties as adultery. Consider the following excerpts from the cases *Knoll v. Knoll* and *Gilbert v. Gilbert*. Both cases were decided under the *Divorce Act* of 1968, prior to the 1985 reconstruction of the legislation. The relevant section was section 3(d), which is virtually identical to section 8(2)(b)(ii) of the current act:

3.   Subject to section 5, a petition for divorce may be presented to a court by a husband or wife, on the ground that the respondent, since the celebration of the marriage . . .

(d)   has treated the petitioner with physical or mental cruelty of such a kind as to render intolerable the continued cohabitation of the spouses.

Knoll v. Knoll was an appeal by the wife to the Ontario Court of Appeal, following the dismissal of her petition for divorce at trial. She had sought divorce on the ground of physical or mental cruelty. Evidence at trial revealed that her husband became very abusive toward her when he drank. He had both assaulted her and verbally abused her on a number of these occasions.

Schroeder, J.A.: Over the years, the courts have steadfastly refrained from attempting to formulate a general definition of cruelty. As used in ordinary parlance, "cruelty" signifies a disposition to inflict suffering; to delight in or exhibit indifference to the pain or misery of others; mercilessness or hard-heartedness as exhibited in action. If in the marriage relationship, one spouse, by his conduct, causes wanton, malicious, or unnecessary infliction of pain or suffering upon the body, the feeling, or emotions of the other, his conduct may well constitute cruelty which will entitle a petitioner to dissolution of the marriage if, in the court's opinion, it amounts to physical or mental cruelty "of such a kind as to render intolerable the continued cohabitation of the spouses." . . .

Care must be exercised in applying the standard set forth in s. 3(d) that conduct relied upon to establish cruelty is not a trivial act, but one of a "grave and weighty" nature, and not merely conduct which can be characterized as little more than a manifestation of incompatibility of temperament between the spouses. The whole matrimonial relations must be considered, especially if the cruelty consists of reproaches, complaints, accusations, or constant carping criticisms. A question most relevant for consideration is the effect of the conduct complained of upon the mind of the affected spouse. The determination of what constitutes cruelty in a given case must, in the final analysis, depend upon the circumstances of the particular case, having due regard to the physical and mental condition of the parties, their character, and their attitudes toward the marriage relationship.

In the present case, it is the cumulative effect of the acts of the defendant upon the petitioner which must be considered and given proper weight. The wife's return to her home after a day's work only to find her husband in an inebriated state, given to quarrelsomeness and abuse, heaping insult upon insult and indignity upon indignity, was clearly conduct amounting to mental cruelty of such a kind as to render intolerable the continued cohabitation of the spouses. I cannot be convinced that our community standards require a wife to tolerate such an intolerable situation.[9]

Consider, on the other hand, the rationale in *Gilbert v. Gilbert*:

Hallett, J.: This is a divorce action, the wife petitioning on the ground of mental cruelty. The petition is opposed by the husband. . . .

The petitioner's principal complaint in support of her allegations of mental cruelty was that the respondent was of a domineering personality and that he had her under constant pressure to the extent that she could not tolerate living with him and left in October 1979. Some of her specific complaints were as follows:

1. At times, the respondent was, as she described it, "moody," in that he would be quiet and she worried about this and

felt upset at the possibility she may have done something to bring on this state. His testimony was that at times, if he had a problem, he would like to think about it and during this period he would be withdrawn and quiet. There was no evidence that this would last any length of time.

2. At times, he was a little late in the morning, causing her to be late for work, which disturbed her and, conversely, if she was late in the evening in getting off work, he would be annoyed because they would be inconveniencing the family with whom they had left their small child.

3. He made her feel guilty after she had stopped work because she was not contributing to the family's finances.

4. On one occasion, in March 1979, he talked of giving up both his education and work and [having] the family go to live in a cottage they owned at Turtle Lake and he would write a book. This upset her and caused her anxiety. His evidence was that this was an idle comment he had made when under pressure studying for his M.B.A. exams. In fact, he did nothing about pursuing this course of activity.

5. As an example of the type of dominance he exercised over her, she complained that he would be critical of her if she placed the cutlery in the wrong direction on the drying board after she washed the knives and forks; this upset her.

6. She complained that from time to time, he would change his mind, and one specific incident related to a proposed purchase of a swing set for their child that he had agreed to buy, but when it arrived, he sent it back. His testimony was that the swing set had been ordered from a catalogue and by the time it had arrived, the summer was over and, as money was tight, he sent it back.

7. She complained that he had induced her to take a drama course at Antigonish which apparently lasted for a week or ten days, and this was an example of his dominance over her. His evidence was that she had expressed an interest in drama and that he had merely pointed out to her that this course was available.

8. She complained that he made her feel guilty when she became involved in outside activities after she stopped working as he felt that, as she had time for these activities,

she could be working, as their financial situation was difficult. He felt she did not take seriously the financial difficulties and that, since commencing her consultations with Mr. Parliament (a psychologist), she seemed to be placing her own interests above that of the family. In my opinion, the evidence indicates this was probably true.

9. She was upset because her husband felt she was being selfish when she indicated she wished to explore her own needs as opposed to those of the family when she became involved in volunteer work and other outside activities.

10. She felt he criticized her unduly for small things after she had worked all day during the period when she was working. There is very little evidence of any specific criticism other than the matter of lining up the cutlery on the drying board.

She testified that since she separated from her husband, she is much happier and this has been confirmed by independent testimony. She felt that at the time she left, she could do nothing right that would satisfy her husband and that they simply were not having any fun as a married couple. . . .

I formed the impression from the evidence and from my observation of the respondent that the worst that can be said about the respondent is that he is a very smug and self-satisfied person, and I accept the petitioner's evidence that she found it intolerable to continue living with him as far as she was concerned, but I do not think that acts of which she complains constituted mental cruelty. The acts complained of were not grave and weighty but merely reflected a concern he had for the family's financial affairs and concern he had to see that his wife and child developed their personalities. It has been said many times that in the test as to whether the actions of a spouse constitute cruelty, one must look at what effect the spouse's actions have had on the petitioner, not what effect they might have on a person of a different temperament. I accept that as a proper principle, but the conduct must be grave and weighty, and there is nothing in the evidence that measures up to this test of cruelty. I can understand that the petitioner was unhappy and that her husband's personality contributed to her unhappiness, but I do not feel his conduct amounted to mental cruelty of such a kind as to render intolerable the continued cohabitation of the parties. . . . The petition is dismissed.[10]

The *Divorce Act* of 1985 and the Question of Support

The question of support for a spouse in the event of marriage breakdown typically generates considerable discussion and controversy. The relevant sections—15, 15.1(1), 15.2(1) to (6), 15.3(1), (2), and 17(7)—of the *Divorce Act* of 1985 state:

> 15.   In sections 15.1 to 16, "spouse" has the meaning assigned by subsection 2(1), and includes a former spouse.
>
> 15.1 (1)   A court of competent jurisdiction may, on application by either or both spouses, make an order requiring a spouse to pay for the support of any or all children of the marriage. . . .
>
> 15.2 (1)   A court of competent jurisdiction may, on application by either or both spouses, make an order requiring a spouse to secure or pay, or to secure and pay, such lump sum or periodic sums, or such lump sum and periodic sums, as the court thinks reasonable for the support of the other spouse.
>
> (2)   Where an application is made under subsection (1), the court may, on application by either or both spouses, make an interim order requiring a spouse to secure or pay, or to secure and pay, such lump sum or periodic sums, or such lump sum and periodic sums, as the court thinks reasonable for the support of the other spouse, pending the determination of the application under subsection (1).
>
> (3)   The court may make an order under subsection (1) or an interim order under subsection (2) for a definite or indefinite period or until a specified event occurs, and may impose terms, conditions or restrictions in connection with the order as it thinks fit and just.
>
> (4)   In making an order under subsection (1) or an interim order under subsection (2), the court shall take into consideration the condition, means, needs and other circumstances of each spouse, including
>
> > (a)   the length of time the spouses cohabited;
> >
> > (b)   the functions performed by each spouse during cohabitation; and
> >
> > (c)   any order, agreement or arrangement relating to support of either spouse.

(5)   In making an order under subsection (1) or an interim order under subsection (2), the court shall not take into consideration any misconduct of a spouse in relation to the marriage.

(6)   An order made under subsection (1) or an interim order under subsection (2) that provides for the support of a spouse should

    (a)   recognize any economic advantages or disadvantages to the spouses arising from the marriage or its breakdown;

    (b)   apportion between the spouses any financial consequences arising from the care of any child of the marriage over and above any obligation for the support of any child of the marriage;

    (c)   relieve any economic hardship of the spouses arising from the breakdown of the marriage; and

    (d)   in so far as practicable, promote the economic self-sufficiency of each spouse within a reasonable period of time. . . .

15.3   (1)   Where a court is considering an application for a child support order and an application for a spousal support order, the court shall give priority to child support in determining the applications.

(2)   Where, as a result of giving priority to child support, the court is unable to make a spousal support order or the court makes a spousal support order in an amount that is less than it otherwise would have been, the court shall record its reasons for having done so.

17.   (7)   A variation order varying a spousal support order should

    (a)   recognize any economic advantages or disadvantages to the former spouses arising from the marriage or its breakdown;

    (b)   apportion between the former spouses any financial consequences arising from the care of any child of the marriage over and above the obligation for the support of any child of the marriage;

    (c)   relieve any economic hardship of the former spouses arising from the breakdown of the marriage; and

    (d)   in so far as practicable, promote the economic self-sufficiency of each former spouse within a reasonable period of time.

Sections 15.2(6)(d) and 17(7)(d) set out an important general principle with respect to claims for spousal support: an expectation of self-sufficiency "within a reasonable period of time." In the mid-1970s, both the Ontario Law Reform Commission and the Law Reform Commission of Canada had called for the reform of spousal maintenance obligations in the event of marriage breakdown. Prior to the passage of the *Divorce Act* of 1985, there was very little guidance as to the principles applicable to spousal support. Section 11 of the *Divorce Act* of 1968 provided for awards of maintenance to husband or wife, "if (the court) thinks it fit and just to do so having regard to the conduct of the parties and the condition, means, and other circumstances of each of them." The current *Divorce Act* provides more guidance, asserting equality between spouses, basing support on the principle of need, and assuming self-sufficiency of each spouse "within a reasonable period of time." In *Lashley v. Lashley*, we see the Ontario Court of Appeal place this phrase in context and give it more concrete meaning.

Cory, J.A.: An appeal has been brought from the judgement of the Honourable Judge Mercier pronounced in Ottawa in November of last year.

Mr. and Mrs. Lashley are a young couple with three children, the oldest born January 8, 1976, the second on May 4, 1980, and the third on November 28, 1981. Mrs. Lashley has not worked during the marriage. She has a Grade 11 education and at one occasion, while her husband was working in Prince Edward Island, she obtained a certificate from the College of Visual Arts in silver-smithing. This marked the successful completion of a two-year course.

Mr. Lashley is a graduate of the Ontario Agricultural College. At the time of the trial, he had an income in the amount of $38 000. He received as well an annual allowance for his car expenses of $2 400. . . .

The trial judge ordered payment of $21 600 annually for main-tenance. This was arrived at by awarding $350 per month for each child and $750 to the wife. There is no doubt that this award is the very maximum that could be made. It is probably greater than any sum any of us would have awarded. Nonetheless, it is not so unreasonable that this court should interfere with it, provided there is a time limit placed on the wife's maintenance. We are of the view that there should be a limit of five years applied to the award of maintenance, commencing with the date the judgement was made.

In this case the wife is young. She is not under any disability. Indeed, she has been and is a ski instructor. She does have a skill and certificate as a silversmith. There is no reason why she should not be able to so arrange her life that she will be in a position to earn an income and maintain herself within the five-year period. One child is in full-time attendance at school. The other two are in day care; yet the wife has not made any serious effort to obtain full-time employment. We do not think this decision is contrary to the principles set forth in *Messier v. Delage*, [1983] 2 S.C.R. 401, 35 R.F.L. (2d) 337, 2 D.L.R. (4th) 1, 50 N.R.16, by Chouinard, J. speaking for the majority. He stressed at p. 352 that each decision must be made on the basis of its facts. In addition, he stated at p. 353 that the decision did not mean that the obligation of spouses should continue indefinitely when the marriage is dissolved.

Many factors will have to be taken into consideration; for example, the age of the spouses and their children, the length of time that one spouse has been out of the work force, the skills, education, health, and capabilities of the parties will all be taken into account in determining whether there should be a time limit placed on the award. The youth, good health, and skills of the wife, together with the very generous award of maintenance, all indicate that a time limit should be imposed in the case at bar.

Paragraph 4 of the formal order will be then amended to provide for that limitation.[11]

Consider, by contrast, the following excerpt from the Supreme Court of Canada's unanimous decision in *Moge v. Moge*,[12] handed down in late 1992:

L'Heureux-Dubé, J.: At the heart of this appeal lies the question of spousal support. Specifically, the Court is asked to determine the circumstances under which spousal support ought to be varied or terminated pursuant to s. 17 of the *Divorce Act*. . . . In a broader sense, however, this case turns upon the basic philosophy of support within the Act as a whole.

Mrs. Moge was born in 1937. The parties were married in Poland in the mid-'50s. It is unclear from the evidence or the recollection of the parties whether the marriage took place in 1955 or 1957, but the discrepancy is immaterial for the purposes of this appeal. They decided to emigrate and moved to Manitoba in 1960. Three children were born of the marriage. The two elder children, Elizabeth and Victor, were born in Poland prior to the family's coming to Canada. The youngest, Edward, was born in 1966 and at the time of the application at issue, was studying at the University of Manitoba.

Mrs. Moge has a Grade 7 education. Prior to coming to this country, she worked briefly as a sales clerk. During the marriage, she was responsible for the day-to-day care of the children and did the laundry, housework, shopping, cooking and so on. She was also employed in the evenings working from 5:00 p.m. until 11:00 p.m. cleaning offices, except for a brief period in 1963–64 when she worked as a seamstress. In his pleading, Mr. Moge attempted to persuade the Court that this was a marriage in which both contributed to the domestic chores, she during the day while he worked as a welder with Motor Coach Industries, and he in the evening while she worked. However, Twaddle J.A., whose reasons in the Court of Appeal I will examine in more detail later, found based on the evidence that:

> There is no suggestion that the wife's outside employment was undertaken for any reason other than the need to supplement her husband's income. Nor is there any suggestion that the husband undertook additional responsibilities at home to counterbalance the wife's efforts in the external work force. In all respects, this was a traditional relationship of the kind which was common then and which was in conformity with the social conventions of the time.

In 1973, the parties separated and on November 22, 1974, Nitikman J. of the Manitoba Court of Queen's Bench granted the separation and made an order awarding custody of the children to Mrs. Moge. Mr. Moge was ordered to pay $150 per month spousal and child support. After the separation, Mrs. Moge continued to work outside the home. From 5:00 p.m. until 11:00 p.m. she cleaned at the Fort Garry Hotel in Winnipeg. During this time she remained responsible for the care of the children, and while she was out of the home in the evenings, the older children apparently helped out with Edward.

A divorce petition was filed by Mr. Moge in 1980. It was not opposed by Mrs. Moge and she did not appear on the hearing of the petition to oppose her husband's proposal that he continue to pay $150 per month toward her maintenance and that of the remaining dependent child. Mr. Moge remarried in 1984 but continued to pay support to his former wife.

Mrs. Moge was employed at the Fort Garry Hotel from 1975 until January of 1987 when it closed down. . . . The evidence disclosed that, at the time she was laid off in 1987, she was earning approximately $795 net per month. Her net monthly income (excluding support) was reduced to $593 in unemployment insurance benefits. The evidence further discloses that during the period she was out of work, she unsuccessfully sought employment with 38 prospective employers. Mr. Moge was then earning approximately $2 000 in gross monthly income and also derived a small amount from investments. He and his second wife had purchased a home.

Mrs. Moge applied to vary the spousal and child support order pursuant to which she was continuing to receive $150 per month. She was successful and a variation order was made by Mullally J. of the Manitoba Court of Queen's Bench on October 14, 1987. The order provided for spousal support of $200 per month and child support of $200 per month, thereby increasing her total monthly support from $150 to $400.

Between December 14, 1987 and June 30, 1989, Mrs. Moge was able to secure part-time and intermittent cleaning work with the province of Manitoba. The longest period of work began on November 14, 1988 and ended on June 30, 1989. During this period, she worked from early to mid-morning for a total of 20 hours per week and received $9.28 per hour or approximately $800 gross per month. By way of comparison, though by no means independently wealthy, Mr. Moge was earning approximately $2 200 per month. His second wife was also employed.

In May of 1989, Mr. Moge applied to vary both the child and spousal support orders of October 14, 1987. This second application also came before Mullally J. By an order pronounced September 29, 1989 and signed on December 7, 1989, child support was terminated and spousal support was to cease on December 1, 1989. The wife appealed on the issue of spousal support only. On April 5, 1990, the Court of Appeal allowed Mrs. Moge's appeal in part and ordered spousal support in the amount of $150 per month for an indefinite period beginning January 1, 1990. Mr. Moge now appeals that decision to this court. . . .

The Trilogy and Its Jurisprudence

The position of Mr. Moge before this Court is that his support obligation to his ex-wife should be terminated on the basis of the reasoning in *Pelech*, supra, *Richardson v. Richardson*, [1987] 1 S.C.R. 857, and *Caron v. Caron*, [1987] 1 S.C.R. 892, the so-called "trilogy." He submits that though those cases specifically concerned situations in which the parties had set out their respective rights and obligations following the dissolution of the marriage by agreement, the Court was advocating a model of support to be relied upon even in the absence of a final settlement.

That model, he says, is characterized by such notions as self-sufficiency and causal connection. Effectively, his position is that his ex-wife should have been self-sufficient by now and, if she is not, no link may be drawn between that lack of self-sufficiency and the marriage (i.e. no causal connection). In other words, her current financial position is no concern of his. . . .

The question that arises is the extent to which the causal connection test articulated in *Pelech*, supra, decided under the 1970 *Divorce Act*, applies to nonconsensual dispositions under the Act, as is the case here. . . .

Introduction

Before dealing squarely with the main issue raised by this appeal, there are a number of preliminary observations that I wish to make.

The first has to do with the argument raised by Mr. Moge that, quite apart from the trilogy, the Act espouses a self-sufficiency model as the only basis of spousal support. . . . Mrs. Moge disagrees. She points out that self-sufficiency is only one of many objectives which the Act directs a court of competent jurisdiction to consider in exercising its discretion under ss. 17(4) and 17(7) and that even then, the objective of self-sufficiency in s. 17(7) is modified by such terminology as "insofar as practicable." She further submits that there is now appellate court jurisprudence which recognizes that in cases such as her own, self-sufficiency will not be practicable, largely due to the residual effects of being outside the labour market for a protracted period of time.

The self-sufficiency model advanced by Mr. Moge has generally been predicated on the dichotomy between "traditional" and "modern" marriage. Often, in order to draw the line after which no more support will be ordered, courts have distinguished between "traditional" marriages in which the wife remains at home and takes responsibility for the domestic aspects of marital life, and "modern" ones where employment outside the home is pursued. . . . [A]s Judge Rosalie S. Abella wrote . . . "it is hard to be an independent equal when one is not equally able to become independent." . . . [C]ourts have frequently been more amenable to finding that "traditional" marriages survive the so-called "causal connection" test (more often) than "modern" ones. . . .

The second observation I wish to make is that, in determining spousal support, it is important not to lose sight of the fact that the support provisions of the Act are intended to deal with the economic consequences, for both parties, of the marriage or its breakdown. Marriage may unquestionably be a source of benefit to both parties that is not easily quantified in economic terms. Many believe that marriage and the family provide for the emotional, economic, and social well-being of [the] members. It may be the location of safety and comfort, and may be the place where its members have their most intimate human contact. Marriage and the family act as an emotional and economic support system as well as a forum for intimacy. In this regard, [they] serve vital personal interest, and may be linked to building a "comprehensive sense of personhood." Marriage and the family are a superb environment for raising and nurturing the young of our society by providing the initial environment for the development of social skills. These institutions also provide a means to pass on the values that we deem to be central to our sense of community.

Conversely, marriage and the family often require the sacrifice of personal priorities by both parties in the interests of shared goals. All of these elements are of undeniable importance in shaping the overall character of a marriage. Spousal support in the context of divorce, however, is not about the emotional and social benefits of marriage. Rather, the purpose of spousal support is to relieve economic hardship that results from "marriage or its breakdown." Whatever the respective advantages to the parties of a marriage in other areas, the focus of the inquiry when assessing spousal support after the marriage has ended must be the effect of the marriage in either impairing or improving each party's economic prospects. . . .

A third point worthy of emphasis is that this analysis applies equally to both spouses, depending on how the division of labour is exercised in a particular marriage. What the Act requires is a fair and equitable distribution of resources to alleviate the economic consequences of marriage or marriage breakdown for both spouses, regardless of gender. The reality, however, is that in many if not most marriages, the wife still remains the economically disadvantaged partner. There may be times where the reverse is true and the Act is equally able to accommodate this eventuality. . . .

The Objectives of the Act

The most significant change in the new Act when compared to the 1970 *Divorce Act* may be the shift away from the "means and needs" test as the exclusive criterion for support to a more encompassing set of factors and objectives which requires courts to accommodate a much wider spectrum of considerations. This change, of course, does not signify that "means and needs" are to be ignored. Section 15(5) [now 15.2(4)] of the Act specifically states that "the court shall take into consideration the condition, means, needs and other circumstances of each spouse." . . .

All four of the objectives defined in the Act (under section 17(7)) must be taken into account when spousal support is claimed or an order for spousal support is sought to be varied. No single objective is paramount. The fact that one of the objectives, such as economic self-sufficiency, has been attained does not necessarily dispose of the matter. . . .

Many proponents of the deemed self-sufficiency model effectively elevate it to the pre-eminent objective in determining the right to, quantum and duration of spousal support. In my opinion, this approach is not consonant with proper principles of statutory interpretation. The objective of self-sufficiency is only one of several objectives enumerated in the section and, given the manner in which Parliament has set out those objectives, I see no indication that any one is to be given priority. Parliament, in my opinion, intended that support reflect the diverse dynamics of many unique marital relationships. . . .

An examination of the economic position of single mothers is also useful in assessing the effects of dissolution of marriage since about 30 percent of single mothers are divorced: Statistics Canada, *Women in Canada: A Statistical Report* (2nd ed.) 1990. In 1987, 57 percent of single mothers lived below the poverty line. . . .

Reports such as these have led many Canadian commentators to draw direct links between female poverty and the financial consequences of the dissolution of marriage. While Eichler emphasizes the limits of family law in addressing poverty in "The Limits of Family Law Reform, or The Privatization of Female and Child Poverty" (1990–1991), *7 C.F.L.Q.*, she recognizes that family law nevertheless has a role to play in alleviating poverty for single mothers when she writes at p. 60:

> *What are the consequences of divorce for women, men, and children, besides emotional pain? They are very different. Men tend to maintain the standard of living they had before the divorce, while women and children sink into instant poverty. . . .*

Findings in the *Report of the Social Assistance Review Committee, Transitions* (1988), show that support can be a significant factor in alleviating some of these negative economic effects. The report notes that recipients of social assistance who receive support payments are more likely to leave the program than those who do not and that the length of time a recipient receives social assistance is inversely proportional to the total amount of support received. At page 44, the report states:

The nearly 50 percent of single parents receiving family benefit allowance who receive no support payments at all averaged between 3.5 and 4 years in the program. The 11 percent receiving between $10 and $100 per month averaged 2.5 to 3 years, while those receiving between $100 and $200 per month averaged 2 to 2.5 years. Finally, the mere 6 percent receiving in excess of $200 per month averaged less than 2 years in the program. . . .

Application to the Case at Bar

. . . The sole remaining consideration is whether the application of Mr. Moge to terminate support ought to have been granted in this case. In my view, it should not have and the majority of the Court of Appeal was right in finding an error of principle on the part of the trial judge. I agree with Twaddle J.A., supra, at p. 177:

. . . even if some degree of economic self-sufficiency is practicable, the level at which the wife can become self-sufficient may be lower than the husband's level of self-sufficiency. This disadvantage will often be attributable to the marriage. In such a case, the court will best meet the objectives prescribed by Parliament by supplementing the wife's earning ability with some maintenance. It would be contrary to those objectives to foreclose a traditional wife from all maintenance.

In the case at bar, the learned judge in Motions Court did just that. In the passage from his reasons which I have quoted, he makes it clear that, in his view, this wife should have achieved total financial independence. With the greatest respect to him, I think that is an error in principle. He failed to consider the disparity between the earning ability of each former spouse: he failed to have regard to the fact that the wife, having married in a traditional arrangement, was disadvantaged by it.

The four objectives of spousal support orders under s. 17(7) of the Act, as explicated above and applied by the Court of Appeal, are met in this case. For this reason, the following specific findings are in order based on the evidence in the record:

1. Mrs. Moge has sustained a substantial economic disadvantage "from the marriage or its breakdown" within the meaning of s. 17(7)(a) of the Act.
2. Mrs. Moge's long-term responsibility for the upbringing of the children of the marriage after the spousal separation in 1973 has had an impact on her ability to earn an income so as to trigger the application of s. 17(7)(b) of the Act.
3. Mrs. Moge continues to suffer economic hardship as a result of the "breakdown of the marriage" within the meaning of s. 17(7)(c) of the Act.
4. Mrs. Moge has failed to become economically self-sufficient notwithstanding her conscientious efforts.

These findings are irrefutable even in the absence of expert evidence relating to the appropriate quantification of spousal support. It follows that in view of all of the objectives of spousal support orders set out in s. 17(7) of the Act, continuing support is in order in this case. Accordingly, there was no error in the Court of Appeal. . . .

McLachlin, J.: Parties sometimes argue that the economic disadvantage of their spouse was not caused by the marriage or its breakdown, or that her economic hardship was not caused by the termination of the marriage. Shades of these arguments surfaced in this case. It was said that Mrs. Moge voluntarily elected to be the primary homemaker and caregiver; that it was her choice and not the marriage that caused the resultant economic disadvantage. Similarly, it was suggested that her present need and lack of self-sufficiency was not the product of the marriage but of her failure to choose to upgrade her education so she could earn more money.

A formalistic view of causation can work injustice in the context of s. 17(7), as elsewhere. The question under s. 17(7)(a) is whether a party was disadvantaged or gained advantages from the marriage, as a matter of fact; under s. 17(7)(c) whether the marriage breakdown in fact led to economic hardship for one of the spouses. Hypothetical arguments after the fact about different choices people could have made which might have produced different results are irrelevant, unless the parties acted unreasonably or unfairly. In this case, for example, Mrs. Moge, in keeping with the prevailing social expectation of the times, accepted primary responsibility for the home and the children and confined her extra activities to supplementing the family income rather than to getting a better education or to furthering her career. That was the actual domestic arrangement which prevailed. What Mrs. Moge might have done in a different arrangement with different social and domestic expectations is irrelevant.

Similarly, in determining whether economic hardship of a spouse arises from the breakdown of the marriage, the starting point should be a comparison of the spouse's actual situation before and after the breakdown. If the economic hardship arose shortly after the marriage breakdown, that may be a strong indication that it is caused by the family breakdown. Arguments that an ex-spouse should be doing more for herself must be considered in light of her background and abilities, physical and psychological. It may be unreasonable to expect a middle-aged person who has devoted most of her life to domestic concerns within the marriage to compete for scarce jobs with youthful college graduates, for example. Even women who have worked outside the home during the marriage may find that their career advancement has been permanently reduced by the effort which they devoted to home and family instead of their jobs, whether the woman be a janitor like Mrs. Moge or a well-trained professional. Sometimes the breakdown of the marriage may have left the woman with feelings of inadequacy or depression which make it difficult for her to do more. In short, the whole context of her conduct must be considered. It is not enough to say in the abstract that the ex-spouse should have done more or be doing more, and argue from this that it is her inaction rather than the breakup of the marriage which is the cause of her economic hardship. One must look at the actual social and personal reality of the situation in which she finds herself and judge the matter fairly from that perspective.[13]

The decision in *Moge v. Moge* shows clearly that the importance and relevance of the factors to be considered in awarding support will depend upon the nature of the marriage, as well as on the relationship between marriage breakdown and the economic status of the respective spouses. Critics have asserted that the decision serves to undermine the principle of equality between men and women; supporters have applauded *Moge v. Moge* for providing a realistic assessment of the consequences of divorce for many, if not most, Canadian women. In any event, the case demonstrates, first, that economic self-sufficiency is only one variable to be considered in awards of spousal support and, second, that the importance of this factor may be eclipsed by the other considerations set out in section 17(7).

After their finding in *Moge*, the Supreme Court of Canada made a similar determination in relation to spousal support in *Hickey v. Hickey*.[14] In this case, the Court was asked to determine the validity of an increase in spousal and child support granted to Patricia Hickey in 1996. The Hickeys (Walter and Patricia) were married in 1971 and divorced in 1987. They had two children, a girl born in 1977 and a boy born in 1980. In 1987, at the time of the divorce, Walter Hickey was paying his wife $1 000 monthly in spousal support and $1 500 in child support ($750 for each of the two children). In March 1996, when the older daughter moved out of her mother's home, her father brought a motion to eliminate support for his daughter, asking that his total monthly payment be decreased from $2 500 to $1 750. His former wife agreed to this removal of support for her daughter, but asked that the remaining spousal and child support be increased. The motions judge agreed and increased her spousal support to $1 300 and child support for her son to $1 500, thereby increasing the original amount of support from $2 500 to $2 800. The Court heard that in 1995 Walter Hickey had an annual income of almost $220 000 and that Patricia Hickey had an income of a little more than $30 000, most of which was from support payments made by her former husband since 1987. She had tried to start a small business, but this enterprise had not been very successful. Mr. Hickey appealed to the Manitoba Court of Appeal, which agreed with him, reducing the amount awarded for child support to $750 and finding the original amount of $1 000 for spousal support to be sufficient.

The Supreme Court of Canada, however, overturned the Court of Appeal's decision and restored the motions judge's decision requiring Mr. Hickey to pay $2 800 per month in spousal and child support. The Court noted that in the instance of child support the increased means of the payor spouse, the increased needs of a child as he or she grows older, and the fiscal reality of inflation all justified an upward variation of the award of support. In the instance of spousal support, the Court noted that all four criteria set out in section 17(7) of the *Divorce Act* must be taken into consideration: the economic disadvantage to the former spouse arising from marriage breakdown, the financial consequences of child care, economic hardship of a former spouse arising from marriage breakdown, and the promotion of the economic self-sufficiency of each former spouse. The Court argued that an upward variation of the support order in this case was consistent with the objectives set out in section 17(7) of the act.

Moreover, the Supreme Court held that appeal courts should not overturn support orders made by trial courts unless there is a significant error in principle, a significant misunderstanding of the evidence, or the award is, on its face, clearly wrong. In other words, the Supreme Court has indicated that in matters of support awards, the discretion of the trial court is to be respected; a trial judge is in the best position to appreciate all the facts in the case. An appeal court is not entitled to overturn a support order simply because it would have balanced factors somewhat differently—to permit such appeals is to create a greater incentive for appeal, to produce added expenses for litigants, and to delay an important need for finality in family law litigation. In any event, both *Moge* and *Hickey* make clear that, at least in certain circumstances, a spouse may well have a lifetime financial obligation to support a former spouse.

A recent decision of the Supreme Court of Canada, *Miglin v. Miglin*, [2003] 1 S.C.R. 303 extends the logic of *Moge* and *Hickey*, at least to some extent. In this case the Miglins separated after 14 years of marriage. They were joint owners of Killarney Lodge in Ontario's Algonquin Park, and they signed an agreement whereby Mrs. Miglin agreed to give up her interest in this lucrative business in exchange for Mr. Miglin's interest in the family home. She believed that she would be able to get by on child support from Mr. Miglin, and on a small annual consulting fee related to the lodge business. As a consequence, she waived her right to any payment of spousal support.

When she found it more difficult than expected to support herself financially, Mrs. Miglin went to court to argue for relief from the agreement that she had signed, saying that it was unfair. Ultimately, a majority of the Supreme Court of Canada did not agree that she should be awarded support, but not before indicating that, while judges should be reluctant to overturn private agreements regarding support, there will be circumstances in which it is legitimate to do so. When there is a significant and unforeseen change in the parties' financial circumstances—one that could not reasonably have been foreseen—it will be appropriate for a court to review and possibly amend the terms of the support agreement, irrespective of the apparent finality of the waiver of rights at the time of the initial agreement. Again, the Supreme Court of Canada has made it clear that there are legitimate circumstances in which a spouse may well have a lifetime obligation of support to a former spouse.

The *Divorce Act* of 1985 and the Question of Custody

Section 16 of the *Divorce Act* of 1985 sets out the terms and conditions applying to orders for custody, pursuant to a petition for divorce. Custody may also be dealt with in provincial courts, pursuant to provincial legislation.

16. (1) A court of competent jurisdiction may, on application by either or both spouses or by any other person, make an order respecting the custody of or the access to, or the custody of and access to, any or all children of the marriage.

(2) Where an application is made under subsection (1), the court may, on application by either or both spouses or by any other person, make an interim order respecting the custody of or the access to, or the custody of and access to, any or all children of the marriage pending determination of the application under subsection (1).

(3) A person, other than a spouse, may not make an application under subsection (1) or (2) without leave of the court.

(4) This court may make an order under this section granting custody of, or access to, any or all children of the marriage to any one or more persons.

(5) Unless the court orders otherwise, a spouse who is granted access to a child of the marriage has the right to make inquiries, and to be given information, as to the health, education and welfare of the child.

(6) The court may make an order under this section for a definite or indefinite period or until the happening of a specified event and may impose such other terms, conditions, or restrictions in connection therewith as it thinks fit and just.

(7) Without limiting the generality of subsection (6), the court may include in an order under this section a term requiring any person who has custody of a child of the marriage and who intends to change the place of residence of that child to notify, at least thirty days before the change or within such other period before the change as the court may specify, any person who is granted access to that child of the change, the time at which the change will be made, and the new place of residence of the child.

(8) In making an order under this section, the court shall take into consideration only the best interests of the child of the marriage as determined by reference to the condition, means, needs, and other circumstances of the child.

(9) In making an order under this section, the court shall not take into consideration the past conduct of any person unless the conduct is relevant to the ability of that person to act as a parent of a child.

The *Divorce Act* does not provide substantial statutory guidance as to the principles that should guide an award of custody, inasmuch as the test of "the best interests of the child" appears to be highly subjective. Family law professor Peter Mnookin has argued as follows concerning child custody adjudication:

> Deciding what is best for a child poses a question no less ultimate than the purposes and values of life itself. Should the judge be concerned with the economic "productivity" of the child when he grows up? Are the primary values of life in warm, interpersonal relationships, or in discipline and self-sacrifice? Is stability and security for a child more desirable than intellectual stimulation? These questions could be elaborated endlessly. And yet, where is a judge to look for a set of values that should inform the choice of what is best for the child? Normally, the custody statutes do not themselves give content or relative weights to the pertinent values. And if the judge looks back to society at large, he finds neither a clear consensus as to the best child-rearing strategies nor an appropriate hierarchy of ultimate values.[15]

In light of these views, how are we to analyze the issues that arise in *Barkley v. Barkley*? Are homosexual and heterosexual relationships treated equally by Canadian courts?

> Nasmith, Family Court Judge: Lynn is a 10-year-old girl whose mother and father are each applying . . . for sole custody of her. The mother is homosexual and much of the evidence has sprung from this fact.
>
> There are serious differences between the parents and I have ruled out the possibility of an order extending the "joint custody" rights with which they both came into this action. It apparently must be determined whether it is in Lynn's best interests for me to order that the mother have sole custody or that the father have sole custody.
>
> Mr. and Mrs. B. were married in 1962 and they adopted three children. They separated in May 1977, shortly after Mr. B returned from a lengthy posting with the armed forces in Egypt. Upon separation, all three children resided with the father, but at the time of trial, only Robert, aged 13, and Douglas, aged 15, remained with their father. There is no dispute about the boys and no order is sought to cover them.
>
> The mother had generous access to the children following the separation, and she often moved back into the house to look after them during extended absences by the father. The evidence is that Lynn became increasingly unhappy living with her father and developed a desire to be with her mother on a full-time basis. The

turning point in this arrangement came when the mother was upset at the father for allegedly leaving the children unattended. In March 1979, she unilaterally decided to keep Lynn with her. That move gave rise to these proceedings to settle Lynn's custody.

There is no allegation by the father as to any deficiencies in the parenting performance of the mother during the period of their cohabitation. The unique feature of the case, I think, is that the father's sole concern arises out of Mrs. B's being a declared homosexual and his case is built on that. From his evidence, I am convinced that he sincerely believes it would be harmful to his daughter to be raised in what he sees as a homosexual environment. . . .

The court made a referral of the family to the family court clinic for an assessment and report on the question of which of the two placements was more likely to serve the best interests of Lynn. Mr. Robert Gardner, M.S.W., has given evidence and has filed a nine-page opinion with a lengthy bibliography of the literature on homosexual parenting. The intimate clinical analysis apparently satisfied Mr. Gardner that both parents had a reasonably good relationship with Lynn. But he concluded that Lynn felt a much greater closeness with Mrs. B, and some distance between herself and her father. The evidence was that Lynn was doing very well, and it was Mr. Gardner's opinion that Lynn's needs could be more adequately met, given a decision to allow her to remain with her mother. It is clear that Lynn's own preference to reside with her mother was a significant part of Mr. Gardner's considerations. . . .

Three Canadian cases have been cited by counsel and from my own research, these would seem to be the only Canadian cases reported.

In *Case v. Case* (1974), 18 R.F.L. 132 (Sask. Q.B.) MacPherson J. stipulated that homosexuality was not a bar to an award of custody and that it was simply a factor to be considered along with others. On the facts, as he found them, custody of a 10-year-old daughter and a 4-year-old son were granted to the father as against the homosexual mother. The court was influenced by what it saw as unfair and exaggerated charges by the mother as to the father's conduct, and I think he was concerned about the fact that the mother slept in the same bed with her homosexual partner and that he had not had the benefit of having the partner as a witness. Reference was made to the mother's hiding her partner from the court. The extent to which the homosexuality weighed against the mother may have been given away by the closing comments. . . .

I greatly fear that if these children are raised by the mother, they will be too much in contact with people of abnormal tastes and proclivities.

In the subsequent case of *K. v. K.* 23 R.F.L. 58 . . . Rowe Prov. J. of the Alberta Provincial Court distinguished the *Case* decision.

His Honour agreed with the Saskatchewan court as to homosexuality being one factor to be considered along with all the others. In awarding custody to a homosexual mother, who also slept in the same bed as her partner, and did not engage in any sexual contact in the presence of the children, the trial judge was supported by strong evidence from a psychologist who testified that the mother and the child had a close relationship, which was one of the best mother–child interactions she had seen in her professional practice. The psychologist noted that the child was happy, well-adjusted, and doing very well in school, and concluded:

> . . . *[T]he manner in which one fulfills one's sexual needs does not relate to the abilities of being a good parent.*

. . . In *D. v. D.* (1978), 20 O.R. (2d) 722, 3 R.F.L. (2d) 327 . . . Smith Co. Ct. J. dealt with an application to vary a decree nisi. The decree had been silent as to custody and the father later sought custody of 13- and 8-year-old children who had been in his *de facto* custody since the separation. It was clear that the father was bisexual but that he was involved in a continuing homosexual relationship. The trial judge treated his homosexuality as . . .

> *a problem which may damage the children's psychological, moral, intellectual, or physical well-being, and their orderly development and adaptation to society. . . . The court's concern ought to be the children's position in their peer group, the children's sexual orientation, and the manner in which the relationship of children to parent is or can be affected by the deviation from the norm in the latter's sexual preferences.*

In awarding custody of the children to the father, which confirmed the status quo, the trial judge's concerns about the "problem" of homosexuality were apparently modified by the following findings:

(a) The father was bisexual;
(b) The father was discreet;
(c) He was not an exhibitionist;
(d) The public did not know about his sexual orientations;
(e) He did not flaunt his homosexual activities;
(f) He was not a militant homosexual;
(g) The court felt that he could "cope with" the problems;

(h) There was no evidence that the children would become homosexual;

(i) The main homosexual partner made a favourable impression on him.

It would appear that the net result of the analysis of the homosexual question was the placing of very little weight on the homosexuality of the father.

In the present case, a focus on the quality of the parent–child relationship here produces a good case for the mother as the more appropriate person to have custody of Lynn.

As in *D. v. D.*, any possible ill effects for Lynn from the mother's sexual orientation have been minimized by the following circumstances:

(1) She is not militant;

(2) She does not flaunt her homosexuality;

(3) She does not seem to be biased about Lynn's orientation, and seems to assume that Lynn will be heterosexual;

(4) There is no overt sexual contact apart from sleeping in the same bed;

(5) The sexual partner has a reasonably good relationship with the child.

Whatever significant risks remain in the area of Lynn's necessary adjustments to our "homophobic" society, they are too esoteric and speculative for me to attach much weight to. I think they must give way here to the more concrete indicia of "best interests."

An order will go granting custody of the child to the respondent with reasonable access to the applicant. . . . [16]

Although *Barkley v. Barkley* was decided before the amendments to the *Divorce Act* of 1985, it remains a valid statement of the law today (the 1985 amendments did not touch upon the issue raised in *Barkley*). For a more recent case that has taken a similar approach to that in *Barkley*, see *Daller v. Daller*.[17] In *Daller*, the Ontario Court of Appeal declined to remove a child from the lesbian mother's custody, on the basis that the homosexual relationship was not having a detrimental effect on the child, and it was not in the child's best interest to grant the father's claim for custody. Similarly, in *Monk v. Doan*,[18] the court awarded custody to a lesbian aunt whose life with a long-term partner was conducted in a manner that was said to be discreet and dignified. At the same time, however, some Canadian courts have used a homosexual lifestyle as a bar to an award of custody. In *Saunders v. Saunders*,[19] a British Columbia judge denied a gay father overnight **access** to his child on the basis that the father's sleeping with another man during these visits was necessarily exposing his child to an "unnatural" relationship.

Conclusion: Family Law as the Crucible of Culture

Legislation and judicial decisions relating to the family in Canada provide us with a lens through which to look back at the changes within our culture over the past 30 years. Perhaps more than any other type of law, family law affords the opportunity of understanding how the way we relate to each other has changed, for better or for worse. We have witnessed legal amendments that permit divorce more easily, strengthen the position of women in the event of marriage breakdown, and endorse same-sex marriage. Whether these kinds of developments will continue is uncertain. What is certain, however, is that family law will continue to be a part of the fabric upon which the evolution of our culture is written.

Web Links

Community Legal Information Association of Prince Edward Island
http://www.isn.net/~cliapei
The website of the Community Legal Information Association of Prince Edward Island has a very good section on common-law relationships, typically a matter of provincial jurisdiction.

Manitoba Justice
http://www.gov.mb.ca/justice/family/familyindex.html
This user-friendly Web page provides information on family law in Manitoba. It contains links to other sites dealing with family law issues.

Gene C. Colman—Family Law Centre
http://www.4famlaw.com
Toronto lawyer Gene Colman's website has extensive information about family law, with an Ontario perspective. Colman has detailed

discussion and references on family law issues with respect to children.

Public Legal Information Association of Newfoundland

http://www.publiclegalinfo.com/about.html

The website of the Public Legal Information Association of Newfoundland offers information about the law, legal processes, and the administration of justice. This association is a component of the Public Legal Education Association of Canada, a national network of legal education societies, to which it has links.

Department of Justice Canada: Child Support

http://canada.justice.gc.ca/en/ps/sup/index.html

This Web page contains the Federal Child Support Guidelines from the Department of Justice, and has links to extensive information on child-support laws.

Duhaime's Canadian Family Law Centre

http://www.duhaime.org/famcentr.htm

The website of Victoria family law lawyer Lloyd Duhaime is extremely useful for its articles on many areas of family law. He also has links to other primary sites for statutes and regulations.

The Alberta Law Foundation

http://www.law-faqs.org/nat/div-act.htm

This Web page provides information on frequently asked questions about Canada's *Divorce Act* and has links to other aspects of family law.

Questions for Discussion

1. In your opinion, what is the most significant feature of contemporary family law? Give reasons for your answer.
2. What are the strengths and weaknesses of the Supreme Court's decisions in *Moge, Hickey* and *Miglin*? As we move into the next century, will spousal self-sufficiency replace notions of spousal support?
3. What do you think of the Canadian Bar Association's insistence that divorce be premised on *whether* a marriage has broken down, not *why*? Take account of the relevant sections of the *Divorce Act* in your response.

Further Reading

Conway, J. *The Canadian Family in Crisis*. Toronto: Lorimer, 1990.
> This book provides a very useful historical backdrop for understanding our contemporary construction of family life, documenting changes in family structure and ideology over the past century. The book is required reading for those who are interested in the social and historical evolution of the family form.

Dekeseredy, W., and R. Hinch. *Woman Abuse: Sociological Perspectives.* Toronto: Thompson, 1991.
> This is a useful introduction to the problems of domestic violence, the difficulties in conceptualizing the problem and in the ability to attach the criminal sanction to various forms of assault and harassment. The book is a useful addendum to the more legalistic materials canvassed within this chapter.

Hovius, B. *Family Law: Cases, Notes and Materials.* 5th ed. Toronto: Carswell, 1998.
> This is the most comprehensive compilation of family law materials in Canada. Professor Hovius covers marriage, divorce, family property, spousal and child support, custody and access, domestic contracts, and the issues of child protection and adoption. Additionally, this text looks in some depth at domestic violence, the rights and obligations of same-sex partners, and the use of the best-interests-of-the-child test in determining custody and access.

Notes

1. J. Conway, *The Canadian Family in Crisis* (Toronto: Lorimer, 1990), 36.
2. J. Snell, *In the Shadow of the Law: Divorce in Canada, 1900–1939* (Toronto: University of Toronto Press, 1991), 9.
3. Statistics Canada, *Income Trends in Canada* (Ottawa, 2002).
4. R. Hamilton, "Women, Wives and Mothers," in *Reconstructing the Canadian Family: Feminist Perspectives*, edited by N. Mandell and A. Duffy (Toronto: Butterworths, 1988), 20.
5. Statistics Canada, *Marriages and Divorces: Vital Statistics*, vol. 2 (Ottawa: Supply and Services, 1985).
6. Ministry of Justice, *Information Paper C-47* (Ottawa: Supply and Services, 1985).

7. Canadian Bar Association, "Submission Regarding Bill C-10 and the Proposed Amendments to the Divorce Act," 1985, 37.

8. *Shaw v. Shaw* (1971), 4 R.F.L. 392 at 392–398, 7 N.S.R. (2d) 77 at 77–84 (T.D.).

9. *Knoll v. Knoll* (1970), 1 R.F.L. 141 at 149–150, [1970] 2 O.R. 169 at 176–177 (C.A.).

10. *Gilbert v. Gilbert* (1980), 18 R.F.L. (2d) 240 at 240–248, 39 N.S.R. (2d) 241 at 242–246 (T.D.).

11. *Lashley v. Lashley* (1985), 47 R.F.L. (2d) 371 at 372–373 (Ont. C.A.).

12. See also, on the issue of economic self-sufficiency, *Messier v. Delage* (1983), 35 R.F.L. (2d) 337 (S.C.C.) and *Richardson v. Richardson* (1987), 7 R.F.L. (3d) 304 (S.C.C.).

13. *Moge v. Moge*, [1992] 3 S.C.R. 813 at 824–882.

14. [1999] 2 S.C.R. 518.

15. P. Mnookin., "Child-Custody Adjudication: Judicial Functions in the Face of Indeterminacy," *Law and Contemporary Problems* 39 (1975): 226.

16. *Barkley v. Barkley* (1980), 28 O.R. (2d) 136 at 136–141 (Prov. Ct.).

17. (1988), 18 R.F.L. (3d) 53, 22 R.F.L. (3d) 96 (Ont. C.A.).

18. (1990), 94 Sask. Rep. 316 (Q.B.).

19. (1989), 20 R.F.L. (3d) 368 (B.C.S.C.).

References

Anderson, M., et al., eds. *Family Matters: Sociology and Contemporary Canadian Families*. Toronto: Methuen, 1987.

Bala, N., et al. *Canadian Child Welfare Law: Children, Families and the State*. Toronto: Thompson, 1991.

Blumberg, A. "Cohabitation Without Marriage: A Different Perspective." *U.C.L.A. Law Review* 28 (1981): 1125.

Conway, J. *The Canadian Family in Crisis*. Toronto: Lorimer, 1990.

Dekeseredy, W., and R. Hinch. *Woman Abuse: Sociological Perspectives*. Toronto: Thompson, 1991.

Divorce Act, R.S.C. 1985, c. 3.

Eichler, M. "The Limits of Family Law Reform, or the Privatization of Female and Child Poverty." *Canadian Family Law Quarterly* 7 (1990–91): 59.

Hamilton, R. "Women, Wives and Mothers." In *Reconstructing the Canadian Family: Feminist Perspectives,* edited by N. Mandell and A. Duffy. Toronto: Butterworths, 1988, Chapter 1.

Herman, J. "Are We Family? Lesbian Rights and Women's Liberation." *Osgoode Hall Law Journal* 28 (1990): 789.

Hovius, B. *Family Law: Cases, Notes and Materials*. 5th ed. Toronto: Carswell, 1998.

Hovius, B., and M. Youdan. *The Law of Family Property*. Toronto: Carswell, 1991.

Hughes, J., and L. Pask, eds. *National Themes in Family Law*. Toronto: Carswell, 1988.

Knetsch, J. "Some Economic Implications of Matrimonial Property Rules." *University of Toronto Law Journal* 34 (1984): 263.

Law Reform Commission of Canada. *Maintenance on Divorce: Working Paper 12*. Ottawa: Supply and Services, 1975.

Mandell, N., and A. Duffy, eds. *Reconstructing the Canadian Family: Feminist Perspectives*. Toronto: Butterworths, 1988.

Parr, J., ed. *Childhood and Family in Canadian History*. Toronto: McClelland and Stewart, 1982.

Rogerson, C. "The Causal Connection Test in Spousal Support Law." *Canadian Journal of Family Law* 8 (1989): 95.

Ryan, H. "Joint Custody in Canada: Time for a Second Look." *Reports on Family Law* (2d) 49 (1986): 119.

Ryder, B. "Equality Rights and Sexual Orientation: Confronting Heterosexual Family Privilege." *Canadian Journal of Family Law* 6 (1990): 39.

Smart, C. *The Ties That Bind: Law, Marriage and the Reproduction of Patriarchal Relations*. London, U.K.: Routledge and Kegan Paul, 1984.

Ziff, J. "Recent Developments in Marriage and Divorce." *Ottawa Law Review* 18 (1986): 121.

CHAPTER 9

Administrative Law: The State and Its Duty to Be Fair

Constitutional law, in its broadest sense, and administrative law are not readily distinguishable. The subject-matter of both is the legal framework within which our system of government operates. Both are concerned with the use, and abuse, of public power and with the design and operation of institutions to check and render accountable its exercise. Both speak to the allocation of government functions and powers among public authorities and officials, and to the procedures followed in the decision-making process. Both also regulate the relationship between the individual and the state, and prescribe the remedies available to those aggrieved by governmental action.

(J.M. Evans et al., Administrative Law, Cases, Text
and Materials, 3d ed. [1989])

Administrative law is a form of public law that, while sharing many of the characteristics of constitutional law, criminal law and family law, is, nonetheless, conceptually separate. It does not spring from the *Constitution Act, Criminal Code,* or *Divorce Act*—from any set of rules in statutory or regulatory form. There are statutes specific to certain realms of administrative law: labour relations, workers' compensation, parole, employment insurance, and radio-television communications, among others. But there is no overarching legislation that defines the essence of administrative law; the quotation that begins this chapter speaks to the heart of administrative law, but not to its origins within a single statute.

The heart of administrative law is, as the quotation notes, to be found in the duty to act fairly in the practice of government, an onus that the state has placed upon itself, both with common law and, more recently and significantly, with the *Canadian Charter of Rights and Freedoms* (the *Charter*). It is a duty that is also found within constitutional law. Most fundamentally, administrative law concerns the relationship between the state, broadly defined, and the individual citizen. Legal scholars Dussault and Borgeat have defined administrative law:

> Administrative law has been termed the "law of the public power in its relations with ordinary citizens," "the day-to-day public law," "the essential incarnation of public law outside of the constitutional sphere." It may be defined as the entire set of rules relating to the organization, operation, and control of the Administration.[1]

Delegation, Interdelegation, and the Powers Accorded within Administrative Law

The legal machinery that makes possible the construction of administrative law—the law relating to various boards, commissions, agencies, and tribunals—is typically referred to as "**delegation**." Parliament, as the supreme authority in Canada, permits the federal government and provincial governments to delegate some legislative powers to these bodies. However, given the division of powers between federal and provincial governments (in sections 91 and 92 of the *British North America Act*), a province may not delegate its powers directly to the federal government; nor may the federal government delegate its powers directly to the provincial legislatures.

The federal government may, however, delegate its powers to a tribunal, board, commission, or agency created by a provincial legislature; similarly, provincial governments may delegate their powers to a body created by federal legislation. This process is known as "**interdelegation**," and it is constitutionally permissible, with two provisos. The first is that not all authority in relation to a given jurisdiction is delegated to the "inferior" tribunal; the second is that there is no further delegation of decision-making power from the tribunal to another decision-making authority. Interdelegation, like any delegation of legislative power, serves a number of important social purposes. Jones and deVillars cite six:

(a) The sheer magnitude of the business of government means that not everything can be dealt with by Parliament or a legislature.

(b) Much of governmental activity is technical in nature, and only broad principles should be contained in legislation.

(c) Delegating power to an administrator allows greater flexibility in applying broad statutory provisions to changing circumstances.

(d) It may not be possible to devise a general role to deal with all cases, which may be more conveniently determined in the discretion of a delegate.

(e) The need for rapid governmental action may require faster administrative response than can be accommodated by the necessity of legislative amendment.

(f) Innovation and experimentation in solving social problems may not be possible if legislation is required.

(g) Someone actually has to apply legislation, and that person has to have authority to do so.[2]

With the governmental duty to act fairly now codified in various sections of the *Charter*, administrative law presents itself as both a relative and a derivative of constitutional law. Administrative law scholars Dussault and Borgeat note:

> Although they are both indispensable tools in analyzing the organization and operation of the Administration, constitutional law and administrative law may be distinguished from each other mainly by the fact that the former provides a skeleton of broad principles which the latter fleshes out. More concerned with the general structure of the State's bodies than with the operation of the Administration on a day-to-day basis, constitutional law seems to be more static when compared to administrative law, which has a more dynamic appearance.[3]

Types and Functions of Tribunals

The nature of the powers accorded within administrative law varies considerably, from the granting of a ministerial or executive authority to the granting of the power to direct public policy (i.e., make binding legal judgments) within the body's particular area of expertise. As recently as the 1970s, there were clear distinctions among types of **administrative tribunals**: the purely administrative tribunal, the administrative tribunal, the judicial or quasi-judicial tribunal, and the fully legislative tribunal. The provincial bodies that issue drivers' licences, for instance, are purely administrative tribunals; they have no discretionary authority beyond the provisions of the motor vehicle licensing statutes. By contrast, labour relations boards and municipal councils can exercise legislative powers. Such distinctions are, however, of limited use; they often overlap and fail to capture the essence of a given tribunal. Law professor Gerald Gall notes:

> [A] given tribunal may exercise different kinds of functions at different times. For example, a municipal council normally exercises a legislative function, but on occasion, a municipal council may be requested to render a decision which could substantially affect the appellant's rights. For this limited purpose, the municipal council will be exercising a quasi-judicial function.[4]

The key issue for an administrative tribunal is not its form, but its obligations to those subject to its findings and the extent to which its decisions are reviewable by a court—the applicability of **judicial review** to an administrative decision. Such designations as administrative, judicial, or quasi-judicial are relevant only in that each one creates different expectations with respect to procedural rights and rights of appeal. Consider, for example, the decision of the Nova Scotia Supreme Court in *Thomas v. Mount Saint Vincent University*.

> An application was made for *certiorari* to quash the decision of Mount Saint Vincent University to deny tenure to the plaintiff, Dr. Antoinette Thomas. [*Certiorari* is a Latin term that translates literally as "to be informed of." Such a writ, issued by a superior court to an inferior court, requires that court to produce a certified record of a specific case, so that the superior court can examine the record of events to determine whether there are any irregularities that would warrant reconsideration.]
>
> **The facts**
>
> Antoinette Thomas is an educator with a doctorate in psychology. On July 1, 1980, she was appointed as an assistant professor in the Department of Education (Child Study) of the university under a two-year-term contract. . . .
>
> This contract was renewed as a probationary contract following a strong recommendation first from the Department of Education to the Committee on Appointment, Rank, Promotion and, Tenure (CARPT) and then a favourable recommendation from CARPT to the president. . . .
>
> In the fall of 1983, Dr. Thomas was again considered for reappointment and she was granted a further renewal, this time with a term contract of just one year, to end June 30, 1985. Although the contract was renewed, Dr. Pauline Jones, chairman of CARPT,

when writing to Dr. Thomas in connection with the committee's recommendation for renewal, expressed some reservations about Dr. Thomas's performance:

> *The Committee has asked me to convey to you our concern over the fact that your contribution in terms of service to the Department is judged to be unsatisfactory, and we would have to be convinced of significant improvement in this area for any subsequent contract renewal. The Committee also feels that it must draw your attention to the need for improved productivity in the area of research and publication, and we would encourage you as well to maintain and improve wherever possible the level of your teaching effectiveness.*

Dr. Margaret E. Fulton, president of the university, in approving the one-year contract, confirmed the concerns of the CARPT committee in a letter dated January 24, 1984:

> *After a review of your file and some discussion, I wish to inform you that I strongly endorse the committee's recommendations.*

Dr. Thomas, in her fifth year at the university, was entitled as of right to be considered for tenure. In September, Dr. Patricia Canning, chairman of the Department of Child Study, initiated the process necessary for the consideration of tenure. She requested the full-time members of her department to examine the files of Dr. Thomas and one other, who was also being considered, and submit their recommendation in writing to her.

In a memorandum dated October 1, 1984, Dr. Canning reported to CARPT that with the exception of one professor who had been employed for too short a time to know very much of Dr. Thomas's work and with the exception of Sister M. Young, who wrote directly to CARPT with a favourable recommendation, the whole of the department recommended nonrenewal of Dr. Thomas's contract. On the basis of these recommendations and her own evaluation, Dr. Canning recommended against the granting of tenure and against a renewal of Dr. Thomas's contract.

On January 31, 1985, Dr. Pauline Jones, chairman of CARPT, wrote to Dr. Thomas to advise her that "the motion to recommend the granting of tenure to you did not carry, and I have accordingly advised the President."

This letter was followed by a letter dated February 22, 1985, from the president, Dr. Fulton to Dr. Thomas, formally refusing tenure.[5]

At this point, Thomas exercised her right to appeal to the Senate Review Committee. A three-person Ad Hoc Appeal Committee was duly formed. It was composed of a representative appointed by Thomas, a representative appointed by the university president, and a third representative selected by the other two. This committee concluded that Thomas should be granted tenure.

> Dr. Fulton refused to accept the recommendation of the Ad Hoc Appeal Committee because, as she said in her evidence given at this hearing, she had to weigh both the original recommendations to deny tenure to Dr. Thomas and the recommendation that came to her from the Appeal Committee to grant it. In her view, the latter recommendation was diluted in that it was not unanimous in all respects. Her decision, on balancing the recommendations, was to refuse tenure.
>
> On June 26, 1985, Dr. Fulton wrote Dr. Thomas:
>
> *In accordance with faculty manual requirements, this is to inform you that I am unable to accept the decision of the Appeals Committee. You will not be granted tenure at Mount Saint Vincent University. As of July 1, 1985, you will no longer be an employee of the University. It would be appreciated if you would vacate your office by that date. . . .*
>
> Does *certiorari* lie?
>
> The threshold issue in this case is whether the refusal of tenure to Dr. Thomas by the president of Mount Saint Vincent University is amenable to *certiorari* proceedings so as to permit scrutiny by this Court.
>
> My conclusion, after examining the various authorities cited to me, is that indeed such actions by a university, through its president, are subject to judicial review.
>
> Mount Saint Vincent University is a creature of statute (see *Mount Saint Vincent Act*, 1966, above). It is a public university, open to everyone with the requisite academic qualifications, and with the enrolment not subject to religious restriction (see s. 22 of the Act). . . . [I]t is quite clear that Mount Saint Vincent has lost its former parochial and private status and has become a "public" institution. According to Dr. Fulton, up to 90 percent of its operating funds come from government. . . .
>
> The argument (of the university) is that since the Faculty Manual is not itself established by the legislation, but only authorized as regulations, it does not have the force of law so as to attract the remedy of *certiorari*.

I do not accept this argument. The Faculty Manual is no less law, whether statutory or delegated, because its establishment was discretionary rather than mandatory. Regulations or by-laws passed pursuant to an authorizing or empowering statute are just as "legal" as the statute itself. . . .

Having reached the conclusion that *certiorari* is applicable, I must now determine whether this Court ought to intervene. . . .

In the result, as we have seen, the Ad Hoc Appeal Committee recommended to the president that she overturn or overlook her earlier decision to refuse tenure to Dr. Thomas, and recommended that Dr. Thomas be granted tenure.

But this very elaborate and outwardly fair "appeal" process was in fact no appeal at all—because all the Ad Hoc Appeal Committee had power to do was to recommend to the very person from whom the appeal was taken that she grant tenure where she had earlier refused it. The committee was advisory only. It had no power to decide, as laid down in the Faculty Manual.

The effect of this whole elaborate process was that the president of Mount Saint Vincent University was sitting on appeal from her own decision. The Ad Hoc Appeal Committee was a mere cypher in the process—window dressing in a flawed procedure euphemistically referred to as an appeal.

The point here is not that Dr. Fulton was in fact biased when she considered again whether or not to grant tenure to Dr. Thomas. I am satisfied that she was not. But the point is rather, whether there was conveyed to others a reasonable apprehension of bias from the involvement of Dr. Fulton in the appeal process. . . . I conclude that there could not help but be a reasonable apprehension of bias in this situation on the part of a reasonable outside observer.

Defects in the Powers Accorded within Administrative Law

Thomas v. Mount Saint Vincent University raises two issues. The first concerns procedural fairness, in this case, of the university's system of tenure and promotion. The second has to do with the circumstances in which an appeal can be launched through Canada's court system to remedy an apparent defect within a decision-making structure such as that of the university. Universities possess the power to make administrative decisions that have the impact of law, and there will always be varying degrees of procedural rigour attached to the range of decisions made by university administrators. For example, students do not have the right to appeal a final course grade to a Canadian court. However, given the circumstance of bias in the *Thomas* case, judicial review appears to have been an appropriate response.

When are judicial scrutiny and intervention appropriate? The simple answer is that when an administrative action is *ultra vires*—outside the legislative jurisdiction of the administration—it can be subject to judicial review. But how is a court or a student of law to determine whether a given administrative action is *ultra vires*? In fact, there is a range of grounds for making this determination: technicalities (failure to conform to enabling legislation), abuse of discretion, and violation of the principles of natural justice or procedural fairness.

Technical Defects

Technical defects may arise in various ways. If, for example, a municipal parks committee decided to spend some of its funds on building transition houses for battered women, the committee would clearly be operating outside its delegated jurisdiction; hence, its actions would be declared *ultra vires*. A more common example is the inappropriate delegation of some of its decision-making powers by an administrative agency. For example, in *Saumur v. City of Quebec*, which was discussed in Chapter 4, the City of Quebec's attempt to make the distribution of literature on the streets subject to permission from the chief of police was seen by the Supreme Court of Canada as an illegal delegation of authority to the police force, and hence was declared *ultra vires*.

Other *ultra vires* defects in the process of delegation can include failure to comply with the terms and conditions of appointment to a board, agency, commission, or tribunal; making a decision in the absence of a prescribed quorum; and appointing individuals to a board, agency, commission, or tribunal who do not meet mandated qualifications. Such technical defects may well include an abuse of discretionary authority or a violation of the duty to be fair, but they are defects in and of themselves, separate from the other grounds for making a determination of *ultra vires*.

Abuse of Discretion

Cases involving alleged abuse of discretion (or violation of the principles of procedural fairness, which will be addressed later) typically turn on the scope of judicial interference with an administrative agency. Consider the decisions of the Ontario Divisional Court and the Ontario Court of Appeal in *Re Sheehan and Criminal Injuries Compensation Board*.[6] As you read, ask yourself whether there was any abuse of the discretion granted the Criminal Injuries Compensation Board.

Holland, J.: This is an application for judicial review of a decision made by the Criminal Injuries Compensation Board, dated January 12, 1973, whereby two applications on behalf of Robert James Sheehan, hereinafter called Sheehan, were refused, A. Roy Wilmott Q.C. dissenting.

The first application arises out of an incident which occurred on January 2, 1970, while Sheehan was an inmate of Kingston Penitentiary, a federal penitentiary. He was assaulted and injured by a fellow prisoner.

The second application arises out of an incident which occurred on April 18, 1971, while Sheehan was an inmate of Kingston Penitentiary and occurred during the Kingston riot. Sheehan had been housed in protective custody and shortly after midnight on April 18, 1971, during the riot, he was forcibly removed, with other inmates, from a cell block, bound to a chair, and assaulted over a considerable period of time by fellow inmates. As a result of this latter series of assaults, Sheehan was most seriously injured. . . .

In refusing the applications for compensation, the Board considered three circumstances:

(1) The fact that Sheehan, before the commission of the criminal assault above referred to, by which he suffered injury, had himself been guilty of criminal behaviour for which he had been convicted;

(2) The fact that the criminal assaults took place within the walls of Kingston Penitentiary, and at all relevant times Sheehan and his assailants were in the official and exclusive custody of another government, under conditions which were totally outside the power and jurisdiction of Ontario to deal with; and

(3) the fact that there was no evidence adduced before the Board to indicate that any application had been made to or proceedings taken on behalf of Sheehan against any other government department, ministry, or agency, to obtain compensation for damages.

The relevant legislation applicable to both of Sheehan's applications is the *Law Enforcement Compensation Act*, R.S.O., 1970, c. 237. The relevant sections . . . are as follows:

3.(1) Where any person is injured or killed by any act or omission of any other person occurring in or resulting directly from

(a) the commission of an offence against any statute of Canada or Ontario . . . the Board may, on application therefor and after a hearing, make an order in its discretion in accordance with this Act for the payment of compensation and the decision of the Board is final and conclusive for all purposes. . . .

5. In determining whether to make an order for compensation and the amount thereof, the Board may have regard to all such circumstances as it considers relevant, including behaviour of the victim that directly or indirectly contributed to his injury or death. . . .

7.(2) An order for compensation does not affect the right of any person to recover from any other person by civil proceedings lawful damages in respect of the injury or death, but, where the Board has granted an order, the Board is subrogated to all the rights of the person in whose favour the order is granted in respect of the injury or death to the extent of the amount awarded in the order.

If the three circumstances set out above, upon which the Board based its decision, are relevant, then any attack on such decision must fail. I will consider the relevance of each of the above circumstances in order.

It appears to me to be completely irrelevant that the victim, before the commission of the criminal assault giving rise to the claim, had himself been guilty of criminal behaviour for which he had been convicted. Counsel for the Board suggested that such was a proper consideration in view of the wording of s. 5, which includes as a proper consideration "any behaviour of the victim that directly or indirectly contributed to his injury. . . . " This surely must be restricted to relevant behaviour. If the victim is, for example, guilty of insulting behaviour that results in an assault, this would be a relevant consideration, but the fact that the victim was guilty of criminal behaviour unconnected with the incident in question to my mind cannot be considered to be relevant.

It is to be noted that the prison guard, on whose behalf an application for compensation had also been made, was not incarcerated by reason of his previous criminal behaviour and yet his application was also refused. . . .

In this case in the assaults to Sheehan arising out of the riot, I think it can hardly be said that Sheehan contributed in any way to such assaults. He was forcibly removed from the cell block by other inmates and severely beaten, after having been tied to a chair. If compensation is to be refused in this case, I can hardly think of any circumstances that would warrant the Board in the future, if it follows its own decisions, allowing compensation to an inmate of a federal penitentiary. As such, the Board, notwithstanding its expression to the contrary, has disentitled inmates of federal penitentiaries, as a class to compensation under the Act.

In my view, the fact that Sheehan was an inmate of a federal institution or "an enclave situate within the Province of Ontario," as referred to by the Board, is not a proper consideration. If the legislature intended to exclude under the Act inmates of federal penitentiaries, it should have said so.

I now turn to the third circumstance considered by the Board and that is that there was no evidence to indicate that any application had been made by or on behalf of Sheehan to any other government department, ministry, or agency to obtain compensation for damages. Section 7(2) of the *Law Enforcement Compensation Act* provides that an order for compensation does not affect the right of any person to recover from any other person by civil proceedings lawful damages in respect of the injury and further provides that where the Board has granted an order, the Board is subrogated to the rights of the person in whose favour the order is granted, to the extent of the amount awarded in the order. No section imposes an obligation on an applicant to make an application or take any other proceedings against any other individual or authority. . . .

For the above reasons, I have come to the conclusion that none of the three circumstances considered by the Board were relevant. The question remains whether this Court can, in view of the wording of s. 3(1) and (5) of the Act, set aside the dismissal of the application and direct that the matter be remitted to the Board for further consideration.

There is no obligation on the Board to award compensation. It could be argued that the payment is an *ex gratia* payment. Even so, the general intent of the Act is clear and that is to provide compensation to victims of crime. Claimants to *ex gratia* payments are entitled to have their claims considered on a proper basis: *Joy Oil Co. Ltd. v. The King* [1951] S.C.R. 624. . . .

I conclude that the Court may properly review the decision of the Board in this case and that the matters considered by the Board were not relevant. In the circumstances, the decision of the Board will be quashed and the matter remitted to the Board for consideration. Application granted.

However, Justice Kelly of the Ontario Court of Appeal had a different view of the matter, holding that the protection of an agency's discretionary authority is more important than subscription to the principles set out above.

Kelly, J.A.: In proceedings in the nature of judicial review, either under the Judicial Review Procedure Act, . . . or upon an application for one of the prerogative writs, the primary consideration is the nature of the jurisdiction of the body whose decision is sought to be brought under review. In this matter, the heart of the issue is this— has the Board, in refusing the application, done so within the proper limits of its discretionary function established by its parent statute, or has the Board, in ascribing its refusal to one or more of the circumstances above referred to, exceeded its statutory jurisdiction so as to bring its decision within the proper reach of judicial review?

The principal argument proffered in support of the contention that the Board had exceeded its jurisdiction and was accordingly subject to judicial review, was that the Board had escalated one or more of the circumstances above set out to the status of statutory conditions of eligibility and had thereby purported to vary the statute under which its authority was to be found. If the Board had said that the presence of any one or more of the factors would disentitle any applicant from receiving compensation, it might be arguable that it had exceeded its authority under the Act. But a clear-cut distinction must be drawn between the Board giving consideration to certain circumstances and the Board holding that a particular circumstance *ipso facto* disqualified an applicant from benefits under the Act. . . .

With respect, I do not construe the Act as authorizing the Court to review the correctness of the Board's decision made within the scope of its authority. The Legislature has expressly assigned to the Board and not to the Courts the discretionary authority to grant or deny compensation.

Within the confines of its convening statute, the Board may, indeed must, perform this function and may do so free from judicial intervention, however a Court may view any particular exercise of its proper discretion.

> In my opinion, the Divisional Court erred when it considered that its task was to determine if the said circumstances were relevant. In the light of the discretion vested in the Board to have regard to all circumstances which it considered relevant so long as it acted in good faith, the decisions of the Board as to what considerations are relevant are unchallengeable: see *C.N.R. et al. v. Canada Steamship Lines Ltd. et al.*, [1945] 3 D.L.R. 417, 420.
>
> I would therefore allow the appeal with costs if demanded, set aside the order of the Divisional Court, and, in its place, substitute an order directing that the application for judicial review be dismissed, also with costs if demanded.
>
> Appeal allowed.

The two decisions in *Re Sheehan* reveal contrasting points of view with respect to the scope of judicial review. The Ontario Court of Appeal decided against any interference with the board's decision to deny compensation, noting that section 3(1) gives the Ontario Criminal Injuries Compensation Board jurisdiction "to make an order *in its discretion* exercised in accordance with this Act for the payment of compensation." (A further appeal by Sheehan to the Supreme Court of Canada was denied.)

A question inevitably comes to mind. Have the courts, in granting such a range of discretion to an administrative agency, allowed that agency to incorporate irrelevant considerations in its decision-making processes? The decision in *Re Sheehan* effectively permits an unrelated criminal record to be used as a bar to compensation for a later criminal injury.

Violation of the Principles of Procedural Fairness

Allegations that an administrative agency has failed to follow principles of procedural fairness typically resemble allegations of abuse of discretion. Consider the following decision of the Ontario Court of Appeal in *Re Sawyer and Ontario Racing Commission*. The applicant, Sawyer, an owner of horses, had been suspended from racing for 10 years, after a hearing before the Ontario Racing Commission. The lawyer who represented the commission also wrote the decision. Sawyer claimed that this was a breach of the principles of **natural justice**.

> Brooke, J.A.: In my opinion, the Commission misunderstood the function of counsel who presented the case against the appellant before them. He was variously described as counsel to the Commission, counsel for the Commission, and counsel for the Commission Administration. But there is no doubt that his role was to prosecute the case

against the appellant and he was not present in a role comparable to that of a legal assessor to the Commission. . . . He was counsel for the appellant's adversary in proceedings to determine the appellant's guilt or innocence on the charge against him. It is basic that persons entrusted to judge or determine the rights of others must, for reasons arrived at independently, make that decision, whether it or the reasons be right or wrong. It was wrong for the Commission, who were the judges, to privately involve either party in the Commission's function once the case began and certainly after the case was left to them for ultimate disposition. To do so must amount to a denial of natural justice because it would not unreasonably raise a suspicion of bias in others, including the appellant, who were not present and later learned what transpired.

In *Re Bernstein and College of Physicians and Surgeons of Ontario* (1977), 76 D.L.R. (3d) 38, when the Discipline Committee of the College had arrived at a verdict that Dr. Bernstein was guilty of the offence charged, the chairman gave to counsel for the college who had prosecuted the case against the doctor a rough outline of the Committee's reasons for its decisions and requested him to prepare formal reasons for the Committee's approval. The original of the rough draft was not available for the Court's consideration. While the Court allowed the appeal because of a lack of sufficient credible evidence to uphold the conviction, of this issue O'Leary J., who delivered the judgement for the majority, said at 63–64:

> In this particular case, Mr. Hunter, though asked by the Court for the same, was unable to locate the rough outline of the reasons for judgement sometimes prepared by the chairman. In my view, it is an unusual and improper practice for counsel to write the reasons for the Discipline Committee, even if the chairman or some member of the Committee has drafted rough reasons to guide him. One who has stood trial before a disciplinary body is entitled to have that body's reasons for its decision and not the reasons the prosecutor composes for the decision. If the Committee has made an error in arriving at its conclusion, the one who has stood trial, in fairness, should learn of it.

In the case before us, the reasons for its decision were never made known by the Commission to anyone, including its counsel. I agree with O'Leary J. What he said is apt here. If it were otherwise, the accused's right of appeal or review would be illusory. . . .

Counsel for the respondent contends that this Court should consider whether the conduct of the Commission has resulted in any prejudice to the appellant and in so doing, have regard to the following factors:

(1) that all of the relevant circumstances surrounding the preparation of the draft reasons for judgement had been disclosed in the affidavit;

(2) that counsel had played no part in the decision-making process of the respondent; and

(3) that the respondent adopted the draft reasons for judgement only after due consideration.

Further, counsel for the respondent contends that the ruling of the respondent ought to be examined apart from the reasons and in light of the record.

I have no doubt whatsoever that the affidavit made by counsel is a frank and accurate statement. However, I do not agree with the above submission. I think Mr. Laskin is right in his submission that justice cannot appear to have been done when the determination of how a case was decided depends, not upon the reasons over the signature of the real author, but rather upon the affidavit of a person who actually wrote the reasons and who now must explain how his thoughts were accepted after the decision of the tribunal. This is not good enough, for the appellant still has not been told by the tribunal why it found him guilty. Similarly, I do not agree that this Court should attempt to test the decision by considering the record. We should not retry the case or simply examine it to find if there is evidence which might support the judgment. This is not what is in issue here. What is in issue is that this man has not been dealt with according to the law.

Appeal allowed.[7]

Judicial Intervention and the Principles of Natural Justice

The phrase "according to the law" in Justice Brooke's decision raises more questions than it answers. Given the scope of administrative discretion, allegations of bias and of failure to provide due process are central to any determination of what constitutes law. While many decisions can be resolved through the correction of technical defects and the application of precedents, other situations exist in which little or no guidance from precedent will be available. Because responsibility for directing policy has been delegated to a given administrative body, the courts are reluctant to intervene in such circumstances unless there has been a fundamental lack of fairness in the state's treatment of its citizens.

In *Thomas v. Mount Saint Vincent University*, the decision to intervene in the internal affairs of the university was based on the apprehension of bias in the university's decision to deny tenure to Dr. Thomas. In *Re Sheehan*, the Ontario Divisional Court held that Sheehan had been excluded from compensation for reasons that were irrelevant to the purpose of the act, in other words, that the board had exceeded its jurisdiction. The Ontario Court of Appeal reversed the decision, arguing that there was no lack of fairness and no excess of jurisdiction. In *Re Sawyer*, the Ontario Court of Appeal concluded that counsel's construction of the Racing Commission's decision failed to provide the appellant with due process.

More recently, the Supreme Court of Canada has elaborated on the notions of procedural fairness and apprehension of bias in *Baker v. Minister of Citizenship and Immigration*. In this case a Jamaican-born woman, Mavis Baker, was ordered deported from Canada after working in the country illegally for more than 10 years. Ms. Baker had four Canadian-born dependent children, and she applied for an exemption to deportation, citing humanitarian and compassionate considerations under section 114(2) of the *Immigration Act*. Her application noted that her departure was likely to have a very significant negative impact on her children.

A senior immigration officer replied to Ms. Baker by letter, indicating that there were insufficient humanitarian and compassionate grounds to warrant processing her application; no reasons were given for this decision—none were required by law. Counsel for Ms. Baker did, however, ask for the notes taken by the investigating immigration officer, notes that were relied upon by the senior officer in making his decision.

These notes were provided, and they revealed the following statements about Ms. Baker and her situation:

> PC is unemployed—on welfare. No income shown—no assets. Has four Cdn. Born children—four others in Jamaica—HAS A TOTAL OF EIGHT CHILDREN. . . . There is nothing for her in Jamaica—hasn't been there in a long time—no longer close to her children there—no jobs there—she has no skills other than as a domestic—children would suffer—can't take them with her and can't leave them with anyone here. . . . Letter from Children's Aid—they say PC has been diagnosed as a paranoid schizophrenic—children would suffer if returned. . . . This case is a catastrophy [*sic*]. It is also an indictment of our "system" that the client came as a visitor in Aug. 81, was not

ordered deported until Dec. '92 and in April '94 IS STILL HERE! . . .
The PC is a paranoid schizophrenic and on welfare. She has no qualifications other than as a domestic. She has FOUR CHILDREN IN
JAMAICA AND ANOTHER FOUR BORN HERE. She will, of course,
be a tremendous strain on our social welfare systems for (probably)
the rest of her life. There are no H&C factors other than her FOUR
CANADIAN-BORN CHILDREN. Do we let her stay because of that?
I am of the opinion that Canada can no longer afford this type of
generosity. However, because of the circumstances involved, there
is a potential for adverse publicity. I recommend refusal but you
may wish to clear this with someone at Region.

Justice L'Heureux-Dubé, in writing the judgment of the court, noted
that the investigating officer had ignored a psychiatrist's letter suggesting
that with consistent treatment, Ms. Baker was likely to be a contributing
member of the community. Justice L'Heureux-Dubé wrote:

[T]he well-informed member of the community would perceive bias
when reading (the investigating officer's) comments. His notes, and
the manner in which they are written, do not disclose the existence of
an open mind or a weighing of the particular circumstances of the
case free from stereotypes. . . . His use of capitals to highlight the
number of Ms. Baker's children may also suggest to a reader that this
was a reason to deny her status. Reading his comments, I do not
believe that a reasonable and well-informed member of the community would conclude that he had approached this case with the impartiality appropriate to a decision made by an immigration officer.[8]

The court held that there was a reasonable apprehension of bias and
allowed Ms. Baker's appeal.

Several expressions are associated with these decisions: due process,
excess of jurisdiction, **doctrine of fairness**, and natural justice. All flow
from a common origin: common-law doctrine developed more than 400
years ago in judgments emanating from the British judiciary.
Constitutional scholar Peter Hogg has noted:

Outside the realm of criminal law, the state and the individual usually come into conflict as the result of the exercise by officials of governmental powers over persons or private property. In Britain,
common-law doctrine early developed that the King and his officials
had no powers other than those granted by the law. With few exceptions, actions which infringe the liberty of the subject require the
authority of a statute. This was settled in the great case of *Entick v.
Carrington* (1765), in which it was held that neither a search warrant

signed by a minister of the Crown, nor a claim of "state necessity" could justify Crown servants in entering the premises of the plaintiff and seizing his papers. The plaintiff's action in trespass against the Crown servants was successful, because they could not show that their actions were authorized by law.[9]

The concept of natural justice has developed over centuries of legal practice founded on the common law. There are two key principles of natural justice, expressed in Latin terminology: ***audi alteram partem*** and *nemo sibi esse judex vel suis jus dicere debet.*

Audi alteram partem means "hear the other side." *Black's Law Dictionary* expands on the definition: "hear the other side; hear both sides; no man should be condemned unheard." The rule requires that parties to a dispute have a fair hearing, which includes being given notice of when and where the hearing is to be held, the opportunity to bring witnesses, and the chance to cross-examine the witnesses brought against them. It flows from claims that the legal process did not afford both sides the right to a fair hearing of their claims.

Nemo sibi esse judex vel suis jus dicere debet, translated literally, means "no person should act as judge on his own behalf or speak the law for his own (ends)." The purpose of the ***nemo judex*** rule is to exclude bias or the appearance of bias from the proceedings of an administrative body. (Both the *Thomas* and the *Re Sawyer* decisions hinged on an appearance of bias on the part of the decision makers—in the former, the university president, and in the latter, the Ontario Racing Commission.) Both principles of natural justice date back to Greek and Roman law. Jones and deVillars note of *audi alteram partem*:

> The rule is an ancient one, known in Greek and even biblical times. It certainly made an appearance in English common law by the seventeenth century, and often appeared thereafter in cases having to do with restoration to offices. It extended to ecclesiastical matters, to societies and clubs, and later to protect members of trade unions from unfair expulsion. As administrative tribunals proliferated in the nineteenth and twentieth centuries, they were required to follow the same rules of fair procedure as their predecessors, the justices of the peace. The identity of the person who exercised the power was not decisive; rather, what mattered was the character of the power being exercised. If it affected a person's rights and interests, then the power had to be exercised in a fair manner.[10]

It is probably fair to suggest, therefore, that the basic principles now underlying administrative law have not changed in more than 2 000 years.

The judiciary has generally required that the state, in exercising powers over citizens and their commercial interests, treat those citizens and their interests fairly. During certain historical and political eras, this duty has been less strictly observed than at other times; but the basic philosophical thrust of the position has endured.

The Doctrine of Fairness

During the late 1960s, the doctrine of fairness, fundamentally an extension of the rules of natural justice, was developed in both England and Canada. The last 30 years have seen increased judicial intervention in the interest of fairness or fair treatment. Evans et al. note:

> One good example of this trend is cases about prisoners, and their claims to hearings decisions about parole, discipline, transfers, and leaves. A lawyer from the 1960s could hardly believe that hearings for these decisions are now commonplace and that the fighting ground is whether hearings will be given for decisions about unescorted temporary absences. The reasons for this change are less clear. The thought that it is simply a response to the pervasiveness and immense complexity of modern government seems hopelessly vague; why, for example, would such a response have occurred at this time and not at almost any other time during the twentieth century? Is it useful to remember the controversy and protest during the 1960s?[11]

In a 1986 Ontario case, Justice Reid noted of the emerging doctrine of fairness:

> It is no longer necessary, as it was before the emergence of the doctrine of fairness, to find that rights were, or might be, affected. The old learning was that if rights were affected, the function of the tribunal was quasi-judicial and therefore subject to the rules of natural justice. It is sufficient now if interests only are affected.[12]

Consider the application of this doctrine to *Cardinal and Oswald v. Director of Kent Institution*. Cardinal and Oswald were inmates in British Columbia's Matsqui Penitentiary. They took a guard hostage at knifepoint and confined him for five hours. After the incident, they were charged with various criminal offences and transferred to the maximum security Kent Institution. The director of that institution placed them in segregation, officially known as administrative dissociation, and planned to keep them there until their criminal offences had been resolved by the courts. A prison Segregation Review Board recommended that the two men be released from segregation and placed in the general population of Kent Institution, but Cardinal and Oswald remained in administrative dissociation. They appealed to the courts, arguing that they had not been given a fair hearing by the director of Kent Institution. The Supreme Court of Canada brought down the following decision:

> LeDain, J.: There can be no doubt, as was held by McEachern C.J.S.C. and the Court of Appeal, that the Director was under a duty of procedural fairness in exercising the authority conferred by s. 40 of the regulations with respect to administrative dissociation or segregation. This Court has affirmed that there is, as a general common-law principle, a duty of procedural fairness lying on every public authority making an administrative decision which is not of a legislative nature and which affects the rights, privileges, or interests of an individual. . . .
>
> The issue then is what did procedural fairness require of the Director in exercising his authority, pursuant to s. 40 of the Penitentiary Service Regulations, to continue the administrative dissociation or segregation of the appellants, despite the recommendation of the Board, if he was satisfied that it was necessary or desirable for the maintenance of good order and discipline in the institution. I agree with McEachern C.J.S.C. and Anderson J.A. that because of the serious effect of the Director's decision on the appellants, procedural fairness required that he inform them of the reasons for his intended decision and give them an opportunity, however informal, to make representations to him concerning these reasons and the general question whether it was necessary or desirable to continue their segregation for the maintenance of good order and discipline in the institution.
>
> With great respect, I do not think it is an answer to the requirement of notice and hearing by the Director, as suggested by Macdonald, J.A., that the appellants knew, as a result of their appearance before the Segregation Review Board, why they had been placed in segregation. They were entitled to know why the Director did not intend to act in accordance with the recommendation of the Board and to have an opportunity before him to state their case for release into the general population of the institution. I do not think the Director was required to make an independent inquiry into the alleged involvement of the appellants in the hostage-taking incident. He could rely on the information he had received concerning the incident from the warden of Matsqui Institution and the personnel at regional headquarters. At the same

time, he had a duty to hear and consider what the appellants had to say concerning their alleged involvement in the incident, as well as anything else that could be relevant to the question whether their release from segregation might introduce an unsettling element into the general inmate population and thus have an adverse effect on the maintenance of good order and discipline in the institution.

These were, in my opinion, the minimal or essential requirements of procedural fairness in the circumstances, and they are fully compatible with the concern that the process of prison administration, because of its special nature and exigencies, should not be unduly burdened or obstructed by the imposition of unreasonable or inappropriate procedural requirements. There is nothing to suggest that the requirement of notice and hearing by the Director, where he does not intend to act in accordance with a recommendation by the Segregation Review Board for the release of an inmate from segregation, would impose an undue burden on prison administration or create a risk to security.

There is the question, suggested by the reasons for judgement of Nemetz, C.J.B.C., whether the breach of the duty to act fairly in this case should be held not to have resulted in an excess or loss of jurisdiction and to have made the continuing segregation of the appellants unlawful because, having regard to the merits of the substantive issue, it did not result in a substantial injustice, or to use the words of Nemetz, C.J.B.C., was not of "sufficient substance." Both Nemetz C.J.B.C. and Macdonald J.A. considered the substantive issue of whether the appellants should be released from segregation and appeared to conclude that the Director's reasons for refusing to follow the recommendation of the Segregation Review Board were reasonable and fair. It is a possible implication of their approach that they were of the view that given the Director's reasons for refusing to follow the recommendation of the Board, a hearing by him of the appellants would not serve any useful purpose. Certainly, a failure to afford a fair hearing, which is the very essence of the duty to act fairly, can never of itself be regarded as not of "sufficient substance" unless it be because of its perceived effect on the result or, in other words, the actual prejudice caused by it. If this be a correct view of the implications of the approach of the majority of the British Columbia Court of Appeal to the issue of procedural fairness in this case, I find it necessary to affirm that the denial of a right to a fair hearing must always render a decision invalid, whether or not it may appear to a reviewing court that the hearing would likely have resulted in a different decision. The right to a fair

> hearing must be regarded as an independent, unqualified right which finds its essential justification in the sense of procedural justice which any person affected by an administrative decision is entitled to have. It is not for a court to deny that right and sense of justice on the basis of speculation as to what the result might have been had there been a hearing.
>
> Appeal allowed.[13]

The decision in *Cardinal and Oswald* is, in most important respects, consistent with the long-established rules of natural justice: the director of the prison must abide by the principle of *audi alteram partem*. What is singular about *Cardinal and Oswald* is that it expanded the rules of natural justice to include life behind the walls of Canada's penitentiaries.

Natural Justice v. Fundamental Justice: The *Charter* and Administrative Law

As mentioned at the outset of this chapter, a critical change in the structure of administrative law in Canada took place in 1982: the enactment of section 7 of the *Canadian Charter of Rights and Freedoms*.

> 7. Everyone has the right to life, liberty and security of the person and the right not to be deprived thereof except in accordance with the principles of fundamental justice.

The wording of this section has caused a great legal conundrum. Section 7 confers a right to be dealt with "in accordance with the principles of fundamental justice" rather than "in accordance with the principles of natural justice." Hogg has noted:

> The legislative history of s. 7 makes clear that the framers thought that "fundamental justice" meant natural justice, and were anxious to avoid judicial review that went beyond issues of procedure. . . . The trouble was that the phrase that was selected to replace due process was not "natural justice," which would certainly have been restricted to procedure, but "fundamental justice," a term that lacked any substantial body of defining case law."[14]

Since the passage of the *Charter*, Canadian courts have wrestled with the meaning to be accorded to the words "principles of fundamental justice." The courts have generally held that section 7 prohibits something more than procedural injustices.[15] Consider the commentary of the

Federal Court of Appeal in *Re Howard and Presiding Officer of Inmate Disciplinary Court of Stony Mountain Institution*. Is this decision simply a logical extension of the principles of natural justice, or a more radical departure from existing common law, necessitated by the *Charter*?

> Thurlow, C.J.: At the material time, the appellant was an inmate of Stony Mountain Institution serving a sentence of two years and four months. On December 31, 1982, he was involved in incidents with officers of the institution as a result of which five charges were laid against him under s. 39 of the Penitentiary Service Regulations. These were, possessing contraband, using indecent or disrespectful language to another person, an act calculated to prejudice discipline or good order of the institution, disobeying a lawful order of a penitentiary officer, and threatening to assault another person. The record does not disclose particulars of the charges other than that the first three occurred at 8:40 hours, the fourth at 9:00 hours, and the fifth at 9:20 hours, all on December 31, 1982. On January 6, 1983, the appellant appeared before a presiding officer and entered pleas of guilty to the charges of possessing contraband and disobeying a lawful order, and pleas of not guilty on the remaining three charges. Disposition of the charges to which he pleaded guilty was held in abeyance pending determination of the remaining three charges. Subsequently, charges of having contraband on January 4, 1983, and failing to obey a lawful order on January 20, 1983, were laid. To these the appellant pleaded not guilty. All the charges were categorized under the Commissioner's Directive No. 213 as "serious" or "flagrant" offences.
>
> On February 3, 1983, by which time he had secured counsel, the appellant appeared before the presiding officer of the inmate disciplinary court who thereupon adjourned the hearing in order to obtain written submissions from counsel for the appellant and for the Department of Justice, on the request of the appellant to have counsel represent him at the hearing. The request was denied on April 11, 1983. The presiding officer held that s. 7 of the *Charter* does not create "a new wave of rights" and, as he was not persuaded that there were circumstances in the particular case which precluded the possibility of a fair hearing in the absence of counsel, he exercised his discretion and denied the request. . . .
>
> I come then to s. 7 of the *Charter* and whether it has the effect of affording an inmate in a disciplinary proceeding a right to counsel that is not subject to denial by the presiding officer on discretionary grounds.

What was said to be at stake in the disciplinary proceedings is the liberty and security of the inmate and his right not to be deprived of them except in accordance with the principles of fundamental justice. The inmate's liberty was said to be at stake because his earned remission was in jeopardy as was also the security of his person since solitary confinement—also referred to as dissociation—was one of the punishments to which he might be subjected. I accept this analysis so far as the appellant's liberty is involved and that, as I view it, is sufficient for present purposes. At the same time, it is to be noted that earned remission, which is a creation of the *Penitentiary Act*, has at all times been conditional in the sense that it has been subject to forfeiture in disciplinary proceedings of an administrative nature and thus has never had the quality of an absolute right to be set free on the completion of the unremitted portion of a sentence. To hold that an inmate's procedural rights have been increased by the enactment of s. 7 is accordingly to hold that its enactment has also enhanced the quality of the less than absolute right conferred by the *Penitentiary Act*.

In the course of their reasons, both the presiding officer and the learned trial judge referred to expression of judicial opinion in a number of reported cases supporting the view that at common law, a prison inmate had no absolute right to have counsel represent him in proceedings before a disciplinary tribunal, that the legal procedures established by law before the enactment of the *Charter* are procedures in accordance with the principles of fundamental justice, and that s. 7 of the *Charter* did not add to the rights of a person in the appellant's position. That may be a legitimate approach to the question. But it appears to me that in interpreting s. 7, and its meaning in the *Charter*, it is desirable to consider the wording of the provision in an effort to determine its ordinary meaning in its context.

The section is cast in broad terms. Its context is that of a constitutional charter. The *Charter* itself is part of the Constitution of Canada. These features suggest a broad interpretation. The extent of the *Charter*'s guarantee of the rights set out in s. 7 may be limited by s. 1, but that does not, as it seems to me, bear on how s. 7 itself should be interpreted or on the breadth of what it embraces. In the present case, no argument was presented on the effect of s. 1 on any right to counsel that may arise under s. 7.

Next, the subject matter of s. 7 is the right to life, liberty, and security of the person. These are matters of prime importance to everyone. Moreover, the fact that liberty and security of the person are lumped together with life itself shows that the importance of the right to them is in the same class with that of the right to life itself. The enjoyment of property is not included in the class as it is in ss. 1(a) and 2(e) of the Canadian *Bill of Rights.*

Further, while the argument in the present case focussed on the meaning and effect of the wording "in accordance with the principles of fundamental justice" as a guarantee of procedural standards, I would not rule out the possibility that the wording may also refer to or embrace substantive standards as well. . . .

I am of the opinion that the enactment of s. 7 has not created any absolute right to counsel in all such proceedings. It is undoubtedly of the greatest importance to a person whose life, liberty, and security of the person are at stake to have the opportunity to present his case as fully and adequately as possible. The advantages of having the assistance of counsel for that purpose are not in doubt. But what is required is an opportunity to present the case adequately, and I do not think it can be affirmed that in no case can such an opportunity be afforded without also as part of it affording the right to representation by counsel at the hearing.

Once that position is reached, it appears to me that whether or not the person has a right to representation by counsel will depend on the circumstances of the particular case, its nature, its gravity, its complexity, the capacity of the inmate himself to understand the case and present his defence. The list is not exhaustive. And from this, it seems to me, it follows that whether or not an inmate's request for representation by counsel can lawfully be refused is not properly referred to as a matter of discretion, but is a matter of right where the circumstances are such that the opportunity to present the case adequately calls for representation by counsel. . . .

This brings me to the question whether the present was a case in which the appellant's request could lawfully be refused. Its principal feature was that the whole of the appellant's 267 days of earned remission was in jeopardy. In my view, that alone suggests his need of counsel. Next, there is the lack of particulars of offences of which three are alleged to have occurred at the same instant. . . . Moreover, one of the three charges is that of an act calculated to prejudice discipline and good order, a notoriously vague and difficult charge for anyone to defend. These features, as well, suggest the need for counsel to protect the inmate.

There is not in the record anything that would indicate that the appellant suffered from physical or mental incapacity which would disable him from conducting his own defence as well as might be expected of an ordinary person without legal training. But he obviously felt the need for counsel because he obtained legal-aid assistance promptly. He must also have been able to persuade those who administer the legal-aid system of his need. Moreover, in a social system which recognizes the right of anyone to counsel in any of the ordinary courts of law for the defence of any charge, no matter how trivial the possible consequences may be, it seems to me to be incongruous to deny such a right to a person who, though not suffering from any physical or mental incapacity to defend himself, is faced with charges that may result in a loss of his liberty, qualified and fragile though it may have been, for some 267 days.

On the whole, I am of the opinion that the refusal of the appellant's request for counsel was a refusal of the opportunity to which he was entitled to adequately present his defence. . . .

Appeal allowed.[16]

Administrative Law in Action: An Example of Decision Making

A recent case from the Ontario Human Rights Commission reveals how administrative law works in action, independent of issues of review. The case hinges on appropriate medical evidence; relevant medical evidence can often be used to determine outcomes, not only in human rights issues, but more commonly in workers' compensation cases. The excerpt that follows is from a recent decision of the Ontario Human Rights Commission, *Kearsley v. Corporation of the City of St. Catharines*, 2004:

The complainant, Antony Kearsley was born May 24, 1962 and is now in his 40th year. He has atrial fibrillation described as an irregular irregular heart beat, discovered as far back as 1993. The cause of his atrial fibrillation is unknown, so his condition is described medically as lone atrial fibrillation. He has no other coronary defect. Further his atrial fibrillation, though persistent, causes him no symptoms, except that at times when he works out, he is aware that his heart beat is irregular.

He applied in 1996 to the Corporation of the city of St. Catharines for work as a fire-fighter. He passed a rigorous physical test designed to weed out those lacking the strength, endurance, conditioning and agility needed in a fire-fighter. In early June 1997 he was told by St. Catharines he was accepted as a fire-fighter with his work to commence July 7, 1997 subject to his passing a medical examination and police clearance.

St. Catharines sent Mr. Kearsley to Dr. D.I. Lorenzen (who happened to be Mr. Kearsley's family doctor) for his medical examination. While the atrial fibrillation had been noted in a hospital record when he was in a hospital in 1993 because of a car accident, Mr. Kearsley did not know he had atrial fibrillation, nor did Dr. Lorenzen, until it was discovered by virtue of an electro-cardiogram test during his medical examination on June 16, 1997. When the atrial fibrillation was confirmed by a second electrocardiogram a few days later, Dr. Lorenzen told Mr. Kearsley that because of the atrial fibrillation, he was not acceptable as a fire-fighter and that he was running the risk of having a stroke. . . .

The Ontario Human Rights Code provides in part:

S 5(1) Every person has a right to equal treatment with respect to employment without discrimination because of . . . handicap. . . .

S 10(1) "Because of handicap" means for the reason that person has or has had, or is believed to have or have had (a) any degree of physical disability . . . that is caused by . . . illness. . . .

S 17(1) a right of a person under this act is not infringed for the reason only that the person is incapable of performing or fulfilling essential duties or requirements attending the exercise of the right because of handicap.

It is obvious at once that a person with very bad eyesight is not discriminated against when refused a job as a truck driver nor a person with inadequate strength when refused a job as a police officer or firefighter. There is no doubt that St. Catharines considered that Mr. Kearsley had a physical disability, namely atrial fibrillation. The issue is whether St. Catharines was justified in concluding that because of this perceived handicap, Mr. Kearsley was incapable of performing or fulfilling essential duties of a fire-fighter. . . .

Prior to attempting cardioversion, Dr. Connolly (asked for his advice as an expert in cardiology) wrote on August 14, 1997 to Dr. Lorenzen in part as following:

The patient is totally asymptomatic, is in a very good physical condition and can run a mile in 5.5 minutes . . . a cardioversion is pending . . . the nub of the issue is that this patient wants to be a fire-fighter and apparently atrial fibrillation will prevent him from doing so. . . . If he has a successful cardioversion and remains free of atrial fibrillation, it appears that he would be a good candidate for going back into the fire fighters. As far as his risk of stroke is concerned I think his stroke risk is very low and certainly is less than 1% per year.

After attempting electrical cardioversion without success, Dr. Connolly on September 10, 1997 sent Dr. Lorenzen a copy of the hospital discharge summary written by him, which reads in part:

> *It looks like this patient is going to remain in atrial fibrillation for the foreseeable future. I do not believe that this will have any effect on his longevity, lifestyle or indeed his ability to work in the fire department. I do not believe he needs to stay on long term anticoagulation. . . .*

The discharge summary seemed to soften Dr. Lorenzen's position. He told Mr. Kearsley on September 22, 1997 that he would "butt out" and defer to Dr. Connolly's opinion, provided Dr. Connolly accepted moral and legal responsibility for the decision that Mr. Kearsley was fit to work as a fire-fighter.

Apparently at the request of Mr. Kearsley, Dr. Connolly wrote a letter to Dr. Lorenzen on October 2, 1997 which reads in part: "I do feel that the patient is not a high risk patient for working for the police force [*sic*] and I would support your decision to allow him to take such a job." No one suggests that by referring to "police force" rather than "fire department" Dr. Connolly caused confusion. It was obvious to all that Dr. Connolly meant the fire-department. . . .

I find that St. Catharines should have hired Mr. Kearsley as of June 8, 1998. Once it was confirmed on June 20, 1997 that Mr. Kearsley had atrial fibrillation, it was necessary to determine whether he had any other cardiovascular problems before he could be found fit for fire-fighting. It is most unlikely that the necessary tests, examinations and opinions could have been accomplished in time for him to commence work on July 7, 1997 or indeed by July 15, 1997. While Dr. Abraham wrote a note on June 30, 1997 stating Mr. Kearsley could work as a fire-fighter, that note was written before any tests had been performed. In his report of June 27, 1997 to Dr. Lorenzen, Dr. Abraham suggested the atrial fibrillation might be due to alcohol or caffeine and those should be avoided. The report of an echocardiogram performed on July 3, 1997 did not reach Dr. Lorenzen until July 7, 1997.

We do not know just when Dr. Abraham might have delivered a full report attesting to Mr. Kearsley's fitness as a fire-fighter, but even if such could have been prepared and delivered to Dr. Lorenzen by July 7 or shortly thereafter, Dr. Lorenzen could very reasonably have wanted the opinion of a cardiologist or expert in arrhythmia such as Dr. Connolly. It is speculation I am not prepared to engage in to find that Dr. Lorenzen could have been satisfied that Mr. Kearsley was fit as a fire-fighter in time for him to commence training with the other recruits in July 1997.

Having failed, without the fault of Dr. Lorenzen or St. Catharines, to pass his medical examination in time to start working in July 1997, he was no more entitled than anyone else to require St. Catharines to hire him until St. Catharines next hired and trained recruits. Dr. Lorenzen was wrong in finding Mr. Kearsley unfit in October, but that meant only St. Catharines was wrong in not taking him on as a fire-fighter when the next hiring took place which turned out to be June 8, 1998.

Order

1) St. Catharines to hire Mr. Kearsley as a first class fire-fighter, his work to commence within 75 days.

2) St. Catharines to pay Mr. Kearsley for his monetary loss resulting from its failure to hire him on June 8, 1998, such loss being his loss of wages, overtime, pension and mileage.

3) St. Catharines to give Mr. Kearsley seniority ahead of those hired on June 8, 1998.

4) St. Catharines to pay Mr. Kearsley general damages of $4,000 for discriminating against him.

Date at Toronto this 2nd day of April, 2002.[17]

Conclusion: Administrative Law—
A Mirror to the State

Over the past three decades, the scope of administrative law, like the scope of government, has expanded considerably. Since 1982, the *Charter* has given a constitutional character to the state's commitment to act fairly in dealing with its citizens, notably those charged with criminal offences or deprived of liberty. Administrative law decisions are required of marketing boards, human rights commissions, labour relations boards, workers' compensation tribunals, children's aid societies, welfare agencies, parole boards, and government ministries from National Revenue to Education. Administrative law is, for better or worse, the most accessible and most pervasive symbol of the fairness of the state in dealing with its citizens. The task for the next decade will be little different from the task of the past century: to give life to the state's obligations to treat its constituents fairly.

Web Links

 W W W ····························

Bora Laskin Law Library, University of Toronto
http://www.law-lib.utoronto.ca/resources/topic/admin.htm
The resources site at the University of Toronto's Bora Laskin Law Library
provides information on administrative law as well as on other areas of law.

Canadalegal.com
http://www.canadalegal.com
A directory of Canadian legal resources on the Internet. Its topical list
of areas of law is extensive and includes headings on administrative law
in general and specifically judicial review.

The Supreme Court of Canada
http://www.lexum.umontreal.ca/csc-scc/en/concept
At the Supreme Court of Canada site maintained by LEXUM (of the
Faculty of Law, University of Montreal), this page provides a list of law
terms linked to SCC cases.

Questions for Discussion

···

1. Which of the two decisions in *Re Sheehan* is more persuasive? Is the
   Ontario Court of Appeal correct in asserting that the protection of
   an agency's discretionary authority (in this case, the Criminal
   Injuries Compensation Board's) is more important than the principle of compensation for a specific criminal injury?
2. Under what circumstances might a dispute over a final course grade
   be subject to judicial review?
3. Should prisoners be deprived of rights other than liberty? If so, what
   specific limitations should be imposed? How would you define the
   responsibility of the state to act fairly in dealings with its imprisoned population?

Further Reading

···

Dussault, R., and L. Borgeat. *Administrative Law: A Treatise*. 2d ed. 5 vol.
Toronto: Carswell, 1988.
    This is an English-language edition of a classic and exhaustive
    five-volume text on the subject of administrative law in Canada.

The authors cover the role of law in the administration (volume one), personal and financial management in public administration (volume two), management of the Crown domain and government information in public administration (volume three), judicial review of the legality of administrative action (volume four), and Crown liability (volume five).

Jones, D.P., and A.S. deVillars. *Principles of Administrative Law.* 4th ed. Toronto: Carswell, 2004.

This text provides the reader with a good statement of the key principles of administrative law. It offers a useful conceptual framework for understanding the basic building blocks within this realm of law. Both authors practise administrative law in Alberta.

McCallum, S.K. *Canadian Journal of Administrative Law and Practice.* Toronto: Carswell, 2000.

This journal is published three times each year. It contains current articles, case comments, practice notes, and book reviews from the realm of administrative law in Canada. It is an excellent source of current information about developments within the field of administrative law, providing a forum for discussion of issues and the critical roles of boards, commissions, and tribunals within this sphere.

Notes

1. R. Dussault and L. Borgeat, *Administrative Law: A Treatise,* vol. 1 (Toronto: Carswell, 1985), 12.
2. D.P. Jones and A.S. deVillars, *Principles of Administrative Law* (Toronto: Carswell, 1985), 58.
3. Dussault and Borgeat, *Administrative Law,* 13.
4. G. Gall, *The Canadian Legal System,* 3d ed. (Toronto: Carswell, 1990), 356.
5. *Thomas v. Mount Saint Vincent University* (1986), 28 D.L.R. (4th) 230 at 246 (N.S.S.C.).
6. *Re Sheehan and Criminal Injuries Compensation Board* (1973), 37 D.L.R. (3d) 336 at 337–343 (Ont. Div. Ct.), rev'd (1975), 52 D.L.R. (3d) 728 (Ont. C.A.).
7. *Re Sawyer and Ontario Racing Commission* (1979), 99 D.L.R. (3d) 561 at 564–566 (Ont. C.A.).
8. *Baker v. Minister of Citizenship and Immigration,* [1999] 2 S.C.R. 813 at 850–851.

9. P.W. Hogg, *Constitutional Law of Canada*, 3d ed. (Toronto: Carswell, 1992), 768.

10. Jones and deVillars, *Principles of Administrative Law*, 3d ed. (Toronto: Carswell, 1999), 197.

11. J.M. Evans, H.N. Janisch, D.J. Mullan, and R.C.B. Risk, *Administrative Law: Cases, Text and Materials* (Toronto: Emond Montgomery, 1989), 70.

12. *Re Collins and Pension Commission of Ontario* (1986), 31 D.L.R. (4th) 86 at 101 (Ont. Div. Ct.).

13. *Cardinal and Oswald v. Director of Kent Institution*, [1985] 2 S.C.R. 643 at 653–661.

14. Hogg, *Constitutional Law of Canada*, 1032–3.

15. See, for example, the Supreme Court of Canada's decision in *Re B.C. Motor Vehicle Act*, [1985] 2 S.C.R. 486.

16. *Re Howard and Presiding Officer of Inmate Disciplinary Court of Stony Mountain Institution* (1985), 19 D.L.R. (4th) 502 at 507–521 (F.C.A.).

17. *Kearsley v. Corporation of the City of St. Catharines*, Canadian Human Rights Reporter D/304, 42, 2002.

References

Arthurs, H.W. "Jonah and the Whale: The Appearance, Disappearance and Reappearance of Administrative Law." *University of Toronto Law Journal* 30 (1980): 225.

Chayes, A. "The Role of the Judge in Public Law Litigation." *Harvard Law Review* 79 (1976): 1281.

Dussault, R., and L. Borgeat. *Administrative Law: A Treatise*. 2d ed. Vol. 1. Toronto: Carswell, 1988.

Evans, J.M., H.N. Janisch, D.J. Mullan, and R.C.B. Risk. *Administrative Law: Cases, Text and Materials*. Toronto: Emond Montgomery, 1989.

Gall, G. *The Canadian Legal System*. 3d ed. Toronto: Carswell, 1990, Chapter 12.

Jones, D.P., and A.S. deVillars. *Principles of Administrative Law*. 3d ed. Toronto: Carswell, 1999.

Kernaghan, K. "Canadian Public Administration: Progress and Prospects." *Canadian Public Administration* 25 (1982): 444.

Mullan, D.J. "The Federal Court Act: A Misguided Attempt at Administrative Law Reform?" *University of Toronto Law Journal* 23 (1973): 14.

Thomas, P.G. "Administrative Law Reform: Legal Versus Political Controls on Administrative Discretion." *Canadian Public Administration* 27 (1984): 120.

Wade, H.W.R. "Crossroads in Administrative Law." *Current Legal Problems* 21 (1968): 75.

Willis, J. "Three Approaches to Administrative Law: The Juridical, the Conceptual, and the Functional." *University of Toronto Law Journal* 1 (1935): 53.

———. "Canadian Administrative Law in Retrospect." *University of Toronto Law Journal* 24 (1974): 225.

CHAPTER 10

Criminal Law: *Mens Rea, Actus Reus*, and Changing Definitions of Intolerable Conduct

The mood and temper of the public in regard to the treatment of crime and criminals is one of the most unfailing tests of any country. A calm, dispassionate recognition of the rights of the accused and even of the convicted criminal, . . . the treatment of crime and the criminal mark and measure the stored-up strength of a nation, and are the sign and proof of the living virtue within it.

(Winston Churchill, public speech, 1910)

The Intent of the Criminal Law and the Definition of Crime

Criminal law is probably the most widely discussed of the many forms of Canadian law. We all have opinions about the operation of the criminal justice system: it is by turns too lenient and too harsh; too intrusive and not intrusive enough; too little and too much concerned with individual rights.

We must always remind ourselves that the criminal law is the most coercive and intrusive form of public law. The task of those who create, enforce, and administer it is to ask continually about the circumstances in which this force should be used. As Winston Churchill observed, the state of a civilized society can be divined from the manner in which it responds to its criminals.

The purpose of the criminal law is to punish certain acts that have been declared in law to be threats to the established social order. Crime can be conceptualized as falling into one of three categories: offences against persons; offences against property; and offences considered to be evil in themselves, irrespective of whether harm befalls another person or the property of another person. Examples of the first category of crime are straightforward enough: culpable homicide, sexual assault, robbery, assault, attempted murder, and the like. Crimes against property are also easily determined: theft, fraud, income tax evasion, insider trading, forgery, and so on. Offences considered to be punishable irrespective of their immediate impact on others include soliciting for prostitution, pornography, the use and distribution of narcotics, and certain gaming activities.

In pre-state societies, no criminal law existed as such. Killings and other serious assaults prompted myriad reactions: revenge executions, compensation from one tribe or clan to another, and conciliation between individuals or collectives. In Canada, no criminal code existed until as late as 1892, when the federal government adopted the British reform code written by Sir James Fitzjames Stephens. Despite its designation, this code was not really reformist, since it did not originate in a fresh reconstruction of principles and practice. As Mewett and Manning noted,

> The *Criminal Code* of 1892 was only . . . the collecting into one more or less comprehensive statute of a multitude of existing provisions and common-law doctrines with some elimination of inconsistencies and tidying up of anomalies. But no attempt was made to find a rational basis for the criminal law or to formulate a new *Code* on that basis. The essential substance of the law was merely adopted as it stood.[1]

Criminal law, unlike tort law, is concerned with public wrongs. The state or the collective has determined that certain kinds of conduct must be responded to with various penalties, both to deter those who might be inclined to engage in these activities and to express community outrage and/or concern about a particular act. The historical distinction between criminal and tort law creates an inevitable tension. A citizen's notion of justice is likely to be compensation for an inflicted harm, but the criminal law makes the state's interest in **conviction** and punishment the objective of prosecution. For victims of crime, the criminal law is typically less personal and less emotionally satisfying than the compensatory imperative of tort. The victim receives no tangible benefit from the penalty imposed, be it a suspended sentence, discharge, fine, probation order, community service order, or imprisonment.

Another way of expressing the intent of the criminal law is to say that it defines what the state regards as intolerable deviance. Over time, the definitions of deviance and the associated penalties have changed markedly, particularly for crimes defined as evil in themselves, the victimless offences listed earlier.

While most legal scholars and the Canadian public agree that the designation of crimes against persons and property can be morally justified, debate continues about the appropriateness of using the criminal law to control such matters as the commercialization of sex, the public-health risks involved in the use and distribution of certain drugs, and the potential economic exploitation involved in certain forms of gambling. But debate also continues about what constitutes crimes against persons and property. Sociologists Herman and Julia Schwendinger have examined the moral criteria employed in defining crime:

> [T]he definition of crime should openly face the moral issues. . . . Traditionally, these issues have been inadequately represented by such unanalyzed terms as "social injury," "antisocial act," or "public wrongs." But how does one confront the problem of explicating "social injury" or "public wrongs"? Is this done by reference to the functional imperatives of social institutions or by the historically determined rights of individuals? . . . Isn't it time to raise serious questions about the assumptions underlying the definitions of the field of criminology, when a man who steals a paltry sum can be called a criminal while agents of the state can, with impunity, legally reward men who destroy food so that price levels can be maintained, while a sizable portion of the population suffers from malnutrition.[2]

A more cautious assessment of the problem of defining what constitutes crime has been advanced by sociologist Steven Box:

> Deviant behaviour is nothing less or more than it has always been: rule breaking. It is behaviour which is proscribed by those who have the institutionalized power, and occasionally the consensual authority, to create rules; it is behaviour which places its perpetrator at risk of being punished by those who have the institutionalized power, and occasionally the consensual authority, to do something to those who do not keep to the rules.[3]

Mens Rea and *Actus Reus*: **Prerequisites for Conviction**

The definitions of crime fluctuate with changes in the social, political, and economic order. But the basic conceptual elements of a crime remain, at least in theory, consistent over time. The concepts of *mens rea* and ***actus reus*** (introduced in Chapter 7) have their origins in the development of the criminal law of England. In order to be convicted of a criminal offence, an individual must have committed an *actus reus*, an evil act, and must simultaneously possess *mens rea,* an evil mind or intention. It is only the coincidence of *mens rea* and *actus reus* that can lead to criminal conviction.

In many contexts, the connection between the two concepts is straightforward. Take the theft of a chocolate bar. The *actus reus* is the taking of the bar from a store without giving payment; the *mens rea* is the intention to do so. However, if a person were forced at gunpoint to steal the bar or were two years old, there would clearly be no intention to commit the offence. If, in another example, the police were to discover marijuana in a person's luggage, they could fairly presume *actus reus*—commission of the act of possession of marijuana. But if the possessor had no knowledge of the presence of the marijuana, and the court believed this to be true, there would be no *mens rea*—no intent to possess the illegal drug.

How does one find a coincidence of *mens rea* and *actus reus* in the commission of the offence of murder? Consider the following excerpt from the Supreme Court of Canada's judgment in *R. v. Cooper.* The Newfoundland Court of Appeal had allowed an appeal by the accused from his conviction for second degree murder; the Crown was appealing that ruling.

Cory, J.: At issue, on this appeal, is the nature of the intent required to found a conviction for murder pursuant to s. 212(a)(ii) of the *Criminal Code,* R.S.C. 1970, c. C-34 (now R.S.C. 1985, c. C-46, s. 229(a)(ii)).

[Section 229(a)(ii) is part of section 229(a), one of three legal definitions of murder. Section 229(a)(ii) reads:

Culpable homicide is murder

    (a) where the person who causes the death of a human being

        (i)   means to cause his death, or

        (ii) means to cause him bodily harm that he knows is likely to cause his death, and is reckless whether death ensues or not.]

Factual background

The respondent Lyndon Cooper and the deceased Deborah Careen lived in Labrador City, Newfoundland. At one time, they had been friends and lovers. On January 30, 1988, they met at a gathering place known as the K-Bar in Labrador City. Although by this time the respondent was living with somebody else, they spent the evening together at the bar. There is no doubt that they consumed a considerable amount of alcohol. Eventually, Cooper, the deceased, and a mutual friend left the bar in a taxi. After they dropped off the friend, they continued in the cab to the residence of another of Cooper's friends, where he borrowed a Jeep. Cooper then drove the deceased to the secluded parking lot of a power station.

At the parking lot, the respondent testified that he and the deceased engaged in some form of consensual sexual activity. He said that they began to argue at one point and that the deceased struck him. At this he became angry. He hit the deceased and grabbed her by the throat with both hands and shook her. He stated that this occurred in the front seat of the Jeep. He then said that he could recall nothing else until he woke in the back seat and found the body of the deceased beside him. He had no recollection of causing her death. He pushed her body out of the Jeep and drove away. Later, during the drive to his home, he found one of her shoes in the vehicle and threw it out the window into the snow.

The expert evidence established that the deceased had in fact been struck twice. However, these blows could not have killed her. Rather, death was caused by "a classic pattern of one-handed manual strangulation." That same evidence confirmed that death by strangulation can occur as quickly as 30 seconds after contact with the throat and that a drunken victim is likely to die from asphyxiation more quickly than a sober one. Nonetheless, the presence of petechial hemorrhages on the neck of the deceased and the finding that the hyoid bone in her throat was not fractured suggested to the expert that death occurred rather more slowly, probably after two minutes of pressure.

The position of the defence was that the respondent was so drunk that he blacked out shortly after he started shaking her with both hands. Thus, it was said that the respondent did not have (i) the required intent to commit murder, or (ii) alternatively, did not foresee that holding someone by the neck was likely to cause death. . . .

What degree of concurrency is required between the wrongful act and the requisite *mens rea?*

There can be no doubt that under the classical approach to criminal law, it is the intent of the accused that makes the wrongful act illegal. It is that intent which brings the accused within the sphere of blameworthiness and justifies the penalty or punishment which is imposed upon him for the infraction of the criminal law. The essential aspect of *mens rea* and the absolute necessity that it be present in the case of murder was emphasized by Lamer, J. (as he then was) in *R. v. Vaillancourt* (1987), 39 C.C.C. (3d) 118. . . . At p. 133 he stated: "It may well be that, as a general rule, the principles of fundamental justice require proof of a subjective *mens rea* with respect to the prohibited act, in order to avoid punishing the "morally innocent". . . .

However, not only must the guilty mind, intent or *mens rea* be present, it must also be concurrent with the impugned act. Professor D. Stuart has referred to this as "the simultaneous principle": see *Canadian Criminal Law 2nd. ed.* (1987), p. 305. This principle has been stressed in a number of cases. For example, in *R. v. Droste* (1979), 49 C.C.C. (2d) 52, 18 C.R. (3d) 64 (Ont. C.A.), the accused had intended to murder his wife by pouring gasoline over the interior of the car and setting fire to it while she was within it. Before he could light the gasoline, the car crashed into a bridge and ignited prematurely. As a result, both his children were killed rather than his wife. He was charged with their murder and convicted. On appeal, Arnup, J.A., speaking for the Court of Appeal in directing a new trial, stated at pp. 53–54:

> . . . the trial Judge did not instruct the jury of the necessity of the Crown showing that at the time of the occurrence at the bridge, the appellant, intending to kill his wife, had done an act with that intention, and in the course of doing so, his children were killed. In short, he did not tell them that the *mens rea* and the *actus reus* must be concurrent. [Emphasis added.]

. . . There is, then, the classic rule that at some point, the *actus reus* and the *mens rea* or intent must coincide. Further, I would agree with the conclusion of James J. that an act *(actus reus)* which may be innocent or no more than careless at the outset, can become criminal at a later stage when the accused acquires knowledge of the nature of the act and still refuses to change his course of action. . . .

Yet, with respect, I do not think that it is always necessary that the requisite *mens rea* (the guilty mind, intent, or awareness) should continue throughout the commission of the wrongful act. There is no question that in order to obtain a conviction, the Crown must demonstrate that the accused intended to cause bodily harm that he knew was ultimately so dangerous and serious that it was likely to result in the death of the victim. But that intent need not persist throughout the entire act of strangulation. When Cooper testified that he seized the victim by the neck, it was open to the jury to infer that by those actions, he intended to cause her bodily harm that he knew that was likely to cause her death. Since breathing is essential to life, it would be reasonable to infer the accused knew that strangulation was likely to result in death. I would stress that the jury was, of course, not required to make such an inference but, on the evidence presented, it was open to them to do so.

Did the accused possess such a mental state after he started strangling the victim? Her death occurred between 30 seconds and two minutes after he grabbed her by the neck. It could be reasonably inferred by the jury, that when the accused grabbed the victim by the neck and shook her, that there was, at that moment, the necessary coincidence of the wrongful act of strangulation and the requisite intent to do bodily harm that the accused knew was likely to cause her death. Cooper was aware of these acts before he "blacked out." Thus, although the jury was under no compulsion to do so, it was nonetheless open to them to infer that he knew that he was causing bodily harm and knew that it was so dangerous to the victim that it was likely to cause her death. It was sufficient that the intent and the act of strangulation coincided at some point. It was not necessary that the requisite intent continue throughout the entire two minutes required to cause the death of the victim. . . .

In the result, I would set aside the order of the Court of Appeal directing a new trial and restore the conviction.

Appeal allowed; conviction restored. . . .

Lamer, C.J.C. (dissenting): It is crucial to a correct charge under s. 212(a)(ii) that the jury understand that there must be intention to cause bodily harm which the accused knows is likely to cause death. Intention to cause bodily harm, without knowledge that such is likely to cause death, is not sufficient. Given the position of the defence in this case, a clear understanding of this aspect was essential to a fair trial. . . .

I do not raise this point to question whether the accused here intended to cause bodily harm. That was conceded in the argument before us. I raise it rather to emphasize that the intention to cause bodily harm by no means leads inexorably to the conclusion that the accused knew that the bodily harm was likely to cause death. It is, of course, this second aspect which is essential to a finding of guilt of murder under s. 212(a)(ii). Particularly with respect to an action such as grabbing by the neck, there may be a point at the outset when there is no intention to cause death and no knowledge that the action is likely to cause death. But there comes a point in time when the wrongful conduct becomes likely to cause death. It is, in my view, at that moment or thereafter, that the accused must have a conscious awareness of the likelihood of death. This awareness need not, however, continue until death ensues.

Cooper intended to choke the deceased and cause her bodily harm. Under s. 212(a)(i), it was open to the jury to infer from his conduct and on all of the evidence that in doing so, he intended to kill her. To be found guilty under s. 212(a)(ii), however, he must have been aware of the fact that he persisted in choking her long enough for it to become likely that death would ensue.

This instruction, given the particular facts of this case and the nature of the defence presented by the accused, had to be given. Additionally, the jury should have been instructed to consider the evidence of drunkenness in relation to this awareness. In my respectful view, upon a reading of the whole charge, this was not done adequately.

I would dismiss the appeal.[4]

The differing judgments of Justice Cory and former chief justice Lamer raise questions about the *mens rea* required to substantiate a conviction for murder. Justice Cory argues that "it could be reasonably inferred by the jury that . . . there was . . . the necessary coincidence of the wrongful act of strangulation and the requisite intent to do bodily harm that the accused knew was likely to cause her death." Justice Lamer argues, on the contrary, that it is not clear that Cooper was "aware of the fact that he persisted in choking her long enough for it to become likely that death would ensue." The difference between the two positions hinges on the inferences that one is willing to draw with respect to intention. Justice Lamer asserts that any conviction for murder requires proof of subjective knowledge of the likelihood of death; it is not sufficient to base criminal conviction under section 229(a)(ii) upon an inference of knowledge of likelihood of death, in the absence of supporting evidence.

The question whether criminal conviction for murder should be premised upon **objective** or **subjective intention** is one that will continue to be debated within criminal law. In essence, the distinction is between what a reasonable person would be expected to intend and what the accused actually did intend. The American jurist Oliver Wendell Holmes set out the following proposition in 1863:

If the known present state of things is such that the act done will very certainly cause death, and the probability is a matter of common knowledge, one who does the act, knowing the present state of things, is guilty of murder, and the law will not inquire whether he did actually foresee the consequences or not. The test of foresight is not what this very criminal foresaw, but what a man of reasonable prudence would have foreseen.[5]

But consider the comments of Justice Dickson in *R. v. City of Sault Ste. Marie*, in direct opposition to Holmes's sentiments:

> Where the offence is criminal, the Crown must establish a mental element, namely, that the accused who committed the prohibited act did so intentionally or recklessly, with knowledge of the facts constituting the offence, or with wilful blindness toward them. Mere negligence is excluded from the concept of the mental element required for conviction. Within the context of a criminal prosecution, a person who fails to make such enquiries as a reasonable and prudent person would make, or who fails to know facts he should have known, is innocent in the eyes of the law.[6]

There are many criminal offences for which the requisite *mens rea* is a subjective intention to commit the given offence, but is founded on "recklessness" or "advertent negligence" rather than a direct intent. Consider the following excerpt from the Supreme Court's decision in *R. v. Hundal*, a case concerned with the criminal offence of dangerous driving causing death:

> Cory, J.: At issue on this appeal is whether there is a subjective element in the requisite *mens rea* which must be established by the Crown in order to prove the offence of dangerous driving. . . .
>
> **Factual background**
>
> The accident occurred at about 3:40 in the afternoon in downtown Vancouver. The streets were wet at the time, a situation not uncommon to that city. The downtown traffic was heavy. The appellant was driving his dump truck eastbound on Nelson Street, a four-lane road, approaching its intersection with Cambie Street. At the time, his truck was overloaded. It exceeded by 1160 kilograms the maximum gross weight permitted for the vehicle. He was travelling in the passing lane for eastbound traffic. The deceased was travelling southbound on Cambie Street. He had stopped for a red light at the intersection with Nelson Street. When the light turned green, the deceased proceeded into the intersection through a crosswalk, continued south across the two lanes for westbound traffic on Nelson Street, and reached the passing lane for eastbound traffic. At that moment, his car was struck on the right side by the dump truck, killing him instantly.
>
> The appellant stated that when he approached the intersection of Nelson and Cambie Streets, he observed that the light had turned amber. He thought that he could not stop in time, so he

simply honked his horn and continued through the intersection when the impact occurred. Several witnesses observed the collision. They testified that the appellant's truck entered the intersection after the Nelson Street traffic light had turned red. It was estimated that at least one second had passed between the end of the amber light and the time when the dump truck first entered the intersection. A Vancouver police officer gave evidence that the red light for Nelson at this intersection is preceded by a three-second amber light and there is a further one-half-second delay before the Cambie light turned green. One witness observed that the deceased's vehicle had travelled almost the entire width of the intersection before it was struck by the truck. Another witness, Mr. Mumford, had been travelling close to the appellant's truck through some 12 intersections. He testified that on an earlier occasion, the appellant went through an intersection as the light turned red. He estimated the speed of the truck at the time of the collision was between 50 and 60 km/h. . . .

The relevant portions of s. 233 read as follows:

233.(1)   Every one commits an offence who operates

(a)   a motor vehicle on a street, road, highway, or other public place in a manner that is dangerous to the public, having regard to all the circumstances, including the nature, condition, and use of such place and the amount of traffic that at the time is or might reasonably be expected to be on such place; . . .

(4)   Every one who commits an offence under subsection (1) and thereby causes the death of any other person is guilty of an indictable offence and is liable to imprisonment for a term not exceeding fourteen years. . . .

The appellant contends that the prison sentence which may be imposed for a breach of s. 233 (now s. 249) makes it evident that an accused cannot be convicted without proof beyond a reasonable doubt of a subjective mental element of an intention to drive dangerously. Certainly every crime requires proof of an act or failure to act, coupled with an element of fault which is termed the mens rea. This court has made it clear that s. 7 of the Canadian Charter of Rights and Freedoms prohibits the imposition of imprisonment in the absence of proof of that element of fault. . . .

Depending on the provisions of the particular section and the context in which it appears, the constitutional requirement of *mens rea* may be satisfied in different ways. The offence can require proof of a positive state of mind such as intent, recklessness or wilful blindness. Alternatively, the *mens rea* or element of fault can be satisfied by proof of negligence whereby the conduct of the accused is measured on the basis of an objective standard without establishing the subjective mental state of the particular accused. In the appropriate context, negligence can be an acceptable basis of liability which meets the fault requirement of s. 7 of the *Charter*. . . .

[T]he wording of the section itself which refers to the operation of a motor vehicle "in a manner that is dangerous to the public, having regard to all the circumstances" suggests that an objective standard is required. The "manner of driving" can only be compared to a standard of reasonable conduct. That standard can be readily judged and assessed by all who would be members of juries.

Thus, it is clear that the basis of liability for dangerous driving is negligence. The question to be asked is not what the accused subjectively intended but rather whether, viewed objectively, the accused exercised the appropriate standard of care. It is not overly difficult to determine when a driver has fallen markedly below the acceptable standard of care. There can be no doubt that the concept of negligence is well understood and readily recognized by most Canadians. Negligent driving can be thought of as a continuum that progresses, or regresses, from momentary lack of attention, giving rise to civil responsibility through careless driving under a provincial *Highway Traffic Act* to dangerous driving under the *Criminal Code*. . . .

The trial judge carefully examined the circumstances of the accident. He took into account the busy downtown traffic, the weather conditions, and the mechanical condition of the accused's vehicle. He concluded, in my view very properly, that the appellant's manner of driving represented a gross departure from the standard of a reasonably prudent driver. No explanation was offered by the accused that could excuse his conduct. There is no reason for interfering with the trial judge's finding of fact and application of the law.

In the result, the appeal must be dismissed.[7]

It is fair to conclude from Justice Cory's reasoning that the very nature of *mens rea* changes as one moves from offence to offence.

Once we leave the realms of subjective intention, recklessness, or wilful blindness, we move into the territories of **strict and absolute liability offences**. Strict liability offences are public welfare or regulatory offences requiring no proof of intention and rarely raising the issue of the liberty of the accused. The prosecutor must prove an objective intent, but an element of reverse onus applies to the accused: the accused must prove that he or she had no intent to commit the crime or, alternatively, that he or she exercised due diligence or had a reasonable belief in the legitimacy of his or her conduct, based on a mistake of fact. For example, the hunting of a particular species out of season, contrary to the *Migratory Birds Convention*, would likely be considered a strict liability offence.

An absolute liability offence is an offence for which intent is irrelevant; the prosecutor need prove only that the person in question committed the offence. Certain parking infractions may be constructed as absolute liability offences, though it may well be that, at least in certain circumstances, courts would hold such an approach to be contrary to the presumption of innocence guaranteed by the *Charter*.[8]

Mens Rea and Parties to an Offence

One final issue with regard to *mens rea* should be discussed: parties to an offence. Under section 21 of the *Criminal Code,* parties to an offence may be held as criminally responsible as the person or persons who actually commit the crime.

> 21.(1) Every one is a party to an offence who
>> (a) actually commits it,
>> (b) does or omits to do anything for the purpose of aiding any person to commit it; or
>> (c) abets any person in committing it.
>
> (2) Where two or more persons form an intention in common to carry out an unlawful purpose and to assist each other therein and any one of them, in carrying out the common purpose, commits an offence, each of them who knew or ought to have known that the commission of the offence would be a probable consequence of carrying out the common purpose is a party to that offence.

In most circumstances, the meaning of this section of the *Code* can be readily understood. If a person provides a gun for the purpose of a crime, drives the getaway car, or keeps a lookout for the police, that person will be held to be as guilty of the crime as the person who pulls the trigger or robs the bank.

What of the following instance, however? Stan is walking down the street and sees his friend Fred beating Jim, whom Stan knows and doesn't particularly like. If he simply walks by and allows Fred to continue the beating, is he a party to the offence? What if he smiles at Fred?

What if he shouts encouragement to him? What if Stan volunteers to hold Jim down? In short, at what point does Stan violate section 21 of the *Code* by doing or omitting to do anything for the purpose of aiding another person to commit an offence? Mewett and Manning provide a framework, if not a definitive answer, for this conundrum:

> Where a person is actually present when the crime is committed by the actor, whether his mere presence will amount to aiding or abetting depends upon the circumstances but, as a general proposition, some act of aiding or abetting must occur over and above mere presence. . . . In the case of *Coney,* the accused were present at an illegal prize fight and were charged with aiding and abetting a battery. The court held that the mere presence of persons at a prize fight, unexplained, is not in itself conclusive proof of the intent to encourage the fight, but where the accused bet on the fight or shouted encouragement to the fighters, then that would amount to aiding and abetting. Thus, while mere voluntary presence, in itself, does not amount to aiding or abetting, presence together with some form of participation might.[9]

Defences to and Mitigations of Criminal Offences

There are many circumstances in which people charged with criminal offences will be able to escape responsibility, or some degree of responsibility, for their crime. For example, they may have inflicted harm in self-defence; they may have been enticed by the police to commit a crime (usually related to illegal drugs or prostitution); they may have been forced at gunpoint to help rob a bank; they may have been mistaken about a woman's consent to sexual relations; or they may have been too intoxicated or too emotionally or mentally disturbed to understand or appreciate the alleged offence.

These "excuses" for crime are highly controversial and are often criticized for supporting unjust societal assumptions. Is it reasonable, for example, that the voluntary consumption of alcohol should diminish an accused's responsibility for the offence of murder? Is it reasonable for a man who sexually assaults a woman to argue that he was mistaken about the woman's consent—that in his world, women "like it rough"? In these contexts—murder and sexual assault—the state of the criminal law often reflects the values of a culture that forgives men their trespasses and lends support to excessive use of alcohol.

In the pages that follow, we look at two specific kinds of defence to a criminal charge—drunkenness and mistake of fact. These are only two of many possible **defences or mitigations of criminal responsibility**. There are many other ways in which a person may defend himself or herself against a criminal charge. It may be possible, first, to negate *mens rea* or *actus reus*—to establish that the accused did not have the "evil intent" to commit the crime in question, or that he did not commit the "evil act" in question. For example, if an illegal substance is found in the accused's apartment, but the accused establishes that he had no knowledge of the presence of this illegal substance, this will negate *mens rea*—he had no evil intent to possess the prohibited substance. Similarly, if it is established that the accused attacked a victim after she was already dead, there can be no *actus reus* for homicide— no "evil act" of killing another human being.

As noted above, there are also a number of justifications for the commission of crimes: acting under duress, necessity, defence of the person, provocation, defence of property, and entrapment. If an accused is attacked on the street by a man wielding a baseball bat and defends himself, assaulting his attacker in the process, the person attacked will typically be able to claim self-defence, provided that his response was reasonable, given its circumstances and the nature of the threat posed by the initial attack.

Section 17 of the *Criminal Code* sets out a justification for the commission of crime under duress:

> 17. A person who commits an offence under compulsion by threats of immediate death or bodily harm from a person who is present when the offence is committed is excused for committing the offence if the person believes that the threats will be carried out and if the person is not a party to a conspiracy or association wherby the person is subject to compulsion, but this section does not apply where the offence that is committed is high treason or treason, murder, piracy, attempted murder, sexual assault, sexual assault with a weapon, threats to a third party or causing bodily harm, aggravated sexual assault, forcible abduction, hostage taking, robbery, assault with a weapon or causing bodily harm, aggravated assault, unlawfully causing bodily harm, arson, or an offence under sections 280 to 283 (abduction and detention of young persons).

In other words, in order for an accused to claim duress as a defence to a criminal charge, the threat must be immediate, the person making the threat must be present when the offence is committed, the accused

must believe that the threats will be carried out, and the person threatened must not be part of a criminal conspiracy. Finally, in most circumstances, Canadian courts have held that duress cannot apply as a defence where serious offences involving personal violence have been committed by an accused. The defence of necessity is somewhat similar to the defence of duress. The distinction is clearly explained by Mewett and Manning in their text on criminal law:

> There may arise the situation where a person is confronted with the choice of two evils. If he is faced with threats of death or grievous bodily harm if he does not commit an offence, he may have the defence of compulsion. Necessity may arise when he has a free choice between one thing and another and chooses the one that amounts to a criminal offence. A starving man may have to choose between starvation and stealing a loaf of bread; a man whose wife is in labour may have to choose between exceeding the speed limit or have his wife give birth in his car.[10]

In the case of *Morgentaler v. R.*,[11] a crime (as it then was) of procuring the miscarriage of a woman through the surgical intervention of abortion, the accused argued that his behaviour was necessary to protect the mental and/or physical health of the woman in question.

The defence of entrapment typically varies in instances of consensual crime. The police often intervene in the underground economy of drugs or prostitution, posing as interested purchasers of the services in question. The argument in some of these circumstances is that, had it not been for the actions of the police in requesting drugs or sex from the accused, the crime would not have been committed. In other words, normally law-abiding accused were "entrapped" by the actions of the police. Canadian courts have generally not permitted entrapment as a defence. Only in circumstances where police conduct amounts to an abuse of process—where conduct, in the words of section 24(2) of the *Charter*, "would bring the administration of justice into disrepute"—can this defence be successfully raised. In other words, it is not technically accurate to think of entrapment as a defence to a criminal charge. Rather, the court is asked to balance the value of illegally obtained evidence with the tendency of police conduct in obtaining that evidence to "bring the administration of justice into disrepute." If the tendency of the conduct to bring our system of justice into disrepute is greater than the value of the evidence obtained, the evidence will be excluded. If not, regardless of whether entrapment has taken place, the evidence will be admitted.

Finally, the *Charter* itself, as in the case of entrapment, can produce a range of potential "defences" to criminal charges, particularly in relation to sections 2 to 7 and section 15: for example, the right to freedom of expression; the right to life, liberty, and security of the person; the right to be tried within a reasonable time; the right to equality before the law; and so on.

The Defence of Drunkenness

Consider the following excerpt from the judgment of the Alberta Court of Appeal in the case of *R. v. Point;* the case makes clear that intoxication must be extreme in order to qualify as a defence to a criminal charge:

> Fraser, C.J.A. (for the Court): The defence appeals Deborah Point's conviction for the second degree murder of Audrey Trudeau. The primary ground of appeal is that the trial judge erred in the application of the "air of reality" test and as a result, wrongly declined to charge the jury on manslaughter, despite the request of both the Crown and the defence to do so. The defence contends that the trial judge ought to have left the lesser charge of manslaughter with the jury on the basis that Point may have been so impaired by alcohol that she lacked the necessary intent required for murder.
>
> Whether the defence of intoxication should be left with a jury is a question of law and is therefore subject to review on a standard of correctness: **R. v. Cinous** 2 S.C.R. 3, (2002) 162 C.C.C. (3d) 129 at 157 (S.C.C.).
>
> In considering whether a defence should be put to a jury, the threshold determination for the trial judge is whether it has an air of reality. Supreme Court of Canada decisions, including, most recently, **R. v. Cinous**, *supra* at 169, have made it clear that there are two components to the air of reality test:
>
> The question is whether there is (1) evidence (2) upon which a properly instructed jury acting reasonably could acquit if it believed the evidence to be true.
>
> The second part of this question requires the trial judge to determine whether the evidence relied upon is reasonably capable of supporting the inferences required to acquit the accused. The forensic evidence here revealed that the victim died from 15 crushing blows to the back of the head caused by either an axe or a hatchet or similar chopping weapon. All these blows were inflicted while she was alive. (Evidence of Dr. Alakija at A.B. 1420, 1459, 1436, and 1428.) This is the context in which the claimed defence of intoxication must be considered.

What then is the evidence of intoxication? Two Crown witnesses testified that on the night of the murder, Point had been drinking. One, Jeanne Revoy, stated that she saw Point for about two hours and that she was "drinking the whole time that [Ms. Revoy] was there," with "the bartender frequenting the table quite often" and "a lot of liquor buying and drinking" (at A.B. 1250). She testified that Point seemed to be "a little bit" under the influence of alcohol and that she "continued to drink . . . heavily" during the time that Revoy was at the bar (at A.B. 1251). Heather Humphrey testified that Point was "drinking, what appeared to be fairly heavily" and was "well on her way" to "getting drunk" (at A.B. 1259). Both witnesses described Point's pacing back and forth, apparently agitated. They also testified that Point threw her keys in the air and caught them repeatedly with a punching motion (at A.B. 1242–3, 1254–5). Point herself denied drinking heavily on the night in question and testified that she was not "a heavy drinker" (at A.B. 2276). Indeed, the most Point would say is: "I may have had a couple of drinks" (at A.B. 2276).

This is the extent of the evidence on intoxication. In our view, the conclusion of the trial judge that this evidence, if believed, could not reasonably raise a reasonable doubt, is correct. The trial judge heard extensive submissions from both the Crown and defence on this issue, carefully considered all the evidence and applicable law, as she was required to do, applied the correct test and determined that in these circumstances, there was no air of reality to a defence of intoxication. We agree.

The core issue is whether the evidence here, if believed, could reasonably support the inference that Point was too drunk to know that 15 forceful blows to the back of the victim's head with an axe or hatchet would likely cause serious bodily harm or death. The evidence on the degree of Point's alleged intoxication is minimal. Since neither Crown witness was cross-examined on the extent of Point's consumption of alcohol and since Point herself denied drinking heavily, there is no evidence as to how many drinks she consumed and over what period of time. Nor is there any evidence as to what Revoy meant when she testified that Point was "drinking heavily" or seemed to be "a little bit" under the influence of alcohol. Similarly, there is no evidence of what Humphrey meant when she testified that Point was "well on her way to getting drunk." Evidence of drinking is not, without more, evidence of intoxication and certainly not the degree of intoxication necessary to raise a reasonable doubt on the primary or secondary intent required for murder.

Nor was there any evidence of Point's physical or mental impairment. The nature, extent and force of the blows Point inflicted speak to physical co-ordination on her part and purposive action. The suggestion that she might not have known what the consequences were of her wielding an axe or hatchet in such a brutal manner because of drunkenness lacks any air of reality. There is nothing in the evidence of what happened when Trudeau was killed that would detract from this conclusion. Point never claimed that when she hit Trudeau with the axe she did not know or foresee that her actions would result in Trudeau's death. Instead, her defence was that she did not kill her.

In the result, there is nothing on the facts of this case that would lend an air of reality to the defence that Point lacked the necessary *mens rea* for the offence of murder because intoxication prevented her from knowing or foreseeing that the blows to Trudeau's head with an axe or hatchet were likely to cause death. This was the trial judge's conclusion and in our view, she did not err in failing to leave the defence of drunkenness vitiating the specific intent for murder with the jury. . . .

Finally, we are satisfied that on the issue of intent, the trial judge's charge, read as a whole, left this issue with the jury as required: ***R. v. Cooper***, 1993 CanLII 147 (S.C.C.), [1993] 1 S.C.R. 146; ***R. v. Evans***, 1993 CanLII 102 (S.C.C.), [1993] 2 S.C.R. 629.

Thus, in the result, the appeal must be dismissed.[12]

The *Point* case indicates that, while drunkenness continues to be a defence to a criminal charge (in order to reduce a conviction for murder to a conviction for manslaughter), such a claim can only be established in relatively restricted circumstances—those circumstances in which an "air of reality" exists. But should we go further? Should drunkenness ultimately be irrelevant to the determination of guilt and have potential applicability only to the sentence to be imposed?

The answer to this question was at least partially decided by the Supreme Court of Canada in the decade-old case of *Daviault v. R.*[13] In this case a 65-year-old woman who was confined to a wheelchair invited Mr. Daviault to her home for a drink. He brought with him a 40-ounce bottle of brandy. The complainant had a drink and fell asleep. When she awoke during the night to go to the bathroom, Mr. Daviault appeared, threw her on the bed, and sexually assaulted her. He had consumed seven or eight beers before arriving at the woman's home and drank the entire 40-ounce bottle of brandy between 6 p.m. and the assault some nine hours later. Mr. Daviault remembered nothing of the assault, having experienced an alcoholic blackout. Testimony at trial by the accused and by a pharmacologist supported the view that Mr. Daviault had lost contact with reality, his brain temporarily dissociated from normal functioning.

The Court held that Mr. Daviault's conviction could not stand, and ordered a new trial. The majority argued that even though voluntary intoxication may be reprehensible, it does not follow that its consequences in every conceivable situation are voluntary or predictable. Accordingly, if on rare occasions the accused can establish on a balance of probabilities that he was so intoxicated as to be in a state akin to automatism or insanity, he should not be held to have the *mens rea* necessary for criminal conviction. Further, the Court argued that a conviction of the accused in such circumstances would offend the presumption of innocence, and could not be saved by section 1 of the *Charter*.

There was, perhaps predictably, a negative public reaction to the Court's decision in *Daviault*. In response to much criticism of the Court's ruling, the federal government enacted section 33.1 of the *Criminal Code*, which states, in effect, that self-induced intoxication is no longer a defence to a criminal charge of "assault or any other interference or threat of interference by a person with the bodily integrity of another person." Drunkenness can, however, serve to reduce a charge of murder to one of manslaughter, as the *Point* case and many others indicate.

The Defence of Mistake of Fact

It is impossible in an introductory book to detail the law relating to all the defences to and mitigations of criminal charges: intoxication, insanity, self-defence, duress, entrapment, and mistake. Consider, however, the ambit of the defence of mistake of fact. If a man has an honest but mistaken belief that a woman has consented to sexual activity, should this preclude a conviction for sexual assault? What can you conclude from the following excerpts of facts in *Pappajohn v. R.*[14] and *Sansregret v. R.*[15]— should either accused be able to avail himself of the defence of honest but mistaken belief in consent, with the *mens rea* of the crime negated by this belief? First consider the case of *Pappajohn v. R.*:

> McIntyre J.: The complainant was a real estate saleswoman employed by a well-known and well-established real estate firm in Vancouver. She was successful in her work. The appellant is a businessman who was anxious to sell his home in Vancouver, and he had listed it for sale with the real estate firm with which the

complainant was associated. She was to be responsible for the matter on her firm's behalf. On August 4, 1976, at about 1:00 p.m., she met the appellant by appointment at a downtown restaurant for lunch. The purpose of the meeting was to discuss the house sale. The lunch lasted until about 4:00 or 4:30 p.m. During this time, a good deal of liquor was consumed by both parties. The occasion became convivial, the proprietor of the restaurant and his wife joined the party, and estimates of the amount of alcohol consumed varied in retrospect, as one would expect. It does seem clear, however, that while each of the parties concerned had a substantial amount to drink, each seemed capable of functioning normally.

At about 4:00 p.m. or shortly thereafter, they left the restaurant. The appellant drove the complainant's car while she sat in the front passenger seat. They went to the appellant's house, the one which was listed for sale, to further consider questions arising in that connection. Up to the time of arrival at the home, at about 4:30 or 5:00 p.m., there is no significant variation in their accounts of events. From the moment of arrival, however, there is a complete divergence. She related a story of rape completely against her will and over her protests and struggles. He spoke of an amorous interlude involving no more than a bit of coy objection on her part and several acts of intercourse with her consent. Whatever occurred in the house, there is no doubt that at about 7:30 p.m., the complainant ran out of the house naked, with a man's bow tie around her neck and her hands tightly tied behind her back with a bathrobe sash. She arrived at the door of a house nearby and demanded entry and protection. The occupant of the house, a priest, admitted her. She was in an upset state and exhibited great fear and emotional stress. The police were called, and these proceedings followed . . .

Dickson, J.: There is circumstantial evidence supportive of a plea of belief in consent: (1) Her necklace and car keys were found in the living room. (2) She confirmed his testimony that her blouse was neatly hung in the clothes closet. (3) Other items of folded clothing were found at the foot of the bed. (4) None of her clothes were damaged in the slightest way. (5) She was in the house for a number of hours. (6) By her version, when she entered the house, the appellant said he was going to break her. She made no attempt to leave. (7) She did not leave while he undressed. (8) There was no evidence of struggle. (9) She suffered no physical injuries, aside from three scratches. . . .

Now consider the Supreme Court of Canada's decision in *R. v. Sansregret*:

> McIntyre, J.: The appellant, a man in his early 20s and the complainant, a woman of 31 years, had lived together in the complainant's house for about a year before the events of October 15, 1982. Their relationship had been one of contention and discord with violence on the part of the appellant: "slappings" or "roughing up" in his description, "blows" in hers. The appellant had left the house for short periods and in September 1982, the complainant decided to end the affair. She told the appellant to leave and he did.
>
> On September 23, 1982, some days after his dismissal, the appellant broke into the house at about 4:30 a.m. He was "raging" at her and furious because of his expulsion. He terrorized her with a filelike instrument with which he was armed. She was fearful of what might occur, and in order to calm him down, she held out some hope of a reconciliation and they had intercourse. A report was made to the police of this incident, the complainant asserting she had been raped, but no proceedings were taken. The appellant's probation officer became involved and there was evidence that he had asked the complainant not to press the matter, presumably because it would interfere with the appellant's probation.
>
> On October 15, 1982, again at about 4:30 a.m., the appellant broke into the complainant's house through a basement window. She was alone, and awakened by the entry, she seized the bedroom telephone in an effort to call the police. The appellant picked up a butcher knife in the kitchen and came into the bedroom. He was furious and violent. He accused her of having another boyfriend; pulled the cord of the telephone out of the jack and threw it into the living room; threatened her with the knife and ordered her to take off her nightdress and made her stand in the kitchen doorway, naked save for a jacket over her shoulders, so he could be sure where she was while he repaired the window to conceal his entry from the police, should they arrive. He struck her on the mouth with sufficient force to draw blood, and on three occasions rammed the knife blade into the wall with great force, once very close to her. He told her that if the police came, he would put the knife through her, and added that if he had found her with a boyfriend, he would have killed them both. At one point, he tied her hands behind her back with a scarf. The complainant said she was in fear for her life and sanity.
>
> By about 5:30 a.m., after an hour of such behaviour by the appellant, she tried to calm him down. She pretended that there was

some hope of a reconciliation if the appellant would settle down and get a job. This had the desired effect. He calmed down and after some conversation, he joined her on the bed and they had intercourse. The complainant swore that her consent to the intercourse was solely for the purpose of calming him down, to protect herself from further violence. This, she said, was something she had learned from earlier experience with him. In her evidence she said:

> *I didn't consent at any time.*
>
> *I was very afraid. My whole body was trembling. I was sure I would have a nervous breakdown. I came very, very close to losing my mind. All I knew was I had to keep this man calm or he would kill me.*

At about 6:45 a.m., after further conversation with the appellant, she got dressed and prepared to leave for work. She had a business appointment at 8:00 a.m. She drove the appellant to a location which he chose, and in the course of the journey, he returned her keys and some money that he had taken from her purse upon his arrival in the early morning. Upon dropping him off, she drove immediately to her mother's home, where she made a complaint of rape. The police were called and the appellant was arrested that evening.

In both *Pappajohn* and *Sansregret,* the Canadian judiciary was divided about the defence of mistaken belief in consent. In *Pappajohn,* Supreme Court Justice Dickson concluded, "It does not follow that, by simply disbelieving the appellant on consent, in fact, the jury thereby found that there was no belief in consent and that the appellant could not reasonably have believed in consent."[16] In other words, the appellant may not have been believed by the jury, but the jury may have been mistaken. And in *Sansregret,* the trial judge concluded:

> [H]is honest belief finds support in the testimony of the complainant. She knows him and, in her opinion, notwithstanding all the objective facts to the contrary, he did believe that everything was back to normal between them by the time of the sexual encounter. His subsequent behaviour as well attests to that fact.
>
> I do not like the conclusion which this leads me to. There was no real consent. There was submission as a result of a very real and justifiable fear. No one in his right mind could have believed that the complainant's dramatic about-face stemmed from anything other than fear. But the accused did. He saw what he wanted to see, heard what he wanted to hear, believed what he wanted to believe.

Both cases were resolved in the Supreme Court of Canada, and in both instances, the accused was convicted. The defence of honest mistake of fact remains as a legal possibility, but it seems clear that it is not to be a purely subjective test of the accused's intention; wholly unreasonable beliefs, however honestly held, are not likely to be viewed as negating the *mens rea* required for conviction.

In 1992, partially in response to cases such as *Daviault, Pappajohn,* and *Sansregret*, the federal government enacted the following definitions of consent with respect to sexual assault:

Meaning of "consent"

273.1(1)   Subject to subsection (2) and subsection 265(3), "consent" means, for the purposes of sections 271, 272 and 273, the voluntary agreement of the complainant to engage in the sexual activity in question.

Where no consent obtained

273.1(2)   No consent is obtained, for the purpose of sections 271, 272 and 273, where

 (a) *the agreement is expressed by the words or conduct of a person other than the complainant;*

 (b) *the complainant is incapable of consenting to the activity;*

 (c) *the accused induces the complainant to engage in the activity by abusing a position of trust, power or authority;*

 (d) *the complainant expresses, by words or conduct, a lack of agreement to engage in the activity; or*

 (e) *the complainant, having consented to engage in sexual activity, expresses, by words or conduct, a lack of agreement to continue to engage in the activity.*

273.1(3)   Nothing in subsection (2) shall be construed as limiting the circumstances in which no consent is obtained.

Where belief in consent not a defence

273.2   It is not a defence to a charge under section 271, 272 or 273 that the accused believed that the complainant consented to the activity that forms the subject-matter of the charge, where

 (a) *the accused's belief arose from the accused's*

  (i) *self-induced intoxication, or*

  (ii) *recklessness or wilful blindness; or*

 (b) *the accused did not take reasonable steps, in the circumstances known to the accused at the time, to ascertain that the complainant was consenting.*

The most recent pronouncement of the Supreme Court of Canada with respect to mistake of fact is to be found in the 1999 decision of *R. v. Ewanchuk*.[17] Steve Ewanchuk was a man in his late thirties, living in Edmonton, looking for staff to work at his retail booths in several shopping malls in the city. The complainant was a seventeen-year-old woman who was looking for work. At Ewanchuk's suggestion, her job interview took place in his trailer, where he stored the custom wood products that he was selling. Ewanchuk was quite friendly with the young woman, touching her hand, arms, and shoulder as he spoke. He asked her to give him a massage, as he was feeling tense. She agreed, but later told the court that she was made uneasy by his request. He then began massaging her, bringing his hands up close to her breasts. She pushed her elbows in between his arms and said "No."

The accused stopped immediately, but later asked the young woman to turn and face him. He began massaging her feet, and his touching progressed up to her inner thigh and pelvic area. She was uncomfortable, but worried that he might become violent. He began to lay himself against her and grind his pelvic area into hers. He asked her to put her arms around him, but she did not. After about a minute of this pelvic grinding, she asked him to stop, which he again did.

Ewanchuk then reached over to hug the complainant, and once again, continued his pelvic grinding. He also moved his hand inside her shorts for a brief time and, while on top of her, fumbled with his shorts and took out his penis. Once again, she asked him to stop, and once again he did, saying something to the effect of, "It's okay. See, I'm a nice guy. I stopped."

The accused then got up, opened his wallet, and gave the complainant a $100 bill, saying that it was for the massage, and asking her not to tell anyone about it. Shortly after receiving the money, she said that she had to go; she left the trailer, walked home, and called the police. At trial, Ewanchuk was acquitted by the trial judge on the basis of "implied consent."[18] More specifically, the judge could not be convinced beyond a reasonable doubt of a lack of consent.

When the case was reviewed by the Supreme Court of Canada, however, Ewanchuk's actions were seen as sexual assaults. As the Court noted,

> [T]he accused relies on the fact that he momentarily stopped his advances each time the complainant said No as evidence of his good intentions. This demonstrates that he understood the complainant's Nos to mean precisely that. ... The trial record conclusively establishes that the accused's persistent and increasingly serious advances constituted a sexual assault for which he had no defence.

This is a reasonable inference. Ewanchuk's first attempt to engage in a physical relationship did not amount to sexual assault, but his persistence in the face of opposition, and his eventual offering of a $100 bill, point to his knowledge that he was engaging in sexual advances that were not wanted.

As the prominent Canadian criminal law professor Alan Young has noted, 20 years ago Ewanchuk would have been labelled a male pig, but never have been convicted of a crime because of the lack of resistance by the complainant—"her passivity would have been taken as a sign of consent." According to Young, Ewanchuk's conviction was probably justified, considering the combination of the age difference, the location of the activity, his persistence, and his indifference to her requests.[19] But consider the precedent set by the language of the Supreme Court of Canada in *Ewanchuk*:

> If the trier of fact accepts the complainant's testimony that she did not consent, no matter how strongly her conduct may contradict that claim, the absence of consent is established. . . . There is no defense of implied consent to sexual assault in Canada . . . the complainant's fear need not be reasonable, nor must it be communicated to the accused in order for consent to be vitiated.

The bottom line, as Young notes, is that "convictions will be obtained even if women do not express or manifest their fears, and even if women do not express or manifest a lack of consent. Criminality is established once the complainant testified that she subjectively and internally felt that way."[20]

The Supreme Court went even further, however, requiring consent to be communicated by the complainant, in order to avoid criminal conviction:

> . . . the evidence must show that he believed that the complainant communicated consent to engage in the sexual activity in question. A belief by the accused that the complainant, in her own mind, wanted him to touch her, but did not express that desire, is not a defence. The accused's speculation as to what was going on in the complainant's mind provides no defence.[21]

The Supreme Court's commentary in *Ewanchuk*, independent of the appropriateness of its decision, raises significant questions about the meaning of consent and the ambit of the defence of mistake of fact in such circumstances.

Self-Defence: *R. v. Lavallee*

A clear defence to a criminal charge of assault and to other offences against persons is to be found in self-defence—the concept that the assault, or, in some circumstances, even the homicide, cannot be labelled a culpable act as the individual in question was only defending him or herself (in the case of a homicide, from a potentially lethal attack). Section 34 of the *Criminal Code*[22] states:

> 34. (1) Every one who is unlawfully assaulted without having provoked the assault is justified in repelling force by force if the force he uses is not intended to cause death or grievous bodily harm and is no more than is necessary to enable him to defend himself.
>
> (2) Every one who is unlawfully assaulted and who causes death or grievous bodily harm in repelling the assault is justified if
>
> > (a) he causes it under reasonable apprehension of death or grievous bodily harm from the violence with which the assault was originally made or with which the assailant pursues his purposes; and
> >
> > (b) he believes, on reasonable grounds, that he cannot otherwise preserve himself from death or grievous bodily harm.

Consider the ambit of this defence in the 1990 decision of the Supreme Court in *R. v. Lavallee*.[23] Lyn Lavallee had been living with Kevin Rust for three to four years. From all accounts it was a highly dysfunctional and violent relationship. Rust beat Lavallee regularly, and had threatened to kill her. She had pointed a gun at Rust on at least two occasions and threatened to kill him if he ever touched her again.

One summer night in August 1986 Lavallee shot Rust in the back of the head as he was leaving her bedroom. She made the following statement to the police:

> He grabbed me by the arm right there. There's a bruise on my face also where he slapped me. He didn't slap me right then, first he yelled at me, then he pushed me and I pushed him back and he hit me twice on the right-hand side of my head. I was scared. All I thought about was all the other times he used to beat me, I was scared. I was shaking as usual. The rest is a blank, all I remember is he gave me the gun and a shot was fired through my screen. This is all so fast. And then the guns were in another room and he loaded it the second shot and gave it to me. And I was going to shoot myself. I pointed it to myself, I was so upset. OK, and then he went

and I was sitting on the bed and he started going like this with his finger (Lavallee made a shaking motion with her index finger) and said something like "You're my old lady and you do as you're told" or something like that. He said, "Wait till everybody leaves, you'll get it then," and he said something to the effect of "Either you kill me or I'll get you," that was what it was. He kind of smiled and then he turned around. I shot him but I aimed out. I thought I aimed above him and a piece of his head went that way.

The arresting officer told the court that en route to the police station Lavallee had said "He said if I didn't kill him first he would kill me. I hope he lives. I really love him."

The Supreme Court of Canada concluded that Lyn Lavallee was not guilty of any criminal offence—that her actions in shooting Kevin Rust amounted to self-defence. The decision has met with mixed reviews. Many women's groups have praised the judgment as an important step forward, a long overdue expansion of the concept of self-defence through recognition that a battered woman does not need to be in immediate danger of being killed to have a reasonable fear of lethal attack. Others have been sharply critical, suggesting that her actions are highly relevant to the sentence to be imposed, but not to the issue of her guilt of the crime of manslaughter. The issue of the ambit of self-defence is particularly difficult to calculate, particularly in cases where there has been a lengthy history of physical abuse. A reasonable conception of danger may vary significantly from one individual to the next.

Sentencing: Does the Punishment Fit the Crime?

The **sentencing** of those convicted of criminal offences is of great interest to Canadians. Discussions about crime in the House of Commons typically centre on the penalties thought to be appropriate for certain kinds of crimes. As discussed in earlier chapters, the *Criminal Code* sets out three categories of criminal offences: summary offences, indictable offences, and **hybrid offences**. A maximum penalty for **summary conviction offences** is stated in s. 787(1) of the *Code:*

> 787.(1) Except where otherwise provided by law, everyone who is convicted of an offence punishable on summary conviction is liable to a fine of not more than two thousand dollars or to imprisonment for six months or to both.

The *Criminal Code* sets punishments for indictable offences according to the nature of the prohibited conduct. A conviction for the indictable offence of first degree murder, for example, carries an automatic term of life imprisonment without parole eligibility for 25 years; conviction for the indictable offence of sexual assault with a weapon carries a term of up to 14 years' imprisonment. All stated punishments are a maximum, unless otherwise indicated.

Sentencing attempts to accomplish a range of potentially complementary purposes: general deterrence, specific deterrence, community denunciation, and rehabilitation. When a court adopts the principle of general deterrence, it imposes a sentence in order to deter the general public from committing the specific crime. Specific deterrence is deterrence particular to the individual offender; the court attempts to find a penalty that is sufficient to deter that offender. Community denunciation, although often conceptualized as state vengeance, can also be understood and appreciated for its educative purpose and impact. As the Ontario Court of Appeal noted in *R. v. Ramdass* social denunciation can fairly be linked to the possibility of a general deterrent effect:

> The sentence by emphasizing community disapproval of an act and branding it as reprehensible has a moral or educative effect and thereby affects the attitude of the public. One then hopes that a person with an attitude thus conditioned to regard conduct as reprehensible will not likely commit such an act.[24]

The sentencing goal of rehabilitation is somewhat more elusive, focusing society's response on the offender rather than on the act committed by the offender. The rise of rehabilitation as a sentencing strategy reflects a belief in the science of corrections. Legislators and the judiciary now share—with social scientists, psychiatrists, and administrators—the responsibility for the control of criminals. As Clayton Ruby notes in his book *Sentencing*,

> the promise has been hollow. Often individual liberty is imperiled by claims to knowledge and therapeutic effectiveness that we do not possess and by failure to candidly concede what we do not know. At times, it is the practitioners of the behavioural sciences who are guilty of these faults; but more often, legislators, lawyers, and public foolishly assume an expertise and an efficacy that simply [do] not exist.[25]

Ruby goes on to discuss the factors considered most important in arriving at an appropriate sentence for a specific crime. He sets out 10 such factors:

1. the degree of premeditation involved;
2. the circumstances surrounding the actual commission of the offence; i.e., the manner in which it was committed, the amount of violence involved, the employment of an offensive weapon, and the degree of active participation by each offender;
3. the gravity of the crime committed, in regard to which the maximum punishment provided by statute is an indication;
4. the attitude of the offender after the commission of the crime, as this serves to indicate the degree of criminality involved and throws some light on the character of the participant;
5. the previous criminal record, if any, of the offender;
6. the age, mode of life, character, and personality of the offender;
7. any recommendation of the trial judge, any presentence or probation official's report, or any mitigating or other circumstances properly brought to the attention of [the] Court;
8. incidence of crime in jurisdiction;
9. sentences customarily imposed for the same or similar offences;
10. mercy.[26]

How these factors are to be interpreted is largely a matter of ideology, with individual judges espousing social and political choices, albeit within the framework of existing statute and case law. Consider *R. v. Horon*, for example.

> Stevenson, J.A.: The Crown seeks to appeal the sentence (a fine, probation, a community service order, and a two-year driving prohibition) imposed upon the accused for impaired driving causing bodily harm.
>
> The issue we must address is the approach to be taken in imposing a sentence for this consequence-related crime.
>
> The accused, respondent, had been drinking at a party. The evidence is that he was in a depressed state and an alcoholic. One witness testified she urged the accused not to drive because of his condition. He drove moving to the wrong side of the road. An oncoming vehicle took evasive action and the accused then turned

toward the right side of the road, resulting in a head-on collision. The oncoming driver suffered a fractured wrist and lacerations to the head and knee. The accused was convicted after a trial. . . .

Parliament has laid to rest any argument about the irrelevancy of the consequences. The wrong is to take control of a motor vehicle when ability is impaired by alcohol. The punishment will reflect the consequences. It will also reflect any other aggravating factors which exacerbate the wrong, such as undertaking that control when the accused has been warned of the risks attendant upon driving in the impaired condition, or the degree of impairment (which may be evidenced by the driving pattern). . . .

A number of appellate authorities deal with punishment for impaired driving causing injury or death. . . . In *R. v. Gutoski,* January 4, 1990, the Manitoba Court of Appeal . . . expressed the view that a sentence of imprisonment is normally required in such cases. They also noted that since the gravamen of the offence is driving while impaired, excuses for the drinking do not excuse the criminal conduct of driving afterwards. I agree with that proposition and add that, once the offence is found, drink-induced inability to comprehend the extent of the impairment or the possible consequences will not be a mitigating circumstance. The Court there imposed a sentence of six months' imprisonment where young children suffered moderately severe injuries as a result of the accused's impaired driving. . . .

I have already outlined the circumstances of this case. The driving pattern was "not bad." Fortunately, the injuries were not serious. What then are the aggravating and mitigating factors applicable to this accused?

In aggravation there was . . . "a serious, significant level of impairment." There is evidence he was cautioned not to drive. There is an old record of impaired driving.

In mitigation, the judge notes the accused to be a fine upstanding citizen except for the drinking problems. He showed remorse and a desire to rehabilitate himself, manifested by a prompt entry into a treatment program which he has followed. There is considerable evidence of rehabilitation and we note that some of his family are dependent upon his ability to continue working. Rehabilitation, reducing the risk of reoffending is relevant, but cannot overwhelm a deterrent sentence. It all lies in the mouth of an accused to plead the hardship his action brings to others. Nonetheless, undue hardship may be a ground for tempering an otherwise appropriate sentence. The judge also cites the special circumstances that led the accused into alcoholism and into drinking on this occasion. Having regard to the gravamen of this offence, namely operating a motor vehicle when impaired, these special circumstances cannot mitigate.

In my view, a jail sentence is necessary in this case. Having regard to the factors I have discussed, the ends of justice would be served by a two-month sentence. The probation and prohibition order remain. The accused may elect to serve this sentence intermittently and may apply through the registrar to any member of the Court to fix reporting times. He will be governed by the probation order when not serving the sentence.

The community service order and fine are vacated.[27]

Sentencing an accused convicted of a criminal offence is a judicial exercise that relies upon a complex matrix of relevant concerns. Offence and offender are placed against the backdrop of existing precedents and are further constrained, to some degree at least, by the mood of legislators and the public, as expressed within a specific historical context. In *Horon,* the judge notes that the accused is a father with dependants and "a fine upstanding citizen"; these are factors that mitigate his punishment. One might ask, however, why men without children who cannot claim to be "fine upstanding citizens" should be treated more harshly for the crime of impaired driving causing bodily harm.

Finally, we should consider the future of sentencing. To date, our courts in Canada and in most other Western jurisdictions have been dominated by a rationale of either punishment or enforced treatment. In the sentencing circles that have recently emerged among Canada's Aboriginal peoples, we see an alternative model, one that stresses restoration, consensus, and the building of community, in response to the offender's crime. Consider the following excerpt from *Canadian Criminology.* Could this kind of approach find an appeal that extends beyond Canada's Aboriginal community?

One of the more innovative approaches to sentencing is "circle sentencing," which is being practised by territorial and provincial judges in the Yukon Territory and in several provinces. In circle sentencing, all of the participants in the case—the judge, prosecutor, defence lawyer, victim, offender, and community residents—sit in a circular arrangement and discuss all facets of the case. The circle, which represents a radical departure from the formal courtroom decorum, is designed to break down the formality of the court process and to provide a forum for the disposition of cases that is based on healing, consensus building, and returning to communities the responsibility for resolving conflicts.

The discussions surrounding the case centre not only on the offender and his or her behaviour, but also on the needs of the victims and the community. Community sentencing is an attempt to empower communities and to provide a mechanism for residents, aboriginal and nonaboriginal alike, to become directly involved in the delivery of justice services.

In cases adjudicated in sentencing circles, the judge sets an upper limit on the sentence that may be imposed. Participants in the circle informally discuss the offender and his or her circumstances. When the discussion has concluded, a consensus on the most appropriate sentence is reached, and this is the disposition that is imposed on the offender. Circle sentencing not only empowers the community, but also expands the information base from which sentencing decisions are made. In addition to considering the facts of the case and the circumstance of the offender, the discussions in sentencing circles often include a dialogue on problems that exist in the community and how these can be addressed and resolved.[28]

An amendment to the *Criminal Code* in 1995 codified the purpose and principles of sentencing in Canada.

Purpose

718. The fundamental purpose of sentencing is to contribute, along with crime prevention initiatives, to respect for the law and the maintenance of a just, peaceful and safe society by imposing just sanctions that have one or more of the following objectives:

    (a) to denounce unlawful conduct;

    (b) to deter the offender and other persons from committing offences;

    (c) to separate offenders from society, where necessary;

    (d) to assist in rehabilitating offenders;

    (e) to provide reparations for harm done to victims or to the community; and

    (f) to promote a sense of responsibility in offenders, and acknowledgment of the harm done to victims and to the community.

This section simply sets out the objectives of the sentencing process, as developed within the common law. A more controversial sentencing principle emerged, however, in the same amendment to the *Criminal Code*. Section 718.2(e) states: "A court that imposes a sentence shall also take into consideration the following principles: (e) all available sanctions other than imprisonment that are reasonable in the circumstances should be considered for all offenders, with particular attention to the circumstances of aboriginal offenders."

This principle was more clearly set out in the Supreme Court of Canada's decision in *R. v. Gladue.*[29] In this case the Supreme Court made it very clear that sentencing judges must take into account the unique circumstances of Aboriginal peoples in sentencing—that the kind of sentence appropriate for an Aboriginal person may well be quite different from the kind of sentence appropriate for a non-Aboriginal person, whether he or she is living on or off a reserve. This decision has, perhaps understandably, provoked a significant amount of discussion, with both Aboriginal and non-Aboriginal support and criticism. Some argue that the decision is a politically correct justification of inequality, while others argue that *Gladue* represents an important first step toward recognizing the distinct nature of First Nations peoples within Canada's criminal justice system.

Conclusion: The Criminal Law as a Barometer of Culture

The criminal law, like all forms of law, is, for better or worse, a barometer of the culture in which we live. In closing, we should recall a point made at the outset of this chapter: the task of those who create, enforce, and administer this law is to continually question the circumstances in which such force should be used. To paraphrase Churchill, how we define and respond to our criminals will tell us a lot about ourselves.

Web Links

International Centre for Criminal Law Reform and Criminal Justice Policy
http://www.icclr.law.ubc.ca/index.htm
This website has an excellent publications page that provides access to documents on issues of criminal law.

Criminal Lawyers' Association
http://www.criminallawyers.ca/links.htm
This is the website for the Criminal Lawyers' Association, an organization of criminal lawyers in Canada. It provides direct links to most

national and many international sites of interest to criminal lawyers, including links to relevant statutes, to Supreme Court decisions, journals, and to other associations of criminal lawyers.

Criminal Code of Canada
http://laws.justice.gc.ca/en/C-46/index.html
The text of the *Criminal Code* is available online from the Department of Justice.

Questions for Discussion

1. What purposes are served by enforcing *Criminal Code* and *Controlled Drugs and Substances Act* provisions relating to the trade in drugs or the trade in sexual services? Are these businesses too exploitive to be capable of public-health regulation? What is the nature of the exploitation in each instance? Can drug distribution and prostitution be seen as similar to other forms of commerce that are not criminalized?

2. Which test of intention for murder is more compelling: subjective or objective? Do you agree or disagree with the former chief justice Lamer's argument that for murder charges, "it is crucial . . . that the jury understand there must be intention to cause bodily harm which the accused knows is likely to cause death. Intention to cause bodily harm, without knowledge that such is likely to cause death, is not sufficient"?

3. Do you agree or disagree with Churchill's observation that the strength of a civilization is to be seen in the way it responds to crime?

Further Reading

Mewett, A.W., and S. Nakatsuru. *An Introduction to the Criminal Process in Canada.* 4th ed. Toronto: Carswell, 2000.

> This text provides an introduction to criminal procedure in Canada, covering all stages of the criminal process from arrest to conviction and sentencing. The text's emphasis on procedure complements this chapter's presentation of the more basic building blocks of criminal law.

Verdun-Jones, S. *Criminal Law in Canada: Cases, Questions, and the Code*. 3d ed. Toronto: Nelson Thomson Learning, 2002.

> This text presents a very useful combination of general principles of the criminal law and an analysis of specific cases. The book's 10 chapters cover subjective and objective liability in the *mens rea* of crime, the *actus reus* elements of a criminal offence, causation, regulatory offences, modes of participation in crime, mental disorder as a defence to crime, and more generally, defences to criminal charges. An excellent source of information for an informed lay reader.

Watt, D., and M. Fuerst. *The 2005 Annotated Tremeear's Criminal Code*. Student Ed. Toronto: Carswell, 2004.

> This annotated code, prepared as a student edition, is an extremely useful source of information about the changing content of Canada's *Criminal Code*. The annotations allow the student to understand, at least in a cursory manner, the changes to law over time.

Notes

1. A.W. Mewett and M. Manning, *Criminal Law* (Toronto: Butterworths, 1978), 11.
2. H. Schwendinger and J. Schwendinger, "Defenders of Order or Guardians of Human Rights?" in *Critical Criminology,* edited by I. Taylor, P. Walton, and J. Young (London, U.K.: Routledge and Kegan Paul, 1975), 132–7.
3. S. Box, *Deviance, Reality and Society*, 2d ed. (London, U.K.: Holt, Rinehart and Winston, 1981), 97.
4. ——.
5. O.W. Holmes [1863], cited in D. Stuart and R. Delisle, *Learning Canadian Criminal Law* (Toronto: Carswell, 1986), 254–5.
6. Cited in Stuart and Delisle, *Learning Canadian Criminal Law*, 255.
7. *R. v. Hundal*, [1993] 79 C.C.C. (3d) 97 at 99–109 (S.C.C.). (Reproduced with permission of Canada Law Book, through the Canadian Copyright Licensing Agency [CANCOPY].)
8. See *Reference re: Section 94 (2) of the Motor Vehicle Act (B.C.)* (1986), 147 D.L.R. (3d) 539.
9. Mewett and Manning, *Criminal Law*, 43.
10. Ibid., 302.
11. (1975), 20 C.C.C. (2d) 449 (S.C.C.).
12. *R. v. Point*, 2003 ABCA 113.

13. [1994] 93 C.C.C. (3d) 21 (S.C.C.).
14. [1980] 2 S.C.R. 120.
15. [1985] 1 S.C.R. 570.
16. *Pappajohn v. R.*, [1980] 2 S.C.R. 120.
17. 131 C.C.C. (3d) 481. (1999).
18. 131 C.C.C. (3d) 494. (1999).
19. A. Young, *Justice Defiled* (Toronto: Key Porter Books, 2003), 73.
20. Ibid.
21. This section on the Ewanchuk case is taken from Neil Boyd, *Big Sister: How Extreme Feminism Has Betrayed the Fight for Sexual Equality* (Vancouver: Greystone, 2004), 177–179.
22. R.S., 1985, c. C-46, s. 34; 1992, c. 1, s. 60(F).
23. 55 C.C.C. (3d) 97 (S.C.C.).
24. *R. v. Ramdass* (1983), 2 C.C.C. (3d) 247 at 249 (Ont. C.A.).
25. C.C. Ruby, *Sentencing*, 3d ed. (Toronto: Butterworths, 1987), 15.
26. Ibid., 21–2.
27. *R. v. Horon* (1990), 58 C.C.C. (3d) 418 at 420–423. (Reproduced with permission of Canada Law Book, through the Canadian Copyright Licensing Agency [CANCOPY].)
28. M.A. Jackson and C.T. Griffiths, eds., *Canadian Criminology; Perspectives on Crime and Criminality,* 2d ed. (Toronto: Harcourt Brace, 1995), 396. (Reprinted with permission of Nelson Thomson Learning, a division of ThomsonLearning.)
29. [1999] 1 S.C.R. 688.

References

Boyd, N. *The Last Dance: Murder in Canada*. Scarborough: Prentice-Hall, 1988.

——. *High Society: Legal and Illegal Drugs in Canada*. Toronto: Key Porter, 1991.

——. *Big Sister: How Extreme Feminism Has Betrayed the Fight for Sexual Equality*. Vancouver, Greystone, 2004.

Boyle, C.M. *Sexual Assault*. Toronto: Carswell, 1984.

Grosman. B., ed. *New Directions in Sentencing*. Toronto: Butterworths, 1980.

Healy, P. "R. v. Bernard: Difficulties with Voluntary Intoxication." *McGill Law Journal* 35 (1990): 610.

Jackson, M.A., and C.T. Griffiths. *Canadian Criminology: Perspectives on Crime and Criminality*. 2d ed. Toronto: Harcourt Brace, 1995.

Law Reform Commission of Canada. *Recodifying Criminal Law: Working Paper 31*. Ottawa: Law Reform Commission of Canada, 1988.

MacLean, B.D. *The Political Economy of Crime: Readings for a Critical Criminology*. Scarborough: Prentice-Hall, 1986.

Mewett, A.W. *An Introduction to the Criminal Process in Canada*. Toronto: Carswell, 1987.

Osborne, J. "Rape Law Reform: The New Cosmetic for Canadian Women." *Women and Politics* 4 (1984): 49.

Packer, H. *Limits of the Criminal Sanction*. Stanford: Stanford University Press, 1968.

Ruby, C.C. *Sentencing*. 5th ed. Toronto: Butterworths, 1999.

Schur, E. *Victimless Crimes*. Englewood Cliffs, NJ: Prentice-Hall, 1974.

Stuart, D., and R. Delisle. *Learning Canadian Criminal Law*. 6th ed. Toronto: Carswell, 1999.

Verdun-Jones, S. *Criminal Law in Canada, Cases, Questions and the Code*. 3rd ed. Toronto: Nelson Thomson, 2002.

Williams, G. *The Mental Element in Crime*. Jerusalem: Magnes Press, 1965.

Zimring, F., and G. Hawkins. *Deterrence*. Chicago: University of Chicago Press, 1974.

Appendix

Canadian Charter of Rights and Freedoms Part 1 – Schedule B of the Constitution Act, 1982

Whereas Canada is founded upon principles that recognize the supremacy of God and the rule of law:

Guarantee of Rights and Freedoms

1.   The *Canadian Charter of Rights and Freedoms* guarantees the rights and freedoms set out in it subject only to such reasonable limits prescribed by law as can be demonstrably justified in a free and democratic society.

Fundamental Freedoms

2.   Everyone has the following fundamental freedoms:
   (a)   freedom of conscience and religion;
   (b)   freedom of thought, belief, opinion and expression, including freedom of the press and other media of communication;
   (c)   freedom of peaceful assembly; and
   (d)   freedom of association.

Democratic Rights

3.   Every citizen of Canada has the right to vote in an election of members of the House of Commons or of a legislative assembly and to be qualified for membership therein.

4.   (1)   No House of Commons and no legislative assembly shall continue for longer than five years from the date fixed for the return of the writs at a general election of its members.
   (2)   In time of real or apprehended war, invasion or insurrection, a House of Commons may be continued by Parliament and a legislative assembly may be continued by the legislature beyond five years if such continuation is not opposed by the votes of more than one-third of the members of the House of Commons or the legislative assembly, as the case may be.

5.   There shall be a sitting of Parliament and of each legislature at least once every twelve months.

Mobility Rights

6. (1) Every citizen of Canada has the right to enter, remain in and leave Canada.

(2) Every citizen of Canada and every person who has the status of a permanent resident of Canada has the right

    (a) to move to and take up residence in any province; and

    (b) to pursue the gaining of a livelihood in any province.

(3) The rights specified in subsection (2) are subject to

    (a) any laws or practices of general application in force in a province other than those that discriminate among persons primarily on the basis of province of present or previous residence; and

    (b) any laws providing for reasonable residency requirements as a qualification for the receipt of publicly provided social services.

(4) Subsections (2) and (3) do not preclude any law, program or activity that has as its object the amelioration in a province of conditions of individuals in that province who are socially or economically disadvantaged if the rate of employment in that province is below the rate of employment in Canada.

Legal Rights

7. Everyone has the right to life, liberty and security of the person and the right not to be deprived thereof except in accordance with the principles of fundamental justice.

8. Everyone has the right to be secure against unreasonable search or seizure.

9. Everyone has the right not to be arbitrarily detained or imprisoned.

10. Everyone has the right on arrest or detention

    (a) to be informed promptly of the reasons therefor;

    (b) to retain and instruct counsel without delay and to be informed of that right; and

    (c) to have the validity of the detention determined by way of *habeas corpus* and to be released if the detention is not lawful.

11. Any person charged with an offence has the right

    (a) to be informed without unreasonable delay of the specific offence;

    (b) to be tried within a reasonable time;

    (c) not to be compelled to be a witness in proceedings against that person in respect of the offence;

    (d) to be presumed innocent until proven guilty according to law in a fair and public hearing by an independent and impartial tribunal;

    (e) not to be denied reasonable bail without just cause;

(f) except in the case of an offence under military law tried before a military tribunal, to the benefit of trial by jury where the maximum punishment for the offence is imprisonment for five years or a more severe punishment;

(g) not to be found guilty on account of any act or omission unless, at the time of the act or omission, it constituted an offence under Canadian or international law or was criminal according to the general principles of law recognized by the community of nations;

(h) if finally acquitted of the offence, not to be tried for it again and, if finally found guilty and punished for the offence, not to be tried or punished for it again; and

(i) if found guilty of the offence and if the punishment for the offence has been varied between the time of commission and the time of sentencing, to the benefit of the lesser punishment.

12.   Everyone has the right not to be subjected to any cruel and unusual treatment or punishment.

13.   A witness who testifies in any proceedings has the right not to have any incriminating evidence so given used to incriminate that witness in any other proceedings, except in a prosecution for perjury or for the giving of contradictory evidence.

14.   A party or witness in any proceedings who does not understand or speak the language in which the proceedings are conducted or who is deaf has the right to the assistance of an interpreter.

Equality Rights

15.   (1) Every individual is equal before and under the law and has the right to the equal protection and equal benefit of the law without discrimination and, in particular, without discrimination based on race, national or ethnic origin, colour, religion, sex, age or mental or physical disability.

(2) Subsection (1) does not preclude any law, program or activity that has as its object the amelioration of conditions of disadvantaged individuals or groups including those that are disadvantaged because of race, national or ethnic origin, colour, religion, sex, age or mental or physical disability.

Official Languages of Canada

16.   (1) English and French are the official languages of Canada and have equality of status and equal rights and privileges as to their use in all institutions of the Parliament and government of Canada.

(2)   English and French are the official languages of New Brunswick and have equality of status and equal rights and privileges as to their use in all institutions of the legislature and government of New Brunswick.

(3)   Nothing in this Charter limits the authority of Parliament or a legislature to advance the equality of status or use of English and French.

17.   (1)   Everyone has the right to use English or French in any debates and other proceedings of Parliament.

(2)   Everyone has the right to use English or French in any debates and other proceedings of the legislature of New Brunswick.

18.   (1)   The statutes, records and journals of Parliament shall be printed and published in English and French and both language versions are equally authoritative.

(2)   The statutes, records and journals of the legislature of New Brunswick shall be printed and published in English and French and both language versions are equally authoritative.

19.   (1)   Either English or French may be used by any person in, or in any pleading in or process issuing from, any court established by Parliament.

(2)   Either English or French may be used by any person in, or in any pleading in or process issuing from, any court of New Brunswick.

20.   (1)   Any member of the public in Canada has the right to communicate with, and to receive available services from, any head or central office of an institution of the Parliament or government of Canada in English or French, and has the same right with respect to any other office of any such institution where

    (a)   there is a significant demand for communications with and services from that office in such language; or

    (b)   due to the nature of the office, it is reasonable that communications with and services from that office be available in both English and French.

(2)   Any member of the public in New Brunswick has the right to communicate with, and to receive available services from, any office of an institution of the legislature or government of New Brunswick in English or French.

21.   Nothing in sections 16 to 20 abrogates or derogates from any right, privilege or obligation with respect to the English and French languages, or either of them, that exists or is continued by virtue of any other provision of the Constitution of Canada.

22.   Nothing in sections 16 to 20 abrogates or derogates from any legal or customary right or privilege acquired or enjoyed either before or after the coming into force of this Charter with respect to any language that is not English or French.

Minority Language Educational Rights

23. (1) Citizens of Canada

    (a) whose first language learned and still understood is that of the English or French linguistic minority population of the province in which they reside, or

    (b) who have received their primary school instruction in Canada in English or French and reside in a province where the language in which they received that instruction is the language of the English or French linguistic minority population of the province, have the right to have their children receive primary and secondary school instruction in that language in that province.

(2) Citizens of Canada of whom any child has received or is receiving primary or secondary school instruction in English or French in Canada, have the right to have all their children receive primary and secondary school instruction in the same language.

(3) The right of citizens of Canada under subsections (1) and (2) to have their children receive primary and secondary school instruction in the language of the English or French linguistic minority population of a province

    (a) applies wherever in the province the number of children of citizens who have such a right is sufficient to warrant the provision to them out of public funds of minority language instruction; and

    (b) includes, where the number of those children so warrants, the right to have them receive that instruction in minority language educational facilities provided out of public funds.

Enforcement

24. (1) Anyone whose rights or freedoms, as guaranteed by this Charter, have been infringed or denied may apply to a court of competent jurisdiction to obtain such remedy as the court considers appropriate and just in the circumstances.

(2) Where, in proceedings under subsection (1), a court concludes that evidence was obtained in a manner that infringed or denied any rights or freedoms guaranteed by this Charter, the evidence shall be excluded if it is established that, having regard to all the circumstances, the admission of it in the proceedings would bring the administration of justice into disrepute.

General

25.   The guarantee in this Charter of certain rights and freedoms shall not be construed so as to abrogate or derogate from any aboriginal, treaty or other rights or freedoms that pertain to the aboriginal peoples of Canada including

   (a)   any rights or freedoms that have been recognized by the Royal Proclamation of October 7, 1763; and

   (b)   any rights or freedoms that now exist by way of land claims agreements or may be so acquired.

26.   The guarantee in this Charter of certain rights and freedoms shall not be construed as denying the existence of any other rights or freedoms that exist in Canada.

27.   This Charter shall be interpreted in a manner consistent with the preservation and enhancement of the multicultural heritage of Canadians.

28.   Notwithstanding anything in this Charter, the rights and freedoms referred to in it are guaranteed equally to male and female persons.

29.   Nothing in this Charter abrogates or derogates from any rights or privileges guaranteed by or under the Constitution of Canada in respect of denominational, separate or dissentient schools.

30.   A reference in this Charter to a province or to the legislative assembly or legislature of a province shall be deemed to include a reference to the Yukon Territory and the Northwest Territories, or to the appropriate legislative authority thereof, as the case may be.

31.   Nothing in this Charter extends the legislative powers of any body or authority.

Application of Charter

32.   (1)   This Charter applies

   (a)   to the Parliament and government of Canada in respect of all matters within the authority of Parliament including all matters relating to the Yukon Territory and Northwest Territories; and

   (b)   to the legislature and government of each province in respect of all matters within the authority of the legislature of each province.

   (2)   Notwithstanding subsection (1), section 15 shall not have effect until three years after this section comes into force.

33.   (1)   Parliament or the legislature of a province may expressly declare in an Act of Parliament or of the legislature, as the case may be, that the Act or a provision thereof shall operate notwithstanding a provision included in section 2 or sections 7 to 15 of this Charter.

(2) An Act or a provision of an Act in respect of which a declaration made under this section is in effect shall have such operation as it would have but for the provision of this Charter referred to in the declaration.

(3) A declaration made under subsection (1) shall cease to have effect five years after it comes into force or on such earlier date as may be specified in the declaration.

(4) Parliament or a legislature of a province may re-enact a declaration made under subsection (1).

(5) Subsection (3) applies in respect of a re-enactment made under subsection (4).

Citation

34. This Part may be cited as the Canadian Charter of Rights and Freedoms.

Glossary

access Considered an "incident of custody" and means that a non-custodial parent may have visiting or contact rights with the child.

actus reus Literally "the evil act," a key component of conviction for any criminal offence. For an individual to be convicted of a crime, *actus reus* and *mens rea* must coincide at the time of the offence. Without a coincidence of an evil act and an evil intent, there can be no conviction for crime.

administrative law A form of public law that obligates the state to act fairly in the practice of government. The law, which applies to decisions of the bureaucracy and of government-appointed tribunals, implies a responsibility to deliver services in an equitable manner.

administrative tribunals Bodies empowered by government to make decisions that range from purely non-discretionary decisions, such as applying the regulations or definitions of a particular statute, to quasi-judicial decisions, such as determining questions of fact or law.

adversarial system This system suggests that "the truth" is most likely to emerge from strong advocacy for opposing points of view. The adversarial system places its confidence in the counsel who appear before the court, in contrast to an *inquisitorial system* (see below in this glossary).

amending formula Sections of the *Constitution Act, 1982* that allow for changes to that legislation. At present in Canada, three sections allow for the Constitution to be changed: sections 38, 41, and 43.

anarchist perspective on law Perspective that emphasizes the role of an oppressive and intrusive state as central to understanding social life. Anarchists typically endorse a non-state-based communitarian ethic, whereas libertarians view the rights of the individual as more deserving of support than the rights of the community.

articling An LL.B. graduate's period of learning in a legal setting and further series of tests referred to as Bar Admissions. Only upon successful completion of these criteria can a person be "called to the bar" of a province, and practise law.

audi alteram partem Latin maxim that means, literally, "hear the other side." This rule requires that parties to a dispute have a fair hearing, which includes notice of when and where the hearing is to be held, the opportunity to bring witnesses, and the right to cross-examine the witnesses brought by the opposing litigant.

bicameral Parliament A legislative body consisting of two houses that jointly enact laws for a country. In Canada, the bicameral Parliament is composed of the elected House of Commons and the appointed Senate.

books of authority Authoritative texts or commentaries on the meaning and development of specific forms of law and their applicable principles.

British North America Act, 1867 British statute that created Canada by politically joining Upper and Lower Canada (now Quebec and Ontario) with Nova Scotia and New Brunswick, and granted constitutional powers to the duly elected representatives of the Canadian people. It is Canada's original and defining source of law and sets out in sections 91 and 92 the respective powers of federal and provincial governments (see below in this glossary). In 1982, it was renamed the *Constitution Act, 1867*.

Canadian *Bill of Rights* Arguably the precursor to the *Canadian Charter of Rights and Freedoms*, the Canadian *Bill of Rights* was a federal statute without the status of a constitutional document. The *Bill* was occasionally used to strike down legislation that offended its principles, but in other judgments it was said to be only a guide to be used by legislators in the construction of statutes.

Canadian Charter of Rights and Freedoms An entrenched charter of rights and freedoms that requires Canada's courts to strike down all federal, provincial, or municipal legislation that fails to conform to the *Charter's* specific provisions.

Canadian Judicial Council Created by Parliament in 1971, its statutory mandate is to set out the *Judges Act*, which states that the council is established to "promote efficiency and uniformity, and to improve the quality of judicial service" in Canada's federally appointed courts. The council, which has 39 members and is chaired by the chief justice of Canada, is responsible for the disciplinary measures concerning all federally appointed judges.

case law Judicially constructed law—that is, law that is established by decisions in specific court cases, with the decisions of the Supreme Court of Canada established as final case law.

Charlottetown Accord An attempt to bring Quebec into the constitutional fold after the province refused to sign the *Constitution Act, 1982*. The accord was put to a referendum of the people of Canada in 1992, but rejected by both Quebec and the rest of the country.

child custody The determination of which parent is best prepared to have custody of a child or children is made in accordance with the admittedly vague standard of "the best interests of the child."

child support The obligation of a parent to contribute to the best of his or her financial ability to the care and costs of raising his or her children. Under federal law, child support is usually determined by applying a quantum from a table set out in the Federal Child Support Guidelines.

common-law relations A statutorily defined term that means a relationship between two people of the opposite sex who, although not legally married to each other continuously, cohabited in a marriage-like relationship for at least three years, or if there is a child of the relationship by birth or adoption, cohabited in a marriage-like relationship of some permanence.

conflict resolution Also known as Alternative Dispute Resolution, this new model for deciding disputes has been developed by communities and the legal profession as an option to the court process. Most common forms are mediation, a form of negotiated settlement between the disputing parties, and arbitration, which has a non-judicial officer determine how the issue in dispute between the parties should be resolved.

consent A defence to allegations that an intentional tort has been committed; can also be used as a defence in criminal law.

Constitution Act, 1982 A constitutional enactment, in 1982, that gave life to the Canadian Constitution as a legal creation of Canada itself. In addition to incorporating the *British North America Act, 1867*, the act also brought into existence both the entrenched *Canadian Charter of Rights and Freedoms* and various amending formulas to enable further change to the governance of the country.

***Constitution Act* of 1791** The British statute that divided Canada into Upper and Lower Canada. At the Canadians' request it also created legislative and executive governments in Canada, although these were both answerable to Britain.

constitutional law The rules that define and interpret the powers of federal and provincial governments and, as a consequence, establish the rights and responsibilities of citizens.

contributory negligence A partial defence for a defendant in a negligence action when it can be shown that the plaintiff was partially responsible for the harm suffered.

conviction In a criminal law context refers to the determination by a court that a person is responsible for or "guilty" of the crime that he or she has been accused of.

Criminal Code The federal statute, first enacted in 1892, which sets out most public crimes (such as assault, murder, and criminal negligence) and their penalties.

custom A source of law that derives from the practices and patterns of behaviour through which society has come to order itself. Sometimes referred to in Canada as "convention."

defences or mitigations of criminal responsibility Used by the accused to demonstrate that they were not criminally responsible for the crime that they committed, or that they had diminished responsibility.

defendant The person against whom a private law proceeding has been brought as well as the term used for the person who is charged in criminal law.

delegation In the context of administrative law, the term for the transfer by federal Parliament and provincial legislatures of some of their legislative duties to non-elected government officials.

dialectical materialism The doctrine or theory of history espoused by Marxism. In ancient Greek "dialectic" means dialogue or conversation, thus the doctrine of dialectical materialism holds that history progresses in stages that are based solely on the supremacy of different economic classes: feudalism replaced aristocracy, capitalism replaced feudalism, and socialism or communism will replace capitalism.

divorce A petition under federal jurisdiction for the dissolution of a marriage; since 1985, granted on the basis of living separate and apart for one year, or on the basis of adultery, mental or physical cruelty, alcoholism, or incarceration.

doctrine of fairness An extension of the principle of natural justice, which requires administrative tribunals to act with both substantive and procedural fairness to all parties.

domestic law The law of a single nation-state, which is different from the domestic laws of other nations and also from international law.

ejusdem generis* and *noscitur a sociis Although theoretically separate, these two Latin maxims essentially make the same point: the meaning of an ambiguous word or phrase within a statute is to be inferred from the context in which it appears.

ex turpi causa, non oritur actio Latin for "an action does not occur (or arise) for a base (or illegal) cause."

expressio unius est exclusio alterius Latin maxim requiring that the express mention of one class of subjects necessarily excludes another class of subjects. If a statute specifies that x is to be the subject of the statute, y is necessarily excluded from the ambit of this law.

Federal Court of Canada Composed of the Federal Court: Trial Division; and the Federal Court: Appeal Division. The Trial Division has original jurisdiction in most cases where relief is claimed against the Crown as well as exclusive jurisdiction for judicial review of most decisions of federal boards, commissions, or other tribunals. The court's jurisdiction also includes interprovincial and federal–provincial disputes, intellectual property proceedings, admiralty matters, immigration proceedings, matters pertaining to the *Charter*, citizenship appeals, and appeals under certain federal statutes. The Appeal Division hears appeals from the Trial Division.

feminist theory of law A theory that places the subjugation of women and denial of the equality of women as central foci of centuries of lawmaking. This perspective views the oppression of women as the unexamined bedrock of the legal process.

feudalism The political and economic system of England that granted the aristocracy nobility and land in exchange for the labour and military service of serfs or vassals on the land. In France and New France, this system was referred to as the seigneurial system, whereby the aristocracy were called "seigneurs" and the serfs, "censitaires."

golden rule The rule of statutory interpretation that softens the impact of the plain-meaning rule, requiring that although the ordinary sense of words is to be adhered to, that ordinary sense may be modified if it necessarily leads to an absurdity or incongruity within the statute.

Hansard The official report of the proceedings of Parliament.

hybrid offences Crimes in the *Criminal Code* for which the Crown attorney may decide (elect) whether to proceed by summary conviction or indictment. In determining whether to proceed by indictment, the Crown will assess the nature of the crime and the facts that are evident before the trial.

indictable offences Those crimes in the *Criminal Code* that are considered to be very serious and that carry substantial penalties.

injustice A word that refers to a situation in which the law or the legal system treats someone or something unfairly. The opposite of *justice* (see below in this glossary).

inquisitorial system A legal system that places its confidence in the judge or arbitrator, who is required to ask relevant questions in an effort to determine "the truth" of the matter.

intentional tort Torts that occur as a result of a wrongdoer intentionally (or apparently intentionally) harming another either physically or mentally. These include the torts of assault, trespass, and defamation, to name a few.

interdelegation A constitutionally permitted process whereby the federal government may delegate its powers to a provincially appointed tribunal, commission, or board; or the provincial government may transfer some of its powers to a federally appointed commission, board, or tribunal provided that not all the delegating authorities are transferred and that the receiving commission, tribunal, or board does not transfer the powers to any other body.

international law A form of law mediated by international institutions such as the United Nations. The law attempts to provide governance and accommodation of nations in relation to global treaties, conventions, and customs. It is usually enforceable through the use of international suasion, not through traditional judicial remedies.

intra vires Latin for "within the power of"; used as the antithesis of *ultra vires* (see below in this glossary).

judicial review The process whereby a court considers whether decisions of administrative tribunals were properly made or *ultra vires* the jurisdiction of the tribunal. Judicial review is not the same as an appeal, which refers to a court of higher jurisdiction rehearing a legal proceeding from a lower court. Administrative decisions can be judicially reviewed for a limited number of reasons, including abuse of discretion, violation of the principles of natural justice or procedural fairness, or failure to conform to the technicalities of the empowering legislation.

jury A panel of one's "peers" that is responsible for fact finding or determining the truth or falseness of facts in evidence at a trial. In Canada, the jury is mostly used in criminal proceedings and is not expected to make determinations on the law, a matter left to the trial judge.

justice A term derived from the Roman term for law, *justicia*, which means "to give each man his due." In modern terms it has come to represent an idea of legal fairness. It is often used to reflect the personal or societal understanding of the upholding of rights and the punishment of wrongs, when undertaken by the law.

laissez-faire capitalism Doctrine that the free market functions to the greatest good when left unfettered and unregulated by government. Some authors give different definitions based on notions of justice and human nature.

law school The term used to refer to Faculties of Law at specific universities. Students gain admission to these institutions after completing an undergraduate degree, or a portion thereof, from a recognized university; one cannot attend directly from secondary school. Some universities now offer a law major in an Arts or Social Science bachelor's degree.

law societies Provincial associations (which can be subsets of the Canadian Bar Association) that license lawyers to practise in each province in Canada. Licences are granted after a period of articling and successful completion of Bar Admission examinations.

legal realism An approach to law that takes account not only of doctrinal developments, but also the social, political, and economic bases of specific law. It is an empirically based system of analysis that arguably has its roots in positivism.

lex iniusta non est lex Latin for "an unjust law is no law at all," the principal tenet of the natural law perspective.

liability What the court decides in a private law action. In this situation, the court assesses fault and decides whether damages are awarded. Liability differs from a "finding of guilt," which is the determination that a judge must make before a wrongdoer can be convicted in criminal law.

limitations clause Section 1 of the *Canadian Charter of Rights and Freedoms* is often referred to as the "limitations" clause because it states that not all the rights guaranteed within the *Charter* are absolute, but are rather subject to "reasonable limits prescribed by law"—limits that "can be demonstrably justified in a free and democratic society."

LL.B. degree Bachelor of Laws degree granted from a law school in recognition that its holder has completed a university-mandated legal education. This degree alone does not entitle the holder to practise law in Canada.

LSAT Law School Admission Test: an aptitude test developed in the United States as a means of determining suitability for legal education and the practice of law. Often criticized for its cultural ethnocentricity and its lack of useful performance indicators, the LSAT remains a requirement for admission to Canada's law schools.

Magna Carta A document attributed to King John of England in 1215 wherein he legally specified that royal powers were not absolute, ceding some power to his barons to change some of his decisions. It is seen as the first movement of English monarchism toward democracy.

marriage The legal definition of marriage currently applies only to state-registered heterosexual unions, though there remains considerable debate both within and outside the homosexual community as to whether same-sex marriages ought to be considered the legal equivalent of heterosexual marriages.

Marxism The theory that espouses the notion that law is created from an irreconcilable conflict between labour and capital. The theory is based upon a view of social life that emphasizes the guiding role of material circumstances, and the inherently contradictory nature of economic inequality.

Meech Lake Accord Part of a multi-pronged attempt to bring Quebec into the constitutional fold, after the province's refusal to sign the *Constitution Act, 1982*. The Meech Lake Accord foundered in the Manitoba legislature.

mens rea Latin for "evil mind," the intent to commit the act complained of. In order for an individual to be found guilty of a crime, he or she must have an "evil mind."

natural justice The written and unwritten rules and procedures to be followed by any person charged with the duty of adjudicating disputes. The chief rules are a duty to act fairly, to act in good faith, and to act impartially or without bias.

natural law A theory that has its roots in Judeo-Christian conceptions of social life. This theory holds that law and morality must be synonymous.

negligence A person or legal entity will be found to be negligent when his, her, or its conduct falls below the standard expected of the reasonable person in the specific circumstances in question, and when damages are incurred as a result of this negligence.

nemo judex This abbreviation of a Latin maxim means, literally, that no person should act as judge on his own behalf. In other words, the apprehension of bias on the part of the decision maker must be excluded from all decision making within an administrative tribunal, board, committee, or commission.

noscitur a sociis See *ejusdem generis*.

notwithstanding clause Section 33 of the *Canadian Charter of Rights and Freedoms*, which allows a legislature to enact laws that specifically "override" the rights and freedoms in the *Charter* by stating that the legislation will operate even though it could or does infringe constitutional rights.

nulla poena sine lege According to *The Concept of Law* by H.L.A. Hart, "there shall be no penalty without a valid law."

***Oakes* case** A rule of Canadian constitutional interpretation first established by the Supreme Court of Canada in *R. v. Oakes* (1986). It applies to the use of the limitations clause and requires that the court apply a two-part test of central importance and proportionality before allowing a validly enacted federal or provincial statute to infringe on a right or freedom set out in the *Charter*.

objective intention An element of *mens rea* that is applied in certain cases and determines whether a reasonable person would have expected a criminal deed to flow from the defendant's actions.

parent Can be a mother, father, or person who has treated a child as if the child were his or her own. All parents have a legal responsibility to provide support for their children.

parliamentary supremacy The doctrine that Parliament is the supreme lawmaker and no person or body (including the courts) has the legal right to override or set aside the laws enacted by Parliament.

patriation A term used to refer to a country's assuming complete control of its own constitution. In Canada, as long as constitutional amendments were made by Britain, the Constitution was not patriated. The *Constitution Act, 1982* patriated the Constitution by creating an "amending formula" that allowed the Canadian legislatures the right and the responsibility to make changes to our constitutional documents.

plain-meaning rule The rule of statutory interpretation that dictates that an ambiguous section of a statute is to be read in accordance with its literal meaning, even if a literal reading appears to lead to an incongruous result.

plaintiff A person who has been harmed by the actions of another and commences a lawsuit to redress the wrong, usually by seeking an award of damages.

positivism The theory that law can be understood as a valid set of rules whose content is to be determined through a logical system of precedents, rather than through the application of moral considerations.

precedent "A judgment or decision of a court of law cited as an authority for deciding a similar set of facts; a case [that] serves as an authority for the legal principle embodied in its decision" (*Osborn's Concise Law Dictionary*).

private law An area of law that responds to matters that are primarily of private interest; a type of law that, at least in theory, regulates not so much the interests of the collective, but primarily various economic relations among individuals and their legal creations.

procedural law Sets out the process, formalities, or mechanisms for enforcing the law. Also referred to as *lex fori,* which means the law of the forum or court in which a case is tried.

provincial court The first stop in the hierarchy of Canada's court system. The trial courts of the province have four divisions: criminal, youth, small claims, and family; 90 percent of all criminal offences are heard in provincial court, criminal division.

public law An area of law that is primarily concerned with the public interest and the regulation of matters of collective rather than individual interest.

punitive damages Damages that are awarded in tort beyond what is necessary to compensate an individual or a legal entity for losses sustained and for pain and suffering. The purpose of punitive damages is to deter the conduct in question, thus bringing a public law objective to the realm of private law.

Quebec Act Statute passed by the British Parliament in 1774 that provided for, among other things, the right of Roman Catholics to participate in government and the use of the French language in civil law.

reasonable person A fictional character who exists in private law (primarily tort) and who decides whether explanations offered by the wrongdoer are rational.

restorative justice Models of dispute resolution, such as sentencing circles, that can apply to Aboriginal populations and are said to more accurately reflect the participants' interpretations of justice than those imposed through the British-based Canadian legal system.

Royal Proclamation of 1763 The Treaty of Paris, signed in 1763, ended the Seven Years' War between the French (and its allies) and the British (and its allies). The British acquired most of the French empire in North America, including Canada. Attempting to resolve the growing dissatisfaction of the First Nations people living in Canada, the British issued the Royal Proclamation, which specified conditions of British contact with Aboriginals; set out political, legal, and religious rights of the French in Quebec; and promised democratically elected institutions for English Canadians.

rule in Heydon's case The rule that states that the intention of a statute is to be derived from an understanding of the "mischief" that the law aims to correct—the "defect" in the common law that existed prior to the implementation of the statute. This rule is often referred to as the "mischief rule."

sections 91 and 92, *British North America Act, 1867* The two sections of Canada's Constitution that define the areas of jurisdiction where the provinces can enact laws (s. 92) and where the federal Parliament can enact laws (s. 91). Section 91 of the act also reserves a residual right to the federal government to enact laws that deal with Canada's "Peace, Order, and Good Government."

sentencing The task of imposing a penalty for a crime. The purposes of sentencing are set out in section 718 of the *Criminal Code*—denouncing unlawful conduct, deterring the offender and others, separating offenders from society where necessary, assisting in rehabilitation, providing reparation for harm done to victims, and promoting a sense of responsibility within offenders, and acknowledgement of the harm done by their actions.

separation A term used in both federal law and provincial law referring to the period after a couple determines that they will no longer live together as husband and wife. Separation is usually followed up with a "separation agreement," which is a document signed by both parties to the separation outlining how the couple intend to resolve the issues arising from their marriage, such as custody, support, and division of assets. If the separating parties cannot reach an agreement, they may apply to a court to resolve the outstanding legal issues arising on separation.

social contract A term usually attributed to Jean-Jacques Rousseau, who in 1762 wrote *Social Contract or Political Right,* in which he states, "The problem is to find a form of association which will defend and protect with the whole common force the person and goods of each associate, and in which each, while uniting himself with all, may still obey himself alone, and remain as free as before." This is the fundamental problem for which the social contract is said to provide the solution.

sovereign The supreme authority in an independent political society. It is now considered to mean the absolute lawmaker. In Canada, the sovereign now refers to the legislative sovereign—Parliament, which can make or unmake any law, subject only to the limitations that Parliament has placed on itself, such as those emanating from the Constitution or the judiciary.

spousal support The provision of support for a spouse in the event of marriage breakdown. Support is to be granted in specific circumstances, depending upon a mix of factors including the economic consequences of the dissolution of the marriage and the efforts made by each spouse to become economically self-sufficient.

spouse As a result of the passage of Bill C-38, a spouse may be one of a man and a woman who are married to each other, or a couple of the same sex. In July 2005 Canada passed this legislation, which provides for the equality of heterosexual and homosexual men and women within civil unions, although religious organizations can continue to bar homosexual men and women from marriage within their churches, synagogues, or mosques.

Star Chamber derives its title from the Court of Star Chamber, which from 1487 to 1640 sat *in camera* (privately) and handed down legal and often arbitrary decisions that were not open to scrutiny by the public.

stare decisis Latin for "to stand by decided things." The term refers to the development of case law within the context of a legal hierarchy.

statute law Law that is enacted by duly elected legislatures, whether federal or provincial.

strict and absolute liability offences Offences that arise from the breach of regulatory or public welfare statutes and that do not typically lead to incarceration; nor is intent a necessary element of the offence. The fact that the action occurred is evidence that the offence was committed. Usually in these situations, the onus is on the defendant to prove that he or she was not the cause of the offence.

subjective intention An element of *mens rea* that asks the question whether the defendant expected that a criminal deed would result from his or her actions.

substantive law The actual law, as opposed to adjectival or procedural law. Substantive laws set out specific penalties for specific kinds of conduct by the public that is prohibited by statute.

suffragette A woman in Britain, Canada, or the United States in the early twentieth century who was a member of a group that demanded voting rights for women and who increased awareness of the matter with a series of public protests. The suffragette Emily Davidson threw herself under the king's horse at the Derby in 1913 to draw attention to the campaign.

summary conviction offences Crimes specified in the *Criminal Code* that are considered to be less serious than others and that carry a maximum sentence of a fine of no more than $2 000 or six months' incarceration.

superior courts of the province There are two divisions within the superior courts of the provinces: the Trial Division, which hears the most significant of criminal and civil cases, and the Appeal Division, which hears all appeals prior to possible consideration by the Supreme Court of Canada.

Supreme Court of Canada The court of last resort in our country since 1949; the Supreme Court has nine justices and hears appeals in relation to significant criminal and civil cases, and references regarding constitutional matters.

tort A private wrong (as opposed to a crime, which is a public wrong punishable by the state). Torts can only be pursued as a private matter by or against another individual, corporation, or arm of government.

ultra vires Latin for "beyond the power." Used in constitutional interpretation when a court strikes down or declares invalid legislation that has been enacted outside a legislature's constitutional authority or jurisdiction.

Index

Credits

This page constitutes an extension of the copyright page. We have made every effort to trace the ownership of all copyrighted material and to secure permission from copyright holders. In the event of any question arising as to the use of any material, we will be pleased to make the necessary corrections in future printings. Thanks are due to the following authors, publishers, and agents for permission to use the material indicated.

Chapter 2. 39: *The Canadian Legal System*, 5th edition by Gerald L. Gall, Figure 2.7, pp. 29 (2004 edition 0-459-24128-1). Reprinted by permission of Carswell, a division of Thomson Canada Limited; **49:** Reprinted by permission of the *Ottawa Citizen*.

Chapter 5. 155: Reprinted by permission of Doug Borch, Calgary Community Conferencing; **166–167:** Reprinted by permission of the University of Toronto Press, Inc.; **179–181:** Reproduced with the permission of the Minister of Public Works and Government Services, 2006.

Chapter 6. 189: Reprinted by permission Harry Arthurs; **200–202:** Published with the permission of the Canadian Bar Association.

Chapter 8. 261: Reprinted with permission from *The Globe and Mail*.

Chapter 9. 300–301: *Principles of Administrative Law,* Fourth Edition, by David Philip Jones, Q.C., and Anne S. de Villars, Q.C., c. 1 "Introduction: What is Administrative Law?", pp. 4–5 (2004 edition 0-459-24130-3). Reprinted by permission of Carswell, a division of Thomson Canada Limited.

Chapter 10. 335: *Critical Criminology* by Ian Taylor, Paul Walton & Jack Young, "Defenders of Order or Guardians of Human Rights?", pp. 132–137, © 1975, Routledge. Reprinted by permission of Taylor & Francis Group.